Founding Mothers

Founding Mothers

THE WOMEN WHO
RAISED OUR NATION

COKIE
ROBERTS

HarperLargePrint
An Imprint of HarperCollins*Publishers*

All photograph credits appear on page 545.

HarperCollins books may be purchased for educational, business, or sales promotional use. For information please write: Special Markets Department, HarperCollins Publishers Inc., 10 East 53rd Street, New York, NY 10022.

FIRST HARPER LARGE PRINT EDITION

Printed on acid-free paper

Library of Congress Cataloging-in-Publication Data

Roberts, Cokie.
    Founding mothers : the women who raised our nation / Cokie Roberts.—1st ed.
        p. cm.
    Includes bibliographical references and index.
    ISBN 0-06-009025-1 (Hardcover)
        1. United States—History—Colonial period, ca. 1600–1775—Biography. 2. United States—History—Revolution, 1775–1783—Biography. 3. United States—History—Revolution, 1775–1783—Women. 4. United States—History—1783–1815—Biography. 5. Women—United States—Biography. 6. Women in politics—United States—History—18th century. 7. Women in politics—United States—History—19th century. 8. Women—United States—History—18th century. 9. Women—United States—History—19th century. I. Title.

E176.R63 2004
973.3'092'2—dc22
[B]
                                                                    2004042873

ISBN 0-06-053331-5 (Large Print)

    04   05   06   07   08   WBC/RRD   10   9   8   7   6   5   4   3   2

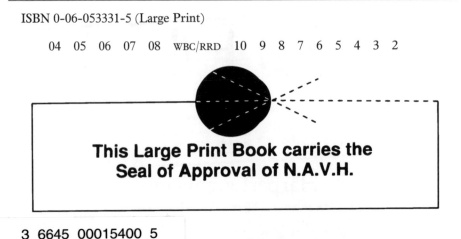

This Large Print Book carries the Seal of Approval of N.A.V.H.

TO MY OWN FOUNDING MOTHERS:

The women in my family, particularly my mother, who told the stories we call history.

And, especially, to the religious of the Society of the Sacred Heart, the RSCJ's, who take girls seriously—a radical notion in the 1950s.

CONTENTS

CHAPTER SIX

1787–1789: Constitution and
the First Election   273

CHAPTER SEVEN

After 1789: Raising a Nation   333

ACKNOWLEDGMENTS AND AUTHOR'S NOTE

First a word about what this book is and what it is not. This is a book of stories—stories of the women who influenced the Founding Fathers. It is not a disquisition on eighteenth-century life. These are by definition elite women. There are many other women of the time whose lives were much harder than the ones described here, but the Founding Fathers weren't listening to them. It is also not an examination of the writings of the Founding Mothers, which can be difficult to read. To make it easier, I have modernized and corrected the spelling and punctuation in their letters.

When I decided to try to find the women who had the ears of the Founding Fathers, I knew I couldn't do it without the help of my friend Ann Charnley. (She's told me to stop saying my **old** friend, but that's the case.) Ann had provided yeoman work on my previous books, but this one was going to be a whole lot harder. So before I agreed to do it, I called to see if she was on board. Her response "Be still, my heart" tells you all you need to know about her commitment to the enterprise. Even so, neither one of us knew just how tough this research would turn out to be. Many of the women in these pages had the lack of grace to burn their letters, Martha

Washington among them. Thomas Jefferson threw away all his correspondence with his wife. Abigail Adams kept telling John to destroy her delightful missives; fortunately, he had the good sense to ignore her. Even the letters that were saved are difficult to track down and to decipher. In many cases, the writings of the men have been transcribed—those of the women still available only in almost-impossible-to-read longhand on fading microfilm. It's required as much detective work as straightforward research to ferret out much of this information. Fortunately, some of these women's descendants understood their ancestors' contributions to early America and wrote biographies based on their letters. And my heroine, Elizabeth Ellet, published her two-volume work **The Women of the American Revolution** in 1848 when there were still people alive who had heard the stories directly from the participants. (At least one woman of the Revolution, Betsey Hamilton, was living at the time of publication.) But even then she found it rough going: "Inasmuch as political history says but little—and that vaguely and incidentally—of the women who bore their part in the Revolution, the materials for a work treating of them and their actions and sufferings, must be derived in great part from private sources." The only difference now is that some of those private letters have ended up in libraries and historical societies where, with a good deal of effort, they can be found. Ann Charnley, though often frustrated, managed to do that magnificently, finding new information right up until publication. Her triumphant hoot when she finally discovered some elusive document was worth the wait.

Along the way, Ann had helpers at many institutions:

At the Library of Congress, where my friend Jim Billington opened the door: Barbara Bair and Janice Ruth in the Manuscript Division; Sheridan Harvey in the Women's Studies Division.

At the Huntington Library, where the Collection of American Historical Manuscripts and Rare Books is truly remarkable: Romaine Ahlstrom, Susi Krasnoo, John Rhodemal, and Barbara Robertson. Paul Zall, the resident reader, was not only personally helpful, but his books provide wonderful sketches of several Founding Mothers, plus their letters.

At the University of Virginia: Holly C. Shulman, editor of the Papers of Dolley Payne Madison.

At the South Carolina Historical Society: Carey Lucas Nikonchuk, research consultant.

At the University of South Carolina, the South Carolinian Library: Sam Fore, manuscript specialist.

At the Mount Vernon Ladies' Association: research specialist Mary V. Thompson.

At the Butler Library of Columbia University: Mary-Jo Kline, the John Jay Papers.

At the Massachusetts Historical Society: Celeste Walker and Ann Decker Cecere, associate editors of the Adams Papers.

At the Historical Society of Pennsylvania: Sharon Ann Holt.

At the John Jay Homestead Historical Site: Allan Weinreb.

The New York, New Jersey, and Virginia Historical Societies were also helpful, as was the New York Public Library. Elise Pinckney, editor of the **South Carolina Historical Magazine**, was a delight. Thanks to her and her cousin Pie Friendly who sent us to her.

Though many Founding Mothers have not been the subjects of full-scale biographies, some books about them for "young readers" have been published over the years. I assigned my own young reader, my niece, Abigail Roberts, to report on several of those books and she did a first-rate job. For a child's book on Mumbet, I asked my great-niece, Charlotte Davidsen, for a book report and she also came through in fine fashion.

Once I started writing, I realized that I would have to deal with footnotes—something I hadn't done since my long-ago college days. Annie Whitworth, who is much more than my assistant, took on that onerous task, along with many others. (As deadlines approached at Christmas time, I was correcting the footnotes surrounded by my four precious grandchildren, all under three at the time. So if there are mistakes, blame me, not Annie.) And my daughter, Rebecca Roberts, carved time out of her very busy life to serve as an enthusiastic and exacting editor. At William Morrow, my friend and editor, Claire Wachtel, has guided me through this book with great patience. Her assistant, Jennifer Pooley, is ever helpful. Jane Friedman, one of the great ladies in publishing, is a terrific cheerleader, as are Cathy Hemming and Michael Morrison. Thanks too to Libby Jordan, Lisa Gallagher, and Kim Lewis. Suzanne Balaban has made sure the world knows this book exists. Barbara Levine found the portraits of the ladies and created the cover. Joyce Wong did a great job copyediting text and footnotes. In this enterprise, as in all my other ones, Bob Barnett served as lawyer extraordinaire.

A project as big as this one naturally takes time away from other work. I am thankful to my bureau chief at ABC News, Robin Sproul, and the executive producer of NPR's **Morning Edition**, Ellen McDonnell, for their understanding, encouragement, and friendship. Kim Roellig kept me from backsliding too much in my personal obligations.

After I had agreed to write this book I was diagnosed with breast cancer. The doctors and nurses at the National Institutes of Health, especially doctors Joanne Zujewski and Rosemary Altemas, plus surgeon Colette Magnant, have taken wonderful care of me both physically and spiritually. So have my many friends and relatives who saw me through a difficult year. Special thanks to Linda Wertheimer, Nina Totenberg, Kitty Roberts, Barbara Boggs, Courtney Kane, Eden Lipson, Millie Meyers, Gloria Borger, Linda Winslow, and Anne Davis. Finally, there's no way I can thank my husband enough. Not only was this book Steve's idea, he has nurtured it and me every step of the way. His devotion knows no bounds. Along with taking over responsibility for our weekly newspaper column, he also took on many household chores. Most important, every day he makes me happy, and many days he brings me flowers.

INTRODUCTION

All of my childhood I heard the stories of my ancestor William Claiborne, who in 1790 went to work for Congress where he met the men we think of as the Founding Fathers. At their urging, Claiborne eventually ran for Congress himself, was seated at age twenty-three, though that was two years younger than the minimum age set by the Constitution, and, as the sole representative from Tennessee, was instrumental in breaking the electoral tie between Thomas Jefferson and Aaron Burr. The next month, in a straight political payoff, Jefferson named Claiborne governor of the Mississippi Territory. When Louisiana was purchased from France a couple of years later, Claiborne took title for America, becoming the first governor of the territory, then of the state. Eventually he was elected to the Senate but died not long after at the age of forty-two. The Claibornes have been active in Louisiana politics in every generation since William's, most recently in the person of my mother, Corinne "Lindy" Claiborne Boggs, who served in Congress for seventeen years.

It was a story I loved to hear. It made me feel connected to the very beginnings of our government. But for me to feel truly connected, I needed to know something more. I needed to know what the women in his life were doing while Claiborne embarked on his many adventures. I know that he had three wives, and that the last one was a great political asset. Her French heritage helped him defeat a man of French extraction when he ran for governor. But that's all I know. I can pull up William Claiborne's letters to James Madison and Thomas Jefferson online. I've never seen anything written by a Claiborne woman before my grandfather's generation.

While the men were busy founding the nation, what were the women up to? Aside from Betsy Ross, I don't remember ever hearing about women as a child. (By the way, some of Ross's descendants still insist that she did in fact sew that first flag.) My courses in American history provided me with a glimpse of Martha Washington's bravery at Valley Forge and gave a brief account of Dolley Madison's daring rescue of the portrait of George Washington as the British marched on the White House. When the modern feminist movement bloomed in the 1960s, women started passing around Abigail Adams's famous advice to John and his colleagues in Philadelphia to "remember the ladies." That was about it.

Then my husband, Steven, and I wrote **From This Day Forward**, about our own marriage and others in American history. We included a chapter on John and Abigail Adams's partnership that opened my eyes to the key role his wife played in the political life of the second president. Not only did John turn to Abigail for information and counsel, she was the person who made it possible for him to do what he did. While he was off in Philadelphia thinking great thoughts, she kept his farm and law business going, coped with the shortages of goods and food caused by war, and cared for the children and the old people, all the while fending off British soldiers. John's advice when Abigail wrote describing the British preparations for war? If it got really dangerous, "fly to the woods with our children." Thank you very much. She must have wanted to throttle him.

As I read through the letters of John and Abigail Adams and became more and more fascinated with her life, I grew curious about the other women who had the ears of the Founding Fathers. These women lived through extraordinary times and must, it seemed to me, have extraordinary tales to tell. Now I know they do. It's safe to say that most of the men who wrote the Declaration of Independence and the Constitution, fought the Revolution, and formed the government couldn't have done it without the women. And it was the women who, by insisting that the men come together for civilized conversations in the early Washington dinner parties, helped keep the fragile new country from falling into fatal partisan discord. The women made the men behave.

It's not easy to track down these stories. Though we thankfully seem to have every grocery list the Founding Fathers ever wrote, most of the women left no written traces. Fortunately, some of them, like Sarah Livingston Jay, sent letters home from travel abroad on their husbands' diplomatic missions. And Eliza Pinckney, the mother of two Founders, was left in charge of three plantations in South Carolina at the tender age of sixteen and wrote to her father to keep him apprised of the business. Among her many accomplishments was the successful cultivation of indigo in South Carolina, which provided a source of income to the Mother Country that one historian of the era judged more important than the silver mines of Peru or Mexico to Spain. When Eliza Pinckney died, George Washington insisted on acting as a pallbearer at her funeral.

As the mother of Founders, Eliza takes us back to the time before the Revolution, to the early 1700s. Her contemporary in the North was the long-suffering Deborah Read Franklin, Ben's wife. While he charmed Europe with his wit and wisdom, her management of the postal service and real estate ventures back in Philadelphia provided him with the money to enjoy the Old World capitals. It was left to Deborah to wield her gun, protecting the Franklin house against an angry mob convinced that her husband had sold out on the Stamp Act. Benjamin Franklin essentially abandoned his wife for sixteen of the last seventeen years of their marriage, returning to America only when it became clear that he had to take over the business because, as he wrote to a friend, "my wife in whose hands I had left the care of my affairs died." All heart, that Ben.

Then there is the war—eight years of war! There

Martha Washington shone as the great heroine, especially to George. First, there was her money, or her late husband's money. "The Widow Custis" was well fixed indeed, and she came through for George over and over again, particularly during the dreadful winter at Valley Forge, when soldiers were deserting in the droves. She cajoled the troops, nursed their wounds, sewed them clothes, and kept them from decamping. She also protected the very attractive George from scandal, as he was prone to indiscretions like dancing the night away with Catharine Greene, the wife of his fellow general Nathanael Greene.

It's possible, though, that the real heroine of that winter was the notorious Betsey Loring. She kept the British general Sir William Howe lustily occupied in Philadelphia when he could have marched on Valley Forge and wiped out the bedraggled Continental army. Their affair was so notorious that it became the subject of popular doggerels like:

Awake, awake, Sir Billy,
There's forage in the plain.
Ah, leave your little Filly,
And open the campaign.

And

Sir William he, snug as a flea,
Lay all this time a-snoring,
Nor dreamed of harm as he lay warm
In bed with Mrs. L——g.

It would be nice to think that Mrs. Loring acted out of patriotism, but in fact she sold her favors in exchange for a lucrative position for her husband with the British army.

Managing through the war proved a daunting task for all but the most stalwart of women. Take the case of Mercy Otis Warren. Her husband, James, was active in Massachusetts politics and friends with John Adams and the other Massachusetts delegates to the Continental Congresses. Had his wife been able to hold down the home front, he would have joined the band of brothers in Philadelphia as they struggled with independence and then government. But if he had, the Warrens would have gone bankrupt. Mercy might not have been a businesswoman, but as a writer and a thinker, she became one of the great philosophers of independence. Her plays, poems, and articles, urged on by John and Samuel Adams, spurred revolutionary sentiment. In her private writings she mused about the place of women and whether it was appropriate for them to venture, as she did, beyond the "domestic sphere."

In fact, women ventured into all kinds of spheres. They went with soldiers to camp. They served as spies. They organized boycotts of British goods. They raised money for the troops. They petitioned the government. As the Daughters of Liberty, they formed a formidable force. They defended their homesteads alone as their husbands hid out, marked men with a price on their heads. The generals on both sides of the Revolutionary War marveled at the strength of the women. George Washington wrote to poet Annis Stockton, "You ladies are in the number of the best Patriots America can boast." The British general Lord Cornwallis paid an even greater tribute: "We may destroy all the men in America, and we shall still have all we can do to defeat the women." And all the while the women were bearing and burying and rearing children.

Then the war was finally over, and there was a country to raise. Martha Washington's special grace was called on once again to choreograph the odd job of first lady—finding a balance that was open and democratic enough to reflect revolutionary principles, but formal and regal enough to win the respect of needed European allies. Other women, like Catharine Greene, whose husband the general died soon after the war, had to make their way in the world. She did it by helping Eli Whitney invent the cotton gin.

When I first started learning about the women who influenced the Founding Fathers, I thought they might represent a unique generation, in the way we have always been told that the men of the era were unique. After all, they lived at a time— declaring independence and fighting a war for it, crafting a constitution, forming a new government—that will never be repeated. John Quincy Adams subscribed to the thesis that his mother's generation was unique when he complained to her that there were no modern women like her. Abigail, God love her, shot back that women might act frivolous and flighty, but only because men wanted them to.

But as I got to know these women, reading their letters and their recipes (I've decided not to dress a whole head of cow, but Harty Choke Pie is delicious), I came to the conclusion that there's nothing unique about them. They did—with great hardship, courage, pluck, prayerfulness, sadness, joy, energy, and humor—what women do. They put one foot in front of the other in remarkable circumstances. They carried on. They truly are our Founding Mothers.

Founding Mothers

CHAPTER ONE

Before 1775: The Road to Revolution

DEBORAH READ FRANKLIN

Stirrings of Discontent

When you hear of a family with two brothers who fought heroically in the Revolutionary War, served their state in high office, and emerged as key figures in the new American nation, don't you immediately think, "They must have had a remarkable mother"? And so Charles Cotesworth Pinckney and Thomas Pinckney did. Today Eliza Lucas Pinckney would be the subject of talk-show gabfests and made-for-TV movies, a child prodigy turned into a celebrity. In the eighteenth century she was seen as just a considerate young woman performing her duty, with maybe a bit too much brainpower for her own good.

George Lucas brought his English wife and daughters to South Carolina in 1734 to claim three plantations left to him by his father. Before long, however, Lucas left for Antigua to rejoin his regiment in fighting the war against Spain, leaving his sixteen-year-old daughter in charge of all the properties, plus her ailing mother and toddler sister. (The Lucas sons were at school in England.) Can you imagine a sixteen-year-old girl today being handed those responsibilities? Eliza Lucas willingly took them on. Because she reported to her father on her management decisions and developed the habit of copying her letters, Eliza's writings are some of the few from colonial women that have survived.

The South Carolina Low Country, where Eliza was left to fend for the family, was known for its abundance of rice and mosquitoes. Rice supported the plantation owners and their hundreds of slaves; mosquitoes sent the owners into Charleston (then Charles Town) for summer months of social activities. Though Wappoo Plantation, the Lucas home, was only six miles from the city by water, seventeen by land, Eliza was far too busy, and far too interested in her agricultural experiments, to enjoy the luxuries of the city during the planting months.

The decision about where to live was entirely hers (again, can you imagine leaving that kind of decision to a sixteen-year-old?), as Eliza wrote to a friend in England in 1740: "My Papa and Mama's great indulgence to me leaves it to me to choose our place of residence either in town or country." She went on to describe her arduous life: "I have the business of three plantations to transact, which requires much writing and more business and fatigue of other sorts than you can imagine. But least you should imagine it too burdensome to a girl at my early time of life, give me leave to answer you: I assure you I think myself happy that I can be useful to so good a father, and by rising very early I find I can go through much business." And she did. Not only did she oversee the planting and harvesting of the crops on the plantations, but she also taught her sister and some of the slave children, pursued her own intellectual education in French and English, and even took to lawyering to help poor neighbors. Eliza seemed to know that her legal activities were a bit over the line, as she told a friend: "If you will not laugh immoderately at me I'll trust you with a secret. I have made two wills already." She then defended herself, explaining that she'd studied carefully what was required in will making, adding: "After all what can I do if a poor creature lies a dying and their family taken it into their head that I can serve them. I can't refuse; but when they are well and able to employ a lawyer, I always shall." The teenager had clearly made quite an impression in the Low Country.

The Lucases were land-rich but cash-poor, so Eliza's father scouted out some wealthy prospects as husband material for his delightful daughter.

The young woman was having none of it. Her father's attempts to marry her off to a man who could help pay the mortgage were completely and charmingly rebuffed in a letter written when she was eighteen. "As you propose Mr. L. to me, I am sorry I can't have sentiments favorable enough of him to take time to think on the subject . . . and beg leave to say to you that the riches of Peru and Chile if he had them put together could not purchase a sufficient esteem for him to make him my husband." So much for her father's plan to bring some money into the family. She then dismissed another suggestion for a mate: "I have so slight a knowledge of him I can form no judgment of him." Eliza insisted that "a single life is my only choice . . . as I am yet but eighteen." Of course, many women her age were married, and few would have brushed off their fathers so emphatically, but the feisty Miss Lucas was, despite the workload, having too much fun to settle down with some rich old coot.

Eliza loved "the vegetable world," as she put it, and experimented with different kinds of crops, always with a mind toward commerce. She was keenly aware that the only cash crop South Carolina exported to England was rice, and she was determined to find something else to bring currency into the colony and to make the plantations profitable. When she was nineteen, she wrote that she had planted a large fig orchard "with design to dry and export them." She was always on the lookout for something that would grow well in the southern soil. Reading her Virgil, she was happily surprised to find herself "instructed in agriculture . . . for I am persuaded .though he wrote in and for Italy, it will in many instances suit Carolina."

By her own account, Eliza was always cooking up schemes. She wrote to her friend Mary Bartlett: "I am making a large plantation of oaks which I look upon as my own property, whether my father gives me the land or not." In years to come the oaks would be, the young entrepreneur explained, "more valuable than they are now—which you know they will be when we come to build fleets." She was anticipating a lumber trade for American ships! Mary's uncle, Charles Pinckney, teased the teenager about her plots and plans, something Eliza acknowledged when she wrote to Mary about her oaks. " 'Tell the little visionary,' says your uncle, 'come to town and partake of some of the amusements suitable to her time of life.' Pray tell him . . . what he may now think whims and projects may turn out well by and by. Out of many surely one may hit."

The project she most counted on to "hit," where she placed the most energy, was the growing of indigo. Through trial and, mostly, error, season after season she attempted to nurture the plants grown for the blue dye used throughout Europe for military uniforms. Determined to turn indigo into a cash crop, Eliza's efforts seemed doomed to failure as the seeds froze in the ground and a dye-maker sent by her father tried to sabotage his female boss. But she persisted, somewhat to the amusement of her neighbors, and the admiration of her father. And she was right—eventually her scheme did hit. But it took years.

Meanwhile, the lively young woman was charming Charleston society. Though Charles Pinckney, a prominent South Carolina lawyer, joked about Eliza's exploits, he and his wife clearly enjoyed her company. They often entertained her at their plantation, Belmont, where she worked her way through the extensive library, including, at Pinckney's suggestion, a study of John Locke (which would turn out to be significant later for her as America contemplated independence). An old biddy in the neighborhood, convinced that the industrious Eliza would never land a husband, threatened, the girl confessed, to throw "a volume of my **Plutarch's Lives** into the fire the other day." (Some things never change—those older women worrying that the younger ones might be too serious for a man have been around forever.) Threats notwithstanding, the letters show a young woman who read everything she could get her hands on, including political news, which she passed on to her father, George Lucas, in Antigua; he was sometimes out of touch, leaving Eliza to her own devices for the better part of a year.

The political news was mostly of England's war with Spain and the problems the colony faced as a consequence. Since no ships were arriving from the Mother Country, Eliza could only assume it was an embargo on shipping (it was) that was greatly interfering with her business. It frustrated her that she couldn't elicit her father's views before she bought another plantation. Irritated with the inconveniences of war, she wished "all the men were as great cowards as myself, it would make them more peaceably inclined." With war, George Lucas rose in the ranks of the military and was soon awarded a post as lieutenant royal governor of Antigua. Realizing that he would never live in Carolina again, at the end of 1743 he dispatched his oldest son, George Lucas the younger, to fetch his mother and sisters and bring them back to Antigua. Eliza was horrified. She loved her life and her friends in Carolina, and her indigo project was on the verge of real success.

The indigo experiment would have discouraged a less determined soul than the teenage girl. But Eliza persisted in planting the crop and trying to turn it into dye despite ridicule from the neighbors, who were all experienced planters and certainly "knew better." When she finally succeeded in harvesting a sizable number of plants, Eliza distributed the seeds among the other planters so that everyone could participate in the plan to make South Carolina a source of important and expensive exports to the Mother Country. The young entrepreneur then managed to jettison the perfidious dye-maker sent by her father and hired his brother, who shipped some of the dye to England in 1744. "If it is as I hope we shall have a bounty from home," Eliza wrote her father, expecting in a few years to supply England "with a manufacture for which she has so great a demand and which she is now supplied from the French Colonies and many thousand pounds per annum thereby lost to the nation." The experiment would succeed, she knew, "if the matter were applied to in earnest."

That same year, not long before the Lucas family was set to return to Antigua, Eliza's friend and protector, Mrs. Pinckney, died. Though the young woman seems to have been truly saddened, it was a death that worked out well for her. It didn't take Charles Pinckney long to realize that having lost his wife, he didn't want to lose the spirited young Eliza as well. (Think **Pygmalion,** or better yet, **My Fair Lady**—the first name's even the same.) A few months after his wife's death, Charles proposed to Eliza and saved her from returning to Antigua. He was forty-five, she was twenty-two, and though it was certainly convenient, it was also a love match. Her father had no dowry to offer except his daughter's own indigo crop. George Lucas must have worried that the young woman he had trusted to run his affairs would now try to run her husband's, that he had created a monster. We don't have George Lucas's letter of concern, but we do have his daughter's reply: "I am well assured the acting out of my proper province and invading his, would be an inexcusable breach of prudence." Fortunately for Eliza, Pinckney, a man of means and speaker of the South Carolina Assembly, showed no desire to force her to retreat to her "proper province," and though he made it clear that no dowry was necessary, he seemed readily to accept the indigo project along with his bride.

And finally Eliza's scheme paid off. By 1747 there was enough indigo to ship to England as a substantial export. The Mother Country responded by paying a bounty to Carolina planters in an effort to cut out the French. Soon the dye became a source of considerable wealth for the colony, with the number of pounds shipped abroad increasing geometrically until the Revolution, when the annual export, according to a nineteenth-century biography of Eliza Pinckney, reached "the enormous quantity of one million, one hundred and seven thousand, six hundred and sixty pounds!" The biographer Harriott Ravenal, who was Eliza's great-great-granddaughter, then adds, "When will any 'New Woman' do more for her country."

In the years right after her marriage, it wasn't just indigo Eliza produced, it was children as well. The first, Charles Cotesworth, came along in 1746. Then George Lucas was born in 1747 but died soon after, the same year that his namesake, Eliza's father, was killed in battle. Then came Harriott in 1749 and Thomas in 1750. Motherhood brought a newfound sobriety to Eliza, who privately put aside a list of "resolutions" that give great insight into women's lives at the time. After declaring her resolve to honor God and obey His commands, she then promised "not to regard the frowns of the world, but to keep a steady upright conduct before my God, and before man, doing my duty." Duty was the byword for all of these women, especially elite women like Eliza. She then pledged to practice certain virtues and avoid certain vices, adding, "I am resolved not to be luxurious or extravagant in the management of my table and family on the one hand, nor niggardly and covetous, or too anxiously concerned about it on the other." Still practical that Eliza, who further resolved: "To make a good wife to my dear husband . . . to make it my study to please him. I am resolved to make a good child to my mother. . . . I am resolved to be a good mother to my children. . . . I am resolved to make a good sister both to my own and my husband's brothers and sisters. . . . I am resolved to make a good mistress to my servants . . . to make their lives as comfortable as I can. . . . I am resolved to be a sincere and faithful friend . . . and a universal lover of all mankind." There, in a pious nutshell, was her life.

Despite the rapid arrival of the babies and the success of the indigo, Eliza kept cooking up more schemes. England's war with Spain, which didn't end until 1748, caused a constant disruption in shipping, as a result all kinds of supplies were hard to come by. The Pinckneys brought looms onto the plantations and set the servants to weaving cotton and wool for their clothes, but then Eliza decided to try her hand at silk as well. She diligently set about this project, as she had all the others, and soon created an assembly line. The slave children collected the mulberry leaves and fed them to the silkworms. Eliza and the adult women wound the threads from silkworm cocoons. The women produced enough raw silk that a few years later, when the family moved to England, Eliza commissioned three dresses; two she gave away (one of them to the Princess of Wales!), one she kept. Though no likeness of Eliza Lucas Pinckney exists anywhere, her silk dress is still intact and, more than 250 years later, goes on exhibit at museums throughout the country.

The Pinckneys' move to England came as a result of a political disappointment. Charles Pinckney expected to be named chief justice of South Carolina, but Parliament gave the job to someone else. As a consolation, the Carolinians made Pinckney their agent in London, where he moved his family in 1753. For the first time in her adult life, Eliza was freed from strenuous work. Since her letter writing in that period is scant, it's hard to tell how she felt about her newfound freedom. She did complain in one missive that the English played cards much too much. The family also seems to have been entertained by English society; one very long letter of Eliza's describes in detail her visit with the Princess of Wales, which she sums up by saying it "must seem pretty extraordinary to an American." An "American"—she was describing herself as a citizen of the collection of colonies in the New World, not yet a country, but in some sense an identity.

The Pinckney children were sent to school in England, as Eliza had been, and the family prepared to stay there until their education was complete, but news from America changed their plans. Yet another war had erupted—this time the French, with their allies the Native American Indians, were trying to wrest land from the English settlers, and the Pinckney properties were in danger. In 1758 Eliza and Charles decided to go home for a couple of years, sell most of their estate, and invest it "in a more secure though less improvable part of the world." In her view, England wasn't doing enough to protect Carolina. The politically savvy Mrs. Pinckney wrote angrily to a friend: "Four years ago we left a fine and flourishing colony in profound peace, a colony so valuable to this nation that it would have been looked upon as absurd to have the least doubt of its being protected and taken care of in case of a war, though war then seemed a very distant contingency. And indeed I looked upon an estate there as secure as in England, and on some accounts more valuable." Since she had played a key role in making the estate and the colony itself so valuable, Eliza's furor is understandable. But the real source of her anguish was the decision to leave the boys in England. She knew she wouldn't see them for two or three years, she worried that she might never see them again, given the dangers of the ocean voyage, the possibility of being captured, and the uncertainty about the hostilities at home. In fact, Eliza was not reunited with her little boys until they were grown men.

As it turns out, Eliza was right to worry. After ten long weeks at sea, she, Charles, and ten-year-old Harriott arrived in South Carolina, where Charles quickly contracted malaria and died. After fourteen years of marriage, at age thirty-six, Eliza was widowed, and devastated. "I had as great an affection for him as ever filled the human heart; that, with his virtues and partiality to me, produced a union as great as ever existed between mortals." Her letters reveal that the only thing that kept her from sinking into a debilitating depression was the requirement that she work. She had to do the business Charles had intended to do. The separation from the boys was more painful than ever, but she had her duty to perform, and " tis' weak to complain."

The work turned out to be harder than expected. In the absence of the owners and the presence of bad overseers, the properties had been run into the ground, so Eliza set about correcting the situation, while keeping a wary eye on political developments, particularly the prospects of Indian attacks. Instead of worrying about the Cherokees, the coastal Carolinians would have done better to concern themselves with their own soldiers, who insisted on going on the attack in Indian Country. They came home with a "Treaty of Peace and Friendship" but also with a raging epidemic of smallpox. The Pinckney family had undergone the dangerous smallpox inoculation in England, putting Eliza in a position to run a little smallpox hospital, which "did not contain more than fifteen patients. I lost only one."

Though concern about the French and Indian wars and complaints about inadequate defense from the Mother Country fill much of Eliza's correspondence, she was also very much a mother in her letters. Her pain in telling the boys about their father's death is wrenching. "You have met with the greatest loss, my children, you could meet with upon earth! Your dear, dear father, the best and most valuable of parents, is no more. . . . His affection for you was as great as ever was upon Earth! And you were good children and deserved it. . . . I hope the almighty will enable me to do my duty in every instance by you, and that all my future life may be spent to do you good." She delighted in hearing from and about her sons, confiding in her friends in England that "it is impossible to tell you how much I long to see them." And she was so proud of them! "I am much pleased with their letters. Charles has long wrote well, but no body but my self will believe that Tomm wrote one of those signed with his name. The writing is so much beyond what they think a child of his age capable." In her letters to England, Eliza also begged for news, complaining that each friend assumed another had written a description of the new queen and of the coronation of George III. "If, Madam," she scolded a friend, "you have ever been witness to the impatience of the people of England about a hundred miles from London to be made acquainted with what passes there, you may guess a little at what our impatience is here." When someone finally told her about the new queen, Eliza concluded: "On the whole I am a very loyal subject, and had my share of joy in your agreeable account of my sovereign and his consort."

But colonial attitudes about loyalty were beginning to change as the Mother Country tried the patience of Americans. Charles was moving on through school and into Oxford University as Parliament passed the Stamp Act in 1765, which, despite their long years in England, drew the same response from the Pinckney boys as it did from any red-blooded American. The law, which imposed a tax on playing cards, newspapers, books, almanacs, and legal documents, became a symbol of the absentee-landlord status of the British government over its American colonies. Taking up the cause of his fellow colonialists, young Thomas Pinckney earned the nickname "The Little Rebel." Still, the Pinckneys stayed in England, where Charles was admitted to the bar. He finally came home in 1769, ten years after his parents had left London. By that time his sister, Harriott, who had been educated entirely by her mother, was married to Daniel Horry and had a baby. And since the end of the French and Indian War in 1763, South Carolina was prospering.

The commerce between England and the colony was steady, and the communication regular. But as Eliza Pinckney's descendant wrote a little more than a century later, "There are, however, principles and rights and sense of wrongs which stir men's hearts and break old bonds, even when the pocket is untouched and the attachment strong." The "taxation without representation" argument was taking hold. In solidarity with their fellow colonists in the North, Carolinians staged a "Tea Party," dumping their taxed tea into the Cooper River. It was 1774, and the stage was set for revolution. Key players in the move to independence and the war that followed would be Charles Cotesworth Pinckney and Thomas Pinckney. Playing important roles on the home front would be their mother and sister, Eliza Lucas Pinckney and Harriott Pinckney Horry.

Everyday Life for Colonial Women

Clearly Eliza Pinckney would have been an exceptional person in any era, but for her to do what she did in eighteenth-century America, given attitudes about women, was truly remarkable. Still, it's important to keep in mind that she couldn't have accomplished what she did without the work of the many slaves who planted and picked her rice and mulberries and indigo, maintained her households, and provided her meals. As with most southerners of her time, there's no evidence that she had any compunctions about the institution of slavery. The most we hear about the subject from Eliza is of her determination to teach slave children to read and write. It's likely that the smallpox hospital she ran was for slaves as well.

Eliza possessed money, education, and the confidence of first her father and then her husband. And because she was single or widowed most of her life, her legal rights were considerably greater than those of married women. She also carried far fewer babies than most and lost only one. All of those advantages set her apart from the vast majority of colonial women. Though the cities on the eastern seaboard, with their shops and conveniences, were growing, most women still lived on farms and produced everything they used. As towns sprouted up, women started specializing—one doing the soap making, another the cheese and butter churning, another the weaving. They bartered with each other for goods and services, creating an off-the-books economy entirely run by women.

When I told friends that I was writing this book, I was often asked about women's literacy. What kind of an education did they have? The answer is, it varied. Eliza seems to have been unusual in that she was sent to school in England and encouraged to continue with her education throughout her life. But almost all of the women who mothered and married the Founders were of the wealthier classes, and even if they had no formal education, they did know how to read and write, and many of them, like Abigail Adams, read extensively, though they never went to school. Abigail never got over the injustice of excluding girls from proper schools, and she advocated vociferously for women's education. John Adams showed how truly thickheaded he could be when he wrote from Paris to his wife running his business and raising his children back in Braintree, Massachusetts. "I admire the ladies here," he oh so sensitively said. "Don't be jealous. They are handsome and very well educated. Their accomplishments are exceedingly brilliant." Abigail had a ready reply: "I regret the trifling narrow contracted education of females in my own country. . . . You need not be told how much female education is neglected, nor how fashionable it has been to ridicule female learning." I suspect he needed not be told because she had told him again and again.

Though many of the marriages of the Founders, like that of Abigail and John Adams, were true partnerships, the women had no legal rights. Under a system called "couverture," their husbands essentially owned women. They had some rights to inheritance, either to the property they brought into a marriage or to a portion of their husband's property, but in the context of the marriage itself they owned nothing, not even their own jewelry. Some colonies allowed for divorce, but since it wasn't legal in England, the subject became another bone of contention between the Mother Country and her colonies. Catharine Littlefield Greene, the widow of Revolutionary War hero Nathanael Greene, caused quite a scandal by living with a man not her husband. Her old friend President Washington (remember, he once danced with Kitty for three hours straight during the war) advised her to marry when she and her gentleman friend came to visit. Kitty was petitioning Congress for repayment of her husband's payouts to clothe his soldiers, and Washington thought her sinful state was causing resistance to the Widow Greene's cause. But Kitty Greene had legal reasons to resist pressure to marry: she wanted to control her property.

The rambunctious, flirtatious, and, eventually,

highly competent Kitty Greene gives us insight into another everyday phenomenon of women's lives at the time—they were constantly pregnant, nursing, and tending babies through illnesses that often ended in death. A woman could expect to have a baby about every two years for as long as she was fertile. It was not at all uncommon for a mother to have children the ages of her grandchildren and to sometimes serve as a wet nurse for her daughter. That is, if a mother lived long enough to see her daughter's children. Many died in childbirth before they ever met a grandchild. For white women who lived, having five to seven living children was the norm, out of five to ten pregnancies. (On plantations, slaves often nursed the babies. In cities there was a thriving wet-nurse business.) **Pioneer Women of America,** a book with barebones facts about the wives of the signers of the Declaration of Independence, is strikingly depressing in its catalog of the births and deaths of the Founders' babies and their mothers.

During the Revolutionary War, while Nathanael Greene was battling the British, Kitty at first stayed home in Rhode Island with her in-laws. She hated it. She took to leaving her children behind and heading with her husband to camp, where she was a popular figure with the troops as well as the generals. But after a couple of winters with the army, she faced a true dilemma—to stay home was to be bored and unhappy, but to go with her husband was to invite, in fact expect, another pregnancy. She opted for camp, much to the delight of the soldiers at Valley Forge and the relief of General Washington, who believed she was good for morale. But Kitty Greene did end up pregnant again. And in later life it was she who would be responsible for the five surviving children.

Despite their lack of legal rights, many pre-Revolutionary women still ruled the roost. There was an elaborate view of "spheres." The men were in the world, while a woman's place was the house, the "domestic sphere." But reading the lives of these couples brings to mind the old joke: The husband says to the wife, "You can handle the small things like where we live and where the children go to school, I'll handle the big things like whether we should recognize Red China." For the women in this book, however, that's exactly what was happening. The men handled relations with England—deciding whether to declare independence and what kind of government should be formed; the women handled pretty much everything else. That's not to say that these women were unaware of the sphere outside of their homes, quite the contrary. Their letters and diaries are filled with political observations and, in the case of Abigail Adams, instructions. Newspapers and magazines of the day kept women as well as men up to date on the news, as well as the fashions, both at home and in England. Visitors from Europe were amazed to see how stylishly their colonial cousins dressed. Given the difficulty of sea voyages, it's astonishing how much commerce and conversation passed between the two sides of the ocean. When Oliver

Goldsmith's **She Stoops to Conquer** opened in London in 1773, it was only a matter of a couple of months before it opened in New York as well.

Theater was popular in New York but banned in Boston. New Yorkers in fact had already performed a show benefiting New York Hospital in 1773, setting the stage for the glitzy benefit performances of today. But Mercy Otis Warren, living in Massachusetts, had probably never seen an actual performance on the stage when she wrote her popular plays. She and her friend Abigail Adams were likely, however, to have attended "lecture day"— the New England practice of going to church on a day in addition to the Sunday service to hear preaching and prayers. Those Puritan ways were foreign to southern women, who entertained incessantly with good food, drink, and dancing as a way to ward off the loneliness of isolated plantation life.

Everyday life for the women in this book depended on where they lived as much as on what their husbands were up to or how much money they had. All of them had household help with the huge amount of cooking, cleaning, and child-raising all women had to do. Many of them, including the northerners, owned slaves. Though the daunting daily duties of these women, including concocting medicines and caring for their servants, were similar regardless of where they lived, what they did in addition to the drudgery varied considerably. Eliza Pinckney's plantation living differed greatly from the life of the mother of another

Founder, Aaron Burr. Esther Edwards Burr's participation in the religious phenomenon known as the "Great Awakening" would have been totally alien to Eliza, though she would probably have sympathized with Esther over the entertaining thrust on her as the wife of a minister who was also the president of Princeton University. Deborah Read Franklin, who ran her husband's many businesses in Philadelphia, would have had difficulty recognizing many of either Eliza's or Esther's endeavors. Still, all of these women would have found familiarity in each other's "domestic sphere." They did what all women who went before them and came after them did when it came to raising children and running households, but they were assigned by history to play other roles as well.

A Solid Citizen

If you want to know why Aaron Burr ended up as the villain in the founding stories, let me introduce you to his family. His father, Aaron Burr, a Presbyterian minister and president of Princeton University, then called the College of New Jersey, died when his son was an infant. His mother, Esther Edwards Burr, daughter of the fiercely evangelical preacher Jonathan Edwards, died when Aaron was two. But she left behind something extremely rare for a colonial woman—a journal. Written as a series of letters to her friend Sarah Prince, Esther Burr's journal reveals an often depressed, almost always exhausted, young woman overwhelmed by her duties as a mother and minister's wife and eternally fearful for her immortal soul.

Jonathan Edwards presided over the Great Awakening, a spiritual movement similar to modern-day revivals. Though the Puritans had fled England in order to practice their beliefs, the generations that followed started slacking off in religious observance, in Edwards's view. The young people were drinking and carousing and doing heaven knows what else. Edwards and his allies railed at them that they were like spiders dangling by a thread over hell, and they better mend their ways. At his meetings, like a latter-day Oral Roberts, he summoned people forth to be converted. After he had been at it a few years, Edwards wrote to a fellow minister, bragging about his accomplishments in the town of Northampton, Massachusetts. "There has been a very great alteration among the youth of the town with respect to reveling, frolicking, profane and unclean conversation, and lewd songs. Instances of fornication have been very rare. There has also been a great alteration among both old and young with respect to tavern haunting. I suppose the town has been in no measure so free of vice in these respects for any long time together for this sixty years as it has been this nine years past."

Those were the years when Esther and her ten brothers and sisters were growing up. Because the Great Awakening came under attack from traditional religions, Edwards exerted a good deal of energy defending his movement. Apparently he could spend up to thirteen hours a day locked in his study, leaving his wife, Sarah, to tend to the books, the household, the parishioners, and, of course, the children. The evangelical movement encouraged women to speak about their conversions, and luckily for Jonathan, Sarah did. At first, she complained about her lot or took to her bed. Then she experienced a series of spiritual epiphanies, stopped fretting, and started testifying for the faith. The evangelical impulse to allow women and blacks a voice was one of the causes of contention with Anglicans and traditional Puritans. But it seems to be the reason Esther kept a journal, as a religious testament, though she had a good deal of trouble on that front.

Jonathan Edwards was eventually run out of Northampton, and settled in Stockbridge, Massachusetts. Without his official pastoral appointment, the family was hurting for money. The three oldest girls soon married, Esther among them. She was wooed and won by Aaron Burr, who traveled from New Jersey to Massachusetts to ask for the hand of the young woman he had met only once, when she was fourteen. (This seems to have been something of a family tradition: Jonathan started pursuing Sarah when she was thirteen, but she staved him off until she reached the ripe old age of seventeen.) After a courtship of a few days, which we can assume included no reveling or frolicking, Aaron returned to Newark, New Jersey. A couple of weeks later Esther and her mother joined him there, and causing quite a bit of gossip among friends and relatives, the Burrs were married. He was thirty-six, the well-established pastor of the First Presbyterian Church of Newark as well as president of the college; she was twenty and, despite her upbringing as a minister's daughter, not ready to take on the tasks of a minister's wife.

Because Esther's letters are to a friend, Sarah Prince, she's much freer with her feelings than Eliza was in her dispatches to her father. Esther gives us some sense of how women of the time felt about the constant childbearing, the loneliness in being cut off from female friends and family, and, always, the ever-present duty. She also provides us with news of the French and Indian War, commentaries on what she was reading (Richardson's romance novel **Pamela** was a favorite; Eliza Pinckney wrote about reading it as well), and gossipy glimpses of the people around her. ("Billy Vance is going to be married—did you ever hear the like? Pray what can he do with a wife? He is more of a woman than of a man." "Mr. Spencer is under petticoat government, that is certain.") But religion was the family business, and much of her writing is about religious matters—the meetings she attended, the preachers she heard, and, especially, the ministers and their wives she was obliged to entertain.

The letters start in 1754, after Esther had been married a couple of years and when her first baby, Sally, was five months old. Sarah Prince had been to Newark for a long stay and, along with Esther's mother, presided over the birth of the baby. With her friend and mother gone and her husband often on the road fund-raising for the college (yes, even then college presidents had to pass the tin cup), she was profoundly lonely. "All solitary! Our house seems so still. I am alone, almost afraid to step about the house for fear of making a disturbance." But more often, she was swamped. "I write just when I can get time. My dear you must needs think I can't get much, for I have my Sally to tend and domestic affairs to see to, and company to wait on besides my sewing, so that I am really hurried." But Esther would try to write a little every day and then send off a packet of her entries with friends traveling to Boston. Sarah regularly wrote back, but those letters have been lost; references to what she had to say show up in her friend's responses. So we hear only Esther's side of the relationship. But it was clearly a close one that seemed to grow closer as the time lengthened since the women had seen each other. Esther pleaded with Sarah to come visit (she never did) and to send love to all their other female friends, a group she referred to as "the sisterhood."

Without any of those women or her mother and sisters around, Esther truly suffered. One entry after another begins with a sad sentiment: "A degree of melancholy has seized me a few days past." "I am of late very low spirited." "Too gloomy to write." "A strange gloom has possessed my mind for some weeks past." "I did not write yesterday because I felt so dull." "I felt like an **old, dead**

horse." Compounding her depression was Esther's sense that she was failing in her religious duty. On one Sabbath eve: "I am carnal, fleshly, worldly minded and devilish." "Oh, how do I fall, **greatly** fall short of the rules, the golden rules, that Christ and his Apostles gave us, not only in words and letter, but in deeds and practice!" Another Sabbath: "A.M. Went to meeting. . . . P.M. Stayed at home with Sally. . . . There is duty at home as well as at the house of God." And on yet another: "Oh, I long for a Sabbath's frame of mind. . . . My heart I see is on the world and not on God."

It would have been pretty tough for Esther's mind to be anyplace else but the world with all the work she had to do. In one week in December 1754, successive entries document the burden: "Dined eight ministers." "Dined ten ministers." "Company stays yet, the weather being very bad." "At last the house is cleared of company." "No sooner is the house emptied but filled again." Then there were her other duties: "Spent A.M. in visiting some sick, and the poor prisoners that you know are very near to me." Plus there was the ironing, spinning, whitewashing, polishing, and child care, and she couldn't find any help. Often in colonial times a young girl from the couple's own or another family would move in to apprentice in domesticity and help in the house. Even well-off families would send a daughter to live with a young family to learn the finer points of cooking and sewing and child-raising. Esther complained that there was no one in Newark to help: "Our young women are all ladies and it is beneath them to go out." (She eventually imported twelve-year-old Sukey Shippen, daughter of a prominent Philadelphia doctor, as a student in housewifery.)

But it was not all gloom and doom. Esther dearly loved her husband and took delight in her little girl. She even enjoyed some of the company, and she certainly thought the married state was for the best. She pestered Sarah Prince to get married and teased her about her single status. This letter in January 1755 is typical: "Miss Abigail is near to marrying, as is usual for all young people **but Miss Prince**. . . . Pray what do you think everybody marries in or about winter for? Tis quite merry, isn't it? I really believe tis for fear of laying cold, and for the want of a bedfellow. Well, my advice to such is the same with the Apostle, LET THEM MARRY—and you know the reason given by him, as well as I do—TIS BETTER TO MARRY THAN TO———." Various of Sarah's beaux were discussed, with code names assigned (one was "the Jesuit!") so that anyone opening the mail wouldn't know for certain whom the young women so thoroughly dissected.

Fears about the mail being intercepted and opened were real given the unsettled state of the colonies. The French and Indian War was raging, causing Esther much concern for her parents, who lived in the frontier town of Stockbridge, Massachusetts, where her father served as a missionary to the large Indian population as well as preacher to the small white one. Keep in mind, the frontier was quite close to major cities, which huddled on the Atlantic seaboard. European settlers had chased the Indians off their land, so resentment understandably ran high, something the French were trying to use to their advantage in their ongoing war against England. Travelers bearing rumors didn't help calm Esther's concerns: "A gentleman from Albany has been here today and brings the certain news that all the Indians in Stockbridge have left the place except two or three families. . . . He said further that they had a mind to send for a neighboring tribe to assist them to kill all the people in Stockbridge. . . . I am almost out of my wits! What will become of my dear father and his afflicted family!" At least as terrifying as the Indians for this pious woman were the Catholic French. "You can't conceive my dear friend what a tender mother undergoes for her children at such a day as this, to think of bringing up children to be **dashed against the stones by our barbarous enemies**—or which is worse, to be enslaved by them, and obliged to turn Papist." To her that was literally a fate worse than death.

Esther kept up with the war news and, like Eliza Pinckney, was furious that the colonies were so poorly protected. Especially vulnerable was her neighboring city. "New York has but two guns that can be fired," she wrote in early 1755. "They have been so neglected that they are rusty and got quite out of order, and more than that they have carried all their gun-powder to the French, and have not enough in the city to fire the guns above twice. Did you ever hear the like!" Clearly, long before the coronation of George III, the Stamp Act, or the Tea Party, the British colonists were losing patience with the Mother Country over the crucial issue of security. The local assemblies weren't ready to put up the cash for their own defense either; Esther sarcastically reported a couple of months later that the Assembly had voted "**500 pounds in full,** to help carry on the war. . . . Our assembly have been in travail these several months, and we all in pain to have her delivered least she should die in the cause. . . . But something is come at last. You my dear remember the mountain that travailed and brought forth a mouse." She was obviously up on the politics, and not happy about what she saw. "Nothing discourages me so much about our public affairs as the growing divisions between the provinces. . . . Our assemblies . . . are extremely divided and set against their governors." And she didn't like what she was reading in the newspapers either: "I conclude you have seen in the New York Mercury such a pack of horrid lies I suppose were never put together before in this country." I'd love to know what they were.

News of the war found Esther rejoicing at the occasional British victories and, more often, despairing at defeats. With some relief she wrote her friend: "We are at last enlisting men here, but not to send abroad. No to be sure, they are only for our own defense. This is much better than nothing." Esther implied that her interest in politics was not always welcomed: "I am perplexed about our public affairs. The men say (though not Mr. Burr, he is not one of that sort) that women have no business to concern themselves about them but trust to those that know better and be content to be destroyed. . . . If I was convinced that our great men did act as they really thought was for the glory of God and the good of the country it would go a great way to make me easy." Sounds like a voter interview today.

The war's main impact on Esther's personal life was to separate her from her family. For a long time she was afraid to visit them: "I am not so certain about going to Stockbridge for the Indians have made their appearance near Stockbridge, and I don't like to be killed by the **barbarous** retches" was her assessment in a July 1755 letter. Soon she must have realized she was pregnant and unable to travel, so it was more than a year later that she and little Aaron Burr, who was born in February, finally set off to see her folks. But they no sooner completed the arduous eight-day trip than Esther's mother decamped for Northampton, where another daughter was about to give birth. Even before her mother left, Esther found Stockbridge terrifying: "Almost overcome with fear. Last night and Thursday night we had a watch at this fort and most of the Indians came to lodge here. Some thought that they heard the enemy last night. Oh how distressing to live in fear every minute." A few days later her mother went to preside over the childbirth. "My Mother gone! It adds double gloom to everything." Esther stuck it out with her father in Stockbridge for another couple of weeks, then rushed home to her husband and daughter, never to see her mother again.

Now the mother of two little children herself, Esther found her already scarce time scarcer still. Soon after Aaron was born, she lamented: "I have had company from early in the morn till late in the eve, and now I write with the son at the breast. When I had but one child my hands were tied, but now I am tied hand and foot. (How I shall get along when I have got half dozen or ten children I can't devise.)" There was every reason for her to believe she would have a baby every couple of years, just like her mother, and she constantly carped about having no help, though the Burrs did own a slave named Harry. If Esther's cries sound much like those of a harassed young mother of any era, she also always had to worry about the children's very survival. Over and over either her son or daughter was on the verge of death. Then there was the question of discipline. When Sally was not even a year old, her mother wrote that she had already been whipped once! "When she has done anything that she suspects is wrong, will look with concern to see what Mama says, and if I only knit my brow she will cry till I smile, and although she is not quite ten months old." These children would learn young that they better behave!

At the end of 1756, the year Aaron was born, the College of New Jersey moved from Newark to Princeton. (Over the summer when Esther had gone to take a look at the magnificent new college building under construction, Nassau Hall, and the house being built for her family, she had to find someone to nurse the baby, but there was a ready supply of wet nurses for hire in Newark.) Once the Burrs moved, Esther was faced with even more entertaining as the ministers and trustees came to call. One week in May, when her sister was visiting, "all the women in Princeton [came] to see me and my sister." "Sundry ministers to dine and a whole room full to tea and three to lodge." "A houseful to breakfast. . . . A drove of women strangers to tea." "An Army to breakfast." Among her guests, however, Esther finally made a female friend close to her own age, Annis Boudinot. An aspiring poet, Annis had recently moved with her parents to Princeton, where before long she married Richard Stockton, an eventual signer of the Declaration of Independence. Soon she became quite famous for her poetry, which was published in newspapers and journals. One of her early efforts, apparently dashed off as Annis was about to go home from visiting Esther, was an ode to the hostess. It begins:

Loveliest of women! Could I gain
Thy friendship, which I prize
Above the treasures of the main
Complete would be my joys.

The friendship was the cause of one of Esther's most memorable letters. "I have had a smart combat with Mr. Ewing about our sex—he is a man of good parts and learning but has mean thoughts of women. He began the dispute in this manner. Speaking of Miss Boudinot I said she was a sociable friendly creature. . . . But Mr. Ewing says—**she and the Stocktons are full of talk about friendship and society and such stuff—and made up a mouth as if much disgusted**—I asked what he would have them talk about—whether he chose they should talk about fashions and dress—**he said things that they understood. He did not think women knew what friendship was. They were hardly capable of anything so cool and rational as friendship**—(My tongue, you know, hangs pretty loose, thoughts crowded in—so I sputtered away for dear life.) You may guess what a large field this speech opened for me—I retorted several severe things upon him before he had time to speak again. He blushed and seemed confused. . . . We carried on the dispute for an hour—I talked him quite silent."

That delightful outburst of a newly confident young woman came in April 1757. The letters continued until September, but often they consisted of only a few dashed-off lines as Esther's days filled with caring for the children and the college. Her husband, Aaron, was working even harder and, without much warning, died three weeks after her last journal entry. Her father, Jonathan Edwards, was chosen to succeed Burr as president of the College of New Jersey. He arrived in Princeton in February 1758, in time for a smallpox epidemic. Their friend Doctor Shippen administered the dangerous inoculation against smallpox to both Edwards and Esther. The inoculation killed Edwards in March. A couple of weeks later Esther died too. She was twenty-six. Aaron Burr was barely two.

In her last letter to her dear friend Sarah Prince, Esther Burr described her nineteen-month-old baby: "Aaron is a little dirty noisy boy, very different from Sally almost in every thing. He begins to talk a little, is very sly and mischievous. He has more sprightliness than Sally and most say he is handsomer, but not so good-tempered. He is very resolute and requires a good governor to bring him to terms." Who knows, if Esther Burr had lived, whether she could have brought Aaron "to terms"? Her own mother, Sarah, might have done so, but on her way to collect her grandchildren and bring them home to raise them, she completed the family tragedy by dying of dysentery in October 1758. The children went to live with their twenty-year-old uncle, Timothy Edwards. Aaron Burr grew up to be a brilliant but "sly and mischievous" man whose lack of a "good governor" almost changed the course of American history.

Philadelphia Business Woman

Benjamin Franklin has come down in history not only as a scientist and statesman but as something of a rogue, a fellow with more than just an eye for the ladies. Much has been made of his relationships with women—a serious scholarly symposium exhaustively explored what Franklin thought of women in general, women in America, women in Europe, women friends, women family members. There's a question left out of all of these studious inquiries: What about the women? What did they think? Of course, it's almost impossible to answer that question—the women didn't conveniently write autobiographies or reveal their attitudes through almanacs. But they did write letters, and since they were letters to a great man, some have actually survived. Plus, Franklin himself provides us with sketches of the women closest to him, though decidedly drawn from his point of view.

For instance, his first meeting with Deborah Read has become famous to followers of Franklin through his charming, probably apocryphal, telling of the runaway seventeen-year-old Boston boy stumbling down the street in Philadelphia with a roll under each arm and one in his mouth. He looked so silly, fifteen-year-old Deborah couldn't stifle a giggle. Franklin soon boarded in Deborah's mother's house and proceeded to woo the girl. Meanwhile, having cut out on his apprenticeship contract to his brother in Boston, Franklin found work as a printer in Philadelphia. The somewhat eccentric governor of the colony took the promising young man under his wing and proposed that Franklin go to England to buy a printing press, pledging to send letters of introduction to pave his way. The year was 1724, and that wasn't the only proposal on the table. Ben had asked Deborah to marry him. Her mother, wary of his prospects and aware of his travel plans, refused to allow the match until he returned. So, though Franklin left for England an engaged man, he soon forgot about the teenager in Philadelphia when there was a whole new continent to conquer. Deborah's mother, justifiably having no faith in the fiancé, married her daughter off to a real ne'er-do-well, John Rogers. He spent her dowry, ran up debts, and took off for the West Indies, where he was rumored to have died. Unfortunately for Deborah, it was not a rumor that could be confirmed.

Having never received the letters of introduction promised by the governor necessary for buying the presses, but having had a very good time, Franklin returned to the printing shop in Philadelphia in 1726 and started looking for a wife. He tried for a couple of girls who would have brought along nice dowries, but they didn't bite. Then he saw Deborah again, suffering in solitude. Whether out of guilt or good sense, he "took to wife" Deborah, meaning that they couldn't legally marry because there was no proof that John Rogers was dead. But the marriage was accepted by all—so much so that his mother-in-law moved in with them to a house on property left by her husband. Deborah had no dowry, but she brought a much heftier down payment to the union: she agreed to raise Franklin's illegitimate son, William, as if he were her own child. (The mystery of William's mother has fascinated historians for centuries, producing as many theories as there are biographers of Franklin.) By the time the couple started living together in 1730, Ben owned (or Ben and the bank owned) the print shop with its newspaper, the **Philadelphia Gazette**. He had also risen in the ranks of prominent men in town. Bringing on the diligent Deborah as a partner so greatly enhanced his prosperity that soon he paid off his debts. After she died, Ben reminisced, "I always discovered that she knew what I did not know; and if something had escaped me, I could be certain that this was precisely what she had grasped."

That was after she died. He was not always so kind while Deborah was alive. But he did rely on her. Mrs. Read ran a sundry shop in the front of the house, Ben's printing shop was in back, and Deborah helped in both, while raising William and taking in various other relatives who crowded the small Market Street home. Everyone contributed to the enterprise. The Boston Franklin family had a recipe for "crown soap," Ben asked for a copy of it from home, and it became a best-seller. (The recipe survives. Let's just say it isn't something kids should try at home.) Since the Read family was well known in the neighborhood, their friends and acquaintances made for good customers. Over the years Deborah took on more duties, including helping run the postal service when Franklin was made postmaster for all the colonies. If Ben married her more out of guilt than passion, his writings show admiration for her: "Frugality is an enriching virtue, a virtue I could never acquire in myself, but I was lucky enough to find it in a wife, who thereby became a fortune to me." At least he talked a good game.

What did she think as she kept the books and helped invest in real estate and expand the business into what were essentially print shop franchises up and down the Atlantic coast and back into the frontier? She probably took some pride in it, but she also was doing what women were expected to do. It would have been unseemly for her to retreat into domesticity when her husband needed her, and it probably never occurred to Deborah that she was doing double duty. Besides, she had too much to do to fret about it. A little boy, Frances Folger, was born two years after they were married, about the same time Franklin started publishing the highly popular **Poor Richard's Almanac.** Franky delighted both of his parents, then broke their hearts when he died of smallpox at age four. It wasn't until seven years later that another child, Sarah, called Sally, was born.

The Franklins did so well in their businesses and real estate investments that Ben was able to retire at forty-two to devote himself to his two real loves—scientific experiments and public affairs. His inventions and discoveries made him famous, and he was called on constantly for public service—meaning that Deborah was called on constantly to keep what was essentially a salon going in the household. She bragged about how speedily she could turn out buckwheat cakes for the unexpected masses. Who knows whether she enjoyed Ben's ascendancy in political life? We do have a reaction, however, from another woman near to Franklin, his mother, Abiah Franklin. On October 14, 1751, she wrote, "I am glad to hear that you are so well respected in your town for them to choose you alderman, although I don't know what it means nor what the better you will be of it besides the honor of it." In other words, nice that you have a fancy title, son, but what good is it? His younger sister, Jane Mecom, added a more gracious postscript: "I rejoice with you and bless God for you in all your prosperity and doubt not that you will bring greater blessings to the world as he bestows upon you greater honors." Greater honors certainly came. Soon Franklin was lobbying for the Pennsylvania Assembly in London in a dispute with the colony's proprietors, and his long years of absence began.

That postscript was typical of Jane Franklin Mecom, the youngest of Ben's sixteen siblings. She could be counted on for emotional support, he could be counted on for financial support, and the two corresponded for decades. Even so, there must have been times, when she wanted to kill him. For her wedding present, on January 6, 1726, he had thought about sending her a nice tea table, but instead, "when I considered that the character of a good housewife was preferable to that of being only a pretty gentlewoman, I concluded to send you a spinning wheel." That was the equivalent of getting a toaster as an anniversary present. You also learn how hard Ben's prominence must have been on his family when you read some of Jane's letters. During his first tour in London for Pennsylvania, which started in 1757, an absurd rumor reached Boston that Franklin had been made a baronet and named governor of Pennsylvania. Jane wrote in horror to Deborah, "Dear Sister, For so I must call you come what will and if I don't express myself proper you must excuse it seeing I have not been accustomed to pay my compliments to governor and baronet's ladies." What a relief it must have been to learn that her brother's honors had not grown quite that great.

Deborah, meanwhile, was left to cope with everything and everybody at home, including the postal system, since it was still her husband's charge. When Lord Loudon, the commander of British forces in America, threatened action against a postal worker for a perceived slight, Deborah stood up to the nobleman, defending the man, who, like almost all of the people Franklin hired for postal jobs, was a relative. But she didn't stop there—once she had the commander's attention, she had a few complaints of her own: "I think I have been treated very unpolitely. I might say insulted in my own house by Sir John Sinclair," and another thing, the postal riders were taking too long in New York and blaming their delay on orders from the commander. Deborah had promised the merchants better mail service; her letter of January 9, 1758, continued: "Since Mr. Franklin went abroad, I have given particular orders that no express on His Majesty's Service be detained in the Post-Office above three hours, and if the post [rider] was not ready to set out, a man and horse have been hired immediately to carry it. This has been expensive and is likely to be more so, as the riders are detained. I therefore hope your Lordship will order the posts for the future to be regularly discharged from New York." Clearly no position of high command intimidated Deborah.

While she was at home fending off officious lords, Ben had taken up residence in London with Margaret Stevenson and her daughter Polly, who provided English equivalents of Deborah and Sally. Deborah had made it perfectly clear that she was not going to brave the Atlantic to be with Franklin for what she thought would be a short stay overseas. Ben's good friend in London, William Strahan, troubled by the relationship with Margaret, wrote to Deborah urging her to make the trip and warning her that women would be after her oh so desirable and temptable husband. "I think you should come over with all convenient speed to look after your interest," he argued. Can you imagine? Now Deborah had to add foxy females to her list of worries. But Strahan's letter didn't budge her—she didn't want to go abroad, she wanted her husband to come home. Deborah supplied Ben with gossip and news but was intimidated when it came to public affairs. She would write a letter and then burn it. He must have at least subtly ridiculed her views for her to be so reticent about politics when she was so assertive about business. And he took the opportunity of his absence to instruct her that women should never "meddle" in politics "except in endeavors to reconcile their husbands, brothers and friends who happen to be on contrary sides. . . . If your sex can keep cool, you may be a means of cooling ours the sooner and restoring more speedily that social harmony among fellow citizens that is so desirable after long and bitter dissensions." There it is—women's role is to come in and calm down the men. His attitude was patronizing beyond belief, but in fact, as the dissensions in the colonies and then the new country grew, it became essential for women to play that civilizing role in order to hold everything together.

In 1760 Deborah reported that her mother had been killed in an awful kitchen fire. That, combined with the length of Ben's absence, made her lonely and suspicious. She finally admitted that she was concerned about what she'd heard about him and other women; he was noncommittal in his response. That might not be particularly surprising—why should he admit to anything at such a distance? But Franklin's next move was out of the ordinary. The man we think of as such a great patriot considered relocating his family permanently to England. When Franklin finally left to go home after five years abroad, he told his friend Strahan that he expected to be back and "I hope I can prevail with Mrs. F. to accompany me."

Not only would she not accompany him to London, but Deborah would not accompany Ben to New York once he returned to America. When he decided to do a grand tour of his postal empire, she opted to stay home. So Sally, who had become a young woman in his absence, went along with her father on what was something of a coming-out party for her. Though Franklin had proudly reported his daughter's achievements to his mother when she was small, he never provided her with the same education he did his son and, later, his grandsons. It just wasn't expected for women. Sally seems to have enjoyed the trip; on it she made friends with a woman with whom her father sustained a decades-long flirtation—Catharine Ray Greene. Franklin had first met Caty Ray several years before, when she was in her early twenties, and he was totally taken with her. She wrote him love letters, he answered by prudently singing the praises of his wife: "If she has any faults I am so used to them that I don't perceive them." When he went to England, Caty wrote to Deborah for advice about her love life. The lively young woman married in due course a man who would become governor of Rhode Island, and she and Franklin wrote to each other regularly and affectionately for decades. But this stop in Rhode Island was the first time he had seen Caty in many years, and the visit gave Sally the opportunity to become friendly with her as well. Then it was on to Boston to sister Jane and a celebration of Sally's twentieth birthday.

When Sally and her father returned to Philadelphia, he embarked on two projects—construction of a new house on Market Street and a campaign for the Pennsylvania Assembly. In a rough race, Franklin finished thirteenth out of fourteen candidates for Philadelphia's eight seats. It must have been a particularly harsh episode from Deborah's perspective. The newspapers and pamphlets of the time hinted at hanky-panky:

**Franklin, though plagued with fumbling age
Needs nothing to excite him,
But is too ready to engage,
When younger arms invite him.**

If Deborah thought his loss would keep her husband home, she was destined to be disappointed. His friends in the assembly chose him to represent them once again in London, this time to petition against proprietary government. Deborah again refused to go with him and refused to let Sally go either. Instead of enjoying her father's position in England, poor Sally had to stay home and suffer the disadvantages of a politician's child. "Your slightest indiscretion will be magnified into crime, in order the more sensibly to wound and afflict me," her father warned. "It is therefore the more necessary for you to be extremely circumspect in all your behavior." What fun. After only a couple of years at home, Franklin set sail again in 1765, and though he told his long-suffering wife that he expected to be home by the end of summer, his sojourn lasted for more than a decade. She never saw him again.

Despite Deborah's insistence on staying home, she missed her husband terribly. After he had been gone a couple of months, she wrote in February 1765 that the town was celebrating a holiday by roasting an ox on the river, "but as I partake of none of the diversions I stay at home and flatter myself that the next packet will bring me a letter from you." A couple of months later she still hadn't heard from him, though she had heard from other people that he had arrived in London safely. "All these accounts are as pleasing as such things can be, but a letter would tell me how your poor arm was and how you were on your voyage, and how you are, and everything is with you."

As it happened, everything was better for him than it was for her. Not long after he arrived in London, Parliament passed the notorious Stamp Act. Ben's daughter, Sally, wrote to him: "The subject now is the Stamp Act, and nothing else is talked of. The Dutch talk of the 'Stamp tack,' the Negroes of the 'tamp'—in short everybody has something to say." Franklin should have listened to his daughter. Even though he had tried to dissuade the English from pursuing the tax on documents, newspapers, almanacs, and other items, he failed to calculate correctly how passionately people felt about the Stamp Act at home. Though Franklin opposed the measure, once it was passed he figured he had to deal with it and suggested a candidate for stamp collector in Philadelphia. When word of the appointment reached America, it incited an angry mob, which marched on his house, ready to raze it. Deborah, determined to protect both her family and her property, first sent her daughter off to stay with her half brother in New Jersey, then prepared to meet the mob. As Deborah recounted the event to her husband, "Cousin Davenport came. . . . Towards night I said he should fetch a gun or two as we had none. I sent to ask my brother to come and bring his gun also, so we made one room into a [fortress]. I ordered some sort of defense upstairs such as I could manage myself. I said, when I was advised to remove, that I was very sure you had done nothing to hurt anybody, I had not given offense to any person at all, nor would I be made uneasy by anybody, nor would I stir or show the least uneasiness—but if anyone came to disturb me, I would show a proper resentment." Resentment at the end of a gun barrel. She faced down the mob and saved her home. He at least had the good grace to say, "I honor much the spirit and courage you showed."

When Jane Mecom heard the news, she dashed off a letter to Deborah. "I am amazed beyond measure at what cousin Davenport tells me that your house was threatened," she wrote on June 25, 1767. "When I think what you must have suffered at the time I pity you; but I think your indignation must have exceeded your fear." Jane knew her sister-in-law well. Ben's London mission might have put Deborah in a precarious position, but it was working out well for Jane. She requested that her brother ask his lady friend, Margaret Stevenson, to pick out some nice English linens so she and her daughter could make flowers to sell for "lady's heads and bosoms." The first shipment so pleased Jane that she wrote directly to Mrs. Stevenson asking for more and "if any new fashion comes out of caps, or handkerchief, ruffles, aprons. Cloaks, hats, shades, [parasols?] or bonnets and you will be kind enough to send me patterns cut in paper with directions how to make them and how they are worn," she would be most grateful. Jane figured she could sell the new English fashions to "our top ladies."

Franklin does seem to have occasionally sent elaborate presents home, but Deborah was much more excited by his letters than his gifts. "I have been so happy as to receive several of your dear letters within these few days and to see a man that had seen you," Ben's wife exulted in October 1765. "He tells me you look well, which is next to seeing you. How am I pleased to read over and over again—I call it a **husband's love letter**." But her pining for him didn't paralyze her. Deborah was wildly busy taking care of relatives from both families and managing the finances, and as the wife of a famous personage, she was expected to entertain prominent people who came to pay their respects. In January 1766, she proudly announced her purchase of real estate in Nova Scotia. "So you see I am a real Land Jobber. I tell Sally this is for grandchildren. She seemed very well pleased at it, and thinks we shall have some in good time. I hope I have done as you would have me or as you would if you had been at home yourself."

Sally continued to report the political news. To her father she wrote: "We have heard by a roundabout way that the Stamp Act is repealed. . . . The bells rung, we had bonfires and one house was illuminated. Indeed I never heard so much noise in my life; the very children seem distracted." To her half brother, William, she wrote: "On Friday night there was a meeting of seven or eight hundred men at Hare's Brew House, where Mr. Ross, mounted on a bag of grain, spoke to them a considerable time." William Franklin's position as royal governor of New Jersey was making things tense for the family. A staunch loyalist to the Crown, William infuriated the nascent revolutionaries, which frightened his stepmother. When Sally went to visit her half brother in the spring of 1767, he was challenged to a duel while she was there. Deborah hesitated about telling Ben but worried that someone else would. "Sally was very much scared and would not let her brother go without her. So you see this daughter of ours is a mere champion and thinks she is to take care of us. . . . I long to see her back again as I could not live another day without her. . . . Oh, that you were at home!"

That spring Deborah desperately wanted her husband home. She had been left to oversee the construction of the new house, and she was sure he was going to criticize her for the decisions about what color to paint a room, or where to hang a picture. But most of all, she needed his advice about Sally, who had a serious suitor. "I am obliged to be father and mother," Deborah complained. She explained that she treated the young man, Richard Bache, in a friendly fashion because if she did not, "it would only drive her to see him somewhere else which would give me much uneasiness. I hope I act to your satisfaction. I do according to my best judgment." Franklin was far from pleased with the match: William had investigated Bache's background and concluded that he was a fortune-hunter. Ben certainly wasn't ready, though, to rush

home to play protective father. Instead, he told
Deborah he left the matter "to you and her
brother." Then he dropped the bombshell that he
wouldn't be there for the wedding, but "I would
not occasion a delay in her happiness if you
thought the match was a proper one."

It was the worst of all possible decisions from
Deborah's point of view. Her husband didn't
straight out oppose the marriage, but it was clear
he wasn't happy about it. And though he refused to
trouble himself to show up for the wedding of his
only daughter, he had plenty of penny-pinching
suggestions: "Do not make an expensive feasting
wedding, but conduct everything with frugality
and economy. . . . I know very little of the gentleman or his character, nor can I at this distance. I
hope his expectations are not great of any fortune
to be had with our daughter before our death."
Then there were more instructions about the
house: "Paint the wainscot a dead white; paper the
walls blue, and tack the gilt border round just
above the surbase and under the cornish. If the paper is not equally colored when pasted on, let it be
brushed over again with the same color." He meanwhile was off to spend the summer in France,
where he dined with the king and queen. Deborah
was probably ready to tack the gilt around his head.
She enlisted allies in support of Bache, including
Jane Mecom and Margaret Stevenson, and Bache
wrote to Franklin as well, explaining the reasons
for his financial setbacks. Ben frostily replied, "I
have told you before that my estate is small, scarce a

sufficiency for the support of me and my wife, who are growing old and cannot now bustle for a living as we have done."

Despite her father's misgivings, Sally married Richard Bache in October 1767, and Philadelphia threw quite a party. According to one newspaper's account, "all the shipping in the harbor displayed their colors on this happy occasion." But Ben refused to be mollified. A couple of months after the wedding, on December 1, 1767, his sister Jane wrote: "You are called to rejoice at the settling in marriage of your beloved daughter to a worthy gentleman who she loves and the only one that can make her happy." But Ben stuck to his guns: "She has pleased herself and her mother, and I hope she will do well, but I think they should have seen some better prospect than they have, before they married, how the family was to be maintained." It took Richard Bache traveling to England to meet his father-in-law in person for Franklin to relent. He greeted Bache warmly, much to the relief of Sally and Deborah. That was the only way the two men would meet, because Franklin showed no signs of ever going home. For a while, Deborah kept up her good cheer, writing gossipy tidbits: "Our Sukey Shippen [the same Sukey Shippen who helped Esther Burr] is married. It was a sort of runaway affair, although it is to a parson." Then she suffered a stroke and started to let him know how unhappy she was. "It is very hard on me, now more than sixty years old," she complained in 1769. Then in 1770: "How I long to see you, but I would not say one word that would give you one moment's trouble." But after he had been away **six years,** she began to pressure him to come home. "You thought it would be but seven months. . . . I hope you will not stay longer than this fall." He paid absolutely no attention.

Another Benjamin Franklin did bring Deborah happiness in her last few years. Sally had a little boy she named for her father. Deborah called the baby "Kingbird" and lovingly recounted his escapades, then those of his little brother. None of it seems to have tempted Franklin to return to hearth and home. Instead, he wrote back about Margaret Stevenson's grandchild. Eventually, old and sick and tired, Deborah had had it. She just stopped writing, telling her husband, "Sally will write. I can't write anymore. I am your affectionate wife D Franklin." That was it—she had signed off.

His sister Jane did keep up her correspondence, with news of unrest in the colonies, which dismayed her. "The whole conversation of this place turns upon politics and religious controversies, both managed with too much bitterness as you will see by the newspapers, if you give yourself the trouble to read them. But they will not infallibly inform you of the truth; for everything that any designing person has a mind to propagate is stuffed into them." So much for the press and the politicians! As the relationship between England and the colonies frayed, questions arose about just what Franklin was doing in London. Whose side was he on anyway? He wrote to Jane about reading a

Boston paper that he was in royal favor, which he hotly denied. "Far from having any promise of royal favor, I hear of nothing but royal and ministerial displeasure." And, he insisted, it would be in America's interest for him to stay at least through the next spring. That was in the fall of 1774; he had been gone ten years and was ready to remain in London indefinitely. But he didn't stay through spring, because Deborah died in December. He had to go home to tend to all of the affairs she had managed for so long.

Franklin finally moved into the house Deborah built. Though his daughter, son-in-law, and grandchildren provided company, he had the audacity to mourn the loss of his "old and faithful companion, and I everyday become more sensible of the greatness of that loss that cannot now be repaired." Years later, when he was living in Paris, Ben wrote a story about a dream. He went to heaven to try to reclaim his wife, but Deborah wouldn't have him. "I have been your good wife . . . almost half a century. Be content with that."

CHAPTER TWO

1775–1776: Independence

MERCY OTIS WARREN

Rebellious Women

The mob that marched on Deborah Franklin's house to object to the Stamp Act was just one of many public protests against what more and more Americans were beginning to see as oppressive rule by England. In Boston, rioters destroyed the stamp collector's office and the lieutenant governor's home. Though Parliament repealed the infamous law the year after it was enacted, other harsher measures followed, provoking the colonists to stronger resistance. The British believed the colonies should pay for the protection afforded by victory in the French and Indian War; the colonists were beginning to formulate the famous concept of "no taxation without representation." Even before the Stamp Act, the Sugar Act of 1764 taxing molasses and sugar, among other products, had led to a sharp decline in the American rum business, to the dismay of many. Then, in 1765, came the Quartering Act, requiring Americans to house and feed British troops (a situation that forced women to serve the soldiers, at best, and to fear rape, at worst); the Townshend Acts soon followed, with their oppressive tax on tea, as well as paint, paper, lead, and glass. As the men in the Old World passed their laws, the women in the New World organized against them.

To fire at British taxes, Americans used the only weapon in their arsenal: the boycott. As shoppers, women were key participants in the movement to shun British goods. The unanimous decision not to use "ribbons and etc. & etc." was agreed to by "a large circle of very agreeable ladies in this town," reported the **Boston News-Letter** in 1767. The Daughters of Liberty, as well as its Sons, were called upon to sacrifice. One of the "Daughters," upset by the merchants' lack of resolve, published a scolding poem in the **Pennsylvania Gazette** in 1768:

> **Since the men from a party, on fear of a frown,**
> **Are kept by a sugar-plumb, quietly down.**

Supinely asleep, & deprived of their sight
Are stripped of their freedom, and robbed of
   their right.
If the Sons (so degenerate) the blessing
   despise,
Let the Daughters of Liberty nobly arise,
And though we've no voice but a negative
   here.
The use of the taxables, let us forebear,
(Then the merchants import till your stores
   are all full
May the buyers be few and your traffic be
   dull.)

Because they knew they would court "dull traffic" if they sold British goods, the Boston merchants signed an agreement forswearing imports. Any who violated the agreement were called to task publicly with flyers, like the one warning, "It is desired that the Sons and Daughters of Liberty refuse to buy from William Jackson." In a revolutionary appeal, women were explicitly summoned to political action.

With the boycott of British cloth, American women were forced to manufacture their own, another chore added to the already onerous domestic duties of the day. Clergymen organized "spinning bees" where groups of women would come together to turn spinning wheels by the hour, creating hundreds of skeins of wool, which would then be woven into cloth. Newspapers heralded the women's activities, regularly writing up the spinning sessions. In 1769 the **Boston Evening Post** wrote that the "industry and frugality of American ladies must exalt their character in the eyes of the world and serve to show how greatly they are contributing to bring about the political salvation of a whole continent." In the **Essex Gazette** of Salem, Massachusetts, a letter of May 23, 1769, told of the Daughters of Liberty of Newport, Rhode Island, "serving their country" by spinning from six o'clock in the morning until six o'clock in the evening. While they spun and gossiped, they also left "the domestic sphere" to talk politics. And their political sensibilities were encouraged by patriots who urged women to celebrate their "homespun" outfits, setting their appeals to song:

> **Wear none but your own country linen;**
> **Of economy boast, let your pride be the**
> **most**
> **To show cloths of your own make and**
> **spinning.**

Women could literally drape themselves in the cause of liberty. At a fancy ball in Williamsburg, Virginia, in December 1769 held for the governor and ladies and gentlemen of the town, the women showed up at the gala affair in simple homespun gowns, leaving their imported silks and brocades at home. The Daughters of Liberty organized up and down the colonies, with hundreds of women spinning their wheels and sipping "Liberty Tea," a mixture of herbs and flowers rather than the real

thing. The **Boston Evening Post** published a boycott agreement on February 12, 1770: women from
three hundred families, including "ladies of the
highest rank and influence," publicly promised
"**totally** to abstain from the use of tea." They continued: "This agreement we cheerfully come into,
as we believe the very distressed situation of our
country requires it."

A woman's place was changing. Sometimes
women found themselves in a very public place.
They joined in the mobs, tarring and feathering
merchants who defied the boycott against British
goods. And they marched in what were in effect
political demonstrations. When, in 1770, her husband was arrested in New York for distributing a
leaflet against the Quartering Act, Hannah Mc-
Dougall "led a parade of ladies from Chapel Street
to the jail, entertaining them later at her home."
Parliament finally repealed the Townshend Acts,
but not until after the Boston Massacre of 1770,
which spurred all of the colonies on to rebellion.

In an effort to control the most obstreperous
colonial city, in 1768 England sent four thousand
troops to occupy Boston, amounting to almost one-
third of the city's population. Not surprisingly, the
presence of so many soldiers stirred resentments.
Women accused them of rape; men complained
that the moonlighting military were stealing jobs
from the locals. A couple of weeks before the inci-
dent that's come down in history as the Boston
Massacre, a British customs officer, trying to break
up a bunch of boycotters, killed an eleven-year-old

boy. Thousands of Bostonians, including thousands of women, marched to the boy's funeral. So the people were primed for protest when British soldiers fired on a mob of young men hurling snowballs and snide insults. Three people were killed, two mortally wounded, and a revolution was conceived. What seemed like the whole city marched six abreast to the funeral of the five victims. Committees of Correspondence formed throughout the colonies with communication established among them, providing a loose framework for what could become colonial government.

Still, the British persisted in the belief that they could tax America into submission. The repeal of the Townshend Acts was followed by the passage of the much-hated Tea Act of 1773, giving a monopoly to the British East India Company in a move that would put many colonial merchants out of business. When the first ships loaded with tea docked in Boston Harbor, patriots dressed as Indians dumped the cargo in the water—the famous Boston Tea Party. The outraged English rushed through the Boston Port Bill prohibiting all shipping into and out of the town until its citizens paid for the tea. It was just one of the so-called Intolerable Acts passed in 1774, including one that outlawed self-government in Massachusetts—making participation in town meetings and the colonial assembly illegal. Thinking it could isolate Boston as the hotbed of hatred against the Mother Country, Parliament made a terrible mistake. The disparate colonies found common cause in defense of their

Massachusetts colleagues. Goods started coming overland into Boston from other parts of America, in another act of defiance against the distant rulers. Thomas Pinckney, who was still studying in England, wrote to his mother, Eliza, in South Carolina about a petition against the laws signed by Carolinians abroad. The Virginia House of Burgesses voted a day of prayer and fasting in solidarity with Boston, causing the royal governor to dissolve that assembly. In Massachusetts, patriots circulated a petition called the Solemn League and Covenant calling on "all adult persons of both sexes" to boycott British imports. The Continental Congress convened in Philadelphia to determine what further steps to take.

Though the Congress, of course, was an all-male affair, women continued their subversive activities in their parsonages and parlors, with the enthusiastic approval of at least some men. One wrote to the **South Carolina Gazette:** "Yes Ladies, you have it in your power more than all your committees and Congresses, to strike the stroke, and make the hills and plains of America clap their hands." Just by abstaining from tea! In **The Massachusetts Spy,** a self-described "aged and very zealous Daughter of Liberty" also urged action:

**Look out poor Boston make a stand
Don't suffer any tea to land
For if it once gets footing here
Then farewell Liberty most dear.**

It was not just Boston that made a stand. In 1774 the **Virginia Gazette** published "A Lady's Adieu to Her Tea Table" because "Its use will fashion slavish chains upon my country." And most famously, in Edenton, North Carolina, fifty-one members of the Ladies' Patriotic Guild met in October 1774 at the home of Mistress Elizabeth King to sign an agreement to boycott tea and British cloth "for the public good." The agreement was published in the **Morning Chronicle and London Advertiser,** causing its English readers great amusement, if a well-publicized cartoon of the time is to be believed. One North Carolinian living in London, Arthur Iredell, saw the mean-spirited drawing depicting incredibly ugly women and wrote with dripping sarcasm to his brother in America: "Is there a female Congress at Edenton too? I hope not, for we Englishmen are afraid of the male Congress, but if the ladies, who have ever, since the Amazonian Era, been esteemed the most formidable enemies, if they, I say, should attack us, the most fatal consequence is to be dreaded."

The English might have found the female protestations funny, but they soon learned to take seriously the formal ban of the Continental Congress on the importation of all British goods. Among other sacrifices, no mourning attire could be worn, since the clothes designated as proper for funerals all came from abroad. In her nineteenth-century biography of Eliza Pinckney, Harriott Ravenal describes a Charleston funeral in 1775 where everyone was colorfully turned out. It was "still remembered as the first **visible** sign of resistance. . . . When one remembers what affairs of solemn state funerals were then; how the kinsfolk came from far and near to attend them, and all walked in strict order of proximity swathed in black from top to toe . . . one comprehends what an innovation this was, and how deep the resolve that inspired it."

Still, George III rebuked any calls for conciliation with the colonies, and he found many supporters loyal to him on the other side of the Atlantic. Before going off to the Continental Congress, John Adams did some legal work in Maine, where he was distressed to see how little sympathy for rebellion against the British he encountered. But he was cheered on the way home when a female tavern keeper refused to serve him even smuggled tax-free tea, shaming Adams by telling him that only coffee was available in her establishment. "I must be weaned," he admitted to Abigail, "and the sooner, the better."

In Virginia and Massachusetts, the radicals continued their resistance. As the Virginia colonists voted to raise a militia, Patrick Henry delivered the "Give me liberty or give me death" oration that has echoed through the centuries. Defying the law, a Provincial Council met in Concord, Massachusetts, to select delegates to a Second Continental Congress. More British troops massed in Boston, causing a militia of minutemen to gather weapons and ammunition surreptitiously. When rumors swirled that the British were searching for a hidden arms cache, women and children helped prevent the soldiers from reaching their goal. That was March 1775. Then, learning of a major supply depot in Concord and the presence of some of the patriot leaders in Lexington, the British decided to take action. It was April 18, 1775. Paul Revere and his cohorts rode furiously to warn of the redcoats' advance, and at dawn the next morning in Lexington the first shots of the Revolutionary War were fired. Much of the support for the Crown instantly evaporated.

Though Massachusetts lost more men than the British on the battlefield of Lexington and the supply depot in Concord was destroyed, as they marched back to Boston, English troops came under incessant fire from farmers and country folk. By the end of the day the British had lost three men for every one American. And everyone in Massachusetts, including the women, seemed ready to rush to support the patriot cause. Some wonderful nineteenth-century books herald the patriotism of women after Lexington and Concord. Elizabeth Ellet's two-volume work, **The Women of the American Revolution**, recounts a story of "the morning after the battle of Lexington, about a hundred American soldiers halted in front of the house of Colonel Pond." Though only Mrs. Pond and a couple of servants were there, they proceeded to feed all those soldiers, with the help of some neighbors who volunteered their cows for milking.

The revolutionary Continental Congress, outlawed by the king, met in May 1775 with a challenge now before it: how to respond to the battles in Massachusetts. The answer came in June with the formation of the Continental army and the appointment of George Washington as its commander. Rebels rallied round in support of liberty from British oppression rather than independence from British rule. The day after Washington's appointment, British movements around Boston met with armed militiamen at Breed's Hill, and the next battle of the Revolution, what's come down in history as the Battle of Bunker Hill, ended in a modest British victory and a major show of willingness by the colonists to fight the Mother Country. But ammunition was in short supply. Elizabeth Ellet tells us that a "Mrs. Draper" responded to Washington's call for lead or pewter to make bullets. "Mrs. Draper was rich in a large stock of pewter, which she valued as the ornament of her house. . . . Her husband before joining the army had purchased a mould for casting bullets, to supply himself and son with this article of warfare. Mrs. Draper was not satisfied with merely giving the material required, when she could possibly do more; and her platters, pans and dishes were soon in process of transformation into balls."

Despite the commissioning of an army, Congress was still not ready to separate from England. In July the delegates sued for peace, sending King George what became known as the Olive Branch Petition, calling for greater liberties but still disavowing independence. The king never even considered it; instead, in August he declared war against America, hiring twenty-nine thousand Hessian mercenaries to help crush the stubborn colonials. Throughout the fall of 1775 Congress learned first that Falmouth, Maine, had been burned by the British navy, then that Norfolk, Virginia, had been destroyed. The voices calling for independence grew stronger and more strident. Most famous among them was Tom Paine, but equally influential with the men making the decisions was Mercy Otis Warren, whose plays, poems, and personal letters fostered the cause. And the private pleadings of Abigail Adams certainly held sway with her husband and his colleagues. By June 1776 John Adams was working with Thomas Jefferson, Benjamin Franklin, Robert Livingston, and Roger Sherman on a draft of the Declaration of Independence. On July 4 the final version was approved. Though the resolution of revolution was read throughout the land, the final signed version was not published until January 1777. By that time members of Congress, each with a price on his head for disloyalty to the Crown, were hiding out from the British in Baltimore. There the signers of the Declaration turned to a woman for the perilous job of printing the document, with their names attached, for the first time. The publisher of the **Maryland Journal,** Mary Katherine Goddard, bravely printed her own name at the bottom of the Declaration, becoming herself a signer of sorts, firmly associating herself with the dangerous cause of the new nation.

Propagandist for the Revolution

No political campaign can succeed without pro-
pagandists. In modern times armies of public
relations firms and media buyers spend millions
to bring a candidate or a cause to the voters via
television, direct mail, or the Internet. In colonial
times the pamphlet was the delivery system of
choice, and one of the great pamphleteers of the
time was a woman—Mercy Otis Warren.

Boston, as the center of rebellious sentiment, saw
both the men and the women caught up in the revolutionary cause. Mercy Warren's writings against
British laws were public, something highly unusual
for women of the day. She also kept up a lively private correspondence with some of the great men of
the era, and with some like-minded women as well.
Abigail Adams was a particular friend—they had
met through their husbands—and the letters between the two women over the years reveal a great
deal about political attitudes on the distaff side.
Fortunately for us, the friends lived just far enough
away from each other in the area around Boston—
Abigail in Braintree, Mercy in Plymouth—to make
regular visiting inconvenient, so letter writing was
necessary for communication. And both women
saw a great need to communicate about everything,
from how to raise the children to how to run the
country. Because of her husband's high positions,
Abigail Adams's writings have survived the centuries. Mercy Otis Warren has been largely over-
looked outside of academic circles. But because

they were published, her very influential works survive as well.

Both the sister and wife of ardent revolutionaries, Mercy Warren had the advantage of what was then considered a masculine education. Growing up in Barnstable, Massachusetts, even as she learned domestic arts from her perpetually pregnant mother, Mercy was allowed by her father to share her brothers' tutors and learn along with the boys until they went off to Harvard. He turned out to be the first of several men who pushed Mercy to venture beyond a "woman's place." James Otis, her brother, involved her in his rebellious activities. James Warren, her husband, fostered her literary endeavors. John Adams, her friend, assigned her topics for propaganda publications. Eventually many of the great men of early America—George Washington, Thomas Jefferson, Alexander Hamilton, and Elbridge Gerry, as well as Adams—corresponded with her.

In 1757, three years after Mercy Otis and James Warren married, they took over the Warren family farm in Plymouth. That same year their first child, James, was born, the oldest of what would be five boys born over nine years. Despite the rapid onslaught of babies, it was a time when the Warrens started running something of a political salon, with the radical Samuel Adams and his milder-mannered cousin John as frequent guests. Since the Otis family had always been involved in politics, Mercy had developed an affection for the subject as a young woman. Also, because of his long-standing feud with her family, she nurtured a hatred of one politician in particular: Thomas Hutchinson, who beat out Mercy's father for appointment as chief justice of Massachusetts. The undying Otis enmity would serve the patriots in good stead as Hutchinson became the symbol in Boston of everything bad about the British.

James Otis, Mercy's beloved brother, took the lead in the fight against the Sugar and Stamp Acts with his pamphlet putting forward the principle of no taxation without representation. His newspaper articles helped stir the populace to mass action, including gutting the house of the lieutenant governor, who just happened to be Thomas Hutchinson. And according to an eighteenth-century historian, it was a meeting of the Otis family at the Warren home that led to the so-called Stamp Act Congress, assembled to resist the law. As the tensions increased and the British sent troops to occupy Boston, Mercy Warren's former loyalty to the Mother Country stretched to the breaking point. She later wrote, in her massive history of the American Revolution, that the day the British troops entered the city, March 1, 1768, was a day marked "with infamy."

Mercy's own entry into the world of political propaganda coincides with her brother's departure from it. James Otis started showing signs of losing his sanity by the end of 1760; then he was permanently put out of commission as a troublemaker by a loyalist officeholder who beat the unruly Otis senseless in a brawl. Mercy took up the pen, producing anonymously published but widely read satirical plays and poems about British sympathizers and their leaders, especially Thomas Hutchinson. The group of men gathered around the Warren family fireside also started plotting action—the plan for Committees of Correspondence in each of the colonies, to provide information and communication, was most likely hatched at the hearth in Plymouth.

Although Mercy's writings, with their classical themes and overwrought style, are fairly tough going for the contemporary reader, they were wildly popular at the time. In 1772 the first play, **The Adulateur,** was published in two installments in the **Massachusetts Spy** newspaper. In it a thinly disguised Thomas Hutchinson, by then the governor, puts personal ambition above all, including the people's liberties. She set the blank-verse play in the fictional kingdom of Servia and gave the villain, the Hutchinson character, lines purporting to reveal his true intentions:

> **To quench the generous flame, the ardent love**
> **Of liberty in Servia's freeborn sons,**
> **Destroy their boasted rights and make them slaves.**

It was not a play written with a stage production in mind—theater was outlawed in Puritan Boston. Mercy, as a deeply religious woman, was unlikely to have ever actually seen a play performed. But the drama fulfilled the propaganda purposes of the patriots, ending as it did with a warning that the struggle for liberty could end in bloodshed.

Hutchinson served as the target of Mercy's next play as well. **The Defeat,** again appearing in two installments, this time in the **Boston Gazette,** chronicled the notorious letters between the Massachusetts governor and a member of the British government. The letters, shown around Parliament but meant for private consumption, were leaked to the conspirators huddled at the Warren hearthside. The correspondence revealed Hutchinson's abandonment of the principles of liberty and provided ample fodder for his enemies. But nowhere near as much fodder as Hutchinson's next act—in his capacity as a representative of the Crown, he insisted on strict adherence to English law. He ordered that the tea coming in from Britain under the newly passed and much despised Tea Act be unloaded at Boston Harbor. Mercy and her compatriots were thrilled when the Boston Tea Party thwarted Hutchinson's decree. At the suggestion of John Adams, Mercy, who was fast becoming the bard of revolutionary ideals, wrote a poem about the heroic deeds at Boston Harbor that Adams convinced a newspaper to publish. Again, it's cast in mythological terms as a "squabble between the Celestials of the sea arising from a scarcity of nectar and ambrosia." But there was no question as to the true meaning of the poem:

The heroes of the Tuskeraro Tribe [the men disguised as Indians],

Who scorn alike, a fetter, or a bribe,
In order ranged, and waiting freedoms nod,
To make an off'ring, to the Watry God.

The poem also included this interesting observation:

For females have their influence over kings,
Nor wives, nor mistresses were useless
  things,
En'e to the Gods, of ancient Homer's page.
Nor when in weighty matters they engage,
Could they neglect the sexes sage advice.

It would be a mistake to see Mercy Warren as some latter-day feminist; she regularly defended the "domestic sphere" as the proper place for women. While she was plotting and propagandizing she was also pursuing the "womanly arts." One of her needlework accomplishments, an elaborate embroidered top for a card table, is still in the collection of the Pilgrim Hall Museum in Plymouth, Massachusetts. She wrote to one young female correspondent that it was possible to do both, raise proper children and write profound chapters, as long as you arranged your time sensibly. Even then the "having it all" question troubled women. Despite her protestations, however, Mercy clearly saw herself as someone with a political role to play. Not only had she been educated "like a boy," but the men in her family valued female opinions. Her brother James Otis was one of the few rebels who equated American liberty with the emancipation of women. In his famous pamphlet attacking the Sugar and Stamp Acts, he raised truly revolutionary questions: "Are not women born as free as men? Would it not be infamous to assert that the ladies are all slaves by nature?" Otis initiated a correspondence with a famous Englishwoman of the era who was an ardent supporter of America as well as a republican—Catharine Macaulay.

As something of a celebrity Macaulay received all the positive and negative attention afforded "celebrities" today—sarcastic criticism from her political opponents, effusive praise from her supporters. As a woman doing serious work, she was something of a curiosity as well. From 1763 to 1771, during the period of deepening division on either side of the Atlantic, her five-volume "republican" **History of England** attracted much notice on both shores, so did her looks ("painted up to the eyes," huffed one critic) and her love life. (She scandalized society by taking up with a rector who placed a life-sized statue of her in his church.) A widow with a tidy inheritance from her physician husband and the mother of one daughter, Macaulay became a fierce fighter in the pamphlet wars, questioning the need for a monarchy and calling for the establishment of more democratic institutions. Her ideas quickly gained currency among the men in America who were beginning to understand their cries for liberty might lead to a new form of government. Several of the Founders regularly corresponded with the beguiling liberal lady.

After James Otis died, his sister started a correspondence with Macaulay where her brother left off. Not to be outdone, Mercy's friend Abigail Adams also started writing to the famous English author, whose ideas about women's rights, particularly women's education, clearly had an impact on Abigail's own thinking. When she would try to enlist Mercy Warren in the cause of their sex, however, Abigail met mostly with silence from the woman who was following in Macaulay's footsteps. Most noticeably, Mercy never responded when Abigail wrote to her about John's brush-off to her "remember the ladies" admonition. It might have been that Mercy was ten years older than Abigail and more conservative, at least at that time, in her views of women's roles; it might have been that she had sons and no daughters so felt less keenly about girls' education; it might have been that she didn't want to risk alienating the men who admired her by taking up the cause of women. Whatever the reason, the position of women in pre-Revolutionary times did not seem particularly to interest America's foremost female writer.

But she did see a role for women in the cause she was worried about—liberty. At the beginning of 1774 she wrote to her friend Hannah Winthrop: "Be it known unto Britain even American daughters are politicians and patriots and will aid the good work with their female efforts." She was at the very center of the resistance. It was James Warren, along with Samuel Adams, who in 1774 promulgated the Solemn League and Covenant calling for a boycott of merchants doing business with Britain. Again, Mercy's poetic prowess was called upon to drum up support for the effort, which citizens of some towns resisted as they waited to see what the coming Continental Congress would do. In anticipation of that Congress, Mercy Warren wrote to John Adams in July 1774, warning the delegates against choosing an ambitious man as their leader: "Such a one might subvert the principles on which your institution is founded, abolish your order and build up a **monarchy** on the ruins of the happy institution." Clearly, she didn't trust the men to be sufficiently republican. A month later she again voiced her concern about the Congress to Abigail, worrying that the men meeting in Philadelphia had in their hands "the future freedom and happiness of a wide extended empire." Only bloodshed, she foretold, would restore the colonies to their rights. Then, to her female friend, Mercy allowed herself to express her worst fears: "No one has at stake a larger share of domestic felicity than myself. . . . I see no less than five sons who must buckle on the harness and perhaps fall a sacrifice to the manes of liberty."

Even knowing what she could lose, Mercy had no illusions that war could be avoided. In December 1774 she wrote to Catharine Macaulay: "America stands armed with resolution and virtue; but she recoils at the idea of drawing the sword against the nation from whence she derived her origin. Yet Britain, like an unnatural parent, is ready to plunge her dagger into the bosom of her affectionate offspring." In that same letter, Mercy staked out new territory for herself, defending her political activities: "You see madam I disregard the opinion that women make but indifferent politicians. . . . When the observations are just and honorary to the heart and character, I think it very immaterial whether they flow from a female lip in the soft whispers of private friendship, or whether thundered in the Senate in the bolden language of the other sex." Of course, Mercy's private friendships were with some of the most influential men in the land.

Catharine Macaulay didn't hesitate to use "bolden language" of her own. In 1775 she issued another of her famous broadsides, this one an "Address to the People of England, Scotland and Ireland on the Present Important Crisis of Affairs." In it she warned her countrymen that they could not expect to continue to "pick the pockets of your American brethren" without defiance. She predicted prophetically: "If a civil war commences between Great Britain and her Colonies, either the Mother Country, by one great exertion, may ruin both herself and America, or the Americans, by a lingering contest, will gain an independency." Britain would then, she cautioned, "be left to the bare possession of your foggy islands."

Despite the stirring sentiments from the female agitator across the seas, the Americans were not yet ready to take up arms. Even as the political situation frustrated Mercy (to Abigail she fretted, "We cannot long continue in this state of suspense. It is and ever has been my poor opinion that justice and liberty will finally gain a complete victory over tyranny"), the personal situation frightened her. What would happen, she wondered to Abigail, to their patriot husbands, "who would be marked out as early victims to successful tyranny." Abigail replied after King George had rejected the Olive Branch Petition: "The die is cast . . . the sword is now our only, yet dreadful alternative." Friends of liberty, she added, would choose "no doubt to die the last British freemen, than bear to live as the first of British slaves." As fearful as they were for their families, these women could not be charged as cowards!

In fact, Mercy was preparing to publish another of her notorious pamphlets. This one, called **The Group,** took on Boston's loyalist community so sarcastically that the poet asked her friend if it was too strident. Not at all was Abigail's answer. Though she could understand that Mercy might worry she had been more severe than "that benevolence which ought always to be predominant in a female character," Abigail assured her that "satire well applied has sometimes found its way when persuasions, admonitions and lectures of morality have failed." Mercy also queried John Adams about his views of her satirical style, wondering whether the times warranted harsh words from a woman: "if a little personal acrimony might be justifiable in your sex," she asked, "must not the female character suffer?" John too reassured her and praised her "genius." And her ever-supportive and devoted husband, James, weighed in with words of praise: "God has given you great abilities; you have improved them in great acquirements. You are possessed of eminent virtues and distinguished piety. For all these I esteem I love you in a degree that I can't express. They are all now to be called into action for the good of mankind, for the good of your friends, for the promotion of virtue and patriotism." Quite an endorsement. Though she continued to publish anonymously, Mercy must have realized that, in all probability, her identity was no secret; otherwise, she wouldn't have feared for her reputation.

The Group was published on April 3, 1775, heaping scorn on those faithful to Britain and predicting that for the patriots

> **Glory and victory and lasting fame**
> **Will crown their arms and bless each hero's**
> **name.**

Though she was clearly calling men to arms, Mercy continued in her private correspondence to plead for peace. On April 5, she wrote to John Adams, "Is there no hope that the dread calamity of civil convulsions may yet be averted, or must the blood of the best citizens be poured out." But it was her public writing that had an effect. **The Group** was reprinted in New York and Philadelphia, and just over two weeks after it first hit the newsstands, the first shots of the Revolution were heard at Lexington and Concord. The war that Mercy Warren had long predicted and helped promote was now a reality.

Hannah Winthrop provided her friend with an eyewitness report on the battle. Time would never erase, Hannah vowed, "the horrors of that midnight cry preceding the bloody massacre at Lexington, when we were roused from the benign slumbers of the season, by the beat of drum and ringing of bells, with the dire alarm that a thousand troops of George the Third had gone forth to murder the peaceful inhabitants of the surrounding villages." She fled from her home and was directed to a place about a mile from town, "but what a distressed house did we find it, filled with women whose husbands had gone forth to meet the assailants, seventy or eighty of these (with numberless infant children) weeping and agonizing for the fate of their husbands. In addition to this scene of distress, we were for sometime in the sight of the battle." The refugees moved on to another town: "thus we began our pilgrimage, alternately walking and riding, the roads filled with frightened women and children, some in carts with their tattered furniture, others on foot fleeing into the woods. But what added greatly to the horrors of the scene, was our passing through the bloody field at Monotong, which was strewed with mangled bodies."

As much as they had anticipated war, now that it was upon them the women were understandably upset. In May, Abigail, holding down the household while her husband was in Philadelphia, lamented, "All our worldly comforts are now at stake—our nearest and dearest connections are hazarding their lives and properties. God give them wisdom and integrity sufficient to the great cause in which they are engaged." She went on to describe the man-of-war ships hovering off her coast and finished with a flourish: "O Britain, Britain how is thy glory vanished—how are thy annals stained with the blood of thy children." Abigail was frightened and she was lonely; she wished for a visit from her friend Mrs. Warren. Mercy would have liked the company as well. James Warren was off serving as speaker of the House of the First Provincial Congress of Massachusetts and as second major general of the militia. Though Mercy missed him and found it hard to manage without him, she was excited that he and his friends—and by extension she—were so central to the action. She told Abigail, "Though I feel a painful concern for their safety I acknowledge I feel some kind of pride in being so closely connected with persons who dare to act so noble a part." Knowing she occupied a privileged position as confidante to so many of the key players in the drama, Mercy Warren decided as early as 1775, with the enthusiastic endorsement of John Adams, to write the definitive history of the American Revolution. Here again Catharine Macaulay provided a model.

In July 1775 George Washington took command of the American troops, such as they were, just a couple of weeks after the next conflict—the Battle of Bunker Hill, near Charlestown, Massachusetts.

After the British took the hill, at great cost in lives, they proceeded to burn Charlestown. James Warren sent his wife a vivid account of the event, telling her of the British defeat of the Americans: "after a stout resistance and a heavy loss of life on their side . . . with a savage barbarity never practiced among civilized nations they fired and have utterly destroyed the town of Charlestown." He gave the sad news of a friend's death and continued: "It is impossible to describe the confusion in this place, women and children flying into the country, armed men going to the field and wounded men returning from there fill the streets." British troops occupying Boston established martial law, imposed curfews, and dealt severely with any patriots who were unable to escape.

Again Hannah Winthrop provided Mercy with a picture of "five hundred householders miserable; involving many a poor widow and orphan in one common ruin. Be astonished, O heavens, at this, and let the inhabitants of America tremble to fall into the hands of such a merciless foe." A couple of months later, in August 1775, Mercy wrote to Catharine Macaulay, repeating much of what Warren and Winthrop had told her and then giving an accounting of the current situation: "We have a well appointed brave & high spirited continental army. Consisting of about twenty two thousand Men. Commanded by the accomplished George Washington . . . a man whose military abilities & public & private virtue, place him in the first class of the Good & Brave." Still, even at that late date as

Mercy hoped some miracle would prevent all-out war, saying that Congress sought reconciliation, as if "wishing for some Benign Hand to interpage and heal the dreadful contest without letting out the blood from the bosom of their brethren."

Mercy Warren trusted her information about the desire of Congress for reconciliation because she was corresponding with members, most notably John Adams. And she was urging them ever onward to action, despite her misgivings. "I have my fears," she told Adams at the same time she wrote to Macaulay, "Yet, notwithstanding the complicated difficulties that rise before us, there is no receding; and I should blush if in any instance the weak passions of my sex should damp the fortitude, the patriotism and the manly resolution of yours." Whew! She helped raise congressional ire against the British with her descriptions of British-occupied Boston. "The desk, the pews, and other encumbrances are taken down in the Old South [church] to make it convenient for the accommodation of General Burgoyne's light horse. . . . I cannot wish to see the sword quietly put up in the scabbard, until justice is done to America."

While the men deliberated in their councils, the women near Boston settled in as "war widows," sometimes frightened by the happenings around them, mostly going about the business of daily life, which now included taking on some of their husbands' business as well. They also occasionally visited back and forth between Plymouth and Braintree, which helped ease the loneliness. In the summer of 1775 Abigail wrote to Mercy apologizing for her tardiness in responding to a letter, but she had been busy and tired, "owing to my having been up all the night before with my sister Adams who about sunrise was delivered of a fine daughter." Life went on and gave some sense of normalcy, as amazing as that was. "I enjoy a good flow of spirits for the most part," Abigail confessed. "I sometimes wonder at myself and fear least a degree of stupidity or insensibility should possess my mind in these calamitous times or I could not feel tranquil amidst such scenes, and yet I cannot charge myself with an unfeeling heart." Often life was disrupted by the war. Mercy and her boys had to move to friends' houses a few times to escape harm's way, the moves serving as a constant reminder of the serious business at hand.

Once, when she went to Watertown for safety, Mercy met the American generals who had set up their headquarters there. She dashed off her impressions to John Adams: "The Generals [George] Washington, [Charles] Lee, and [Horatio] Gates with several other officers dined with us three days since. The first of these I think one of the most amiable and accomplished gentlemen, both in person, mind and manners that I have ever met with. The second, whom I never saw before, I think plain in his person to a degree of ugliness, careless even to unpoliteness—his garb ordinary, his voice rough, his manners rather morose; yet sensible, learned, judicious, and penetrating. . . . The last is a brave soldier, a high republican, a sensible companion, an honest man, of unaffected manners and easy deportment." Not content to write about the people she had met, Mercy wanted to know about those she hadn't as well. She actually had the audacity to ask Abigail for John's letters to his wife, because "I have a curiosity to know a little more about certain public characters and particular transactions." Mercy was already thinking of the history she would write. Needless to say, Abigail did not comply.

George Washington's presence in Boston excited everyone. A local Boston woman, Phillis Wheatley, composed a poem about him, which was published in newspapers in Pennsylvania and Virginia. It ended with the rousing cry:

Proceed, great chief, with virtue on thy side,
Thy ev'ry action let the goddess guide.
A crown, a mansion, and a throne that shine,
With gold unfading, WASHINGTON! be
thine.

The poet Phillis Wheatley's story can truly be called unique. She started life in America as a young slave owned by an elite Boston family. The Wheatleys bought Phillis when she was only seven or eight years old, fresh off the boat from Africa. They soon learned that she was extraordinarily gifted, and allowed her to stop working in order to spend her time studying. Members of the Wheatley family taught her English and Christianity and even threw in some Latin and ancient history. Her great talent turned out to be writing poetry. When Massachusetts newspapers published her work, she became a Boston celebrity—no one had ever heard of a slave writing poetry, since most slaves were not allowed to learn to read and write, much less a female teenage slave. When her book of poems appeared in England (with an introduction attesting to her authentic authorship signed by some of Boston's leading citizens), she became an international phenomenon. One of her widely published poems specifically brought her slave sensibilities to the cause of American liberty. Addressed "To the Right Honorable William, Earl of Dartmouth," it read:

> **Should you, my lord, while you peruse my
>   song,**
> **Wonder from whence my love of freedom
>   sprung,**
> **Whence flow these wishes for the common
>   good,**
> **By feeling hearts alone best understood,**
> **I, young in life, by seeming cruel fate**
> **Was snatched from Afric's fancied happy
>   seat:**
> **What pangs excruciating must molest,**
> **What sorrows labor in my parents' breast!**

Washington sent a letter to Phillis Wheatley praising her poetic talent and inviting her to visit: "If you should ever come to Cambridge, or near Head Quarters, I shall be happy to see a person so favoured by the Muses." Washington was doing a good bit of entertaining at the time, among his guests on different occasions: Mercy Warren and Abigail Adams.

Meanwhile, as Congress continued its deliberations, still far from being ready to declare independence from Britain, Mercy fought for separation. Anticipating the day when tyranny would be "driven from our land," she wrote to a female friend in 1775: "Then may the western skies behold virtue (which is generally the attendant of freedom) seated on a throne of peace, where she may ever preside over the rising Commonwealth of America." The women regularly wrote each other of their strong views on war and politics, as well as which children were sick and what babies were being born. In one letter, early in 1776, Mercy apologized to Abigail: "I write in a great hurry or I should touch a little on politics, knowing that you love a little seasoning of that nature in every production."

Things were heating up politically. Thomas Paine's famous pamphlet **Common Sense** was published and read by just about anyone who could read. The American army, trying to build on victory at Fort Ticonderoga, had invaded Canada and been routed but had defeated British loyalists in North Carolina. George Washington, from his camp in Cambridge (where the troops were housed in Harvard dorms) staged a brilliant military maneuver. A key player in Washington's officer corps, Colonel Henry Knox, dragged the cannons captured at Fort Ticonderoga all the way to Massachusetts and then stealthily mounted them behind secretly built fortifications on Dorchester Heights. When the British encamped in Boston awoke to the sight of cannons staring down at them from the hill above and understood that their warships in the harbor could also be hit by heavy fire from Dorchester Heights, they knew the game was up. Rather than fighting their way out of Boston, after what amounted to a six-year occupation, the British simply packed up, taking everything they could carry, plus about a thousand loyalist families, marched out to their ships, and sailed off to Canada. The American troops triumphantly entered the looted and laid-bare city amid the cheers of the citizens.

War, politics, independence—the women were dying to know what the men were doing on all fronts. But they were most concerned with the home front, where they were left to do everything. In April, Abigail, who seemed so brave to her husband, confided her cares to her female friend: "I find it necessary not only to pay attention to my own indoor domestic affairs, but to everything without, about our little farm, etc. . . . frugality, industry and economy are the lessons of the day—at least they must be so for me or my small boat will suffer shipwreck." Even as she fretted, however, Abigail was eager for the news, asking Mercy, "How do you like Mrs. Washington. Any other person you have seen and **noticed** should be glad of your opinion."

Mercy happily obliged, regaling Abigail with an account of her meeting in Cambridge with Martha Washington: "Her affability, candor and gentleness qualify her to soften the hours of private life or to sweeten the cares of the hero and smooth the rugged scenes of war." Martha took Mercy to see the ruins of Charlestown after the British retreat: "A melancholy sight . . . which evinces the barbarity of the foe, and leaves a deep impression of the sufferings of that unhappy town."

With the British gone, there was the question of what to do with the loyalist, or Tory, women left behind. "A number of gentlemen who were together at Cambridge," Abigail wrote John, "thought it highly proper that a Committee of Ladies should be chosen to examine the Tory's ladies." The committee: Mercy, Abigail, and Hannah Winthrop. But that's all we know. History doesn't tell us if the Committee of Ladies ever met. And in her letter, Abigail quickly moved on to the trials of the moment: "Your brother has lost his youngest child with convulsion fits. Your mother is well and always desires to be remembered to you. Nabby is sick with the mumps, a very disagreeable disorder." The women might be filling new roles, but the old ones took precedence.

Finally, the Congress did what Mercy and Abigail had been agitating for—it declared independence from Britain. Mercy Warren must have known she played no small part in accomplishing that remarkable end. Her poems and plays and pamphlets helped sway public opinion to take up arms against the Mother Country. Now it was all-out war with incredibly high stakes. In early 1777 Mercy dramatically declared to her mentor Catharine Macaulay: "The approaching spring appears big with the fate of empires, and the wheels of revolution move in swift progression. They may smite the diadem from the brow, and shake some tyrant from his throne before he is aware."

For all their prominence before the war, James and Mercy Warren retreated to more private pursuits once the battles were under way. Unlike the women whose sacrifices made it possible for their husbands to be Founding Fathers, Mercy did just the opposite. Her distress at James's leaving home made it impossible for him to become as involved in the rebellion as his friends the Adams cousins were; though he was asked to serve in several jobs, Warren refused. When he turned down the Superior Court in 1776, Abigail told John, "Our friend has refused his appointment. I am very sorry. I said everything I could think to persuade him, but his Lady was against it. I need say no more." Later, when Warren was asked to join the Continental Congress, he again demurred, giving as part of his reason his wife's disapproval. Though she retreated from center stage, Mercy Warren continued to correspond with the men playing the starring roles in the evolving American drama. And she reemerged on the public scene later in the century when she parted ways with some of those men over the government they were inventing.

Political Philosopher

Remember the ladies" might be the most well-known phrase ever written by an American woman. It was, of course, Abigail Adams's warning to John while he was off creating a new country. There's been much speculation over the centuries about whether this was some tongue-in-cheek, playful banter between husband and wife, or whether Abigail was seriously promoting women's rights. I personally think the ardently patriotic Mrs. Adams was more serious than not. This was a woman with emphatic views. Once, when her husband was a delegate to the Continental Congress, she wrote to him of a meeting with another member's wife, a "Sister Delegate," according to Abigail. "Why should we not assume your titles when we give you up our names," she demanded. And after John dismissed her request to "remember the ladies" when writing the new code of laws, with the curt "I cannot but laugh," Abigail huffily defended herself to her friend Mercy Warren: "I ventured to speak a word in behalf of our sex, who are rather hardly dealt with by the laws of England." She resented the fact that married women could neither own property nor enter into contracts, and it doesn't sound like she was kidding to me.

Abigail Smith Adams seems to have been a feisty female from the beginning (rather like the only other woman to be both the wife and mother of presidents, Barbara Bush). A preacher's daughter from a prominent Massachusetts family, Abigail was born in 1744. She and her two sisters never went to school but were given a solid education in the classics by their father and his students. When she was fifteen years old, Abigail met John Adams, who was almost ten years older and first found the teenager a little too sharp-tongued for his taste. But soon the young lawyer fell in love. The letters back and forth between the two while they were courting are filled with teasing talk and pent-up passion. They were the beginning of what would become a highly interesting and historic correspondence. Sadly for them, but happily for us, Abigail and John spent so much of their early married lives separated from each other that they wrote regularly, and most of those letters have survived, despite Abigail's persistent instructions to John to burn all her letters. He knew better, telling her often that she was a far better writer than he. Her writing—to him, to her sisters, to Mercy Warren, to Catharine Macaulay, and later to some of the most prominent men of the time—is a delight to read. Her lively letters serve as snapshots of the times as well as frank renditions of her own fears and fortunes. She once told John, "My pen is always freer than my tongue. I have written many things to you that I suppose I never could have talked."

Though there survive a few letters from the early days of their courtship, the decades-long letter writing began in earnest in 1764, before they were married, when John went from Braintree to Boston to undergo the smallpox inoculation and Abigail stayed home with her family in Weymouth. This was an extremely unpleasant procedure, and Abigail's parents had apparently decided not to subject their children to it. The course of treatment involved days of medication before the inoculation, and then weeks of confinement with other sufferers. The serum gave patients a mild case of smallpox, which made them quite sick but protected them from the ravages of an epidemic, assuming they lived through the treatment. Since smallpox was so deadly, many Americans decided the inoculation, with all its perils, was preferable to contracting the disease itself, or living in dread of it.

In his letters from quarantine, John teased Abigail that he was going to send her an "account in minute detail of the many faults I have observed in you." Not to be outdone, she beat him to it, saying some found him haughty, unsociable, displaying what "sounds like a lack of breeding." He then gave her his list of her "faults, imperfections, defects, or whatever you please to call them." He told her she paid little attention to playing cards, that she lacked bashfulness, that she couldn't sing, that she read, wrote, thought! and she crossed her legs and walked funny. Abigail took the "criticisms" in the joking manner they were meant, but she still wouldn't give any quarter, reminding him that "a gentleman has no business to concern himself about the legs of a lady." John Adams knew when he married Abigail a few months later that she could give as good as she got.

The young couple set up housekeeping in John's hometown of Braintree, Massachusetts, where he, a member of the newly established Sons of Liberty, soon defeated an ardent British loyalist in a campaign for selectman. His political career was launched, and so was the family. A baby girl, Abigail, was born in 1765, then a boy, John Quincy, two years later. In those years, even as Boston was roiled by the fallout from the Sugar and Stamp Acts, Abigail's letters stick closely to domestic themes. The family moved from Braintree to the city for a few years to be closer to others involved in the patriot cause, and a third child, another girl, was born and then died fourteen months later, not long before another son, Charles, was born in 1770. That same year John took on two dangerous tasks—one was his election to what was seen by the British as the treasonous Massachusetts legislature; the other was representing the British captain in the Boston Massacre case, a highly unpopular decision with his patriot friends. John's diary tells us that Abigail burst into tears when she heard of his election to the legislature, fearing for his life as well as hers and the children's. But her own correspondence of the time didn't deal with politics, though she did call the Mother Country "cruel" in a 1770 letter to a cousin in London.

It was to this same cousin, Isaac Smith Jr., that Abigail the next year explained that she would have liked to travel abroad, but "the natural tenderness and delicacy of our constitutions, added to the many dangers we are subject to from your sex, renders it almost impossible for a single lady to travel without injury to her character. And those who have a protector in a husband have, generally speaking, obstacles to prevent their roving." Though she hadn't seen other countries, she was convinced that America was the best because of the equality of its people, "there being none so immensely rich as to lord it over us, neither any so abjectly poor as to suffer for the necessaries of life." Still, she feared for America's liberty and was eager to know more of that renowned republican, Catharine Macaulay: "One of my own sex so eminent in a tract so uncommon naturally raises my curiosity. . . . I have a curiosity to know her education, and what first prompted her to engage in a study never before exhibited to the public by one of her own sex and country." Abigail was clearly interested in what was going on politically, even if she wasn't writing much about it in those years.

That would change markedly when John went off to ride the circuit on court cases, and then to the Continental Congresses, and as she began her correspondence with Mercy Otis Warren, a woman known to espouse political views. Also, the children were getting a little older; the last, Thomas, was born in 1771, and the first letters to Mercy Warren started in 1773. By the end of that year the Tea Act and its consequences were on the women's minds. Abigail reported that "the tea that baneful weed is arrived. Great and I hope effectual opposition has been made to the landing of it." Even as early as 1773 she feared the outcome of the struggle would be war: "Although the mind is shocked at the thought of shedding human blood, more especially the blood of our countrymen, and a civil war is of all wars the most dreadful, such is the spirit that prevails." The Boston Tea Party had not yet happened, and Abigail was eager for news that the patriots had successfully defied the British and prevented the unloading of the East India Company tea. While she was snowed in at her parents' in Weymouth and unable to get home to John, she begged for news because "we have not heard one word respecting the tea." When it finally happened, Abigail saw the Tea Party as a great triumph and joined her husband in asking Mercy Warren to celebrate it with a poem.

But the aftermath of the Tea Party brought tough times for Boston and created a rough financial situation for the Adams family. In the spring of 1774 John wrote his wife that the town was suffering martyrdom, that there was no prospect of business there: "I don't receive a shilling a week." But still, their family would be called on to help those even less fortunate. In the next couple of months, building up to his departure for the First Continental Congress in Philadelphia, Adams traveled around Massachusetts and Maine, trying to drum up legal business, without much success. He wrote home regularly, instructing Abigail on managing the farm and reporting to her the lack of revolutionary fervor he found outside of Boston. People were so hostile to the Bostonians, he began to worry that the loyalists would win: "I confess myself to be full of fears that the ministry and their friends and instruments will prevail and crush the cause of the friends of liberty." If that happened he knew he was finished. But still, he told his wife, he had to persist, and he needed her help: "I must entreat you, my dear partner in all the joys and sorrows, prosperity and adversity of my life, to take a part with me in the struggle." There it is. She would have to play her part. If he was to be what would come to be called a Founding Father, she would have to be a Founding Mother.

John's morose messages about Tory sympathizers continued from every town he stopped in until he finally went off to Congress in Philadelphia. It was his first trip out of New England, and he was dependent on her not only to manage his affairs but to keep him apprised of the news. She had little doubt of where the path he was following would lead: "Did ever any kingdom or state regain their liberty, when once it was invaded, without bloodshed? I cannot think of it without horror." Abigail's sister and confidante, Mary Cranch, from her home in Boston, also feared for the worst: "I am full of apprehensions of—I don't know what. What unnumbered distresses has Lord North brought on thousands of innocent creatures." The women were clearly politically engaged. And their news from Boston of the British destroying American munitions and powder supplies enraged the men meeting in Philadelphia and united them behind their compatriots in Massachusetts. More and more John turned over decisions about running the farm and educating the children to Abigail, who was forced to cope even as she watched the British readying for war. "The governor is making all kinds of warlike preparations such as mounting cannon on Beacon Hill, digging entrenchments upon the Neck, placing cannon there, encamping a regiment there, throwing up breastworks, etc. etc." John responded that the Congress was ready to support the colony, and urged his wife to have no fear: "Frugality, my dear, frugality, economy, parsimony must be our refuge. I hope the ladies are every day diminishing their ornaments, and the gentlemen too. Let us eat potatoes and drink water. Let us wear canvass, and undressed sheepskins, rather than submit to the unrighteous and ignominious dominion that is prepared for us." It was a little easier to voice those noble sentiments while being wined and dined by patriot families in Philadelphia than to swallow them back in Braintree, where, Abigail wrote in September 1774, the men between fifteen and sixty were being called to take up arms and start training. She also told John about "a conspiracy of Negroes" in Boston who would fight for the British if promised liberation. She didn't know the outcome of the plot but had some sympathy with its instigators: "I wish most sincerely there was not a slave in the province. It always appeared a most iniquitous scheme to me— fight ourselves for what we are daily robbing and plundering from those who have as good a right to freedom as we have. You know my mind upon this subject." I suspect he did.

The mail was also filled with news of the children, his mother, his law business—or lack of it—and Abigail's longing for him. She loved John and missed him and was glad to welcome him home when Congress adjourned later that year. But the situation in Boston continued to deteriorate. Abigail wrote to Catharine Macaulay, "The only alternative which every American thinks of is liberty or death." That was several months before Patrick Henry's famous speech. Mercy Warren and Abigail were writing back and forth to each other about the buildup of troops in their neighborhoods, ending with Abigail's dramatic letter after Lexington and Concord announcing her determination to stay put in Braintree "as long as it will be safe for any person to tarry upon the sea coast." Once again she was the one making the decisions—John had left for the Second Continental Congress. From the road he advised her, "Keep your spirits composed and calm, and don't suffer yourself to be disturbed by idle reports and frivolous alarms." But as more news reached him, John realized that she could in fact be facing more than "frivolous" scares. "In case of real danger . . . fly to the woods with our children. Give my tenderest love to them, and to all." Clearly, she was on her own.

For a few weeks all was calm—no redcoats showed up in Braintree, but there was also no business for his law associates and no school. Abigail wasn't sure what to do with eight-year-old John.

Then more British ships arrived in Boston Harbor, and everyone was placed under alarm. Patriots escaped the city with whatever goods they could carry, and men called to join the militia stopped at friendly homes along the way. The scene at the Adams house was one of "confusion . . . soldiers coming in for lodging, for breakfast, for supper, for drink, etc. etc. Sometimes refugees from Boston tired and fatigued, seek an asylum for a day or night, a week—you can hardly imagine how we live." With all of that, Abigail was glad of the news from Philadelphia that an army was being assembled. "In Congress we are bound to secrecy," John wrote in June, but he confided to his wife that "ten thousand men will be maintained in Massachusetts, and five thousand in New York at the Continental expense." A few days later he added, "I can now inform you that the Congress have made choice of the modest and virtuous, the amiable, generous and brave George Washington Esqr., to be the General of the American Army, and that he is to repair as soon as possible to the camp before Boston."

Though he was occasionally writing, Abigail didn't receive any of John's letters for five harrowing weeks while she battened down in Braintree, with anxieties rising daily. "We now expect our seacoasts ravaged. Perhaps the very next letter I write will inform you that I am driven away from our yet quiet cottage." And though she was fearful for herself and her children, Abigail was also fearful for her cause. "Courage I know we have in abundance, conduct I hope we shall not want, but

powder—where shall we get a sufficient supply."
Here she was, hunkered down waiting for the enemy to attack, worrying about whether the Americans had enough ammunition! And in fact, the "very next letter" informed John of the Battle of Bunker Hill: "Charlestown is laid in ashes. The battle began upon our entrenchments on Bunker Hill, a Saturday morning, about 3 o'clock and has not ceased yet and tis now 3 o'clock Sabbath afternoon. Tis expected they will come out over the neck tonight and a dreadful battle must ensue."

Abigail was able to provide a play-by-play account of the battle, since she, with little John Quincy in tow, had watched from a perch on nearby Penn's Hill. Much later, just a couple of years before his own death in 1848, John Quincy Adams remembered the terrible times of 1775: "For the space of twelve months my mother with her infant children dwelt, liable every hour of the day and night to be butchered in cold blood, or taken and carried to Boston as hostages [by the] same hands which on the 17th of June lighted the fires of Charlestown. I saw with my own eyes those fires, and I heard Britannia's thunders in the Battle of Bunker's Hill." Despite the American loss, Abigail rallied quickly. Two days after it was over she cheered her husband with the message: "The spirits of the people are very good. The loss of Charlestown affects them no more than a drop in the bucket." She was trying to put on a brave face but wanted to make sure the Congress knew the hardships: "Does every member feel for us? Can they realize what we suffer?" Soon John was able to send her the good news that indeed the members understood and George Washington was on the way.

Though John's letters were disappointingly short and uninformative from Abigail's perspective, he pushed her to give lengthy descriptions of all that was happening at home. She told him that "the present state of the inhabitants of Boston is that of most abject slaves under the most cruel and despotic of tyrants," then cited chapter and verse of English strictures on the citizens of the city. Still, she went on, "I would not have you be distressed about me. Danger they say makes people valiant. Hitherto I have been distressed but not dismayed. I have felt for my country and her sons, I have bled with them and for them." Then she continued, in the most matter-of-fact way, to ask for some knitting needles and pins and report on the crops and the weather. At least John was aware that she was indeed remarkable: "It gives me more pleasure than I can express to learn that you sustain with so much fortitude the shocks and terrors of the times. You are really brave, my dear, you are an heroine."

Abigail was tough, but she was still sentimental. In one letter she could give a complete report on the reaction to the American generals ("I was struck with General Washington. . . . The people have the highest opinion of Lee's abilities, but you know the continuation of the popular breath, depends much upon favorable events") and the scarcities of wartime ("You can hardly imagine how much we want for common small articles which are not manufactured among ourselves") while complaining that she didn't hear enough by way of romance from her husband ("I want some sentimental effusions of the heart. I am sure you are not destitute of them or are they all absorbed in the great public"). If she was going to manage everything alone, the least he could do was tell her he loved her.

It was a complaint that Abigail would repeat much of their married life, but John never really obliged. Soon after that letter, written in July 1775, he had an experience that affected the tone and content of his correspondence forever. Much to John's embarrassment, his mail was intercepted when the British captured the courier he had entrusted with it, and the letters were published in the **Massachusetts Gazette** and reprinted in British newspapers. It was bad enough that he had written about the difficulties of members of Congress needing to "form a Constitution for a new empire, at the same time that they have a country of fifteen hundred miles extent to fortify, millions to arm and train, a naval power to begin, an extensive commerce to regulate, numerous tribes of Indians to negotiate with," but he also revealed some quirks and foibles of his colleagues (one he described as a "piddling genius"). The letters, with the implication that Congress was considering forming a separate nation long before the country was ready, caused quite a stir. He was probably grateful that they didn't also include some "sentimental effusions" for his enemies to ridicule. John's letters were understandably, but to his wife infuriatingly, circumspect from then on.

Though it was unfortunate that the letters were made public, the contents were nothing new to Abigail. When she asked his opinion of the famous Dr. Franklin, John answered that the distinguished scientist "thinks we have the power of preserving ourselves, and that even if we should be driven to the disagreeable necessity of assuming a total independency, and set up a separate state, we could maintain it." Abigail didn't find the prospect of independence so disagreeable. As the summer of 1775 dragged on with British occupation of Boston, she wrote, "Our Army are restless and wish to be doing something to rid themselves and the land of the vermin and locusts which infest it." Chief among the "vermin" was General John Burgoyne: "I am not master of language sufficient to give you a true idea of the horrible wickedness of the man." And she was disgusted with the Olive Branch Petition—Congress's attempt at reconciliation with Britain. "Your petitioning the King again pleases (forgive me if I say the timid and the weak) those persons who were deemed the Lukewarms." To Abigail, there was no going back to subject status.

As much as she supported his work, Abigail truly missed John and was grateful when he came home for a brief visit in August. As he departed again she told her friend Mercy Warren, "I find I am obliged to summon all my patriotism to feel willing to part with him again. You will readily believe me when I say that I make no small sacrifice to the public." She had signed on for the struggle, but she didn't have to be happy about it. Soon she had a great deal to be unhappy about as an epidemic of dysentery swept through the area, making her terribly sick and threatening the life of one of her children. When John heard of it, he was distressed but felt helpless to do anything but praise her: "I am charmed with your admirable fortitude, and that divine spirit of resignation which appears in your letters. I cannot express the satisfaction it gives me, nor how much it contributes to support me." But she was bereft of his support when the epidemic took her mother; all he could do was sympathize long-distance, regretting that his children would not benefit from the "forming hand of their grand-mother." It was all, finally, beginning to get Abigail down. She told Mercy Warren, "I feel but little in-clination to go into company. I have no son big enough to accompany me, and two women cannot make out so well." And she lamented to John, "In the 12 years we have been married I believe we have not lived together more than six."

Even as she mourned, however, Abigail contin-ued to report and request news. And she never stopped sharing her views. When she learned the British had bombarded the town of Falmouth, she judged, "We have done evil or our enemies would be at peace with us. The sin of slavery as well as many others is not washed away." Though John so-licited and respected his wife's opinions, he didn't completely accept the notion that women should participate in political conversations. His colleague John Hancock married while in Philadelphia, which meant the new Mrs. Hancock lived amid all the men at the Continental Congress. Adams assured his wife that the female addition was modest and genteel, and that "she avoids talking upon politics. In large and mixed companies she is totally silent, as a lady ought to be—but whether her eyes are so penetrating and her attention so quick to the words, looks, gestures, sentiments etc. of the company, as yours would be, saucy as you are this way, I won't say."

Whatever he thought, Abigail had no intention of shying away from her positions. When the parson at church prayed for reconciliation with Britain, she refused to join in, proclaiming, "Let us separate, they are unworthy to be our brethren . . . let us beseech the Almighty to blast their counsels and bring naught to all their devices." In her own mind, Abigail had already settled the question of independence and moved on to the question of what kind of government the new country would adopt. She first raised the question with John in November 1775: "If we separate from Britain, what code of laws will be established. How shall we be governed so as to retain our liberties? . . . When I consider these things and the prejudices of people in favor of ancient customs and regulations, I feel anxious for the fate of our monarchy or democracy or whatever is to take place." The strong, she feared, would always lord it over the weak. Then **she** apologized to **him:** "I believe I have tired you with politics." But of course she kept it up: "I suppose in Congress you think of everything relative to trade and commerce, as well as other things." But she had some ideas of her own on those subjects as well. She gave a list of what taxes should be imposed and suggested that America hold on to its gold and silver because inflation was making paper money worthless. Finally, she castigated the Congress for not being sufficiently committed to separation from Britain.

John came home for Christmas and actually thought about not returning to the Congress so he could tend to his business and his family. In what was a no-win proposition for her, he asked Abigail to decide. As hard as it was for her, she told Mercy Warren, "I could by no means consent to his resigning at present, as I was fully convinced he must suffer if he quit." The momentous year 1776 had arrived. Adams wrote of preparations for war in other parts of the country and sent his wife the newly published **Common Sense,** which she greatly admired. She heard the cannons boom for days on end before the Americans took Dorchester Heights, and then, to her amazement, watched the British leave Boston. Abigail saw the hand of Providence in the departure, transferring the "seat of war . . . from this to the Southern colonies that each may have a proper sympathy for the other, and unite in a separation."

Having never left her native New England, Abigail held a somewhat dim view of the "Southern colonies." She told John that she suspected that their "passion for liberty" could not be as strong as that of the North because they deprived their slaves of liberty. Even though members of her family held slaves, Abigail had long opposed the institution of slavery. She always took up the cause of the weak against the strong, whether it was the colonies against England, slaves against masters, or women against men. And it was in that spirit, in the same letter of March 31, 1776, questioning the southerners, that she penned her most memorable words: "I long to hear that you have declared an independency—and by the way in the new Code of Laws which I suppose it will be necessary for you to make I desire you would remember the ladies, and be more generous and favorable to them than your ancestors. Do not put such unlimited power into the hands of the husbands. Remember all men would be tyrants if they could. If particular care and attention is not paid to the ladies we are determined to foment a rebellion, and will not hold ourselves bound by any laws in which we have no voice or representation."

Was she being playful? I don't think so. She went on to say that some men give up the "harsh title of master for the more tender and endearing one of friend." Clearly, she included her husband in that number, but wondered, "Why, then, not put it out of the power of the vicious and the lawless to use us with cruelty and indignity and with impunity." Remember, men legally owned their wives under English law. Abigail was bound to have seen some abusers of their "property." But John chose to answer in a joking manner. "As to your extraordinary Code of Laws, I cannot but laugh. We have been told that our struggle has loosened the bands of government everywhere. That children and apprentices were disobedient—that schools and colleges were grown turbulent—that Indians slighted their guardians and Negroes grew insolent to their masters. But your letter was the first intimation that another tribe more numerous and powerful than all the rest were grown discontented."

He then delivered the age-old put-down: you women don't need power, you already have all the real power. "We know better than to repeal our masculine systems. Although they are in full force, you know they are little more than theory. We dare not exert our power in its full latitude. We are obliged to go fair, and softly, and in practice you know we are the subjects. We have only the name of masters, and rather than give up this, which would completely subject us to the despotism of the petticoat, I hope General Washington and all our brave heroes would fight." Very funny. It would be decades before women could control their own property.

Abigail tried to enlist her friend Mercy Warren in her campaign. After all, Mercy's brother had written about the emancipation of women more than a decade earlier. "I think I will get you to join me in a petition to Congress. I thought it was very probable our wise statesmen would erect a new government and form a new Code of Laws. I ventured to speak a word in behalf of our sex, who are rather hardly dealt with by the laws of England which give such unlimited power to the husband to use his wife ill. . . . I thought the most generous plan was to put it out of the power of the arbitrary and tyrannical to injure us with impunity by establishing some laws in our favor upon just and liberal principles." She then told her friend of John's response. Mercy never replied.

So Abigail was left to shoot off one last volley to her husband. "I can not say that I think you very generous to the ladies, for whilst you are proclaiming peace and good will to men, emancipating all nations, you insist upon retaining an absolute power over wives. But you must remember that arbitrary power is like most other things which are very hard, very liable to be broken." In a couple of centuries she would be right.

If John wasn't about to take on the legal status of women, he was happy to give his own wife her due and to allow his daughter certain latitude. When he discovered that Nabby, as young Abigail was called, was studying classical languages, he simply asked her not to tell many people about it, "for it is scarcely reputable for young ladies to understand Latin and Greek." As for Abigail, he praised her abilities as a farmer, "or anything else you undertake." In another letter he judged that the "neighbors will think affairs more discreetly conducted in my absence than any other time." He added, somewhat in awe: "You shine as a stateswoman, of late as well as a farmeress. Pray where do you get your maxims of state, they are very apropos."

John began to count on Abigail for everything. When she asked him what to do with their house in Boston now that the British had left, he told her to decide. He sought out her opinions. To her he could vent his frustrations with the men who talked forever in the Congress and with their failure to adequately fortify his hometown. After she wrote telling him that she had been appointed to a committee to judge the Tory ladies, he responded with an assignment: "As you are a politician, and now elected to an important office, that of judgess of the Tory ladies, which will give you naturally an influence with your sex, I hope you will be . . . exhorting them to use their influence with the gentlemen to fortify."

Above all, Abigail provided John with peace of mind. He knew she was running things well at home and supporting his endeavors in Philadelphia, even though she missed him terribly. "Nothing has contributed so much to support my mind as the choice blessing of a wife, whose capacity enabled her to comprehend and whose pure virtue obliged her to approve the views of her husband." As for Abigail, she saw her work as her contribution to the cause, a gift that made it possible for John to serve the country. But she was getting impatient with the others who were serving. She was of the opinion that independence was long overdue. So it was with great satisfaction that John was finally able to write to her on July 3, 1776: "Yesterday the greatest question was decided, which ever was debated in America, and a greater perhaps, never was or will be decided among men. A resolution was passed without one dissenting colony 'that these united colonies are, and of right ought to be, free and independent states.'" Finally the moment had come. The next day Congress issued a defense of the causes for the decision—the Declaration of Independence.

When Abigail got the news, she was elated. "Your letters never fail to give me pleasure," she told her husband, who was one of the drafters of the document, "yet it was greatly heightened by the prospect of the future happiness and glory of our country." But as thrilled as she was, Abigail had the fate of the family, rather than the nation, foremost in her mind. She and the children had moved to Boston to undergo the dangerous smallpox inoculation. It was going to take weeks, and the outcome was far from clear. Having gone through it himself, John was horribly worried for his wife and children. He fretted about the fact that no one in Boston was sending him word of how his family was doing: "Do my friends think I have been a politician so long as to have lost all feeling? Do they suppose I have forgotten my wife and children? . . . Or have they forgotten that you have a husband and your children a father?" It would have been easy to do. John was gone so long that one of Abigail's uncles had teasingly advised her to find another husband.

It tells you something about John's total reliance on Abigail that the period of the smallpox inoculation was the only time he seems to have asked male family members how his wife and children were doing. In all his other correspondence during the time he was in Philadelphia, Adams wrote about affairs of state. There was never a hint of "check on the family for me." It wasn't that he didn't care. His anguished letters to several friends during the smallpox episode show that he cared desperately. He simply trusted Abigail to handle everything without masculine oversight, and she did.

While she was suffering through the smallpox ordeal, Abigail left her sickbed to celebrate independence. With great excitement, she wrote John of the day the Declaration was read from the balcony of the State House in Boston to the throngs assembled below. She reported that "great attention was given to every word," and then, when it was done, "the cry from the balcony was God Save our American States and then 3 cheers which rended the air, the bells rang, the privateers fired . . . the cannon were discharged . . . and every face appeared joyful."

As far as Abigail was concerned, John's mission was accomplished. But still he didn't come home. He wrote ominously of impending British attacks on New York and New Jersey and started concerning himself with what the new country's government would look like. "You love to pick a political bone," he teased his wife in late July, "so I will even throw it to you." Then he posed questions that would stump the men writing the Constitution more than a decade later: How should the states vote, equally or in proportion to their populations? And what control would Congress have over the states? He admitted to being perplexed on these subjects. Perhaps his politically astute wife could help.

Abigail had ideas of her own about what the Congress should be up to. She wanted the men to work on education, and once again she put forth a radical notion: "If we mean to have heroes, statesmen and philosophers, we should have learned women." She acknowledged that the world would probably laugh at her, but she made the case convincingly. This time she received her husband's endorsement: "Your sentiments on the importance of education in women are exactly agreeable to my own. . . . In reading history you will generally observe, when you light upon a great character, whether a general, a statesman, or philosopher, some female about him either in the character of a mother, wife or sister who has knowledge and ambition above the ordinary level of women, and that much of his eminence is owing to her precepts, example or instigation in some shape or other." Behind every great man, there's a great woman. It was a remarkable view at the time, but Adams was hoping to achieve greatness, and he knew the role Abigail played in his life.

She had carried on valiantly, but now she was ready for him to come home, at least for a little while. "You may serve them again," she told him in September 1776, "but unless you return what little property you possess will be lost." Abigail could manage the farm, but she needed him to do some legal work to bring in a little cash; the Congress was paying him nothing. "I know the weight of public cares lie so heavy upon you that I have been loathe to mention your private ones." When it came to the "public cares," the news was not good. The British had taken New York. Still, Abigail reassured John that by all accounts the American men had fought honorably. "We are in no way dispirited here, we possess a spirit that will not be conquered. If our men are all drawn off and we should be attacked, you would find a race of Amazons in America."

John Adams probably didn't doubt that. Finally, in October 1776, he briefly went back to Braintree, to his own Amazon, before taking on more assignments for the new nation, which was now engaged in all-out war.

CHAPTER THREE

1776–1778:
War and a Nascent Nation

ABIGAIL SMITH ADAMS

At the Front

America was now a country, but a country in name only, required to fight for its life. And in this first war as a nation, as in every war since, women played a significant but unsung role. In addition to the legions of women taking over for their husbands at home, often under perilous circumstances, there were genuine Revolutionary War heroines—women who served as soldiers and spies, women who tricked the enemy, women who were tricked by the enemy. Their stories are told in romantic song and story and in dust-dry pension records of the U.S. Army.

The most well-known of these women, Molly Pitcher, may not have ever existed. According to the famous story, a woman called Molly was bringing water to thirsty soldiers (that's where the "Pitcher" comes from) during the Battle of Monmouth, New Jersey, when she saw her husband shot, then took his place firing a cannon. There's a good bit of historical debate about who this woman might have been, and whether "Molly Pitcher" became a generic term for the female water carriers on the battlefield. But it's pretty clear that a woman was working a cannon at Monmouth, according to at least one eyewitness account. And a person named Mary Hays, who many believe to have been Molly Pitcher, was present at Monmouth and was later granted a pension by Pennsylvania "for her services in the Revolutionary War."

Another account of a woman warrior is considerably clearer. Margaret Corbin's husband, John, was killed firing artillery from Fort Washington, New York. His wife moved into his battle station and fought bravely, sustaining three gunshot wounds, until the British captured the post. Because her wounds disabled her, the Continental Congress awarded Margaret half the pay of a soldier and a complete outfit of clothing, or its value in cash; eventually she also received an annual clothing allowance. Not willing to leave it at that, as a member of what was called the Invalid Regiment, Margaret Corbin petitioned and won a full ration, including rum or whiskey. Many years after her death the Daughters of the American Revolution were granted their request to rebury Margaret Corbin at West Point, making her the only Revolutionary veteran to receive that honor.

What were these women doing on the battlefield in the first place? They, along with many thousands of others, went to war with their husbands and brought their children as well. Most of these so-called camp followers were extremely poor; they hadn't the wherewithal to survive at home alone. Though there's been some behind-the-hand snickering about these women for centuries, they were not prostitutes. The American camps maintained strict rules about consorting with "bad" women, in contrast to the British, who hired women to "service" the troops. Though he knew he couldn't turn away these destitute women, they were the bane of George Washington's sense of an orderly and disciplined army. Still, no army could do without women. They foraged for and cooked food for the soldiers, sewed and laundered their clothes, and nursed their wounds. Women were assigned battle chores as well, such as swabbing down the cannons with water. Recognizing that they were indispensable, the army paid the women for their work and issued them rations—only a fraction of what the men received, of course. Washington just wished the ragged, motley assortment of women and children weren't so visible. He issued order after impotent order attempting to regulate the women trying to keep them out of the wagons, off of the main streets on marches through towns, relegated to walking with the baggage wagons. The fact that he had to issue the orders to stay off the wagons repeatedly indicates that the women weren't paying much attention to the good general. When he set up a Green Beret–like ready response team, "fit for action and free from every encumbrance," Washington advised the troops to leave behind "such of their women as are not able to undergo the fatigue of frequent marches." Notice, he didn't even try to exclude all women, just the weak ones.

Women spies didn't present the commander in chief with any of the problems that camp followers did, as long as they were American spies. During the dread winter at Valley Forge, he warned, on February 11, 1778, of the "pernicious consequences" of allowing women "to pass and repass from Philadelphia to camp, under pretence of coming out to visit their friends in the Army . . . but really with an intent to entice the soldiers to desert." But there were women in Philadelphia working their wits and their wiles for the patriot cause as well, most notably Lydia Darragh, a local mortician. She used a vantage point from a window in her house to record British troop activities, then wrote them up in coded messages, which she would hide behind her son's coat buttons. He would then bring the messages to his big brother serving in Washington's army. When the British officer Major Andre arrived at her door to commandeer her house for fellow officers, Lydia asked permission to stay there as well, with some of her children. One night she heard the enemy generals plotting a surprise attack on Washington's camp. She devised a ruse to receive a pass out of the city, traveled on foot until she met up with a friendly soldier, and delivered the information to the American army in time to thwart disaster.

A journal kept by a surgeon in the Continental army tells of General Putnam's retreat from New York. As Putnam was leading his small force of Americans out of the city, unbeknownst to him the British were moving toward him eight thousand strong. Fortunately, the British generals stopped for a bite at the home of Robert Murray, described by the American surgeon as "a Quaker and friend of our cause." Mrs. Murray plied the redcoats with Madeira so that they stayed long enough for the Americans to pass by without encountering the vastly superior enemy force. The journal entry concludes, "It has since become almost a common saying among our officers that Mrs. Murray saved this part of the American army."

Down through the decades, probably much embroidered in the telling, have come dramatic stories of women riding their horses through the night, wading through dangerous waters, skirting enemy lines, braving almost certain death in order to impart crucial information to the Continental army. Emily Geiger was carrying intelligence from one American general to another when she was intercepted by the British, who summoned a woman to search her. Before the searcher arrived, Emily swallowed her sensitive paper rather than relinquish it.

After her release, she continued on, despite the danger, and delivered the information verbally. Sybil Luddington was another damsel on horseback. Only sixteen years old, she rode forty miles to reach the local militia in Danbury, Connecticut, and alert them to an impending attack. An even younger midnight rider, Behethland Moore, was fifteen when she carried a message to the American troops in South Carolina. In Massachusetts, Deborah Champion, at age twenty-two, spent two days on her steed bringing information to George Washington. And sixteen-year-old Dicey Langston forded a neck-deep river in South Carolina to get to her brother's camp with news of enemy troop movements.

Then there were the women who disguised themselves as men and fought right alongside their male brethren. It's impossible to know how many there were—a few names are preserved in the military records, but their stories are lost. There is one account of Prudence Wright, who rustled up a troop of women shortly after the battle at Lexington. Armed with pitchforks and muskets, and dressed in men's clothes, the women prepared to defend the town of Pepperell, Massachusetts. They were able to ambush a British spy and deliver his intelligence to the Americans.

The most famous of the women who fought as men was Deborah Sampson, who reveled in her tales of derring-do, regaling audiences on the speaking circuit for years after the war. A poor girl in Massachusetts, she was swept up in the patriot cause and had no family to hold her back when, as Elizabeth Ellet later wrote, "the zeal which had urged the men to quit their homes for the battle-field, found its way to a female bosom." Deborah secretly sewed a suit of men's clothes, snuck into the woods to change out of her dress, and, for all intents and purposes, became a man. She enlisted in the army as Robert Shurtliff and went off to war. In her three years' service, Deborah, or "Robert," was twice wounded but continued to volunteer for hazardous duty. Apparently tall and strong, the other soldiers called their beardless brother "Molly," but it never occurred to them that someone who could do her work and survive her wounds really **was** a girl. Finally, after she contracted a fever and nearly died, a doctor discovered her disguise when he unwrapped the tight bandages around her breasts. But he told no one. As her health improved, the doctor brought her home, allowing her to continue the deception, until she was well. Then he sent "Robert" with a letter to George Washington. The general read the letter and, according to Ellet, "handed her in silence a discharge from the service, putting into her hand at the same time a note containing a few brief words of advice, and a sum of money sufficient to bear her expenses to some place where she might find a home." Years later Washington invited her to come see the Congress, which then voted her a pension and some land in recognition of her military service. After she died her husband petitioned Congress for survivors' benefits. The House Committee on Revolutionary Pensions declared that the record of the American Revolution "furnishes no other similar example of female heroism, fidelity and courage" and that Deborah's husband "has proved himself worthy of her, as he has sustained her through a long life of sickness and suffering, and as that sickness and suffering were occasioned by the wounds she received and the hardships she endured in defense of the country . . . the committee do not hesitate to grant relief."

Because the Revolutionary War was fought in cities and towns, the home front could be more hazardous than the battlefield, and it was often women who were left to defend a family's turf. Nancy Hart, a sturdy frontierswoman in Georgia, helped a patriot escape from his loyalist neighbors and then tricked his pursuers into searching in the wrong place. When the Tories came to confront her about aiding their enemy, she shot a couple of them, killing one and wounding the other, and held the rest at gunpoint until her husband arrived with reinforcements. Then, with the assistance of the men, she took the Tories outside and hung them. Years later Elizabeth Ellet was shown the hanging tree by a neighbor of the fierce Mrs. Hart who clucked, "Poor Nancy, she was a honey of a patriot, but the devil of a wife." Another Georgia woman dealt with the Tories in a somewhat more genteel fashion. Ann Gwinnett, widow of the president of Georgia and signer of the Declaration of Independence, informed on them. In a decidedly political move, she wrote to John Hancock and "the other

Members of the Grand Continental Congress" telling them that the officers in the Georgia militia were not to be trusted—they were Tory sympathizers. "These things (though from a woman, and it is not our sphere, yet I cannot help it) are all true," she warned.

Rampaging British troops were notorious for rape, and both armies were ravaged with disease, making word of a military approach cause for civilian panic. One woman in New York dealt with the oncoming British by setting fire to the city, stopping the march. Her bold move caused the famous English statesman Edmund Burke to taunt the House of Commons with the news that "one miserable woman . . . arrested your progress, in the moment of your success." When the woman was found, "knowing she would be condemned to die," Burke told Parliament, "upon being asked her purpose, said, 'to fire the city!' and was determined to omit no opportunity for doing what her country called for." Another New York woman, Catherine Schuyler, wife of General Philip Schuyler (and later mother-in-law of Alexander Hamilton), ignored threats of Indian attacks and traveled to her family's estate to burn the wheat fields so the enemy could not harvest them. No wonder Cornwallis voiced his lament that even if he destroyed all the men in America, he'd still have the women to contend with.

When Cornwallis was himself defeated, one of the women witnesses told of the surrender in her deposition written to obtain a veteran's survivor's benefit from Congress. Sarah Osborn marched with her husband from Philadelphia to Baltimore to Yorktown, cooking for him and a few other soldiers and baking for the army. When they reached York-town, she "cooked and carried in beef and bread and coffee (in a gallon pot) to the soldiers in the entrenchment. On one occasion when [Sarah Osborn] was thus employed carrying in provision, she met General Washington, who asked her if she was 'not afraid of cannonballs?' She replied . . . that it would not do for the men to fight and starve too." The deposition went on to describe the drumrolls and cheers that accompanied the British surrender, adding Sarah Osborn's observation that "the British General at the head of the army was a large, portly man, full face, and the tears rolled down his cheeks as he passed along."

But the war dragged on for years before that surrender, and still more years before peace was finally achieved. They would be years when the Founding Mothers took charge at home, often in dangerous conditions, or took their places beside their men at camp, where the men, especially the man in charge, found them invaluable. George Washington might have regretted the presence of so many women in the army, but he wanted his own wife with him. Martha Washington later said that she had heard the opening and closing gun of every military campaign of the Revolution.

At Camp with the Generals' Wives

My Dearest," began the letter from Philadelphia written June 18, 1775. "I am now set down to write you on a subject which fills me with inexpressible concern—and this concern is greatly aggravated and increased, when I reflect on the uneasiness I know it will give you—It has been determined in Congress that the whole army raised for defense of the American Cause has been put under my care, and that it is necessary for me to proceed immediately to Boston to take upon me the command of it." It was signed, of course, "George Washington."

So began what would be for Martha Dandridge Custis Washington, as well as her husband, eight long years of life at war. On the face of it, nothing in her background had prepared her for the difficulties of living in army camps, ministering to the troops, but she turned out to be the perfect person for the part. Forty-three when the war began, Martha Washington was a mature woman who had managed through tough times. Over the opposition of his family, she had married into one of the richest fortunes in Virginia in 1750 when, at age twenty, she wed Daniel Parke Custis. In the next six years, four children were born and one died. Then, in rapid succession, she lost both another child and her husband, leaving her a widow, albeit a very rich widow, with two tiny children. After her initial shock, she took it upon herself to manage the vast estates, initiating correspondence with suppliers in England, informing them that she was now in charge. But with money like that, the young widow soon found suitors lining up at her door. According to a nineteenth-century biographer, Martha turned them all away. "Content in her singular freedom from authoritative restraint, conscious of her ability to conduct unaided her own business affairs and those of her children . . . the beautiful widow remained immovably relentless, while each enamored lover pressed, in turn, his glowing and disinterested suit!" That was, until she was introduced to the very good-looking but debt-ridden hero of the French and Indian War named Washington. "No common wooer, no ordinary mortal," swoons Martha's Boswell. Though Martha probably had a less exalted view of the man, after only a few meetings they arranged to marry, and George soon brought her and the children to live at his work in progress in northern Virginia—Mount Vernon.

And there they might have stayed for the rest of their days, adding to the house, planting large gardens, inviting guests for hunting, occasionally going off to Williamsburg for sessions of the House of Burgesses. Washington wrote to a relative: "I am now I believe fixed in this seat with an agreeable consort for life and hope to find more happiness in retirement than I ever experienced amid a wide and bustling world." But that life was shattered by the public unrest over the Intolerable Acts and the private unhappiness caused by the death of Martha's teenage daughter. George Washington was soon selected by his rebellious compatriots as a member of the Continental Congress. When his fellow Virginia congressmen stopped at Mount Vernon on the way to Philadelphia, Martha told one of them, "I hope you will stand firm—I know George will."

The next year, after Lexington and Concord, the Congress put Washington in charge of the army. Though he sought to assure his wife that "far from seeking this appointment I have used every endeavor in my power to avoid it," she might have suspected that his departure for Philadelphia in his full military dress constituted a form of lobbying. Washington's new job was not only unsettling for Martha, who wasn't sure when she would see her husband again, it was also potentially perilous for her. Virginia's royal governor sailed up the Potomac River apparently intending to capture her and hold her hostage. He was stopped by the militia, but Washington's friends were sufficiently alarmed that they begged Martha to leave home. Dismissive of the threat, she succumbed to their pleas for only a few days before returning to Mount Vernon. Her husband seemed to agree with Martha that the governor wasn't anyone to be feared when he wrote to his cousin Lund Washington, whom he had left in charge of Mount Vernon, that he didn't think "Lord Dunmore can act so low, so unmanly a part, as to think of seizing Mrs. Washington by way of revenge on me."

Still, the talk of kidnapping was bound to make Martha think she might be better off accepting George's invitation to join him at camp in Cambridge. While she was considering it, she was slapped with an untrue but possibly very damaging attack in the press: "It is said that Mrs. Washington, being a warm Loyalist, has separated from her husband since the commencement of the present troubles, and lives very much respected in the city of New York." That did it. Off to camp in Cambridge she went, starting a pattern that was to last throughout the war. To put the lie to the rumors that she was a Tory, Martha launched a public relations offensive. Bringing her son, daughter-in-law, and nephew with her, the usually elegant plantation mistress donned homespun as she set out on the long trip north in the dead of winter. All along the way she met with leaders of the patriots and so won over the doubters that the tolling of church bells soon signaled her progress toward Massachusetts. She knew then, if she hadn't before, that she was now well and truly a public figure. She wrote a friend that she had departed from Philadelphia "in as great pomp as if I had been a very great somebody."

When she arrived in Cambridge, Martha was startled by what she heard ("I confess I shudder every time I hear the sound of a gun"), but she was comforted by the people around her, especially other officers' wives, two of whom would become lifelong friends, Lucy Knox and Catharine Greene. They came from very different circumstances, and Martha was considerably older than the other two, but they had something in common few other people did: their husbands were marked men, traitors to the Crown, none more so than the Virginia gentleman George Washington. Even though that put Martha in the most danger, she remained the most composed, the most ready to accept unpleasant conditions, the most sympathetic to the soldiers throughout the war. But Lucy Knox and Catharine Greene became great favorites of the troops as well.

Lucy Flucker Knox was the headstrong daughter of a loyalist officeholder. The Flucker family adamantly opposed her engagement to a young Boston bookstore owner, Henry Knox, both because he was "in trade" and because he was a patriot. But as in most things, Lucy had her way, and she and "Harry" Knox were married in 1774, not long before his twenty-fourth birthday; she was not quite eighteen. Then, less than a year later, Knox and his young bride escaped from Boston in the aftermath of the Lexington battle, with his sword sewn into the lining of her coat. He then presented himself to the head of the militia in Cambridge and was there waiting when Washington arrived.

Catharine Littlefield Greene was raised in an unconventional family on the somewhat wild Block Island, off the coast of Rhode Island. Her greatgrandfather had moved there to evade the religious orthodoxy of Massachusetts, and the family was considered quite free-spirited in those puritanical times. (The women wore pants to ride horses!) Catharine's mother died when she was seven, and three years later the little girl was sent to the mainland to live with her aunt, Catharine Ray Greene.

(Yes, the same Catharine Ray Greene who was Benjamin Franklin's flirtatious friend—it was a small country.) When she was about twenty, and quite charming, Kitty Littlefield met and married Nathanael Greene, thirteen years her senior, at just about the same time the Knoxes were married. Less than a year later, when he heard the news from Lexington and Concord, Nathanael, though a Quaker, immediately saddled up and headed for Massachusetts. Soon named a brigadier general in charge of the Rhode Island brigade, he left his forge business and his pregnant wife in the care of his brother and sister-in-law. The vivacious young woman hated her confined life, and when she heard that Martha Washington was expected to join her husband at camp, Kitty Greene, despite her pregnancy, decided to do the same.

The Washington, Knox, and Greene couples entertained one another along with some of the notables of Massachusetts society, like Mercy Otis and James Warren and Abigail and John Adams. The occasional visiting congressmen dropped by as well; one was Benjamin Franklin, who was in Massachusetts as part of a committee from Congress appointed to confer with Washington about maintaining the army. (On his way back to Philadelphia, Franklin collected his sister, Jane Mecom, who was a refugee in Rhode Island, having been forced from her home in British-occupied Boston.) In January 1776 Martha reported on the enemy troops to her sister: "They have been kept in Boston so long that I suppose they will be glad for a place where they may have more room as they cannot get out anyway here but by water. Our navy has been very successful in taking their vessels." It was Henry Knox, a self-educated expert in artillery, who came up with the plan of using the cannons from Fort Ticonderoga to capture Dorchester Heights and drive the British from Boston. Among the thousand loyalists who left with the British was Lucy Knox's whole Flucker family. She never saw them again.

Once the enemy had evacuated, Boston was attacked again—this time by a smallpox epidemic. There was no reason for the Continental army to stay headquartered in Massachusetts, so it was on to New York to prepare for the next siege. In April 1776 Martha wrote Mercy Warren to decline a dinner invitation, explaining that they were too busy packing to take time out for entertainment. Martha went briefly to Philadelphia to be inoculated against smallpox, both to set an example for the troops who needed inoculations, and to be able to brave army camps despite the disease. It was about this time that George Washington, along with Robert Morris and George Ross, were supposed to have called on Betsy Ross, the upholsterer. According to the story, the trio was part of a secret committee of the Continental Congress formed to commission an American flag. Betsy's daughter also claimed that her mother was well acquainted with the Washingtons because they attended the same church in Philadelphia and the general had hired her to embroider "ruffles for his shirt bosoms and cuffs, and that it was partly owing to his friendship for her that she was chosen to make the flag." And George Ross was her late husband's uncle. As Betsy's grandson first told the story, Washington supposedly showed the seamstress a flag design that included six pointed stars; she demonstrated for him how to cut a five-pointed star instead, with a single snip, and her assignment was secure. Over the centuries the legend has been debunked by historians who insist there never was a flag committee, that the Flag Resolution wasn't passed by Congress until a year later, in June 1777, and that even then the United States did not fight under a single standard. But it's a story that hasn't died since it was first published in **Harper's Monthly** in 1873, and I'm inclined to believe there's at least some truth to it. In **Pioneer Mothers of America,** the niece of Roger Sherman, one of the drafters of the Declaration, is quoted talking about her aunt Rebecca Sherman's excitement about independence: "When, a little later, George Washington designed and ordered the new flag to be made by Betsy Ross, nothing would satisfy Aunt Rebecca but to go and see it in the works, and there she had the privilege of sewing some of the stars on the very first flag of a Young Nation. Perhaps because of this experience, she was chosen and requested to make the first flag ever made in the State of Connecticut. . . . This fact is officially recorded." That's fairly close to a contemporaneous account.

Flag or no flag, George and Martha Washington moved on to New York in the early summer of

1776. Nathanael Greene brought Kitty and the new baby, George Washington Greene, home to Rhode Island, but before long Kitty deposited the baby with his Greene relatives and moved in with Lucy and Henry Knox in New York, while Nathanael camped in Brooklyn. When the British fleet sailed into New York Harbor in late June, Martha Washington and Lucy Knox left the city, but Kitty Greene, who had gone home briefly to take care of her sick baby, returned to the action, much to her husband's dismay. That's why she was in New York on July 9 when the Declaration of Independence was read on the Bowling Green to a crowd of soldiers and civilians who triumphantly toppled the equestrian statue of George III in a scene made familiar in many revolutions since. The exaltation didn't last long. Soon the British swarmed into the city, and even Kitty Greene was persuaded to go home.

Neither Martha nor Lucy could be convinced to travel far from their husbands. Martha went to Philadelphia, Lucy to New Haven. Henry thought his wife should be in Fairfield, Connecticut, instead and wrote her a series of letters excoriating her for not listening to him. She furiously and sarcastically replied, "You are pleased frequently in your letters to remind me of my incapacity of judging for myself—I now assure you—that I have a deep sense of my own weakness and ignorance and a very high opinion of him—in whose eyes mine are so contemptible." She could be biting, and she could get into all kinds of trouble—a family she stayed with in Connecticut reported to the general that the crockery was broken, the furniture damaged, and the rum, twenty-five gallons of it, missing—but Henry Knox loved his fat and funny Lucy.

In August, Martha Washington thought the war was still going well when she wrote to her sister from Philadelphia, "I thank God we shan't want men—the army at New York is very large and numbers of men are still going there." But the British force was overpowering. New York fell, the Americans fled to New Jersey, and as the troops' commissions ran out, they abandoned the army in droves. Things looked bleak for the Americans when Nathanael Greene sent his wife a letter from Trenton in December: "The enemy have pressed us very hard from place to place. The time for which our troops were engaged expired, and they went off by whole brigades. . . . The distress they [the British] spread wherever they go exceeds all description. I hope to God you have not set out for this place. . . . Continue at home, my dear, if you wish to enjoy the least share of happiness." Nathanael kept sending her reports of enemy atrocities, including rape, as the American army retreated into Pennsylvania. Even the spirited Kitty was understandably terrified when the British landed in Newport, Rhode Island, and took the town without a struggle. She was pregnant again and afraid she had nowhere to hide. So it was with much relief that the news came that Washington's army had crossed the Delaware River on Christmas Day, surprised and soundly defeated the British at

Trenton, and marched on to Princeton, where the Continentals routed the enemy officers out of their headquarters in Nassau Hall. Men started reenlisting, the army settled in Morristown for the winter, and Martha Washington was able to join her husband again.

She had spent the fall and early winter back at Mount Vernon turning it into a fabric factory. In contrast to her life at camp, at home Martha had the service of many slaves, and there's no evidence that she ever questioned the institution of slavery, though George Washington eventually did. During the war Martha employed her slaves on behalf of the soldiers. She set them spinning and weaving and knitting and sewing to provide clothes for the troops, because she had seen that Congress wasn't putting up the money for uniforms. And she herself, in her homespun, unraveled silk stockings and pillow covers and wove the thread into silk stripes. When word reached her that George was terribly sick in New Jersey, she determined once again to chance the roads in winter, arriving in March 1777 in Morristown where she found a much-improved husband. Nathanael Greene wrote to Kitty: "Mrs. Washington is excessive fond of the General and he of her. They are very happy in each other." Lucy Knox joined her husband as well, and several women from the prominent Livingston family of New Jersey, forced from their homes by the British, took up residence with relatives in Morristown. Poor Kitty Greene was having difficulty with her pregnancy and was trapped in Rhode Island when all she wanted on earth was to be with her husband and flirt with his friends.

When Martha saw the miserable condition of the troops and the hostility of the townsfolk to the sickly wretches in their midst, she quickly devised a solution to both problems. To help the soldiers, she started sewing shirts and knitting socks out of the materials she had brought from home. As for the townspeople, they were invited to call on the famous general's wife, and when they did, Martha sent them a not-so-subtle message. One prominent woman from the town described the visit where she found her hostess **"knitting, and with a speckled apron on!** . . . And this was not all. In the afternoon her ladyship took occasion to say, in a way that we could not be offended at, that at this time it was very important that American ladies should be patterns of industry to their countrywomen because separation from the mother country will dry up the sources where many of our comforts have been derived." How could the locals complain if "her ladyship" was so devoted to the troops and the cause?

Kitty Greene had a hard time recovering from the birth of her little girl, Martha Washington Greene, delaying the much-longed-for reunion with Nathanael, who had written: "There is not a day or night, nay not an hour, but I wish to fold you to my heart." As soon as she was able, Kitty made the perilous four-day trip past enemy territory, to New Jersey. No sooner had she arrived than Nathanael was off to do battle. The news he sent from the front was all bad, but Kitty couldn't face a return to Rhode Island. She and the children stayed on in New Jersey with friends while the other women returned home for the summer. After a series of victories, most notably at the Battle of Brandywine, the British marched into Philadelphia, forcing the Continental Congress to flee to the Pennsylvania countryside and seriously demoralizing the Americans.

When Lucy Knox went home, she found that her brother-in-law had made a bad deal on some horses Henry asked him to sell. She wrote to her husband, berating him for the low price they got for the horses "owing to your not entrusting me with the sale of them." She wondered why he didn't assign her as "your future agent" because she was, she said, "quite a woman of business." A couple of months later, in August 1777, Lucy wrote Harry a long love letter, telling him what her days were like, how much she missed him, and how much she missed her family. "When I seriously reflect that I have lost my father, mother, brother and sister, entirely lost them, I am half distracted." She then went on to tell her husband that she was scrupulously saving "what little gold we have" in case she needed it to ransom him if he were taken captive. Finally, Lucy speculated on what life would be like after the war, worrying that Harry had become so "accustomed to command" that he might be "too haughty for mercantile matters—though I hope you will not consider yourself as commander in chief of your own house, but be convinced that there is such a thing as equal command." At least Harry was forewarned.

When she went home to Mount Vernon in the fall of 1777, Martha learned the sad news that her favorite sister had died leaving a daughter, Fanny. As much as Martha wanted to collect the little girl and raise her in the Washington household, the general's wife felt her duty lay elsewhere. She told her grieving brother-in-law: "The General has written to me that he cannot come home this winter, but as soon as the army under his command goes into winter quarters he will send for me, if he does I must go." It was a constant tension for Martha, who was torn between her duty to family at home, especially as her son's wife continually suffered through difficult pregnancies, and her duty to her husband at camp. She always chose camp, and in the winter of 1778 it was at Valley Forge, Pennsylvania.

When she arrived there in February, Martha found a horrific situation. Fifteen hundred horses had died from starvation, and the human condition was not much better. Cold, hungry, sick, and dirty men threatened desertion, chanting, "No bread, no soldier." Washington's position as commander in chief was threatened as well, so Martha had her work cut out for her when she arrived on the scene. Once again she brought supplies from Mount Vernon, which were even more welcome than the year before. She set up a sewing circle of officers' wives, including Kitty Greene and Lucy Knox, who had both left their children at home and joined their husbands. One witness to Martha's activities later wrote: "I never in my life knew a woman so busy from early morning until late at night as was Lady Washington, providing comforts for the sick soldiers. . . . Every few days she might be seen, with basket in hand . . . going among the huts seeking the keenest and most needy sufferers, and giving all the comforts to them in her power." When she wrote about the conditions to Mercy Otis Warren, perhaps fearing that her letter would be intercepted by the British, Martha put a much brighter face on the situation: "The army is as healthy as can well be expected in general—the General's [Washington] apartment is very small. He has had a log cabin built to dine in which has made our quarters much more tolerable than they were at first." Martha joked with Mercy: "It has given me unspeakable pleasure to hear that General Burgoyne and his army are in safe quarters in your state, would bountiful providence aim a like stroke at General Howe, the measure of my happiness would be complete." British General Burgoyne was being held prisoner in Massachusetts. General Howe, on the other hand, was living it up in Philadelphia with his friend Mrs. Loring—the infamous woman who traded her favors for a position for her husband with the British army—and a city full of prosperous American Tories. The gaiety of Philadelphia that winter stood in stark contrast to the bleakness at Valley Forge, and had Howe decided to attack, it's possible the Continental army would have been wiped out.

The women tried to bring some lightness and

laughter to Valley Forge. They gathered in the Washingtons' little log dining room and encouraged everyone to sing, with the high-spirited Kitty Greene working especially hard to keep up morale. Martha even found some musicians to help celebrate George's birthday. And then they heard news that was cause for real celebration—the French had recognized America and signed a treaty pledging assistance. Washington issued an order on May 5, 1778, "to set apart a day for gratefully acknowledging the divine Goodness and celebrating the important Event," which included a parade, cannon and gun salutes to the king of France, and a gill of rum for each soldier. The festivities took place the next day. Soon after that good news, more reached the army at Valley Forge: the British had left Philadelphia, heading north. The Continental army moved into the city, the Congress returned from its exile in York, Pennsylvania, and the women went home for the summer, when the serious battles were fought, knowing they were likely to see each other again in camp the following winter.

On the Home Front

The news that the Continental army had reclaimed Philadelphia was joyously received by the Congress holed up in York. Josiah Bartlett (yes, the folks at **The West Wing** found the real name of a signer of the Declaration of Independence for their president), a congressman from

New Hampshire, wrote to his wife, Mary: "This town is not large enough to accommodate the multitude of people that have constantly business with Congress." Business with Congress continued even as war was waged; there was a need to form a government for the nascent nation.

Some Founding Fathers were trying to codify Americans' freedoms in the same years that others fought for them. Josiah Bartlett, a physician from New Hampshire, had signed up early with the patriots, heading the Committee of Correspondence in his colony, and suffered dire consequences for his allegiance to the cause. In 1774 Tories burned his house to the ground—leaving him, his wife, Mary, and their eight children to find a new home. Despite the violence against him, Bartlett went off to serve in the Provincial Congresses and then, in 1776, the Continental Congress, where he readily endorsed the Declaration of Independence—his name comes first under John Hancock's. Through the many months that he was gone, Mary, who was pregnant again, gave him regular reports of what was going on in that momentous year, telling him of the progress of "your farming business." Though the farm was doing fine, she had less positive reports about the country: "I hear some British lords have laid a plan to attack Philadelphia by land, if impracticable by sea. However I believe they can plan more than they will be suffered to accomplish." He gave her reports of actual troop movements; the New Hampshire regiments were headed for Canada, where they ended up surrendering, much to both Josiah's and Mary's dismay. "The people in general amongst us seem cool and backward about enlisting and going to war; they hear so much bad news about the war in Canada," she told her husband. Though she was managing well, she worried that "the times look dark and gloomy upon the account of the war. I believe this year will decide the fate of America." It would have been considerably easier for Mary Bartlett if history had worked out that way. As it was, she spent a good deal of the next few years on her own.

Soon her letters detailed some of the problems: "The men among us are very backward about going into war, they are not content with the province bounty. . . . We hear of wars and tumults from one end of the Continent to the other; I should be glad to know if your courage holds out yet about keeping and defending America." As the months wore on she wrote of scarcity and high prices and then finally begged Josiah to come home, "before cold weather, as you know my circumstances will be difficult in the winter if I'm alive." In addition to all of their other fears through the years of war, the fear of death in childbirth was something every woman of childbearing age faced.

Abigail Adams faced childbirth alone. John's brief sojourn in Massachusetts at the end of 1776 was long enough for her to become pregnant. And it was with heavy heart that she saw him leave again to join the Congress meeting in Baltimore in January 1777. Abigail wrote to her friend Mercy Warren, "I had it in my heart to dissuade him from going and I know I could have prevailed, but our public affairs at that time were so gloomy . . . that I thought if ever his assistance was wanted, it must be at such a time." When John arrived in Baltimore in early February, he was full of chatty news about the town, but then, reflecting on how long he would be gone, he added, "it makes me melancholy. When I think on your **circumstances** I am more so, and yet I rejoice at them in spite of all this melancholy." That's about as close as they ever come to talking about pregnancy in the eighteenth century.

Despite her "circumstances," Abigail remained as stalwart a patriot as ever, wishing, like Mary Bartlett, in one letter that "there was a little more zeal shown to join the army" and asking in another, "I wish to know whether the reports may be credited of the Southern regiments being full." John, in turn, told her, "I am very anxious to hear from you, and to know the state of public affairs in your part of the world." Abigail was not only running the farm but overseeing the manufacture of cloth. Mercy Warren sent her wool to help in her efforts, with the message that Abigail was a woman "to whom the females in the United States, must in the future look up for the example of industry and economy." As Abigail worked hard, making do with little and missing her husband, all for the good of the country, she wondered to John whether future generations would care: "Posterity who are to reap the blessings, will scarcely be able to conceive the hardships and sufferings of their

ancestors." It was not just posterity that was unlikely to be grateful—the Founding Fathers, like
all the politicians who have come after them, knew
they couldn't possibly do enough to please the
electorate of the time. "I live like a miser and a
hermit to save charges," John complained, "yet my
constituents will think my expenses beyond all
bounds." Not much has changed there. But the
constituents had problems of their own. "There is
such a cry for bread in the town of Boston as I suppose was never before heard," Abigail reported.
Still, she remained in good spirits, explaining that
she was in better health than usual for her "situation"—"a situation I do not repine at, tis a constant reminder of an absent friend, and excites
sensations of tenderness which are better felt than
expressed." She did love him.

The Congress returned to Philadelphia and John
Adams gave encouraging reports on the progress of
state governments in establishing laws and enlisting
armies, though he fretted about the expense of his
living arrangements and wondered how his family
would manage. "What will become of you, I know
not. How you will be able to live is past my comprehension." Still, he saw no choice but to serve.
Abigail too was somewhat concerned about making
ends meet. She went over his books, found some legal fees owed her husband, and tried to collect; she
rented out the house in Boston and in April, at
home in Braintree, began "the farming business."
Her letters show much more concern about how
the country was faring than how the family was do-

ing, causing John to joke, "You think I don't write politics enough! Indeed I have a surfeit of them. But I shall give you now and then a taste, since you have such gust for them." In letter after letter, he served up full meals of politics—news from Benjamin Franklin's mission to France, news from the battlefields in New Jersey of English atrocities, news from the Congress, where all thirteen states finally had sent representatives, and occasional news of the social scene in Philadelphia. She supplied news from home, mainly about politics, but also about people, including the disquieting report that a friend had died as a consequence of childbirth, adding, "Every thing of this kind naturally shocks a person in similar circumstances."

Though Abigail was managing well—neighbors told John his farm looked better than ever—she was much more frightened of invasion by British troops than she had been earlier in the war, since stories of rape and ravage had spread through the states. "I should dare not tarry here in my present situation, nor yet know where to flee for safety; the recital of inhumane and brutal treatment of those poor creatures who have fallen into their hands freezes me with horror." If Abigail was apprehensive about the fast approaching birth of the new baby, John was excited about it. In among reports on war and politics he interspersed instructions on naming the new addition to the family. His wife wanted to know more of the military movements and was frantic that General Howe's army might be descending on Boston: "If you hear of our being invaded this way, I think you must return. I used to have courage, but you cannot wonder at my apprehensions when you consider my circumstances." She was having trouble just moving around in the late stages of pregnancy; she couldn't imagine what she would do when she and the four children were in danger. John tried to reassure her, promising her that this would be his last year away from home, where he knew her burden was heavy: "I know not what would become of me and mine if I had not such a friend to take care of my interests in my absence." As the time for delivery drew near, Abigail asked her husband, "Would you willingly share with me what I have to pass through? . . . I wish the day passed, yet dread its arrival." She was frightened, despite words of encouragement from her friend Mercy Warren, who wanted news of "the birth of a young patriot." Then, in early July, it seemed that Abigail's fears were not in vain: "I was last night taken with a shaking fit, and am very apprehensive that a life was lost. As I have no reason today to think otherways, what may be the consequences to me, Heaven only knows." Clearly, the baby had stopped moving.

Not only was John not there, he was so far away that the mail took forever. Every letter Abigail opened over the next couple of weeks must have broken her heart. "Before this shall reach you I hope you will be happy in the embrace of a daughter as fair and good and wise and virtuous as the Mother, or if it is a son I hope it will resemble the Mother in person, mind and heart." He wrote that the same day that Abigail delivered a stillborn baby girl. A few days later the sorrowing mother roused herself to write: "Join with me my dearest friend in gratitude to Heaven, that a life I know you value, has been spared and carried through distress and danger, although the dear infant is numbered with its ancestors." She had lost the baby, but she was alive to take care of her other children, and for that Abigail was grateful. But John hadn't heard the news, so his next letter, filled with dispatches from various battlefields, expressed his hope that the letter would find her "happy in the embraces of a little female beauty." Abigail was mending, but grieving. She told John that she had dreamed of presenting him "a fine son or daughter" when he came home, but those "dreams are buried in the grave." Finally, more than two weeks after the baby was born, John heard the news and was devastated. After thanking God for saving a life "dearer to me than all other blessings in this world," he asked, "Is it not unaccountable that one should feel so strong an affection for an infant that one has never seen nor shall see? Yet, I must confess to you, the loss of this sweet little girl has most tenderly and sensibly affected me."

Abigail recovered faster than she had feared and was soon back at the business of the farm, reporting to John on good crops but complaining about the shortage of farmhands, the high price of everything, and the scarcity of sugar and coffee, "articles which the female part of the state are loathe to give up." She told John about a rumor that an "eminent, wealthy, stingy merchant (who is a bachelor)" had a supply of coffee, which he refused to sell at a reasonable price. "A number of females, some say a hundred, some say more, assembled with a cart and trucks, marched down to the warehouse and demanded the keys, which he refused to deliver, upon which one of them seized him by his neck and tossed him into the cart. . . . He delivered the keys when they tipped up the cart and discharged him, then opened the warehouse, hoisted out the coffee themselves, put it into the trucks and drove off. It was reported he had a spanking among them, but this I believe was not true. A large concourse of men stood amazed, silent spectators of the whole transaction." (A month before twenty-two women in Poughkeepsie, New York, broke into a store to steal tea. The owner, they believed, was hoarding it to drive up the price.) To Abigail's delightful tale, John replied, "You have made me merry with the female frolic with the miser. But I hope the females will leave off their attachment to coffee. . . . We must bring ourselves to live on the produce of our own country." This to a woman who was growing her own food and spinning her own wool! Soon Abigail informed her husband that the good folk of Boston had learned to make molasses out of cornstalks, which meant, much to their relief, that they could make rum. John must have thought better of his admonishments; in his next letter he reiterated his view that behind every great man there's a great woman, then lamented, "I wish some of our great men had such wives . . . it seems the women in

Boston begin to think themselves able to serve their country. . . . I believe the two Howes [British generals] have not very great women for wives. . . . A smart wife would have put Howe in possession of Philadelphia a long time ago." It would not be long, however, before that general, wife or no wife, would take the city.

Howe's occupation of Philadelphia during that dreadful winter when the Continental army was starving at Valley Forge came after a series of British victories that took the Americans by surprise. John wrote one confident letter after another about the prowess of Washington's army. He believed the march through Philadelphia (that's the march where General Washington had insisted that camp follower women go on back streets) had been impressive to friend and foe alike, and he was convinced that the British could never make it north from Chesapeake Bay, where the royal fleet had landed, all the way into Pennsylvania. Washington's defeat at Brandywine on September 11 ended those illusions. James Lovell, a colleague of Adams's in the Congress, sent Abigail a map of the war zone, beginning an odd and somewhat flirtatious correspondence that went on for years. But when she got that first letter, Abigail was scared to death that Lovell was writing with bad news about John. She was so relieved when it was just bad news about war. More of that bad news soon came from John himself, who wrote from York that the Congress had gathered up its papers and fled Philadelphia, getting out just as Howe's army took over the city. Only a couple of weeks later, however, the British general Burgoyne was forced to surrender at Saratoga, creating much public cheer. When Abigail went into Boston to celebrate and give thanks with friends and family, it was the Adamses' thirteenth wedding anniversary. She reflected on their long years apart and deemed it her offering to her country. Little did she know then that a much bigger gift would soon be asked of her.

Fortunately, she loved America passionately and equally passionately hated England. After Burgoyne's defeat, Abigail wrote to a loyalist cousin who had moved to London that each state had felt "the cruel depredations of the enemy . . . and this so far from weakening has served to strengthen our bond of union. . . . To this cause I have sacrificed much of my own personal happiness." She thought that sacrifice had ended in November when John finally came home. Soon he was back to his legal work, traveling on the circuit for his cases. While he was away in December, an official-looking packet came for John from James Lovell, who was still in Congress. Abigail opened it and, in horror, immediately responded to her congressional friend: "How could you contrive to rob me of all my happiness?" The Congress had appointed John Adams commissioner to France, causing Abigail great sorrow: "My life will be one continued scene of anxiety and apprehension, and must I cheerfully comply with the demand of my country?" But Lovell had no doubt that Adams would take the job, and when John got the news that he was being asked to join Benjamin Franklin in Paris, he didn't hesitate to accept, despite all his protestations that he was ready to return to private life. The only question was whether Abigail would go too. At first that was the plan; then, fearing his capture at sea, the couple thought better of it. Many years later Adams said, "I never would have gone anywhere without my wife. Nothing but the **deadly** fear that I might be in the Tower [of London] and she not permitted to be there with me prevented my taking her." Instead, at the child's insistence, little ten-year-old John Quincy Adams went along.

Abigail must have shown her unhappiness, she got a scolding letter from Mercy Otis Warren. "I know your public spirit and fortitude to be such that you will throw no impediment in his way. Why should you. You are yet young and may set down together many years in peace after he has finished the work." Mercy, who wouldn't let her own husband go as far as Philadelphia, knew she was skating on thin ice: "Something whispers me within that you will justly say we are very ready to give advice when we but illy practice upon the principles we lay down. True—but we may profit by the advice though we despise the weakness of the advisor." A week later Mercy responded to a letter from Abigail asking for arguments to convince her it was all right for John to go. "Is it really necessary to muster up arguments to prevail with my dear Mrs. Adams to consent to what she knows is right, to what she is sensible will contribute much to the welfare of the public. No, surely she has already consented." And, of course, she had. In February 1778 John and John Quincy Adams set sail. Adams was to join Benjamin Franklin in Paris to try to hammer out an alliance between the United States and France, but unbeknownst to him, the Franco-American alliance had just been signed. (The announcement of the alliance took a while to cross the ocean. That's why Washington didn't proclaim a day of rejoicing until May.) A few days later Abigail received a sympathy note from her friend Hannah Storer: "Examining my heart I can't say that I should be willing to make such sacrifices as you have done. I hope that my patriotism will never be proved in the way that yours has."

That spring Josiah Bartlett returned to Congress from New Hampshire, having contributed his medical services to the New Hampshire militia the previous year. When he arrived in York, he wrote Mary that "our public affairs wear a very favorable aspect. General Washington thinks the British army is about to quit Philadelphia." Then he added, "The Lottery is drawing, but can get no account at present of your tickets." Even then, the government was supplementing its coffers with gambling money. Mary, who was once again in charge of the farm, reported that a late freeze had hurt the beans and corn, but not killed them, and that "I hear the enemy is expected this way from Philadelphia." It was all in a day's work. By his next letter, Josiah was less optimistic about public affairs. British commissioners appointed to "settle the dispute with America" had sent letters stating that Parliament refused to recognize American independence, so "I suspect a peace will not soon take place, though I suspect the fighting business is chiefly over." Too bad his optimism was thoroughly unjustified. The good news arrived that the British had decided to leave Philadelphia to head to New York. (On the way they suffered massive losses at the Battle of Monmouth, New Jersey, where Molly Pitcher fought.) Congress could return to the city, and Josiah speculated that "a very short time now will determine whether the Enemy will remove their armies and make peace or whether they will try the fate of another campaign." But meanwhile, he wanted to know the condition of the hay, the English and Indian corn, the flax, "and etc. etc."

Soon the answer about another campaign was clear, and the American army was having a tough time of it in Rhode Island. Josiah wrote that the Congress had "received no account from that place . . . we are anxious to hear the event." Mary too was eager to know what was going on in Rhode Island, since, she told Josiah, many of the men in New Hampshire had gone there to join the battle. With all of those men gone, it must have been difficult for her on the farm. But she said they were preparing to sow the winter rye. Still, she hoped, "in a short time there will be an end to these written conveyances by seeing you at home." Josiah wanted to be able to impart important news to his wife but had still heard nothing from Rhode Island by the time he wrote his next letter, and apparently he didn't consider his appointment to the committee to draft the Articles of Confederation newsworthy. So he decided "to fill my letters with smaller matters." He reported on laws and loyalty oaths, the arrival of the French ambassador, the price of everything in Philadelphia, and the scarcity of cider (something John Adams continually complained about as well). And "now for fashions," he wrote. "When the Congress first moved into the city, they found the Tory ladies who tarried with the Regulars [the British] wearing the most enormous high headdresses after the manner of the mistresses & wh——s of the British officers; and at the anniversary of independence they appeared in public dressed that way." That must have been something for the wife tending the farm back in New Hampshire to wrap her mind around.

For her part, Mary was ready for Josiah to come home, though he had been gone only a few months. She advised him to write "where you think proper (as the General Court is adjourned to the last of October)" to request that the other congressional delegates relieve him. She acknowledged: "This is my judgment; but you must do as you think best." And Mary again assured him that "our farming business goes on middling well." When he had first left home, she called it **"your"** farming business, then changed to **"the"** farming business. Now it was **"our"** farming business. I should think so.

By September the news from Rhode Island was bad, and Mary didn't know whether it was that "disappointment" or "something else" that had caused a huge rise in prices. Josiah's next letter brought the welcome news that he was planning to come home, as soon as someone came to replace him in Congress. Until that happened, he advised her to "order some wood" and, if necessary, hire someone "to tarry with you till my return in order to prepare for the winter." It wasn't easy to convince people to serve in Congress, but New Hampshire eventually prevailed on a couple of men to take on that duty. Josiah Bartlett went home.

Mary Bartlett's story is not one of high drama, at least not after she was burned out of house and home for her husband's political views, but it is one that shows how crucial a role these women played while their husbands fought the battles and formed the laws of the new nation. It was not just that they were making it all work at home, they were also passionate patriots themselves, engaged in the government and the war just as their husbands, sons, brothers, fathers, and friends were.

For some women, there was no choice—the war came to them. At the least they were reduced to refugee status, at worst they were killed. Jane Mecom, Benjamin Franklin's sister, was first a refugee from Boston, where she had been run out by the British occupation in 1775; she eventually went with her brother to live in Philadelphia. When that city fell to the enemy two years later, she moved in with her old friend Catharine Ray Greene in Rhode Island. But then the British landed there as well, and Greene's household filled with refugees, so Jane moved in with her grandchildren nearby and anxiously awaited the removal of the

British. "What success we will have in expelling them from Rhode Island is uncertain," she wrote Franklin in August 1778. "They have fortified themselves strongly."

New York and New Jersey were particularly hard hit in the early years of the war. Not only were Americans fighting the British, they were fighting each other. Loyalists and rebels were engaged in what was essentially a civil war. Families would move from place to place as one group and then the other took over towns. Sarah Livingston Jay, daughter of the governor of New Jersey and wife of John Jay, a member of the Continental and New York State Congresses, gave some sense of how unsettling the situation was in a letter to her husband: "I long to know my destination next winter, and yet I could wish not to wait so long as winter . . . before your abode is mine." But her situation was nothing compared to that of her mother and sisters, who insisted on staying at Liberty Hall, the family home in Elizabeth, New Jersey, in an attempt to protect it. William Livingston, the governor, was considered a prime prize by the British, who continually sought to capture him. One particularly hair-raising night, the Brits arrived at Liberty Hall, acting on what turned out to be bad intelligence that the governor was, for once, in residence. Livingston's daughter Susan couldn't convince them that he wasn't there until they had searched the house, terrifying her mother and sister. When the soldiers failed to find the governor, they decided to go for second prize—his papers. A successful search would have sent the British back to their commanders triumphant even without Livingston. Stored in a locked desk in the house was his correspondence with George Washington, with Congress, and with the state government. As a soldier approached the desk, a quick-thinking Susan intervened. Telling him that the letters in there were her private correspondence and appealing to his sense of chivalry, she begged him not to embarrass her by looking at the papers in the desk. He did as she asked, in exchange for her promise to produce what he was looking for. Susan led him to a stack of official-looking files, and the soldiers departed with an armful of old legal briefs, leaving the Livingston women, the house, and the sensitive documents unmolested.

That wasn't the case for the man William Livingston had defeated for governor of New Jersey, Richard Stockton. Annis Boudinot Stockton, the young poet who befriended Esther Edwards Burr, had grown up to see her family take leadership in America's cause. Her husband and son-in-law both signed the Declaration of Independence, her brother served as a high-ranking soldier in the Continental army, she herself produced patriotic poetry. When the British took Princeton in 1776, General Cornwallis took over the Stockton home, called Morven. But before he got there, Annis hid important state papers, plus the names of the members of the American Whig Society of Princeton College, a treasure trove for the English, who wanted to punish patriots. Her husband, who was serving in Congress in Baltimore, rushed home to try to take his family to safety, but he was arrested, imprisoned, and abused in captivity. Annis got word of his treatment to the Congress, and the British were threatened with retribution, but their tactics had succeeded. Stockton was the only signer of the Declaration to swear an oath to take no further action against the king. He was released, a broken man who never again participated in the cause. His house was used by the British, who destroyed the interior, burned his books and some of the papers they found, and stole others. But Annis continued to write her poems and eventually reestablished herself at Morven.

Margaret Beekman Livingston, matriarch of a whole family of Founders, saw her New York estate burned to the ground, but she refused to leave, moving into a cottage on the property until she could rebuild. Remarkably, the British left her alone there. That wasn't always the way they treated respectable ladies. One of Margaret Livingston's daughters married Morgan Lewis, whose father, Francis, was another man marked by the Crown for signing the Declaration of Independence. When the British learned that Francis Lewis's wife and property were unprotected on Long Island, they decided to launch a full-scale attack. A man-of-war fired on the house from the Sound, while soldiers arriving on horseback ransacked everything in it, then seized Elizabeth Lewis and carted her off to prison, where she was treated miserably. It turns out that George Washington was wrong when he judged that the British would not go after his wife to get at him. When Elizabeth's plight was brought to the attention of Washington, he ordered that the wives of two British officers be put under house arrest in Philadelphia until an exchange could be worked out. Eventually that happened, and Elizabeth Lewis, after months in jail, was released. But her health was destroyed, and she died a couple of years later, leading a descendant to observe, "Mrs. Lewis could not have been more a victim to the Revolution had she been slain in battle."

The battles were nowhere near over, but the theater of conflict shifted at the end of 1778—Savannah surrendered to the British, and the South was under siege.

CHAPTER FOUR

1778–1782: Still More War and Home-front Activism

SARAH FRANKLIN BACHE

On the Home Front

Once the city of Savannah fell, the British were able to establish a firm foothold in the South. Government loyal to the Crown returned to Georgia in 1779 for the rest of the war—Ann Gwinnett's warning about traitors in the ranks seems to have been borne out. With Georgia securely in their hands, enemy soldiers moved on South Carolina, plundering and pillaging as they marched, with the aim of taking Charleston. British forces had made a concerted attempt to capture the city early in the war but had been embarrassingly defeated when their ships ran aground. This time they were determined to succeed. Eliza Pinckney's sons had returned to America from their many years of schooling in England as dedicated patriots, each having been instructed in his father's will to devote "all his future abilities in the service of God and his country, and in the cause of virtuous liberty." Both Thomas and Charles Cotesworth Pinckney rose to high rank quickly in the army, along with their sister Harriott's husband, Daniel Horry. Charles Cotesworth Pinckney had served as George Washington's aide in 1777, but with the war shifting to his home territory, Charles shifted with it, joining his brother in the unsuccessful campaign to thwart British attacks north from Florida.

By 1778 Eliza Pinckney had been widowed for twenty years and had been managing on her own since she was a girl. With the men off at war, her daughter Harriott found herself a virtual widow as well, but she stayed at her plantation on the Santee River in Hampton with her little children, to keep the family business going. In her isolation she was desperate for news. "I have not had a line to inform me of anything," Harriott wrote her mother. "I am now here entirely alone." Eliza soon joined her as the British rampaged through South Carolina in 1779. Of course the women weren't really alone on their plantations; there were scores of slaves as well, but that would soon change. While she was at Hampton, Eliza received word from her son Thomas that both her plantation house and his had been destroyed. "I have just received . . . the account of my losses and your almost ruined fortunes by the enemy, a severe blow!" The British had gutted Eliza's house, burned Thomas's place, and taken the slaves. (In plundering South Carolina's plantations, the British rounded up about three thousand slaves, many of whom were still treated as property—just the property of new owners— and sold to the West Indies. Neither side in this fight for freedom was ready to grant it to the slaves.) Charles Cotesworth Pinckney had offered to divide his property with his mother and brother, but Thomas had said he couldn't accept the offer; Eliza agreed with that decision, adding, "Nor can I take a penny from his young helpless family. Independence is all I wish, and a little will make us that." Several families of women and children moved in with Harriott at Hampton, hoping to find safety there while their husbands and sons hopelessly tried to save Charleston. In the end they failed, and the British finally achieved their long-awaited goal—they captured Charleston, the South's preeminent city culturally and economically, in May 1780, gaining major tactical and psychological victories plus control of the vast regions of Georgia and South Carolina.

Charles Cotesworth Pinckney was taken prisoner; Thomas had escorted the governor out of the city as it came under siege and so escaped captivity for a little while longer. As the British moved into Charleston, they evicted women from their homes, or worse. Tales of the occupation were handed down as part of family lore; in the next century Eliza's great-great-granddaughter Harriott Ravenal would write, "Two sisters who remonstrated against some order were thrown into the dungeon under the old post-office, with the worst felons of the town." Women were also summoned to grace British balls, which they could refuse only so many times before they faced retaliation. Some, of course, enjoyed the whirl of social events, but those who dallied with the British soldiers ended up marked for life. Ravenal tells of a "very respectable woman" who lived to be almost one hundred; she was "pointed out to the young people: '**We** don't think much of Miss X—— Y——, my dear. **Quite** too fond of the British officers.'" Still, Charleston was safer for women than life on the plantation, with the British barreling through the state. Despite the danger, the great South Carolina warrior Francis Marion urged the women to remain on their property, "to take protection, make provisions, keep up communications, and send information to the men in camp."

He had enlisted the women in the cause, so Marion knew he was likely to find Harriott at home at Hampton one night when he showed up exhausted from the fight and hungry for a meal. While dinner was cooking, the sound of horse hooves alerted them that the British were approaching. Harriott rushed Marion out the back door, showing him the creek at the foot of the property and telling the "Swamp Fox" that he could swim over to an island and hide there until it was safe to rejoin his men. Then the plantation mistress opened her front door to General Banastre Tarleton, the British persecutor of South Carolina, who proceeded to search the premises. According to the family story, Harriott prolonged the search as much as possible, then fed Tarleton the dinner prepared for Marion, who was safely on his way. As he departed Tarleton appropriated "a fine volume of Milton, of a beautiful Baskerville edition, bound in crimson and gold." The family showed the second volume as they passed the story from generation to generation.

On their next visit to Hampton, which was full of refugee families, the British walked away with a far more important prize. Both Thomas Pinckney and Daniel Horry were there for brief visits, and the enemy came looking for them. Thomas escaped, Daniel was captured, and, as Harriott wrote to a friend, "we have lately been well plundered by the enemy." Thomas returned to his unit, and his wife, Elizabeth, went home to join her sisters and their mother, Rebecca Motte. Eliza traveled to her house in Charleston for the summer and wrote to her young daughter-in-law, "chiefly to beg you to keep up your spirits, and imitate your husband's fortitude." Probably not what she wanted to hear from her mother-in-law, but the pregnant Elizabeth gamely replied, "I do all in my power to keep up my spirits and hope for the best." As for her husband, "I have not heard from him since he left

Camden, but hope ere now he is safe with Gen. Washington." Unfortunately for Thomas, that was not the case.

He was still in Camden, South Carolina, where the Americans were routed a month later. Shortly after the battle, Eliza got word of Thomas's fate and wrote to him of "your leg being shattered, and you yourself a prisoner. Gracious God support me in this hour of distress! . . . how readily I would part with life, could it save your limb." Eliza was eager to go take care of her son, but he had already sent word that she should not come. His mother acquiesced, but she wasn't happy about it. "I suffer more from . . . my own anxiety and melancholy apprehensions than if I was near you." Since Thomas's wife had just had a baby, she was also unable to take on the nursing duties, which fell to a woman in Camden, a town described by Eliza as a "filthy, wretched" place. Thomas was chafing at the bit to go home as soon as the British would let him, even if he wasn't sufficiently healed. Word from his mother that a friend had seen his baby and pronounced him "a fine fellow, hearty and well," must have been comforting, but the father probably wanted to see for himself. To her daughter-in-law, Eliza offered her wish "that we may meet in more comfort than we have lately known!" In October, Cornwallis allowed Pinckney to return to his in-laws', under what was essentially house arrest, to await a prisoner exchange. His mother worried that caring for both him and the baby would wear his wife out. "Poor Betsey is a young nurse, I feel

much for her." It was well-placed sympathy—"poor Betsey" almost died taking care of her severely wounded husband.

Because the British had too few soldiers in the South to maintain prison camps, they released officers on parole, placing them under house arrest until an exchange could be effected. While they were on parole, both Thomas and his brother Charles were wooed by their loyalist friends but remained staunchly in the patriot camp. Eventually they were shipped to Philadelphia, where the prisoner swap later occurred. The brothers then served in George Washington's army for the rest of the war. The Pinckneys' patriotism was more than supported by their spouses. Charles Cotesworth Pinckney was married to Sarah Middleton, sister of a signer of the Declaration of Independence and daughter of a president of the Continental Congress. Thomas's wife, Elizabeth Motte, was the daughter of one of the great heroines of the Revolution, Rebecca Motte.

After Thomas Pinckney left his in-laws, but was still being held prisoner, the British moved in, establishing a garrison on the Motte property and forcing Rebecca Motte, a widow, and her children to take up residence in a farmhouse nearby. American troops, under Francis Marion and Henry Lee, surrounded the British encamped on her estate and demanded they surrender. The British, expecting reinforcements at any moment, refused to give up, leaving the Americans with just one choice—to destroy the Motte mansion, thus depriving the enemy of a bastion for defense. Since Rebecca Motte had been housing the Americans, caring for the sick and wounded, and since her son-in-law was considered a hero in the Continental army, Lee was loath to destroy the house. He took the problem to Rebecca, who "gave instant relief to his agitated feelings by declaring that she was gratified with the opportunity of contributing to the good of her country." Lee devised a plan to shoot flaming arrows into the roof of the Motte house, setting it on fire. When Rebecca was informed of the strategy, she told the general that she could help—she had some East Indian arrows that burst into flame when they struck their target. So she herself provided the weapons of destruction. When the flares started flaming, the British made a brief attempt to put the fire out but soon surrendered, making it possible for the Americans to save most of the mansion. Afterward, Rebecca served up a meal to the officers of both armies, which General Lee later remembered: "The deportment and demeanor of Mrs. Motte gave a zest to the pleasures of the table. . . . Conversing with ease, vivacity and good sense, she obliterated our recollection of the injury she had received." The sheath for the arrows became the case for Rebecca Motte's knitting needles.

The British occupation of South Carolina left the state destitute. Explaining to a doctor why she could not pay his bill, Eliza Pinckney, the great entrepreneur, described her situation: "It may seem strange that a single woman, accused of no crime, who had a fortune sufficiency to live genteelly in any part of the world . . . should in so short a time be so entirely deprived of it as not to be able to pay a debt under sixty pound sterling, but such is my singular case." She went on to detail how her plantations had been plundered, her house in Charleston appropriated by the British, and her wood all cut down to build a garrison, "for which I have not got a penny." Remember how as a girl she plotted to plant those trees in hopes that they would someday supply an American shipping business? Now they were gone.

At Camp

While some British forces marched through the South, others occupied New York, and George Washington camped his army nearby in order to keep the enemy contained on the isle of Manhattan. After a few months at Mount Vernon in 1778, Martha Washington wrote to her brother in November, "I am very uneasy at this time—I have some reason to expect that I shall take another trip northward." And soon she did, once again traveling in the winter, this time in a creaky carriage that stopped first in Philadelphia while George fixed up quarters for them at camp in Middlebrook, New Jersey. Washington met his wife in Philadelphia in late December so they could spend Christmas together for the first time in four years. The couple visited in Philadelphia, enjoying themselves for a few weeks, despite the bad news that the British had captured Savannah, and celebrated their twentieth wedding anniversary in January. That night Washington danced with Sally Bache, Benjamin Franklin's daughter, who reported to her father in France, "I have lately been several times invited abroad with the General and Mrs. Washington. He always inquires after you in the most affectionate manner, and speaks of you highly." It was a pleasant idyll, but at the beginning of February, while the British were moving from Savannah into South Carolina, the Washingtons joined the army at camp in New Jersey. Lucy Knox and Kitty Greene and their children were there as well.

Kitty Greene recently had delivered a third child, but as always, she was ready to leave Rhode Island relatives and reunite with her husband as soon as possible after the birth. And Nathanael wanted her to come: "I don't believe half a kingdom would hire you to stay away," he wrote to her before she arrived in New Jersey, and then admitted, "It will greatly contribute to my happiness to have you with me." Washington hoped the lively young woman would come to Middlebrook as well; he thought she was good for troop morale. It was a festive season at camp; soon after Martha arrived, Lucy and Henry Knox threw a party to mark the one-year anniversary of the alliance with France. It wasn't the same as the big celebration thrown at Valley Forge the year before, but it gave everyone a lift. Then the Greenes hosted a dance. This was the famous night when George Washington bet Kitty

Greene that he could win the stamina contest, and they "danced upwards of three hours without sitting down," Nathanael told a friend. (As for Lucy Knox, General Greene wrote, "Mrs. Knox is fatter than ever.") Three tiny children notwithstanding, Kitty Greene was having such a good time that her husband finally took her aside and scolded her, telling her she had become too fond of wine. Still, with the winter hiatus in fighting, partying filled a lot of the time at Middlebrook, where conditions were considerably more comfortable than they had been the year before at Valley Forge. The weather was much milder, and the soldiers better clothed and generally healthier. One regiment styled itself "Lady Washington's Dragoons" and turned out in white uniforms trimmed in blue. Though things were peaceful in New Jersey, the reports from the South were worrisome, and Martha was fearful for her family in Virginia. In March she wrote to her son: "All is quiet in these quarters. It is from the southward that we expect to hear news, we are very anxious to know how our affairs are going in those quarters." As one loss in the South piled on top of another, there was at least one promising development—Spain joined the war on America's side in May 1779. With the arrival of spring, winter camp disbanded, the women went back home, and Kitty Greene once again was pregnant.

When they came together again the next winter at Morristown, New Jersey, it was a far less pleasant experience. Snowstorms buried the camp, with drifts reaching twelve feet. The soldiers' clothes were worn, and many of them slept outside, their feet circling a campfire. Wartime inflation had made their salaries in paper currency practically worthless. They "ate every kind of food but hay," wrote their distraught commander in chief. When Martha Washington arrived in January, the troops cheered her into camp, but mutiny was in the air, with whole regiments threatening desertion. Kitty Greene, hugely pregnant, brought her son George through a blizzard, leaving her little girls behind with relatives, and made it to camp in time to give birth to her fourth child, Nathanael Ray Greene. The baby provided a nice diversion that dreadful winter, with the women working hard to improve conditions. Martha once again assembled her sewing circle, and the occasional party brightened spirits somewhat, though one evening's entertainment ended unhappily for General Washington. A teetotaling visitor decided the men were drinking too much, so he joined the ladies in another room. When the men organized to retrieve him and make him take a drink, the ladies refused to surrender him. Washington himself then tried to capture the stubborn visitor, whose wife was holding on to him. When, as part of the joke, Washington grabbed her wrist, she screamed, "Let go of my hand or I'll pull every hair out of your head! Even if you are a general you are still just a man!" So much for wartime attempts at levity, Washington kept being challenged by unsubmissive women.

Martha made her own efforts at lightening up the dark winter. She adopted a tomcat and named him

"Hamilton" after George's handsome young aide, Alexander Hamilton, who had quite an eye for the ladies. One of those ladies, Elizabeth Schuyler, came calling at camp, trying to get a glimpse of her beloved. She sent Martha a gift of cuffs, for which she was thanked: "Mrs. Washington presents her best respects to Miss Schuyler. She sends her some nice powder, which she hopes will be acceptable to her." Even in those trying times, the ladies tried to keep up appearances. It wasn't easy—with the British close by, there was constant fear of attack. Occasionally alarms in the night sent soldiers scurrying into Martha's room, with guns at the ready. One night, when George was away, a soldier assigned to guard "Lady Washington" found some volunteer congressmen "assisting" him. He wrote his brother that he was honored by the assignment: "I am happy with the importance of my charge, as well as the presence of the most amiable woman upon Earth." But he was not so thrilled with the congressmen: "The rations they have consumed considerably overbalance all their service done as volunteers, for they have dined with us every day almost and drank as much wine as they would earn in six months." Martha remained safe throughout the long winter but was happy when it finally ended. As she told her brother after she left Morristown, "there was not much pleasure there, the distress of the army and other difficulties . . . the poor General was so unhappy that it distressed me exceedingly." In June, Martha went to Philadelphia, where she found women mounting a nationwide drive to help with her cause of improving the lot of the common soldier.

Political Activism

On the commencement of the war, the Women of America manifested a firm resolution to contribute as much as could depend on them, to the deliverance of their country." Those words, under the heading "The Sentiments of an American Woman," greeted newspaper readers in Philadelphia on June 10, 1780. It was a call to action. In remembering female heroines of the past, the broadside exhorted women of the present to sacrifice some luxuries for the "armies which defend our lives, our possessions, our liberty." The plan: a fund-raising effort on behalf of the soldiers. "Let us not lose a moment; let us be engaged to offer the homage of our gratitude at the altar of military valor, and you our brave deliverers . . . receive with a free hand our offering." The piece was signed "By an American Woman." In fact, the woman who wrote the stirring "sentiments" had been an American for only ten years, since her marriage to Joseph Reed, who was then the president, or governor, of Pennsylvania.

Esther DeBerdt was born in London in 1747, the daughter of a merchant made prosperous in trading with America and acting as the lobbyist before Parliament for the business and political interests of Delaware and Massachusetts. His colonial connec-

tions put Dennis DeBerdt in contact with Americans studying in London, including law student Joseph Reed. When Reed met young Esther, he was immediately smitten, but he would be returning to America, and she could not break her parents' hearts by going with him. Despite her parents' disapproval, seventeen-year-old Esther started a secret correspondence with Joseph while he was still in London, questioning his determination to return home. Eventually her parents dropped their opposition to the match after it appeared that Reed would, after all, live in England, where he would work with his father-in-law as an agent of the colonies. He returned for what he thought was a short visit to America in the troubled year 1765, the year the Stamp Act was passed, and found his own father's business in shambles. Esther followed what was happening in the colonies from her side of the Atlantic as she kept up a five-year correspondence with her absent love. "You in America, as you feel the worst of the difficulties, are certainly most chagrined at them. We are in great hopes something will be done to relieve you," she told him in August 1765. The "difficulties" were affecting her father's business as Americans boycotted anything from England, and Joseph was afraid the family might blame him for their losses. Esther assured him otherwise: "We are surrounded with Boston men, who are so hot about these new regulations, that we have heard of little else for a long time." In fact, DeBerdt was so sympathetic to the Americans, and so dependent on their business, that he became instrumental in getting the hated Stamp Act repealed. His daughter clearly knew what was going on politically, telling Reed at one point, "The House of Lords are most your enemies. There were but five who voted for your right of taxing yourselves." At another point she said that her father "bids me tell you his opinion of Dr. Franklin—that he stood entirely neuter until he saw which way the cause would be carried, and then broke out fiercely on the side of America." (The mob that marched on Franklin's house, thinking him too sympathetic to the Stamp Act, might have gotten it right.) Esther was so savvy that her father hired her as his clerk. "I tell him I believe I must not marry, as he will hardly know what to do without me."

The prospects for marriage anytime in the near future were looking dim as the couple tried to figure out a way to be together. Before Joseph could assume a job in London, DeBerdt needed another commission from Boston, and a salary to go with it, but the Massachusetts Assembly was taking forever about the hire. "How hard it is," Joseph sighed to Esther, "that the happiness of two lovers should depend on the slow debates and the wary counsels of politicians." The reprieve in sour relations created by the repeal of the Stamp Act soon ended with the passage of the tax on tea, and in eerily familiar words, Esther wrote, "There is a storm gathering, which will break over England as well as America, and what will be the consequence is impossible to say." One consequence was that her father's trade with America dried up. "To be an American or a friend of America is a great disadvantage," she reported in January 1769; she added later, "It is impossible for anyone to stem the tide against America." Still, once his father died and he put everything in order, Joseph decided to move to England to join his true love and work for her father. When he arrived in May 1770, he learned that Esther's father was dead, his business bankrupt, and the English attitudes toward the colonies even worse than expected. A few weeks later, after their five-year separation, Esther and Joseph were married in London and soon sailed with her mother to America. In appraising Esther's move from sophisticated London to small-town Philadelphia, her grandson William Reed wrote in 1847: "To marry an American eighty years ago, must have seemed more inappropriate for a gentle and refined British maiden, than nowadays it would be for a New York or Philadelphia young lady to follow the fortunes of a California settler, or an emigrant to Oregon."

It wasn't easy for Esther to adjust to her new home, as we learn from a regular correspondence with her brother, Dennis DeBerdt, Junior, in England. "I cannot say America is agreeable," she wrote. "I should be very glad to change this fine sky for our heavy one." After she had been in the country a little less than a year, her daughter Martha was born, a sickly little girl. "If she lives, it will make me more anxious than ever to return to dear England," Esther told her brother, "as the education of girls is very indifferent here." A year later, after another baby, a boy, arrived, his mother confided, "I wish I could stop with that number, but I don't expect that." As she got used to her new home, and as the political rift with England grew wider, Esther's attitudes about the country started to change. When the British punished the people of Boston by closing the port, she warned, "The Provinces are determined to stand by them, and make it a common cause." She knew that her brother would "feel the bad effects of it in your trade affairs. I am distressed on your account as well as for the public." By November 1774 she had had a third child, but all she could write about was politics: "The next news from England after Parliament meets, I imagine, will be decisive. . . . A determination to proceed and enforce [the Tea Act] must inevitably plunge New England into a scene of blood and all the horrors of civil war." Again she emphasized that "the whole continent is in the cause." Esther clearly knew what was coming. As the situation worsened, she urged her brother, in early 1775, "You must not forget to write us every piece of intelligence concerning American affairs you can pick up, especially what is said in the House, and who is on our side, and who against." She had chosen sides. She was now an American, no longer a Brit like her brother. But, like most patriots before the Battles of Lexington and Concord, Esther Reed saw America's cause as "dependency on the Mother State on proper terms, and to be secure of their liberties; you may depend on it that the accounts given that this country is aiming at independence are false." She realized that it was unusual for a woman to concern herself so with public affairs. "You may judge my dear Dennis, how interesting politics are when they employ so much of my thoughts and attention, now I am surrounded with family concerns." She slyly then asked her brother, "Do tell us what part the great Doctor Franklin is taking; whether he has the openness to declare his sentiments before he sees which way affairs will terminate." Esther didn't like politicians who put their fingers in the air to test the wind.

Once the war began in 1775 and Washington was named commander in chief, Joseph Reed was appointed to a committee to escort the general out of Philadelphia. Esther thought her husband would be gone for only a few days, but he soon wrote to her that Washington had convinced him to join the army, so off Reed went to Cambridge, without so much as saying farewell to his wife or tidying up his law practice. She wrote to her brother that "civil war, with all its horrors, stains this land . . . the people are determined to die or be free." And she informed him that now she could not return to England because it would be "totally improper." In her next letter Esther gave the news that Joseph had been appointed secretary to Washington, and she didn't expect him home anytime soon. Though she was concerned for herself, she was proud of her husband. "Every heart and every hand almost, is warm and active in the cause, certainly my dear brother, it is a glorious one. You see every person

willing to sacrifice his private interest in this glorious contest." It was a cause, she concluded, that
"has at least a chance to be victorious." Esther and
the children moved about between friends and relatives that summer. Writing to her brother from
New Jersey in September, while Joseph was still at
camp in Cambridge, she was sanguine about their
disrupted family life: "I cheerfully give up his profits in business (which were not trifling), and I ac-
quiesce . . . at his being so long absent from me. I
think the cause in which he is engaged so just, so
glorious, and I hope so victorious, that private interest and pleasure may and ought to be given up,
without a murmur."

The newly minted patriot recounted for her
brother detailed news of military actions, "because
the newspapers are not always to be depended on as
to particulars, though true in general." And she
plaintively asked, "But where sleep all our friends
in England? Where sleep the virtue and justice of
the English nation?" The answer to those questions
came in a letter from Dennis DeBerdt to his
brother-in-law, Joseph Reed: "It is not easy to
know the sense of the Nation, but, excepting those
connected with the government, I believe the majority clearly for America." Without the tools of
political polling, DeBerdt ventured a breakdown of
English public opinion: "One-fourth may be said to
be always on the side of Government; one-fourth
sunk in sensuality and pleasure; one-fourth im-
mersed in business; and the remainder inattentive
and indolent to all public matters, provided a

grievance does not actually happen in their families or circles of acquaintance." It doesn't sound very different from today's scientific studies. But then those attitudes resulted in dire consequences for Britain, as Esther predicted in October 1775. Long before the men in Congress were ready to take this step, even before Abigail Adams was urging it on John in her letters, Esther was considering a complete break with the country she had left so reluctantly only five years before. If the last petition from the Congress to the king was rejected, she boldly conjectured, "I imagine WE SHALL DE-CLARE FOR Independence, and exert our utmost to defend ourselves."

Joseph came home briefly and then rejoined Washington's forces in New York, leaving Esther to get the household out of harm's way in Philadelphia. She moved first to Burlington, New Jersey, but then, as the enemy approached, she fled with her mother and four young children (she had recently had another baby) to a farmhouse in Evesham, near the frontier, where they were cut off from communication with the family in England. (During the war patriots would either move in with friends or take over a loyalist's house in patriot-controlled areas, and vice versa.) Another soldier's wife went with them, as well as a fourteen- or fifteen-year-old boy to help out. As the British and, even worse, their hired Hessian soldiers swarmed over New Jersey, Esther devised an escape plan to pile their little group into a wagon kept at the ready and head west into truly wild territory. Elizabeth

Ellet expressed her horror at the situation when she wrote about it a few decades later: "The wives and children of American patriot-soldiers thought themselves safer on the perilous edge of an Indian wilderness, than in the neighborhood of soldiers . . . commanded by noblemen."

Fortunately, Esther and company stayed safely at their farmhouse until the American victories at Trenton and Princeton routed the British out of New Jersey, when the fugitives went home to Philadelphia. In March 1777 Esther was finally able to write to her brother and tell him that "an army of foreigners" had been only a few hours away from her for several weeks, "and since they have been driven back we have understood they had planned a visit to our retreat." She attributed British successes to "the horrid blunder our rulers made" by enlisting soldiers for only four or six months. But, she said, things were looking up for the Americans, for which she was grateful, since her husband had had a couple of very near misses. Once a deserting soldier tried to shoot him, and once "his horse was shot under him." (It turned out that Joseph Reed's horses were magnets for bullets—three of his mounts were killed during the Revolution.) With the British occupation of Philadelphia, Esther and the children were once again on the run, and all communication with England interrupted. When Joseph Reed wrote to his brother-in-law in May 1778, his letter was filled with distressing news—his family had been forced to move four times, his house had been plundered, and "we lost a fine little girl near two years old, about a fortnight ago, but your sister made me a present of a fine boy the day before." When the British weren't threatening, smallpox was, and it claimed their child. Esther had a terrible time dealing with the loss. "I ought to take blame to myself," she wrote a friend. "Teach me to say that God does **all** things well."

Later that year Joseph Reed was elected president of the Executive Council of the State of Pennsylvania, a state that was embroiled in bitter factional politics. Benedict Arnold, who had been named commander of the military in Philadelphia after the British left, opposed Reed at every turn. Esther told her brother in 1779 that she couldn't really talk about public affairs, "Since our life is so entwined in politics." But she was clearly active in them. In May 1780 Esther gave birth to her last child, George Washington Reed, and in June her "Sentiments of an American Woman" hit the presses. Her idea that women should "wear clothing more simple, hair dressed less elegant," and give the money saved to the troops as **"the offering of the ladies"** might have been suggested by Martha Washington, who was always worrying about bolstering troop morale. Whatever the origin, it was an idea that immediately caught on. Women in Philadelphia set about finding ways to carry out the campaign within days of the publication of the "Sentiments." On June 21, the **Pennsylvania Gazette** printed the original call to action, with an addendum: a set of proposals on how to proceed. "1st. All Women and Girls will be received without exception," newspaper readers were told. A "Treasuress" would be chosen by the women in each county, and when the Treasuress thought it appropriate, she would send the money to "the wife of the Governor or President of the State, who will be the Treasuress-General of the State," and she in turn would send the contributions on to "Mistress Washington." There were provisions if the governor was unmarried, and if "Mistress Washington" was not at camp when the money arrived, it would be delivered to General Washington as a "Father and Friend of the Soldiery." The general could spend it as he saw fit, except "the American Women desire only that it may not be considered as to be employed to procure the army the objects of subsistence, arms or clothing, which are due them by the Continent." It was to be something extra to "render the condition of the Soldier more pleasant." The general would have his own ideas about that.

Newspapers around the country printed the documents, and women started organizing. The Ladies' Association of Philadelphia elected Esther as their leader and kept records of exactly how the fund drive proceeded. Women set out in pairs, dividing up the city among them, and went door-to-door asking for donations. The wives of some of the most prominent men in Philadelphia took up the collection, and it was considered an honor to participate. One account was provided by an anonymous letter writer to a friend in Annapolis and later published in the **Maryland Gazette**. She described how the women had met after the publication of the "Sentiments" and signed up for the task of fund-raising, "notwithstanding the fatigues and cares which it was natural to think would accompany such employment. . . . Those who were in the country returned without delay to the city to fulfill their duty; others put off their departure; those whose state of health was the most delicate found strength in their patriotism." She related the story of one woman who wanted to "discharge the patriotic task" but needed to nurse her baby. Another woman took up the nursing while the new mother went soliciting. "They have not omitted one house," she wrote, and told of poor women insisting on giving something. "It is an honor to the women of America," she concluded, and a blow to "the hopes of the enemies of our country, whose expectations of conquest are more founded in divisions of America, than in any superiority of strength and courage." The women were relentless. Sarah Bache, Benjamin Franklin's daughter, wrote to a Mistress Gray on July 1 that attempts to reach her had failed because of where she lived. "We all know your attachment to the cause of Liberty," Sarah wrote, and asked her "to collect the donations of the good women on that side of the water." Sarah was sure she'd get a receptive response, as she wrote to a friend at the time that the "sums given by the good women of Philadelphia" had been much greater than expected, "and given with so much cheerfulness, and so many blessings, that it was rather a pleasing than a painful task to call for them."

Not everyone was so pleased with the determined ladies. Anna Rawle wrote to her mother, whose husband had been exiled as a loyalist, "Of all absurdities the ladies going about for money exceeded everything." Rather than patriotic sentiment, Anna insisted, it was the fund-raisers' insistence that caused women to cough up cash: "people were obliged to give them something to get rid of them." Whatever the reason, the women were highly successful. In just a few days they collected about $300,000, only slightly less than the merchants of the city had put together to establish a bank. The contributors ranged from a housemaid to the Marchioness de Lafayette, who, the carefully recorded ledger shows, gave the largest amount. Lafayette sent the donation to Esther Reed, in his wife's name. "Without presuming to break in upon the rules of your respected Association, may I humbly present myself as her Ambassador to the confederate ladies," he wrote, asking that "Mrs. President be pleased to accept her offering."

The women's movement rapidly spread to other states. On July 4 "The Ladies of Trenton, in New Jersey," announced in a newspaper that they were "emulating the noble example of their Patriotic Sisters of Pennsylvania." A committee was appointed to correspond with ladies in different counties throughout the state "for the purpose of promoting a subscription for the relief and encouragement of those brave men in the Continental

Army." Julia Stockton Rush, daughter of the Princeton poet Annis Stockton and wife of Benjamin Rush, a prominent signer of the Declaration, became so involved in the drive for donations that her husband wrote a somewhat sarcastic letter to his friend John Adams. Julia, Rush said, who once "had all the timidity of her sex as to the issue of the war and the fate of her husband, was one of the ladies employed to solicit benefactions for the army. She distinguished herself by her zeal . . . in this business, and is now so thoroughly enlisted in the cause of her country that she reproaches me with lukewarmness."

The women of Maryland got into the act as well. The governor's wife, Mary Digges Lee, had taken up the plan and perhaps was the moving force behind convincing the **Maryland Gazette** to publish the anonymous letter from the woman in Philadelphia. And Molly Carroll, the wife of Charles Carroll of Carrollton, another signer of the Declaration, though pregnant with her seventh child, also enthusiastically enlisted in the cause. One of Carroll's congressional colleagues expressed his support, hoping "Mrs. Carroll will succeed to the utmost of her wishes in the laudable business she is at present engaged in." Soon the Philadelphia Ladies were famous. When an American army officer in Baltimore bragged to a compatriot in North Carolina about the activities of the Maryland women, he cited the example set for them by the women of Philadelphia.

A "Letter from an Officer at Camp" in late June

was printed in newspapers up and down the continent. The "officer" reported that the soldiers who had felt "neglected" were pleased by the "mark of respect" shown by the Philadelphia women. That was exactly what Esther Reed had in mind when she penned her "Sentiments," which had become known throughout the land, not only through the newspapers but through what we would now call "direct mail." Esther sent form letters to ladies of note in all of the states and, as governor's wife, especially tried to engage other "First Ladies" in behalf of the soldiers. The wife of the governor of Virginia, Thomas Jefferson, heard directly from Martha Washington about the appeal. The **Virginia Gazette** published Martha Jefferson's announcement of a collection in churches, since it would be impractical to go house to house in rural Virginia. She sent the plan to a friend, explaining, "Mrs. Washington has done me the honor of communicating the enclosed proposition of our sisters in Pennsylvania and of informing me that the same grateful sentiments are displaying themselves in Maryland. . . . I undertake with cheerfulness the duty of furnishing to my country women an opportunity of proving that they also participate of those virtuous feelings." It is the only letter of Martha Jefferson's that survives.

Unfortunately for Esther Reed, Martha Washington went home to Mount Vernon that July and so was not at camp to receive the money. So General Washington was in charge of determining how it would be spent, and he had never liked the women's avowed intention to provide "an extraordinary bounty" instead of the things the soldiers should "receive from Congress or the states." As soon as he learned of the drive, Washington wrote to Esther's husband—not to her—that, "although the terms of the association seem . . . to preclude the purchase of any article" the Congress was supposed to provide, the general "would, nevertheless, recommend a provision of shirts in preference to anything else." As commander in chief, Washington would have his way, but not until after a power struggle with Esther Reed. On July 4, 1780, only a few weeks after her broadside first appeared, she sent the general a letter telling him that the ladies had raised more than $300,000 in paper money, and that they expected "considerable additions from the country," since she had written to the other states. Then she offered to complete the task by spending the money "agreeably to the intention of the donors and your wishes on the subject." Unfortunately for Esther, those two goals came in conflict. Washington's reply praised "the patriotism of the Ladies," which, he said, "entitles them to the highest applause of the country." But, he added, "I would propose the purchasing of coarse linen, to be made into shirts." That wasn't at all what Esther and her fellow females had in mind. Then Washington came up with another idea: the women could put the money in the new bank, giving that institution a much-needed infusion of cash, and use banknotes to "purchase the articles intended," since, he concluded, "I should imagine the ladies will have no objection to a union with the gentle-men." Wrong. The women wanted this to be a special "offering of the ladies" that the soldiers could point to with pride.

At the end of July, Esther tried once more to have her way, responding to Washington that Pennsylvania was already preparing to provide new shirts to its troops and "an idea prevails among the ladies that the soldiers will not be so much gratified by bestowing an article to which they are entitled from the public, as in some other method which will convey more fully the idea of a reward for past services and an incitement to future duty." Her suggestion: that the inflated paper money be converted to hard currency (gold or silver coins) and every soldier be given two dollars, "to be entirely at his own disposal." Washington adamantly opposed that proposal, fearing that the soldiers would use the money for liquor and that "a taste of hard money may be productive of much discontent as we have none but depreciated paper for their pay." One more time he insisted that the contributions be used to buy linen for shirts. Esther, who was again alone with her children while Joseph served with the Pennsylvania Volunteers, told her husband about Washington's decision. "I received this morning a letter from the General, and he still continues his opinion that the money in my hands should be laid out in linen; . . . his letter is, I think, a little formal, as if he was hurt by our asking his opinion a second time, and our not following his directions, after desiring to give them." Poor Washington, he was always having trouble getting the women to do what he wanted. Remember how he railed at the army camp followers about not riding in the wagons? Esther and her compatriots finally complied, and she set about buying the linen. "I shall now endeavor to get the shirts made as soon as possible," she told her husband. Reed responded: "The affair of the donation will require your attention, or slander will be busy on that score; the General is so decided, that you have no choice left, so that the sooner you finish the business the better." He then advised his wife to give a public accounting of "your stewardship in this business, and though you will receive no thanks if you do it well, you will much blame, should it be otherwise." Joseph, who was embroiled in nasty political disputes, knew that no good deed goes unpunished. That was August 1780.

A few weeks later, just shy of her thirty-fourth birthday, Esther Reed died. A virulent wave of dysentery had spread through Philadelphia and claimed the "American Woman," who was still nursing her four-month-old baby. For once the politicians of Philadelphia put aside their personal differences and came together in grief. "The Council and Assembly adjourned and attended her funeral in a body," her grandson later wrote. "A large number of citizens followed." A year later Joseph sadly told Esther's brother in England, "I never knew how much I loved her till I lost her forever."

The work of the Ladies' Association was unfinished. Sarah Franklin Bache took over from Esther

Reed and assigned the shirt-making for the soldiers to individual women. That fall, when a Frenchman visited the Bache household, he was shown into a room "filled with needlework, recently finished by the ladies of Philadelphia." There were 2,200 shirts, and "on each shirt was the name of the married or unmarried lady who made it." Even while bowing to Washington's wishes, the women had found a way to make an individual mark. The soldiers would know whom to thank. The general's gratitude to Sarah Bache and her committee of ladies was gracious: "The Army ought not to regret its sacrifices or its sufferings when they meet with so flattering a reward as in the sympathy of your sex; nor can it fear that its interests will be neglected, while espoused by advocates as powerful as they are amiable."

But the sacrifices and sufferings continued, both in the army and at home. When Catharine Littlefield Greene received Esther Reed's letter asking for a contribution from Rhode Island, she responded, "The distressed exhausted state of this little government prevents us from gratifying our warmest inclinations." The British were occupying much of the state, including Newport. It was a low point in the war: the Americans were losing in the South, out of money and dependent on the still-absent French for salvation, and one of George Washington's most trusted generals had been unmasked as a traitor.

Enemy Agent

By all accounts, Peggy Shippen was a delightful, fun-loving girl from an old Quaker family when she met the man assigned as American military commander in Philadelphia, Benedict Arnold. Soon she was also recruited as a spy. For decades historians debated whether Arnold's wife was a coconspirator in his treachery—she pulled the wool over the eyes of George Washington, Alexander Hamilton, and Lafayette, among others. But the letters between the man whose name is synonymous with traitor and the English who controlled him make it abundantly clear that Margaret Arnold was part of the plot from the start. At the same time that the other ladies in Philadelphia were working to raise money for the soldiers, she was maneuvering to sell them out.

Peggy Shippen and her sisters were quite popular with the British officers when they occupied Philadelphia. Edward Shippen, her father, was a Tory sympathizer, but not a particularly ardent one. The British who regularly visited his house came not for political discourse but for pretty daughters. And the girls enjoyed the round of dances, plays, and musical evenings staged for and by the occupiers. At the middle of all the entertainments—working on costumes and sets and befriending the ladies—was Major John Andre, who was quartered in Benjamin Franklin's house when the patriot family was driven out. Andre was one of the many men who came calling at the Shippen

household and one of the organizers of the infamous farewell celebration, called the Meschianza,
that the British threw for their commander, Lord
Howe. It was an over-the-top festival complete
with a regatta, a mock-tournament, a ball, and a
fireworks display. (This all while the American
troops were starving at Valley Forge.) The Shippen
girls were invited to participate, but, according to
some accounts, their father forbade it because of
what he considered the shocking "Turkish" costumes, designed by Andre. It was just as well—
when the Americans came to town, they didn't take
too kindly to the women who had been partying
with the enemy.

But Benedict Arnold, a thirty-four-year-old widower with three boys and a wounded leg, did take
kindly and instantly to eighteen-year-old Peggy
Shippen. He had been wooing one Betsy DeBlois
(introduced to him by Lucy Knox), writing dramatic, passionate love letters, to no avail. But the
blond, beautiful Peggy soon replaced Betsy in
Arnold's affections, and he simply recycled the letters, only changing the names. It gives you some
idea of what kind of character he was. The Shippen family seems to have been somewhat taken
aback by the not so subtle suitor. "We understand
that General Arnold, a fine gentleman, lays close
siege to Peggy," wrote one relative. She apparently
resisted the siege at first, if a letter from Sarah
Bache to her father is any indication. Writing to
Benjamin Franklin in Paris about her one-year-old
daughter, Sarah joked, "You can't think how fond

of kissing she is, and gives such old-fashioned smacks. General Arnold says he would give a good deal to have her for a schoolmistress to teach the young ladies how to kiss." At the same time he was waging his whirlwind romance, Arnold was alienating the fine folks of Philadelphia. His conduct of his command had brought charges of corruption and mismanagement and placed him in constant conflict with the Pennsylvania Executive Council and its president, Joseph Reed. Rather than bring civil action against the general, the army took over and court-martialed Arnold. In that more sympathetic venue the military man eventually received no more than a slap on the wrist for his disregard for the Executive Council and civil authority.

But the complaints against Benedict Arnold made him bitter, and his marriage to Peggy in April 1779 threatened to make him poor. She loved luxury and was used to it, coming from one of the richest families in town. And he was ready to indulge her, even if he couldn't afford it. Those two reasons probably drove him to strike his nefarious deal with the British, with Peggy as his ally. It has been hard for historians to believe that the flighty young woman would be trusted with secrets by her husband or anyone else. Elizabeth Ellet thought that Peggy Arnold "was utterly unfitted for the duties and privations of a poor man's wife." But not a traitor. Perhaps a different wife would have kept the general on the straight and narrow. "Arnold had no counselor on his pillow to urge him to the imitation of homely republican virtue, to stimulate him to follow the rugged path of a Revolutionary patriot." But the correspondence between Andre and Arnold tells a different story.

One month after the wedding the American general approached a loyalist shopkeeper in Philadelphia who later declared that Arnold offered "his services to the commander-in-chief of the British forces in any way that would most effectually restore the former government." The loyalist, in turn, went to a fellow traveler in New York, who introduced him to the aide to the British commander, Sir Henry Clinton. The aide was Major Andre. Realizing what an opportunity he was being presented, the offer of information from one of Washington's most trusted generals, Andre quickly drafted a letter promising ample compensation and outlining how the convoluted espionage would work, including how to encode messages and how to indicate what kind of invisible ink was being used. The instructions ended with this note: "The Lady might write to me at the same time with one of her intimates, she will guess who I mean, the latter remaining ignorant of interlining and send the letter. . . . The letters may talk of the Meschianza and other nonsense." In other words, Peggy would suggest to a friend that she write to their old buddy Andre about social happenings, and the friend would give the letter to Peggy, whose general husband could probably see to its delivery. With the letter in hand, Peggy would ink in the true message literally between the lines, and her identity would be protected. Arnold's first coded letter to Andre included the greeting "Madam Arnold presents you her particular compliments." Peggy was in it from the beginning.

When Arnold started pressing the British for more money than they were willing to pay, the negotiations broke off. Andre tried to restart them through a letter to Peggy. In it, true to the original scheme, he talked about the Meschianza and hoped she would "infer a zeal to be further employed." That letter was found among the papers in Arnold's house after he joined the British and was used as evidence against Peggy, but her defenders took it at face value, as a chatty conversation about clothes. Her reply—"Mrs. Arnold begs leave to assure Captain Andre that her friendship and esteem for him is not impaired by time or accident"—was essentially a turndown. It would be up to Arnold himself to get back in touch, which he did in May 1780, about the time of the siege of Charleston. To show his worth, the general, who was at camp in Morristown, sent along some secrets—including news of the French fleet on its way. All the while, Arnold was lobbying for command of West Point, a fort where large numbers of supplies had been laid in over three years' time. The general's plan was to take command of West Point and hand it to the British, for a sum of twenty thousand pounds sterling. Before the deal was sealed, he headed for his new post, leaving Peggy in charge of delivering his correspondence to the British. Instead of sweet nothings, the letters from Benedict to his wife gave her the news that Washington was on the way to

West Point: "I believe we shall have near ten thousand men together, who will probably move towards N.Y. in order to draw the attention of Sir Henry Clinton from Rhode Island." In his next letter the absent husband wrote of Washington's plan to "build works, which will confine the British within narrower bounds and shorten our communication with New England." Peggy dutifully passed the letters along to the enemy.

It was not just a business arrangement, however. Arnold seemed solicitous of his wife, who by now had a baby boy. And he wrote lovingly of her to a friend as he awaited her arrival at West Point. While she was back in Philadelphia without him, Peggy went to dinner at the home of their friend Robert Morris. In a story told by Morris, another friend arrived and congratulated her on Arnold's assignment; it was an important post, the friend reported, but not West Point. Peggy erupted into a fit of hysterics the likes of which the rest of the party had rarely seen. Later it occurred to the other guests that she might have been mourning what she feared was the loss of the lucrative deal arranged for the surrender of West Point. But the friend's information was wrong. Arnold was ensconced at the fort, where she and the baby soon joined him. In disguise, Andre made his way through the American lines to West Point as well and left with an armload of sensitive documents for his British commander. Waylaid by the Americans on the way, Andre was arrested and the papers were confiscated. They clearly implicated Benedict Arnold as a traitor.

As all of this was transpiring, George Washington, with Lafayette accompanying him, was heading for West Point. Instead of going directly there, he decided to take a detour to check the fortifications on the Hudson River. Lafayette protested that Mrs. Arnold would be waiting breakfast for them, causing Washington to tease his French friend, "I know you young men are all in love with Mrs. Arnold, and wish to get where she is as soon as possible. You may go and take your breakfast with her, and tell her not to wait for me." Lafayette stayed with Washington, so neither one was there at breakfast when Arnold received word of Andre's arrest. The general excused himself and went upstairs, where he was joined by Peggy. He told her what had happened and quickly made his escape to a British man-of-war docked in the Hudson, allowing Peggy to feign surprise and protest her innocence. Washington arrived, learned everything that had happened, and found a completely out-of-control Peggy Arnold. She accused the men of a plot to kill her baby, she tore her hair, she yelled, she screamed. She appeared a raving lunatic, certainly not a scheming coconspirator. And she melted the hearts of the men around her. Alexander Hamilton, who had been dispatched to try to catch Arnold, the next day wrote to his fiancée, Elizabeth Schuyler, "All the sweetness of beauty, all the loveliness of innocence, all the tenderness of a wife, and all the fondness of a mother, showed themselves in her appearance and conduct. We have every reason to believe that she was entirely unacquainted with the plan." Hamilton had failed at capturing Arnold but returned with two letters from the traitor, one to his wife, one to Washington. To the commander in chief Arnold insisted on his wife's innocence and asked that she be protected. Washington told an aide to tell Mrs. Arnold that "though my duty required that no means should be neglected to arrest General Arnold, I have the great pleasure in acquainting **her** that he is now safe." She had convinced all these warriors that she was an innocent lamb, ready to be delivered back to her father in Philadelphia.

On the way she stopped at the home of Theodosia Prevost, the wife of a British soldier and the lover of Aaron Burr. Supposedly, once inside the door, Peggy wiped off her haggard look and confessed that she was sick to death of acting, that she had not only known of the plot but been a key player in it. The story wasn't told until years later, after both Arnolds had died. And it was told by Aaron Burr, a man few people trusted, so the debate over Peggy Arnold's guilt continued. Her old friends and neighbors in Philadelphia, and the Executive Council her husband had so vilified, were not interested in listening to arguments pro and con. When Arnold's household was searched, the letter from Andre to Peggy surfaced, the **Pennsylvania Packet** editorialized against her, and she was run out of town. The Executive Council resolved,

"That the said Margaret Arnold depart this state within fourteen days from the date hereof, and that she do not return again during the continuance of the present war." Off she went to New York, where her husband was now a general in the British army. She soon was back in the thick of things, and Arnold had received a tidy sum "sufficient for every demand in genteel life." Major Andre was hanged.

After the war the Arnolds moved to England, where they were never really accepted by polite society. But the country took good care of all of them, especially Peggy, who received a five-hundred-pound annual pension "for her services, which were very meritorious."

Waiting for Peace

Benedict Arnold's treachery had not only international implications—combined with the fall of Charleston, it made the French question the wisdom of committing to the American cause—but also strategic consequences. Now the British numbered among their generals one who knew both the army they were fighting with and the land they were fighting on better than any of them. At the end of 1780, Arnold took a force south from New York and started staging raids into Virginia, while the British army in South Carolina made its way toward North Carolina. George Washington needed one of his best officers to take over the Southern Command. His choice: Nathanael Greene.

Kitty Greene and the children were back in Rhode Island, which had been ransacked by the British. She was devastated when she received her husband's announcement: "What I have been dreading has come to pass. . . . How unhappy is war to domestic happiness." Domestic happiness seemed a distant memory to Kitty, who was already struggling to make ends meet and learned from Nathanael that he had no cash to send her, just some probably worthless stock certificates. What she decided to do and where she decided to live were up to her; "choose for yourself and act for yourself," he told her as he departed for the South without even having a chance to see her and say good-bye. Kitty, who loved to join the other families at camp, would have to spend the winter in Rhode Island, though she kept hoping she could somehow meet up with her husband in the South. The other regulars did show up at Washington's encampment in New Windsor, New York, near West Point. Lucy and Henry Knox were there, and Martha Washington arrived before Christmas, finding once again a deprived and surly army. George was forced to dip into his own funds to keep his staff fed, and Martha took on some secretarial duties to help lift the load. Mutiny was in the air, with troops in Pennsylvania and New Jersey threatening desertion, and America's prospects looked grim. Martha was also worried about what she had left behind at Mount Vernon. Her daughter-in-law was perennially pregnant and often experienced difficult childbirths; her son continually made bad financial decisions; her brother-in-law had died, leaving a wife with six children and a large mortgage; and other members of her family, especially her sister's child, were also in need of her. It couldn't have been easy to decide her greatest duty at the time was to her husband.

As Benedict Arnold swept through Virginia, Martha had more reason for concern. The governor, Thomas Jefferson, had moved the capital from Williamsburg to Richmond, thinking it was better protected from invasion. But in January 1781 Arnold, buoyed by good winds, sailed up the James River with 1,500 men. They roared into Richmond burning everything in sight. Jefferson had sent his wife and daughters, including a not yet two-month-old infant, scurrying out of the city to safety. He barely escaped capture himself. Washington dispatched Lafayette to Virginia with a sizable force, but they were unable to contain the British, who struck again in April. Then the dreaded Tarleton, who had terrorized South Carolina, brought his band of marauders to lay waste to Virginia, raping, stealing, and murdering along their path. They docked on the Potomac River at Mount Vernon and demanded provisions for the ship. Though Washington was humiliated when he learned of it, his cousin complied with the British demands rather than risk having the house razed. Tarleton then went after Jefferson, hoping to capture the governor and the Virginia legislature. In

June, as the British moved on Monticello, the Jefferson home, Martha once again was forced to gather up her remaining children—the baby had died a few weeks before—and flee. Jefferson also ignominiously escaped, and some members of the legislature were captured.

But not all the news was bad. After months of guerrilla warfare in the South, enemy fortresses started falling in the face of American onslaughts. Nathanael Greene forced the British out of Camden in May; his forces retook Augusta in June, leaving the Crown in control only of Charleston and Savannah. Cornwallis's foray into Virginia, where he left devastation in his wake, succeeded in enraging the population, making it easier to incite the militia to action. And most important, Washington received word that a large French fleet loaded with marines was headed for the West Indies. If the admiral could be convinced to sail north, the revolutionaries would control the water.

Despite the fighting in Virginia, Martha Washington was eager to get there but was too sick to travel. Her letter home explaining her situation, as so often happened during the war, was intercepted by the British, who tried to score a propaganda victory over "Lady Washington's" illness. The widow of a British soldier sent a basket of goodies under a flag of truce, along with a note wishing Martha well. George, already smarting from his cousin's succumbing to the enemy, turned down the gift of some sorely missed items—including fresh oranges and lemons and "fine Hyson tea"—claiming that his wife was doing fine. In fact, Martha was still quite sick when she set out for Mount Vernon in late June. Then, in September, for the first time in six years, her husband came home, though only for a brief visit on his way south to meet the enemy at Yorktown.

Cornwallis had settled his troops on a peninsula between the James and York Rivers, where he proceeded to build fortifications at Yorktown for his 7,500 soldiers, plus a few hundred loyalists. Washington learned that the French fleet had come through—thirty ships and 3,000 men strong—and was on the way to Chesapeake Bay; the ships still in Rhode Island set sail to meet their compatriots. The general instructed Lafayette to move secretly to secure the area south of the British, cutting off the possibility of escape into North Carolina. Then Washington's forces combined with the French, numbering together more than 15,000 troops, moved from Williamsburg, and dug in around the peninsula, ready to wait the British out. The French fleet blocked the ability of Sir Henry Clinton in New York to send reinforcements to Cornwallis. The Americans moved closer and closer to the surrounded British, sending bombardment after bombardment into their fortifications, and on October 19 Cornwallis officially surrendered. The major fighting in the long war for independence was over.

But no one really knew that at the time. It would be years before the armies disbanded and the British finally evacuated New York, Charleston, and Savannah. And the heartache of wartime continued on for some time. Martha Washington's son, her only surviving child, had gotten caught up in the excitement when George and the other generals stopped over at Mount Vernon. For the first time, Jack Custis signed up and went off to Yorktown as his stepfather's aide-de-camp. Unaccustomed to the rigors of combat, he soon contracted a fever, and just a couple of weeks after the joy of the British surrender the Washington family met with the grief of Jacky's death. He was not yet twenty-seven years old, and he left his twenty-three-year-old widow with four children under the age of five. Fearing that she couldn't cope with all her burdens, George and Martha adopted the youngest two Custis children and brought them to live at Mount Vernon. But they had very little time for making arrangements or for mourning. It was already November, and time to go to winter camp, though no one was quite sure what the course of the war would be from here on out. The Washingtons first traveled to Philadelphia for George to report to Congress. And now that the South seemed subdued, Kitty Greene was finally able to join Nathanael. She stopped in Philadelphia on the way.

Kitty was always able to cheer everyone up, and Martha Washington was glad to see her. George wrote to Nathanael, now hailed as a hero for his victories in the South, that Kitty "is in perfect health, and in good spirits, and thinking no difficulties too great not to be surmounted." A snowstorm kept her in Philadelphia a little longer than she expected, giving Washington time to convince Kitty to leave her son, George Washington Greene, behind so that he could receive a good education in Philadelphia or Princeton rather than lead the vagabond life of a child at camp. She reluctantly agreed, then got word to her husband that she was on her way and expected to be "met by him personally at least five miles from headquarters." But she didn't exactly rush into Nathanael's arms. First Kitty stopped at Mount Vernon, where Lucy Knox was presiding in Martha's absence. With Henry Knox a key figure in the operation at Yorktown, Lucy had joined Martha at her home and stayed there when the Washingtons left. The two old friends had such a good time together enjoying the splendors of the estate that Kitty didn't leave for South Carolina for more than a month. When she did finally hit the road, with her military escort, she was shocked at the sights of war-torn towns, burned-out buildings, and stripped-bare fields all along the way. Finally, in April, her party approached Greene's camp on the Santee River above Charleston. As she had instructed, some men on horseback awaited her carriage on the road outside of camp. One of them broke from the rest and rode to her, giving her escort his horse, as he took a seat in the carriage. It was the first time Kitty and Nathanael Greene had seen each other in almost two years.

What Kitty Greene found when she arrived at camp was a warmer version of Valley Forge—men hungry for both food and fun. As usual, she was able to bring some cheer. Her husband wrote to a friend, "She is a great favorite even with the ladies." But the troops were still restive and threatening mutiny. Merchants in Charleston had evaded the British and sold Nathanael fabric for uniforms, but the general had to sign for them on his own credit. Even with such gestures, some soldiers made common cause with the British, who attempted to capture Nathanael and Kitty while they were at dinner away from home base. The couple was warned and escaped before the British arrived, but Greene was forced to deal with turncoats in his camp. The time dragged on, with no action but no peace. With summer came the usual diseases of the Carolina Low Country, making evacuation to the oceanfront island of Kiawah a sensible solution for the ailing soldiers. The nurse who accompanied them: Kitty Greene. By the officers' accounts, a good time was had by all as everyone recovered, with the general's wife serving in her accustomed role as the life of the party.

All this happened while Greene was negotiating with the British to evacuate Charleston. Finally, in December 1782, two and a half years after they had captured the beautiful colonial city of Charles Town, the occupiers left it in shambles. Still, the departure was cause for great celebration as the Americans, with several South Carolina statesmen in their parade, marched in to reclaim the city and rename it "Charleston," in order to sound less English. Kitty Greene, who "had the spirit of the military about her," was decked out in a uniform she had made for the occasion, "deep blue with yellow buttons and gold facings." The triumphal procession did not include, however, the tolling of church bells. The British had stolen them along with everything else they could carry. At first the people of Charleston welcomed the conquering heroes, especially General Greene and his lady, who insisted on hosting a great victory ball. Soon the soldiers were already doing what old soldiers do—telling war stories. Kitty Greene related some of these to friends at home, including the one about Nathanael and the governor of South Carolina, John Rutledge, finding shelter in some miserable spot in North Carolina after a defeat on the battlefield. "Sometime after the General and governor who both occupied one bed got into it the General complained that the governor was a very restless bedfellow. Yes General—says the governor—you have much reason to complain who have been kicking me around this hour. They both denied the charges which put them upon examining who was at fault. And behold the General of the southern department and the Governor of the rich state of South Carolina—and how shall I write it—**a hog**— (who thought perhaps he had a right to take a place with a defeated General) had all crept into one bed together."

After the initial excitement, the people of Charleston began to grow cool toward the army's continued presence in the city as it dragged on and as Greene tried to force the reconstituted state legislature to support the troops. Soon the American military was seen as yet another set of occupiers rather than liberators. But still, there was no word of a peace agreement, so there was no way to disband the army. Kitty, who missed her children and once again found herself pregnant, left her husband in the spring of 1783 to sail back to Philadelphia.

While Greene was struggling to keep the army together in the South, George Washington was having the same problem in the North. He had established camp at Newburgh, New York, where he and Martha spent the spring of 1782. Martha, still grieving over the loss of her son, went home for the summer to Mount Vernon, hoping George would soon be able to join her for good. On her way south from Newburgh she was treated again as "a very great somebody"—the Pennsylvania Assembly made a gift of William Penn's coach, and in Williamsburg she was honored with gold medals. But Martha's wish of moving home and staying there was not to be—she would first have to spend one more winter in camp. Other generals realized that they too might as well summon their wives. Horatio Gates told a friend, "Upon talking with the General, I have sent for Mrs. Gates to keep me from freezing this winter. . . . Mrs. Washington is, I understand, upon the road." Now the challenge was keeping busy. Martha did her best to prevent the enlisted men, who adored her, from deserting the inactive army. George had her at his side when he pardoned all American military prisoners in February 1783 in an attempt to placate the troops.

And she occupied herself with a garden and with sewing projects. In March, Martha sent two hair-nets to Henry Knox (to bind up the little ponytails the men wore!), apologizing that "they would have been sent long ago but for want of tape." The summer dragged on, and this time Lady Washington remained in camp with her husband while everyone waited to hear from the negotiators assembled in Paris that peace was finally at hand.

CHAPTER FIVE

1782–1787:
Peace and Diplomacy

SARAH LIVINGSTON JAY

Widows and Orphans to Diplomacy

On June 11, 1781, Congress appointed Benjamin Franklin, John Jay, Thomas Jefferson, and Henry Laurens as additional negotiators to John Adams in the quest for peace with Great Britain. Behind that simple sentence lies a story of months of intrigue and unhappiness—on both sides of the Atlantic. In the years leading up to treaty talks, the person who seems to have been the least perturbed by the infighting among Americans, and the most pleased by the indulgences of the French, was

Benjamin Franklin. "Doctor" Franklin's sojourn in America after his wife Deborah's death lasted less than two years before he was dispatched by his fellow congressmen to enlist the French in the American cause. He arrived in France at the end of 1776 with two grandsons in tow, leaving his daughter and sister, along with his longtime correspondent Catharine Ray Greene, to fend off the British in Philadelphia and Rhode Island and wait for his letters.

As a widower, Franklin was able to openly enjoy the company of Parisian ladies—and enjoy he did. He wrote to a female friend in Boston that France was a most agreeable country where people "endeavor to find out what you like, and they tell others. . . . Somebody, it seems, gave it out that I loved ladies; and then everybody presented me their ladies (or the ladies presented themselves) to be **embraced,** that is to have their necks kissed. For as to kissing of lips or cheeks, it is not the mode here, the first is reckoned rude, and the other may rub off the paint. The French ladies have however 1000 other ways of rendering themselves agreeable." He was clearly having a very good time. The folks at home were having a much tougher time of it. Soon after he left, his sister Jane Mecom wrote that the family in Philadelphia had escaped to Chester County, Pennsylvania, "on hearing the enemy were advancing towards us." She didn't complain much about their circumstances, but his daughter, Sally, did: "I never shall forget nor forgive them for turning me out of house and home in the middle of winter." But, she assured her father, "your library we sent out of town well packed in boxes, a week before us." Sally added, "I send you the newspapers; but as they do not always speak true," she enclosed some of her husband's letters with more accurate news. The family briefly returned to Philadelphia, only to flee again right after the birth of Sally's second daughter. This time Jane Mecom made her way to the Rhode Island home of her granddaughter, Jane Greene. Just to give you a sense of how convoluted these family relationships were—this Jane was married to Elihu Greene, who was Nathanael Greene's brother, so she and Catharine Littlefield Greene were sisters-in-law. And that Catharine Greene, Kitty, was the niece of Catharine Ray Greene, Caty, who was Jane Mecom and Benjamin Franklin's great friend. Got that? Caty Greene and Benjamin Franklin saw each other only five times in their lives, but they corresponded for forty-five years.

While the women in his family were seeking refuge from the British, Franklin was writing home about the good life in Paris. He told his sister in October 1777, "I live in a fine airy house upon a hill, which has a large garden with fine walks in it." A few months later, after hearing of his family's distress, he admitted to Caty Greene, "I pity my poor old sister, to be so harassed and driven about by the Enemy. . . . I live here in great respect, and dine every day with great folks; but I still long for home and for repose." Franklin not only lived in "great respect" but was a genuine celebrity. The

French idolized the famous inventor as the embodiment of the American cause. Everywhere he went he could see himself on medals, in paintings, in engravings, on snuffboxes. He was so omnipresent that, as he wrote his sister, "my face is now almost as well known as that of the moon." He sent French fabric home for Jane to sell to help support herself, but when his daughter requested a little finery to dress up in after the British withdrawal from Philadelphia, he blew up: "Your sending for long black pins, and lace, and **feathers!** disgusted me as much as if you had put salt into my strawberries. . . . If you wear your cambric ruffles as I do, and take care not to mend the holes, they will come in time to be lace; and feathers, my dear girl, may be had in America from every cock's tail." This to a woman who had been twice run out of her home by the British but had taken care of her father's prize books before she fled! Sally was clearly hurt by his outburst: "How could my dear papa give me so severe a reprimand for wishing a little finery. He would not, I am sure, if he knew how much I have felt it. . . . My spirits, which I have kept up during my being drove about from place to place, much better than most people's I meet with, have been lowered by nothing but the depreciation of the money, which has been amazing lately."

Franklin's letters home were few and far between, but occasionally a newsy missive would arrive in America. He told his sister that he had sent his grandson, Benjamin Franklin Bache, to school in Geneva, "where he will be educated a republican and a Protestant, which could not be so conveniently done at the schools in France." But Jane wanted to hear more about his work: "The few friends I have here flock about me when I receive a letter and are much disappointed that they contain no politics. I tell them you dare not trust a woman with politics, and perhaps that is the truth but if there is anything we could not possibly misconstrue or do mischief by knowing from you, it will gratify us mightily if you add a little to your future kind letters." Future letters were slow in coming, and Jane teased her seventy-three-year-old brother Benjamin: "I now and then hear of your health and glorious achievements in the political way, as well as in the favor of the ladies." Caty Greene kept scolding Franklin to write to his sister: "I grow very jealous of you. I fear the French ladies have taken you entirely from us for we don't have a single line from you this very long time." Franklin had held out the prospect that when he returned the brother and sister might retire together, but at age sixty-seven, Jane feared she might never see her brother again: "America knows your consequence too well to permit your return if they can possibly prevent it, and your care for the public good will not suffer you to desert them till peace is established." Peace seemed a long way off. In the fall of 1779 Franklin finally wrote sympathetically: "The enemy have been very near you indeed. When only at the distance of a mile you must have been much alarmed." He then recounted the exploits of John

Paul Jones taking on the British fleet: "Had not contrary winds and accidents prevented it, the intended invasion of England, with the combined fleet and a great army might have taken place, and have made the English feel a little more of that kind of distress they have so wantonly caused in America." As it was, Jones had headed to Holland with four hundred prisoners, the war was still on, and Franklin had a request—he wanted his sister to send him some of the Franklin family's famous crown soap.

While the women were suffering on the home front, Franklin was having problems of his own on the diplomatic front. He had served as one of three American commissioners most of his time in France. Silas Deane and Arthur Lee had worked with him, and it was the three of them, with Franklin as the lead negotiator, who achieved the all-important treaty of alliance with France. But they had a hard time allying with one another. Reports of constant rivalry and backbiting among them made their way to Congress, which heard from the partisans of one man and then another. Finally, Silas Deane was recalled and John Adams sent to replace him. Adams arrived in the spring of 1778, after the alliance had been forged, but with commercial treaties and loans still to be negotiated. This tripartite commission also proved to be essentially unworkable, something each of its members reported to Philadelphia, and on September 14, 1778, Franklin was named sole U.S. representative in Paris. Arthur Lee had already received an assignment in Spain; John Adams returned to America. But after a very few months Congress decided that peace with Britain might soon be at hand and redeployed Adams to Paris so he'd be in place to negotiate when the time came. He brought with him the bars of Jane Mecom's crown soap.

Jane was still at her granddaughter's in Rhode Island when she heard about the Ladies' Association of Philadelphia's fund-raising effort for the soldiers. She wrote to her niece, Sally, one of the major organizers, that "we would follow your example but I fear what my influence would procure would be so diminutive we should be ashamed to offer it. I live in an obscure place, have but little acquaintance and those not very rich." Poor Jane, it was a rough time. One after another, her children died off from various diseases. Her son-in-law, who was a seaman, was repeatedly captured by the British, and she had no home. She told Sally that normally her best bet for a female fund-raiser would be Caty Greene, since her husband was governor, but "they have suffered extremely in their fortune."

But fortunes were beginning to turn. The French fleet had arrived in Newport, and Caty Greene was thrilled that they would now be protected from the British. "Tongue cannot express the one half of the distresses they have made us feel. Murdering, butchering, starving, stealing—there is no evil can be named but they have practiced in America, this once peaceful happy land. But in our state we are happily delivered from them since the arrival of our new allies." That must have been particularly gratifying for Franklin, since he had forged the alliance. But then there was the bad news that "the wicked, wretched [Benedict] Arnold is in Virginia with 18 hundred men and has ravaged Richmond." Then, finally, Jane Mecom exulted: "The Glorious News we have received from the South makes us flatter ourselves you may return to us soon." Cornwallis had surrendered. But Franklin would stay on in Paris until the peace was signed. Jane was once again in a tenuous living situation. The granddaughter she lived with had died "of a consumption," leaving three tiny children behind with the tired old lady. "My Dear Child urged me earnestly not to leave them as long as I live," Jane wrote her brother, "and though I made her no promise I find the request to be very powerful." As the negotiations dragged on, Caty Greene grew impatient, asking repeatedly, "When is this cruel war to be at an end?" Rhode Island, Caty fretted in June 1782, was feeling the pressure of guarding its seacoast until the British were safely gone: "Our hope is now that the time is just at hand when we shall drive them root and branch from our land."

At least as impatient for final peace as Caty Greene was Abigail Adams, who had been a virtual widow in Braintree for all but a few months since John Adams and their son John Quincy had sailed for Paris in February 1778. Because the war had long since moved out of Massachusetts, Abigail was no longer in physical danger, but she was far from happy as she fretted about the safety of her husband

and son, struggled to stretch her dollars, and pestered the politicians for news. Her cousin, John Thaxter, who had served as her children's tutor and was working as a secretary to the Congress, turned out to be a good source of information, along with John Adams's former colleague James Lovell. The day after her husband left, Abigail wrote a long letter to Thaxter, telling him that she had wanted to "run all hazards" and accompany John, "but I could not prevail upon him to consent." Then she launched into one of her favorite arguments, the need for equal education for women: "It is really mortifying Sir, when a woman possessed of a common share of understanding considers the difference of education between the male and female sex." With pen still hot, she told him to ask Lovell to "permit you to communicate to me all the news and intelligence from your quarter of the world which may be communicated to a **woman**." And he did. Thaxter regularly provided her with reports of the political and military situation, and he engaged in her arguments, mainly by agreeing with her: if she thought "jealousy of rivalship is the foundation of neglect of your sex Madam, I am positive it is too often the case." Wise man.

When John Adams arrived in France in April 1778, he moved in with Benjamin Franklin and wrote home happy letters about how much he liked the country, including his famous admission, "I admire the ladies here." How dumb can you get? It took a couple of nerve-wracking months for that letter to reach Abigail. It was June before she knew whether her husband and ten-year-old son had safely landed in France. When she was assured of their arrival, her anxiety abated and she took on the French ladies: "I can hear of the brilliant accomplishment of any of my sex with pleasure. . . . At the same time I regret the trifling narrow contracted education of the females of my own country." It was a flash of her old feisty self, but Abigail was truly miserable. She had not realized how completely out of touch with her husband she would be, how many of their letters to each other would never reach their destination, how seldom she would hear about him or from him. And the few letters she did receive seemed cold and distant. Pronouncing herself "depressed," Abigail told John, "If I had realized before you left me that the intercourse between us would have been so hazardous, I feel my magnanimity would have failed me."

He could, or would, do nothing to cheer her up. Horrified that his letters might be intercepted and printed in newspapers, he wrote so perfunctorily that she exploded, "Could you after a thousand fears and anxieties, long expectation and painful suspenses be satisfied with my telling you that I was well, that I wished you were with me, that my daughter sent her duty, that I had ordered some articles for you which I hoped would arrive etc., etc. By Heaven if you could you have changed hearts with some frozen Laplander or made a voyage to a region that has chilled every drop of your blood."

She didn't buy the argument that he was worried about interception. What difference did it make? "The affection I feel . . . is the tenderest kind, matured by years . . . and approved by heaven. Angels can witness to its purity, what care I then for the ridicule of Britains should this testimony fall into their hands, nor can I endure that so much caution and circumspection on your part should deprive me of the only consoler of your absence." He wouldn't give an inch: "If you write me in this style I will leave off writing entirely, it kills me. . . . Am I not wretched enough in this banishment without this. . . . I beg you would never more write to me in such a strain for it really makes me unhappy." Maybe he was thinking twice about mentioning the French ladies. But Adams had been burned once by the British intercepting his letters from Philadelphia, and he wasn't going to let it happen again: "I never know what security I have against appearing in the newspapers and I assure you I don't wish to see any more of my love letters there."

While this personal drama played out, Adams was dealing with professional distress as well. The triumvirate of Benjamin Franklin, Arthur Lee, and John Adams was breaking up with the naming of Franklin as the sole minister to France, and Adams didn't know what the Congress wanted him to do. Abigail did her best to find out. She asked James Lovell, "Where is my Friend to be placed? I would fain hope not at a greater distance than he is at present." She knew John would stay in public service, wherever it took him, "whilst I must endeavor to act the part allotted to my sex—patience and submission." Patience and submission weren't her strong suits; she wanted to be more involved in the decision making. She asked Lovell, "Am I entitled to the journals of Congress, if you think so, I should be much obliged to you if you would convey them to me." Then she embarked on a discourse about what to do about the currency. Lovell answered that no decision had yet been made about Adams. That winter their daughter Abigail—Nabby, as the family knew her—was spending some time with Mercy Otis Warren, helping out in her household. Thirteen-year-old Nabby's mother wrote her daughter a long chatty letter—the subject? Politics. She reported that John informed her peace was not likely to come anytime soon, even though all of Europe now saw Great Britain as an oppressor nation. The American diplomats were doing what they could do to win allies and isolate the British, but this was two and a half years before Yorktown—peace was not even slightly at hand. And John was getting more and more frustrated by the unsettled nature of his situation. He first picked up rumors that he was headed for Holland, then learned he had no assignment; in February 1779 he claimed he was coming home. He was in a lighthearted mood, teasing Abigail, "I must not write a word to you about politics, because you are a woman. What offense have I committed?—a woman! I shall soon make it up. I think women better than men in general, and I know you can keep a secret as well as any man whatever. But the world doesn't know this. Therefore if I were to write any secrets to you and the letter should be caught, and hitched into a newspaper, the world would say, I was not to be trusted with a secret." But light-heartedness was soon supplanted by suspicions: "There are spies upon every word I utter, and every syllable I write—spies planted by the English— spies planted by stockjobbers—spies planted by selfish merchants—and spies planted by envious and malicious politicians." He didn't trust the people around him, he didn't know how Congress viewed him and what it meant to do with him, and he was taking out his frustrations on her: "You want me to unravel to you all the mysteries of the politics of Europe, and all the intrigues of the Courts. This would make Madam a Lady of Consequence no doubt and enable her to shine in a Circle of Politicians of either sex." Finally, in a huff, John Adams decided to sail home, without waiting for word from Congress.

But Abigail didn't know that. She must have been miffed to receive a letter from her friend Mercy Otis Warren announcing there was "no expectation in Congress that your Mr. Adams will return yet. There is a large majority in that body who highly esteem him and wish his continuance in Europe." It couldn't have been pleasing to Abigail that Mercy claimed to be in the know and she wasn't. She tried to remedy that by asking James Lovell exactly what was being said about her husband, "whether the conduct of Mr. A. has been impeached either directly or indirectly? . . . Was he ever requested to tarry in France or any notice of any kind taken of him after his commission was vacated?" Lovell replied that Arthur Lee had written that Adams was leaving France; the congressman then told his friend's wife, "The sacrifices you have made to the public good and the manner in which you have made them have given you a despotic command over my affections." Then he signed off, "Very platonically to be sure, but very, very affectionately." Lovell's the one who should have been worried about intercepted letters. Then suddenly, with no advance warning, on August 3, 1779, John and John Quincy Adams showed up at home in Braintree. Abigail must have thought she was seeing ghosts.

John's political ambitions were briefly redirected to the state level. Massachusetts was holding a constitutional convention in Cambridge, and he was appointed to write a draft of the new charter, which would turn out to be a rough blueprint for the federal Constitution eight years later. Abigail was once again happily involved in her husband's work. But it was a soon interrupted idyll as October brought the news that Congress had named John negotiator of peace with Great Britain. He was to leave as soon as possible for Paris so he would be available when the time for talks came.

John Adams's work on the Massachusetts constitution eventually had a momentous impact, thanks to the courage of a woman. The charter that was adopted in 1780 stated that "all men are born free and equal." A slave woman named Elizabeth Free-man, called "Mumbet," took the words to heart. She worked for the Ashley family in Sheffield, Massachusetts, and often served the men who were instrumental in the passage of the constitution, so she heard them discussing its contents, including the declaration of freedom. It was probably some-thing she had thought a good bit about, since her husband had been killed fighting with the Conti-nental army, in the cause of liberty. Elizabeth Free-man's sister was also owned by the Ashley family, and one day when the mistress of the house went after the servant with a heated fireplace shovel, Mumbet intervened to deflect the blow and de-cided then and there she'd had enough. She went to one of the men she had served, lawyer Theodore Sedgewick, and asked him to take her case suing for freedom under the Massachusetts constitution. He agreed to the highly unusual request, and in August 1781 the municipal court in Great Barring-ton decided in Elizabeth's favor, liberating her and another slave owned by the Ashley family. It was a precedent that soon led to the abolition of slavery in the state of Massachusetts. The court awarded Elizabeth Freeman damages of "thirty shillings lawful silver money" and charged John Ashley legal costs of "five pounds fourteen shillings and four pence." As a free woman, Mumbet worked for the Sedgewick family and did business in the town as a nurse and midwife. She's buried in Stockbridge, Massachusetts, where her tombstone reads: "She was born a slave and remained a slave for nearly thirty years. She could neither read nor write yet in her own sphere she had no superior or equal. She neither wasted time nor property. She never violated a trust nor failed to perform a duty. In every situation of domestic trial, she was the most efficient helper, and the tenderest friend. Good mother, farewell."

By the time Elizabeth Freeman brought suit under the constitution he helped draft, John Adams had been back in Europe for almost two years. When he sailed on November 15, 1779, this time taking both John Quincy and Charles with him, he could not have guessed that it would be close to nine years before he'd be home again. After a hair-raising detour to Spain in a leaky ship and an arduous trip by land to France, John and the boys arrived in Paris and Abigail took up again her lonely life in Braintree. Her main complaint, other than missing her husband and sons, was the high cost of everything. She had worked all these years to keep the family from going into debt, overseeing the farm, collecting law fees owed Adams, living as frugally as possible, but it was getting harder to make ends meet, particularly with taxes continually rising. John started sending her European goods—lace, ribbons, fans, handkerchiefs, tumblers—to sell either directly from her little house or to local merchants, and she became quite proficient at predicting what would fetch a price and what wouldn't. The market was "glutted" with Barcelona handkerchiefs; Irish linen sold better than Dutch. (But Mercy Warren told her that she was charging too much for some handkerchiefs.) Eventually John suggested that Abigail cut him out as the middleman and deal directly with the European suppliers herself. She was able to do well enough to buy some property. Of course, she had to do it in John's name. Abigail picked up some parcels of land in Vermont; John had no interest in such a rustic scene.

Abigail also kept John informed about news of the war and politics, especially politics in Massachusetts, where the new constitution called for the election of a governor. She told her husband that the right man (James Bowdoin) would lose to "the tinkling cymbal" (John Hancock). "What a politician you have made me! If I cannot be a voter on this occasion, I will be a writer of votes." She kept up her correspondence about Congress with James Lovell; John Thaxter had gone with Adams to Europe, so that correspondence became less frequent. (Abigail teased Thaxter about the broken hearts he left behind. When the Philadelphia Ladies' Association was formed, she exuberantly described it to Thaxter: "Public spirit lives—lives in the bosoms of the fair daughters of America, who . . . unite their efforts to reward the patriotic, to stimulate the brave, to alleviate the burden of war, and to show that they are not dismayed by defeats or misfortunes. Read the Pennsylvania papers, and see the spirit catching from state to state.") To Mercy Warren, Abigail expressed her fears for John: "I view him beset with the machinations of envy, the snares of treachery, the malice of dissimulation and the clandestine stabs of calumny."

It turned out Abigail's suspicions were well founded. Benjamin Franklin was undermining Adams, arguing to his own allies in Congress that the man from Massachusetts was alienating the French court. Franklin had been in Paris a long time and understood the French ways—he saw Adams as a rambunctious American bull in the French china shop. The affable Dr. Franklin figured he had yet one more difficult colleague on his hands, after suffering through endless battles among America's envoys, added to by the "ambassadors" to other countries who weren't received in the capitals of Europe and hung out in Paris offering their two cents' worth. Adams, in turn, thought Franklin too ready to do the bidding of the all-important ally. In part to try to diffuse France's power, Adams traveled to Holland in July 1780, taking his sons, to see if he could entice the Dutch into recognizing American independence and providing a loan. The next year a letter from Arthur Lee's sister (who resented Franklin's handling of her brother) intended for Betsy Adams, Samuel's wife, reached Abigail by mistake. From it she learned of Franklin's perfidy where Adams was concerned. Lee's sister, Alice Shippen, accused Franklin of "blackening the character of Mr. J.A. to Congress more than he did Mr. L———'s, and he has got the French minister to join him." Abigail immediately fired off a volley to Lovell: "It needs great courage Sir to engage in the cause of America, we have not only open but secret foes to contend with. . . . It wounds me Sir—when he is wounded I bleed." She railed to Elbridge Gerry, "The independent spirit of your friend abroad does not coincide with the selfish views and inordinate ambition of your minister [Franklin], who in consequence of it, is determined upon his destruction." And then she pleaded, "Will you suffer female influence so far to operate upon you as to step forth and lend your aid to rescue your country and your friend." Lovell tried to assuage Abigail by telling her that the disagreement with Adams was a policy dispute, not a personal one: "There is no idea here as any criminality in Mr. A——. He is much esteemed. But such is the uncouth way of proceeding here at times that unintended chagrin must arise." But Abigail wasn't buying it. She seethed to John when she wrote him about what was happening: "I will not comment upon this low, this dirty, this infamous diabolical piece of envy and malice as I have already done it where I thought I might be of service—to your friends Lovell and Gerry." So much for the notion that wives "meddling" in politics is a modern-day phenomenon.

Abigail was distressed by the news she was getting **about** John as well as by the fact that she got no news **from** him. It was almost a year between letters, so she didn't know that fourteen-year-old John Quincy had gone to Russia as secretary to the newly appointed ambassador, Francis Dana. And she didn't know that eleven-year-old Charles, who was desperately homesick, was coming back to her.

Her friends in Congress confirmed Abigail's fears that John had been sabotaged by Franklin. Instead of serving as the sole negotiator with Great Britain, Adams would be part of the five-member team along with Benjamin Franklin, John Jay, Henry Laurens, and Thomas Jefferson. When, after almost a year, Abigail finally heard from John in the fall of 1781, he warned her that peace would not come anytime soon.

As it turned out, Thomas Jefferson declined the appointment to the peace commission because his wife was too sick for him to leave home. And Henry Laurens barely made it to Paris for the negotiations. Laurens was a wealthy South Carolinian who had made his money mainly in the slave trade, though he was always guilt-ridden about it and eventually turned against slavery. Married in 1750, his wife bore thirteen children before her death at age thirty-nine from complications of the last birth. Henry, distraught with grief, was left to raise the five surviving children, writing to a friend, "I am Father, Mother, Nurse, Tutor and Companion." Deciding that the schools in Charleston weren't good enough for his three boys, in 1771 Henry convinced his brother and sister-in-law to move into his mansion to look after the girls while he took his sons to London for schooling. Martha was a precocious eleven-year-old who had learned to read when she was three, and her sister Polly was still an infant. At the end of 1773, when Martha was fourteen years old, she signed a "covenant with

God," which she wrote in a journal. (Over the rest of her life she jotted reflections on religion into the journal, and her husband's publication of it after her death made her posthumously quite famous as an author.) A couple of years later her uncle decided he needed to take a sea voyage for his health, so he and his wife took sixteen-year-old Martha and five-year-old Polly to London, where the girls saw their brother John for the first time in four years. To determine whether she was the same "Spartan girl he had left her," John arranged for the driver of their carriage to race at terrifying speed through the countryside, testing whether she was free from "womanish fears." Martha passed this strange examination of stoicism, but her family was always torn about just how much she should venture out of a woman's place. When she asked for some globes of the world, her father sent them with instructions: "When you are measuring the surface of this world, remember you are to act a part on it, and think of a plumb pudding and other domestic duties."

It was the crucial year 1776. Henry Laurens was back in South Carolina fomenting rebellion, putting his children in England in a difficult position. John was chafing to go home and join the army, which he soon did as an aide to George Washington. Martha's job, Henry told her, "will be to join with the sons and daughters of piety and pray incessantly for peace." But he warned her not to "give offense to any body by interposing your opinions concerning these matters." Henry might not want his daughter talking about politics, but she was hearing plenty about it, especially after he was elected president of the Continental Congress in 1777. Her aunt and uncle decided to take the girls to France, where they would not be subject to English attacks on their father as a "fomenter of disputes between Britain and her colonies." After the family established itself in Vigan, in the south of France, Martha opened a school for the local children and used a gift from her father to buy Bibles for her students. Her enterprising abilities soon would be called on in behalf of her father.

Henry Laurens had sailed for Holland in 1780, having been named by Congress the minister to that country. On his way to assume his post, his ship was hijacked by the British, and he was locked up in the Tower of London. John Adams's fears about an American Founder being taken on the high seas turned out to be justified. It was left to twenty-year-old Martha Laurens to petition the Americans in Paris, Benjamin Franklin and John Adams, to work toward her father's release. She argued that it was an insult to the country of the United States for the British to hold someone of as high a rank as her father. Word reached the family that Henry was receiving egregious treatment, and Martha wanted to travel to England to work for his release. Her brother John told her to "reconsider the matter" because traveling to the enemy country could have "a very ill effect both in France and

America, from a public point of view, and I do not conceive any good that can arise from it to our dear and respectable father." In her correspondence with Adams and Franklin, Martha learned the awful news that the British, continuing to hold Laurens, expected to "hang him at the peace, if the war should end in their favor." It was while Henry was in the Tower that he was appointed as a peace commissioner, and finally, at the beginning of January 1782, the pressure from the Americans, stimulated by Martha, resulted in his release. Annis Boudinot Stockton, who had become something of a chronicler of the Revolution, wrote a poem in celebration.

After a bout with the gout, Laurens made his way to Paris, where he wanted Martha to join him. She resisted, saying that she had to stay in Vigan to take care of her sick uncle and help her aunt manage in a foreign country. Her father insisted, telling her, "You are already grown old by nursing and I wished to relieve you." She was twenty-two. And she had another reason for wanting to stay in Vigan—a man. Without first consulting her father, who was somewhat indisposed in the Tower, a merchant in town had committed the unforgivable sin of discussing marriage with Martha. Henry was livid when she told him, and he suspected his brother and sister-in-law were in cahoots with his daughter, with the motive of keeping her "in servitude." Henry dispatched his son Harry to fetch his sister, with many dramatic predictions about how she would fare if she disobeyed her father. And, he warned, if she didn't accompany her brother to Paris, Henry would have to go to Vigan himself, "at the hazard of my life and the risk of my reputation at home." Henry wrote a similarly overwrought letter to Martha, conjuring up tragic consequences if she married the Frenchman Caladon deVerne. Fearing that she would spend the rest of her life in Europe, the outraged father scathingly rejected deVerne's request for his daughter's hand. Then true tragedy struck. John Laurens was killed in battle. Henry begged his brother to save him from "the living death of another child." While the family was at war, Laurens was negotiating peace. In November 1782 he and Franklin, Adams, and Jay signed a preliminary peace agreement in Paris, and then Henry left for England. Martha made her choice. She decided she could not let her father suffer over her brother's death alone, so she left her French love to play the dutiful daughter. When she reached Paris and found her father had gone to England, she followed him there. He had planned to send Harry to accompany her across the Channel, but Martha's father later bragged to a friend, "She had, with her maid, traveled upwards of 900 miles, like a true American woman." Martha served as her father's hostess both in Europe and after he went home to South Carolina until 1787, when she married the widower David Ramsay, a historian friendly with many of the Founders.

Wives and Daughters to Diplomacy

John Jay, the fifth member of the peace commission meeting in Paris, was the only one who brought his wife with him. Sarah, called Sally, Livingston Jay was a daughter of the governor of New Jersey, William Livingston. It was his home, Liberty Hall, and his papers that had been protected from a British raid, by his daughter Susan. Susan was the oldest of five spirited Livingston daughters; Sally was the fourth. Spending the winter of 1772–73 visiting some of her many Livingston relatives in New York, the sixteen-year-old Sally took the city by storm. A family friend, Gouverneur Morris, wrote to her older sister Kitty, "I would make you laugh," as he described the young men surrounding Sally: "One being forwards rolling up his eyes and sighing most piteously. Another at a distance setting side long upon his chair. . . . A third his shoulders drawn up to his ears . . . and the corners of his mouth making over his chin a most rueful arch. In the midst of all this sits Miss with seeming unconsciousness of the whole. One would be led to imagine she is unconcerned. I shall dispose of her before the winter is out I believe provided Mamma has no objections." Morris wasn't far off. Sally accepted the proposal of the already prominent young lawyer John Jay in January 1774. That April, about the same time New York was becoming active in the resistance against British law, the couple was married at Liberty Hall. She was eighteen, and he was thirty.

Soon John Jay was serving in the Continental Congress along with his father-in-law, William Livingston, and writing letters to Sally in New Jersey complaining about life in Philadelphia, letters that took weeks to arrive. At Christmastime, 1775, he reported that the New York Convention had decided to pay its delegates to Congress four dollars a day: "The allowance indeed does by no means equal the loss I have sustained by the appointment." (Members of Congress regularly voice the same complaint today.) Jay needed to have some money coming in, since Sally would produce a baby boy in January 1776. As the war moved into New York and New Jersey from Massachusetts, Sally, as well as her parents and John's, often moved from place to place for safety's sake, bunking with friends and relatives or occupying deserted loyalist homes, sometimes escaping the British by a matter of minutes. But the young mother didn't seem to let anything get her down; instead, she was always ready to make light of the most dire situations. From Fish Kill, New York, she reported, "This very instant the Doctor came into the room, his look bespeaking the utmost discomposure. Bad news Mrs. Jay, aye Doctor what now? The regulars Madam are landed at Peekskill. . . . Wherever I am, I think there are alarms. However I am determined to remember your maxim, prepare for the worst and hope the best." From Troy, New York, she put a sunny face on her situation, "although retired is by no means unpleasant," because "when alone of an afternoon a play of Shakespeare furnishes an elegant amusement." Sally had made something of a name for herself playing Kate in **The Taming of the Shrew** back home in New Jersey before she was married.

Though she was upbeat about her situation, she saw the irony in the fact that the patriot families' whereabouts were determined by the British army. "Is it not a mortification to us who disclaim the tyranny of the King of England, that even the most interesting actions of our lives are controlled by his minions." By the winter of 1778 Sally had joined John near Poughkeepsie, New York, where he was working on the state charter. Two-year-old Peter stayed home with the Livingstons, and John wrote a joking letter to his sister-in-law Susan: "His mother expects that by the time she sees him his education will be considerably advanced, and that he will by that time have been taught to d——n the King." Then he added, "Sally says that if I write such things she wishes I would conclude my letter." The postscript was written by Sally: "What a critical situation, my dear Susan, is that of your sister at present, to contradict the assertions of my Lord and Master may for ought I know be esteemed Petty Treason in the eye of every man who has the **honor** of being a husband." Guess that put John in his place.

By the end of that year, on December 28, 1778, John's place had become quite exalted—he was named president of the Continental Congress, the highest position in the land. Sally was none too pleased to learn of his new job by reading about it in a newspaper: "Permit me to remind you that there is a Post that takes letters from Morristown for Philadelphia and returns every week." Had she known in advance, she added, "I should not have been **Roman matron** enough to have given you so entirely to the public." She was good-natured about it, but Sally wasn't keen on her "state of widowhood." Her still single sister Kitty was feeling even more isolated: "Poor Kit is very anxious to know her fate, as she calls it, whether she shall spend the months of March and April agreeably in Philadelphia or waste them in obscurity and dullness." There was something to look forward to, however: the sisters were invited to the ball Lucy and Henry Knox held to celebrate the anniversary of the French alliance. George Washington's camp at Morristown did provide some amusement. In March, Sally was irritated that she hadn't heard from John for a while until she learned that "I had been deprived of that pleasure by a British Officer, who Susan writes me to her . . . great regret had taken two letters of yours from the mantelpiece." It's the only mention of Susan's heroic defense of Liberty Hall.

Soon Sally Jay would be saying good-bye to Liberty Hall for many years. Congress named John Jay minister to Spain, with the mission of persuading that country to join the Franco-American alliance, to grant unconditional navigation rights to the Mississippi River, and to lend the cash-strapped United States $5 million at 6 percent interest or less. In return, Florida would be Spain's if the Americans succeeded in recapturing it from the British. Essentially, it was a mission impossible. Spain had entered the war against Great Britain in March as part of a secret agreement with France, but the Spanish court had not recognized American independence. (The French had promised there would be no peace treaty with the British until Gibraltar was in Spanish hands.) Twenty-three-year-old Sally Jay, alone among the American wives during the war, decided to make the treacherous trip with her husband. Three-year-old Peter would stay in America, dividing his time between grandparents. It was clearly a sacrifice, but one Sally was ready to make for both her husband's sake and her own. Her brother William congratulated his sister for her decision: "To gratify a laudable curiosity and to travel in the pursuit of knowledge under the advantages that will attend you . . . are motives that appeal to your friends and yourself with equal force." If Sally was looking for a learning opportunity, she was definitely about to have one.

In October 1779, after John had resigned his post as president of Congress, the couple set sail with Sally's brother Brockholst, an aide named William Carmichael, and John's young nephew Peter Munro. As a good-luck talisman, Sally had asked for a lock of George Washington's hair, which the general sent with the wish "that prosperous gales, unruffled sea, and everything pleasing and desirable may smooth the path she is about to walk in." It was a wish that would not come true. Two months later, still aboard the ship and nowhere near Spain, Sally recounted their adventures to her mother. After being at sea a couple of weeks, she heard a terrible noise on the deck in the middle of the night: "We had been deprived of nothing less than our bow-spirit, main-mast and missen-mast . . . however our misfortunes were only begun, the injury received by our rudder the next morning served to complete them." The ship was dismasted and rudderless, the seas were high, and winter was on the way. A council of ship's officers concluded that there was no way to reach Europe under those conditions, so they set course for the island of Martinique. It took a couple of weeks for the winds to get them going in the right direction, but, Sally cheerfully reported, "we are now in smooth seas having the advantage of trade winds which blow directly for the island . . . while our American friends are amusing themselves by a cheerful fireside, are we sitting under an awning comforting ourselves with the expectation of being soon refreshed by some fine southern fruits." She was looking forward to the "crabs, fresh fish and oysters." Sally luckily was possessed of remarkable equanimity. What she didn't tell her mother was that she was pregnant. Stranded at sea, Sally and John threw a party, surprising and delighting fellow passengers. Finally, at the end of December, the ship limped into port in Martinique, where Sally was able to send off her letter home. A few days later the Jays found another vessel to take them to Cadiz, Spain. If she hated the thought of getting on another ship, Sally certainly didn't reveal it in a letter to her father-in-law: "Our voyage from America to Martinique was rather an unpleasant one, rendered so by several accidents and the degree of uncertainty naturally attending them." How's that for understatement? But, she continued, "the variety, verdure and fertility of the island afforded me not less pleasure than the hospitality, good breeding and cleanliness of the inhabitants." Sally could always find the silver lining, even when they arrived in early 1780 at Cadiz, where her brother wrote home about the fleas and other vermin.

They were lucky to have reached Spain at all. In a letter to her sisters Kitty and Susan, Sally wrote: "Two or three days before we made the Bay of Cadiz, we were chased by an English frigate and while a number of sailors were preparing the cabin for the expected engagement, I went on deck and stayed there until the chase was over." She was happily situated, she said, and the view from her window reminded her of home. "Do you think, girls, that distance diminishes my affection for Americans, or my concern for their interests? Oh! no; it increases my attachment even to enthusiasm. Where is the country (Switzerland excepted) where justice is so impartially administered, industry encouraged, health and smiling plenty so bounteous to all as in our much favored country? Are not those blessings . . . worth contending for? But whither, my pen, are you hurrying me? What have I to do with politics? Am I not myself a woman and writing to ladies? Come then, ye fashions to my assistance!"

Right. Jay had sent his aide, Carmichael, ahead to Madrid to try to detect how the Americans would be received. The answer: they could come as private citizens to talk to representatives of King Charles III; the issue of recognizing independence had still to be determined, so John Jay would not be officially received. It was enough to allow the Jays and their party to proceed to Madrid, which was a horrendous excursion later described by Sally to her sister Susan. The traveling party had been advised to bring with them everything needed for the journey, including beds and bedding, but the first night out, "we found that a broom was absolutely essential." After carting out loads of dirt and lice, the group settled down to sleep. Sally soon learned that "the adjoining apartment to ours was allotted to our mules," which wouldn't have been so bad if the animals weren't wearing bells, "but unluckily for us they slept not much and we had the mortification of being serenaded with the tinkling." Remember, Sally was pregnant. They journeyed on, not stopping long enough for Sally's taste in the charming city of Cordova, where she would have liked to linger for a while before getting back on the road, where "we very frequently passed little wooden crosses on the highway which had been placed there to denote the burying places of those who had been found murdered there." Finally, six scary months after leaving home, the Jays arrived at their destination of Madrid.

The king liked to move his court from place to place, so John was on the road a lot, and in financial straits, leaving Sally unofficially recognized and friendless in Madrid. Still, the Spanish took notice of her. One wrote about John Jay: "This woman, whom he loves blindly, dominates him and nothing is done without her consent, so that her opinion prevails." Clearly the tall, blue-eyed, brunette charmer had made her mark, which she seemed to do wherever she went as "a woman of considerable natural ability, of great charm of manner, as well as of distinguished beauty," according to a nineteenth-century social historian. Mrs. Jay's letters make clear she was also a woman of wit. After Sally left for Spain, Mercy Otis Warren received a letter about her from a Livingston cousin, describing her attributes and saying she "has a great fund of knowledge, and makes use of most charming language; added to this she is very handsome, which will secure her a welcome with the unthinking, whilst her understanding will gain her the hearts of the most worthy. Her manners will do honor to our countrywomen; and I really believe please even at the splendid court of Madrid." No need to fear, in other words, that Sally would come across in the castles of Europe as some country bumpkin American. Her letters showed more interest in the situation in America than in her own circumstances. Having read in a newspaper that it was a particularly harsh winter in New Jersey, she wrote home: "How I pity our soldiers for the sufferings they so much have sustained, and yet that pity is mingled with admiration. . . . May peace and tranquility soon succeed those scenes of war and toil that at present occupy my countrymen and may they long enjoy the liberty for which they have so nobly struggled." Sally delighted in news from home, even the news that the British sympathizers had once again invaded Liberty Hall. This time drunken Hessian soldiers were headed to the second floor, ready to rape and pillage, when a bolt of lightning illuminated the intrepid Susan, who had posted herself at the top of the stairs. When the soldiers saw this apparition, dressed in a white nightgown, they took off out of the house, thinking they had seen a ghost. Susan Livingston had foiled the enemy again. What Sally most wanted was news of her little boy Peter, who had turned four. She asked her mother, "Is he amiable? Is he healthy?" She missed him terribly, she said in every letter, but knew he was in good hands. And Sally's second baby was due soon.

On July 9, 1780, Susan Jay was born. She died three weeks later. "When I used to look at her every idea less pleasant vanished in a moment," Sally mourned to her mother, "and while I clasped her to my bosom my happiness appeared complete. . . . Excuse my tears—you too Mamma have wept on similar occasions." In her grief, Sally also revealed how hard life was for her in Madrid, "excluded from the society of our most intimate friends, behold us in a country whose customs, language and religion are the very reverse of our own, without connections, without friends." John was away again, and she was missing everyone at home, especially her little boy. "Oh! Mamma, I never fully comprehended the affection of parents for their children 'till I became a mother."

Nothing was going right for the U.S. mission to Spain. The Congress had already borrowed against the loans they expected John Jay to produce, so he was in the position of beggar before the Spanish court, and the king still refused to receive him. The American team itself was at each other's throats— Sally's brother, Brockholst Livingston, had aligned himself with William Carmichael in nonstop attempts to undermine Jay. And the news from America in the awful year of 1780 was all bad, with the fall of Charleston, the betrayal of Arnold, and the collapse of the currency. The one bright spot: the Philadelphia Ladies' Association, which delighted Sally. Her mother, as first lady of New Jersey, had been active in the fund-raising, and sister Kitty sent Sally a copy of "The Sentiments of an American Woman." Sally gleefully forwarded it to John, with the message "I am prouder than ever of my charming countrywomen." Sally was, as always, looking at the positive side. But in Spain it was hard to find. The Americans were useful to the Spanish only as pawns on the European chessboard. Contemplating peace with England, Spain tried to keep the British guessing by giving the Americans a small loan. The entire experience was humiliating for John Jay.

Sally's sisters kept her spirits up even from afar, though often she'd receive a letter referring to another letter she'd never seen—many never made it to Spain. Despite her determination to stay cheerful, it must have been an awfully tough time for the seldom complaining Sally. She was lonely. Her brother had turned against her husband. Her little boy went back and forth between her family and John's, both of which were often in danger. In May 1781 Susannah Livingston described the situation: "Our house was between two fires, for the enemy's point was a little below us. . . . Mamma had a forced march 5 miles across the country. . . . Your little **hero** was here when they first pushed into the country, and was much amused at the sight of such an army. . . . I hope we shall not be favored with another such visit this summer." But there was good news as well: their youngest sister, Judith, had married the year before, and oldest sister Susan told Sally that their friend Aaron Burr was set to bring more news from their little sister: "I expect to hear from Judy every moment by Colonel Burr, who I suppose will announce a little stranger in the family." But, Susan also reported, sister Mary's husband was sick and might not recover. Susan was clearly the mainstay of the family. She didn't marry until she was in her forties and took care of everything and everybody until then. Among her assignments: tutor of Sally's little boy Peter. When he was five years old, Sally received a letter from her son: "Aunt Susan teaches me to read; every hour the bell rings, and then I go in and say my lesson. Aunt Kitty sends me books from Philadelphia."

To escape the dangers of New Jersey, Kitty had moved in with friends of the Livingstons, Mary and Robert Morris, in Philadelphia, where she was wooed by just about every eligible bachelor. Kitty eventually married Matthew Ridley, whom she met while staying at the Morrises. (Robert Morris was the moneyman in the Revolution, using his own wealth and his contacts as a trader to supply the army and pay off some loans. Sally and Mary, called Molly, kept up a chatty correspondence while the Jays were abroad.) With a family as close as the Livingstons, it must have been doubly hard for Sally to write her father about brother Brockholst's disloyalty to John Jay. It was a long letter, citing chapter and verse of the brother's sins, including his public dismissal of the Congress that had appointed Jay as a bunch of drunkards worse than any monarchy. Brockholst was young and opinionated and apparently didn't like to be bossed by his brother-in-law. (Later he went into New York politics, where he issued unsigned diatribes against the distinguished John Jay; still later Thomas Jefferson appointed him to the Supreme Court.) Sally's brother had decided to go home, and she was afraid he would slander her husband. The letter went to her sister Kitty, to be shown to their father only if Brockholst started spreading lies. Thankfully for the family, Brockholst behaved once he arrived in America.

When the tide of war turned, in 1781, William Livingston wrote a detailed description of current events to his daughter abroad. Robert Morris was making progress in improving the country's finances, and the military was finally making progress as well: "Our success in the southern states has been astonishing. . . . General Washington with the Troops of our Allies is besieging New York, and we hourly expect a French fleet to co-operate with him. . . . If we succeed in this enterprise, I think the British must abandon America, and Lord North, may if he pleases, go and hang himself. If the nation had any virtue remaining, they would spare him that trouble." Clearly, Sally had been raised with the expectation that women would care about politics. (Her father later included the sad news that her younger brother John's ship had been lost at sea, and the happy news that her little boy had been "delighted with the water" when he crossed the Raritan Bridge.) The belief that the end was near in terms of the war concentrated the minds of the American Congress on the peace. The fight between Benjamin Franklin and John Adams over France's role was now something for America to confront. John Jay, who had been dealing with a cantankerous European monarchy, seemed an ideal addition to the commission assigned to negotiate with Great Britain. Jay was nowhere near achieving his mission in Spain, and after Cornwallis surrendered at Yorktown in October 1781, a friend of Jay's suggested he move on to Paris, where he might be able to do some good.

First, there was a baby to be born. Maria Jay arrived healthily in Madrid on February 20, 1782. Her father's rejoicing must have been short-lived. The next month the United States defaulted on its loan from Spain. Soon after that demoralizing event, however, the French miraculously provided a loan to cover the debt. Benjamin Franklin had helped convince Versailles to come through with the cash; now he wanted Jay to join him in Paris. John Adams was in Holland, Henry Laurens locked in the Tower of London, Thomas Jefferson home with a sick wife, and Franklin could use a hand in peace negotiations that were about to become more urgent. On June 17, 1782, the British Parliament passed the Enabling Act, allowing its envoys to discuss the terms of peace. A few days later the Jay family arrived in Paris. Meanwhile, two years of effort by John Adams in Holland were finally bearing fruit—he had succeeded in convincing the Dutch to recognize America as a nation, with Adams as its minister plenipotentiary. He bought what amounted to the first U.S. embassy at The Hague, and he extracted a sizable loan from the Dutch bankers. It was a great triumph for Adams after his humiliation the year before when Congress had removed him as the sole negotiator of peace and instructed its team of negotiators to follow the wishes of the French court in settling with Britain. Fearful of alienating its one true foreign friend, Congress had acceded to Franklin's insistence on appeasing Versailles at all costs. With Jay on the scene, Adams had an ally in his desire to resist French attempts to diminish the United States in both size and importance. Jay's hard line at the negotiating table might not have made him the most popular diplomat in Paris, but his wife, Sally, was charming everyone she met.

Benjamin Franklin loved Sally, Lafayette and his wife loved Sally, the growing American expatriate community loved Sally. And Sally loved Paris. "I am very much pleased with France," she pronounced to her mother in August 1782, except, "I sincerely wish my dear boy was with me, but have not resolution to send for him." Peter was six, and Sally asked her mother to look into the grammar school run by the College of New Jersey (Princeton). Even though peace negotiations were under way, Sally was still concerned about the safety of her family back at Liberty Hall: "I should have possessed more tranquility of mind had all the family abandoned that seat for the present. But Mamma's ideas and mine differed on the subject and I wish the event may prove that I was too timid." (After all the raids against Liberty Hall, it still stands as a museum today.) While she worried about the family back home, Sally thoroughly enjoyed life where she was. She told a friend back in Philadelphia that Queen Marie Antoinette was "so handsome and her manners are so engaging, that almost forgetful of republican principles, I was ever ready while in her presence to declare her born to be a queen." (It was long enough before the French Revolution that the queen's reputation had not yet been ruined by the "Let them eat cake" line.) Sally didn't add that she herself had been mistaken for the queen one night when she entered a box at the opera with Benjamin Franklin. Though she often wrote about the "pleasures Paris affords," Sally was eager to see her family again, and by the end of 1782, after the American and British negotiators signed the Preliminary Articles of Peace, she believed she would be going home soon. "Let us my dear Kitty rejoice together and bless God!" she wrote to her sister, "for the prospect of approaching peace. I already begin to enjoy in imagination some delightful scenes." Kitty's hostess, Mary Morris, described to Sally the effect of the tentative agreement: "I congratulate you on peace being restored to our country; it was hardly announced to us before the flags [ships] of different nations crowded into our port and made us immediately sensible of its great advantages."

But the final peace treaty would take some time to hammer out, and some fancy footwork on the part of John Jay, who ignored congressional instructions to follow Versailles's lead and struck a much better deal with the English than the French minister would have approved. While the negotiations dragged on, Sally and John were regular guests of the Lafayettes, who sent their invitations, written in English, via an American Indian messenger. They also visited with other Americans like Angelica Church, the sister-in-law of Alexander Hamilton; and Robert and Molly Morris's sons, who were at school in Geneva with Benjamin Franklin's grandson, spent their holidays with the Jays in Paris. Among the merry messages sent home was one in July 1783 from John Jay to his sister-in-law Kitty announcing, "Mrs. Jay promises us a welcome guest next month." Anne Jay was born at Benjamin Franklin's house in Passy just a few weeks before September 3, 1783, when the Treaty of

Paris was signed, bearing the signatures of Benjamin Franklin, John Adams, and John Jay. Henry Laurens was ill in England. The new baby prevented Sally from hosting the ball she had planned to celebrate the signing, but the exuberant patriot did raise a "Toast to America and her Friends":

1. The United States of America, may they be perpetual
2. The Congress
3. The King and Nation of France
4. General Washington and the American Army
5. The United Netherlands and all other free States in the world
6. His Catholic Majesty and all other Princes and Powers who have manifested friendship to America
7. The Memory of the Patriots who have fallen for their Country—May kindness be shown to their Widows and Children
8. The French Officers and Army who served in America
9. Gratitude to our Friends and Moderation to our Enemies
10. May all our Citizens be Soldiers, and all our Soldiers Citizens
11. Concord, Wisdom and Firmness to all American Councils
12. May our Country be always prepared for War, but disposed to Peace
13. Liberty and Happiness to all Mankind

Amen, Sally. Official word of the treaty signing reached America on November 1, 1783. The British, who had spent the summer helping loyalists leave New York City, finished evacuating their troops from New York on November 25. Jay's parents were able to return to their home in Rye, and a friend wrote that the reentry of patriots to the city had gone without a hitch. George Washington, after two long years of keeping an army ready to fight in case negotiations faltered, was finally able to send the troops home. Washington's farewell toast to his remaining officers on December 4 was raised at Fraunces Tavern in New York, where the American flag now flew: "With a heart full of love and gratitude, I now take leave of you. I most devoutly wish that our latter days may be as prosperous and happy as your former ones have been glorious and honorable." (The tavern still stands as a museum and restaurant.) On December 23 the general submitted his resignation to Congress, "to surrender into their hands the trust committed to me, and take my leave of all the employments of public life." On Christmas Eve, 1783, eight long years after he had been named commander in chief of the Continental army, George Washington arrived home at Mount Vernon. The war was finally well and truly over.

There was, however, still diplomatic tidying up to be done. It took several months for the documents ratifying the treaty to make their way back to Paris. On May 12, 1784, Britain and the United States exchanged ratifications. Four days later, his mission accomplished, John Jay, with Sally and their two little girls, left Paris to start their journey home. Henry Laurens, whose daughter Martha had been serving as his hostess in London, went back to America a short time later. Congress authorized Benjamin Franklin, Thomas Jefferson, and John Adams to negotiate "a great number of commercial treaties, which will detain them about two years in Europe." John Adams decided it was time to send for his wife.

After all those long years of absence, Abigail Adams surprisingly had a terrible time making up her mind to join her husband. As much as she missed John, and she missed him terribly, what she wanted was for him to come home. When Charles had arrived in Braintree after a harrowing five months of travel, Abigail hadn't heard from her sons for more than a year, and she had had it with living apart: "I cannot reconcile myself to living in this cruel state of separation . . . eight years have already passed since you called yourself an inhabitant of this state." What kept her going was the conviction that she was selflessly serving her country, and she was proud of it. "Patriotism in the female sex is the most disinterested of all virtues. Excluded from honors and from offices, we cannot attach ourselves to the state or government from having held a place of eminence. Even in the freest countries our property is subject to the control and disposal of our partners," this woman who was buying property in her husband's name told him. "Deprived of a voice in legislation, obliged to submit to those laws which are imposed upon us, is it not sufficient to make us indifferent to the public welfare? Yet all history and every age exhibit instances of patriotic virtue in the female sex; which considering our situation equals the most heroic of yours." She had clearly been chewing on the question of women's political place and wanted to talk about it with John. Still, despite her political sophistication, Abigail had never traveled. Even without enemy ships threatening capture, a trip to Europe without her husband was a frightening prospect. And, she told John, she had heard that Mrs. Jay was very unhappy in Paris. A scurrilous rumor, to be sure, but one Abigail had apparently heard.

Until he received notice from Congress that he was to stay in Europe, John was unsure about what to do. Should his wife come or not? Would he be going home or not? Still smarting from having been replaced as sole peace negotiator with Great Britain, he didn't know what Congress had in mind for him. He assigned Abigail to find out, knowing she always did a better job of digging out political intelligence from her congressional sources than he did. ("I always learn more of politics from your letters than any others.") John was truly torn: "I am so unhappy without you that I wish you would come at all events. . . . I must however leave it with your judgment, you know better than I the real intentions of Philadelphia." It was not just congressional intentions that made John hesitate about sending for Abigail once the seas were safe. "The question is whether it is possible for a lady to be once accustomed to the dress, show, etc. of Europe without having her head turned by it." He actually thought the woman who had scrimped and sacrificed to keep the family out of debt would become a spendthrift fashion plate! Abigail had her own concerns: she worried about embarrassing her husband. "A mere American as I am, unacquainted with the etiquette of courts, taught to say the thing I mean . . . I am sure I should make an awkward figure, and then it would mortify my pride if I thought I should be a disgrace to you." Adding to the difficult decision making was her daughter's love life. Young Abigail, called Nabby, was being courted by a young man her mother liked but who sounded unreliable to her father. Bringing the young woman to Europe might be just the thing to end the relationship. John wrote his daughter: "Nothing in this life would contribute so much to my happiness, next to the company of your mother, as yours. . . . You have reason for a taste of history, which is as entertaining and instructive to the female as to the male sex. . . . It is by the female world, that the greatest and best characters among men are formed. I have long been of this opinion to such a degree, that when I hear of an extraordinary man, good or bad, I naturally . . . inquire who was his mother?"

It was a good strategy. Nabby was engaged to her young man before she left America, but the separation killed the romance. After learning of John's new appointment from Elbridge Gerry, the Adams women sailed for England on June 20, 1784. Abigail's sisters filled in for her at home—Charlie and Tommy went to live with Betsey Shaw; Mary Cranch agreed to take care of John Adams's mother. In the same way Abigail made John's public service possible, her sisters made it possible for her to be with him. In taking her sister's sons, Betsey Shaw promised that the boys would have "the watchfulness of parents," but it was also a business arrangement. Abigail agreed to pay "$2 per week for each child including teaching." The day before the Adamses were scheduled to sail, Thomas Jefferson arrived in Boston suggesting the women wait to sail so they could accompany him on a ship to France. But Abigail had finally made up her mind, and nothing was changing it now. It had been a painful farewell, but mother and daughter, a couple of servants, and a cow were on their way across the Atlantic.

Trust Abigail Adams to take over the ship once she recovered from seasickness. She was appalled at its filth and decided, she wrote Betsey, "to exert my authority." Abigail organized "all the boys I could muster, with scrapers, mops, brushes, infusions of vinegar etc." to scrub the ship down. Then she moved on to the kitchen, where she "taught the cook to dress his victuals, and have made several puddings with my own hands." However, "we met with a great misfortune in the loss of our cow." The "poor creature" had to be killed after being badly injured during a storm. With the ship all tidied up, Abigail could enjoy what turned out to be a monthlong voyage. When she arrived in England on July 20, John Adams wasn't there. She and Nabby made their way from Dover to London and got word to John, who was in Holland, that they had arrived. He was ecstatic: "Your letter of the 23rd has made me the happiest man upon Earth. I am twenty years younger than I was yesterday." But after all that time, Abigail would have to wait still a while longer. As always, John's work came first: he had to stay a little longer finishing up some diplomatic duties in the Netherlands, so he sent John Quincy to greet his mother and sister. But for his mother to see John Quincy was incredibly gratifying. To her sister Mary, Abigail exclaimed, "His appearance is that of a man," and it was something for her to get used to, "not feeling 20 years younger as my best friend says he does, but feeling myself excessively matronly with a grown up son on one hand, and daughter upon the other." She was not yet forty. Abigail didn't know what John wanted her to do—go to The Hague, go to Paris—but "the sooner we meet the more agreeable it will be to me. I cannot patiently bear any circumstance which detains me from the most desirable object in my estimation that hope has in store for me." Soon her hope was realized. John came to London to collect his wife and daughter and bring them to Paris. Abigail, who had written about so much else in her life, chose to remain silent about the reunion. Months later she wrote to Mary: "Poets and painters wisely draw a veil over those scenes which surpass the pen of the one and the pencil of the other."

The day after Adams arrived in London the family left for Paris to meet Thomas Jefferson. Twice before the Congress had named Jefferson an envoy to Paris, and twice the Virginian had refused to serve because of his wife's illness. Jefferson had married the twenty-three-year-old widow Martha Wayles Skelton in 1772 and brought her to live at his always under construction hilltop home outside of Charlottesville. Over the next ten years at Monticello, Martha Jefferson bore six children and saw three of them die. (Though some women expressed their distress at the repeated pregnancies, it was what women expected, and the men didn't seem willing to do anything about it. That started to change at the end of the eighteenth century, perhaps as a result of women feeling somewhat more in charge of family decisions after their wartime experiences forced them to take charge of so much else. There are letters from mothers advising their daughters to nurse babies longer in order to stave off another pregnancy. And birthrates did start declining in the last couple of decades before the turn of the nineteenth century.) As Jefferson watched his wife grow sicker with each birth, and more distressed after each death, he cut back more and more on his national political activities, much to the dismay of his compatriots. As early as July

1776, only a few weeks after his triumph as the author of the Declaration of Independence, Jefferson was begging a Virginia colleague to replace him in Philadelphia: "For God's sake, for your country's sake and for my sake, come. I receive by every post such accounts of the state of Mrs. Jefferson's health, that it will be impossible for me to disappoint her expectation of seeing me at the time I have promised."

Jefferson would have liked to take on some of his assignments, and he told Franklin that Paris seemed awfully appealing, but he felt he couldn't leave his wife, and she couldn't travel. He concentrated his political activities in Virginia, as a member of the legislature and then as governor, but came under a good deal of criticism for his absences, which generally happened around the birth or death of a child. His handling of the defense of Virginia during the British invasion, and his own ignominious escape, also provided fodder for his political enemies. But Jefferson's harshest critics were his allies who wanted him to serve. When he turned down both the appointment to the peace commission and then service in the Continental Congress in 1781, a friend railed against Jefferson's "unpardonable rage for retirement." But Martha was pregnant again, and her husband knew how dangerous childbirth was for her. The baby was born in May, and Martha Jefferson never recovered. For four months Thomas stayed by her side. As she lay dying, Martha wrote out some lines from **Tristram Shandy:**

Time wastes too fast: every letter I trace tells me with what rapidity life follows my pen. The days and hours are flying over our heads like clouds of windy day never to return— more everything presses on—

Then her handwriting stops and her husband's picks up:

—and every time I kiss thy hand to bid adieu, every absence which follows it, are preludes to that eternal separation which we are shortly to make.

Jefferson saved the scrap of paper, along with a lock of his wife's hair, for his daughter to find many years later. Though he knew he would lose his love, the knowledge didn't lessen the pain. When Martha died on September 6, 1782, Jefferson was inconsolable. His daughter Martha, who was ten years old at the time, recalled his reaction many years later: "He nursed my poor mother . . . sitting up with her and administering medicines and drink to the last," and after she died, "he kept his room for three weeks and I was never a moment from his side. He walked almost incessantly every night and day only lying down occasionally. . . . When at last he left his room he rode out and from that time he was incessantly on horseback rambling about the mountain . . . in those melancholy rambles I was his constant companion, a solitary witness to many a violent burst of grief."

Young Martha Jefferson would remain her father's companion for much of her life.

His wife's death allowed Thomas Jefferson to reenter public life, which he did readily. He sent his two younger daughters, Mary, called Polly, and Lucy, to live with their mother's sister. And he and Martha, called Patsy, headed for Congress in Philadelphia, where Jefferson hired teachers and tutors to provide a first-rate and highly unusual education for a girl child. In a letter to a French friend, Jefferson explained his actions: "The plan of reading which I have formed for her is considerably different from what I think would be most proper for her sex in any other country than America. I am obliged in it to . . . consider her as possibly the head of a little family of her own. The chance that in marriage she will draw a blockhead I calculate at about fourteen to one." Jefferson didn't say why he thought a blockhead son-in-law was in his future, but he was determined that Patsy study rigorously. He sent her a detailed schedule for her day:

> From 8 to 10 o'clock practice music
> From 10 to 1 dance one day and draw another
> From 1 to 2, draw on the day you dance, and
>   write a letter the next day
> From 3 to 4 read French
> From 4 to 5 exercise yourself in music
> From 5 to bedtime read English, write, etc.

Jefferson told his daughter that "the acquirements which I hope you will make under the tutors I have

262 / Cokie Roberts

provided for you will render you more worthy of my love." But that wasn't the end of it. Patsy's father also instructed her in personal appearance: "Nothing is so disgusting to our sex as a want of cleanliness and delicacy in yours. I hope therefore the moment you rise from bed, your first work will be to dress yourself in such a style as that you be seen by any gentleman without his being able to discover a pin amiss." Jefferson was clearly preparing his daughter for public life. And soon she would be thrust into it. When Congress offered him a third opportunity to go to Paris, he jumped at the chance. He and twelve-year-old Patsy set sail on July 5, 1784. She wrote home to a friend that their cabin was "not more than three feet wide and about four long . . . the door by which we came in at was so little that one was obliged to enter on all fours." Fortunately, it was a quick trip by eighteenth-century standards—they arrived in Paris on August 6. Patsy was quickly enrolled in a convent school, causing some criticism in America. But Jefferson argued that there were plenty of Protestants at the posh school, and he knew his daughter wouldn't be indoctrinated by the nuns. (Abigail wasn't so sure.) Patsy ended up loving the school, but for the first month, until she was adjusted, her father visited her every day.

Thomas Jefferson and John Adams had worked closely together drafting the Declaration of Independence, and Jefferson had once met Abigail in Boston. Now the two families established an intimate friendship. (Sally and John Jay had left a few months before, in May 1784, after John spent some time writing down conversations with Benjamin Franklin, what we would now call an oral history.) Abigail Adams especially enjoyed Jefferson's company, since she was having a hard time adjusting to Paris. John had rented a thirty-room mansion in the suburb of Auteuil, and keeping a house of that size was something of a challenge to Abigail, whose little saltbox house in Braintree had only seven rooms. (The house is still there in what is now Quincy, Massachusetts, and it's hard to believe so many people both lived and worked there.) Abigail found Paris dirty and her servants both lazy and very particular about their assignments, sticking strictly to their own departments. She did find the method of polishing the tile floors funny—a servant attached brushes to his feet and skated around the room, "dancing here and there like a Merry Andrew." Another challenge: keeping up with French fashions. "To be out of fashion is more criminal than to be seen in a state of nature, to which the Parisians are not averse," she told her sister Mary. "Poor Mr. Jefferson had to hie away for a tailor to get a whole new black silk suit made up in two days." Still, being with her husband and older children made Abigail very happy, and she learned to appreciate theater and opera and even, though she found it shocking, the ballet. And the whole Adams family enjoyed Jefferson's company.

They grieved with him when he received the news in January 1785 that yet another child had died. Little Lucy, the baby whose birth caused

Martha Jefferson's death, had not been able to survive a bad case of whooping cough. Nabby Adams wrote in her journal: "Mr. J. is a man of great sensibility and parental affection . . . this news has greatly affected him and his daughter." When Jefferson learned in May that he was to replace Franklin, who at age seventy-eight was ready to retire as minister to France, he determined to send for his daughter Polly, who was six. The defiant little girl answered with a firm no: "I want to see you and sister Patsy, but you must come to Uncle Eppes house." The little girl's father pleaded with her from across the Atlantic and offered her bribes of dolls and toys, but he couldn't stop himself from sending harsh instructions as well: "Remember too . . . not to go out without your bonnet because it will make you very ugly and then we should not love you so much." No wonder the child wanted to stay home with her aunt and uncle. Poor Jefferson soon had another parting to deal with—John Adams was named the first United States ambassador to the Court of St. James's, and the family was moving to London. Their departure put him "in the dumps" and saddened his friends as well. "I shall really regret to leave Mr. Jefferson," Abigail wrote Mary. "He is one of the choice ones of the earth." She also had to say good-bye once again to her son John Quincy—it was time for him to go home to Harvard.

With the English Channel between them, Abigail Adams and Thomas Jefferson struck up a lively correspondence, full of news and opinions. Now that he was to replace Franklin, Jefferson wanted to know whether he could charge Congress for his house rent, because he knew his expenses would exceed his allowance. "I ask this question of you, Madam, because I think you know better than Mr. Adams what may be necessary and right." It's not clear whether the envoys ever asked for a housing allowance; the Adamses, who rented a house in Grosvenor Square, were strapped for cash the whole time they were in London. For Jefferson, Abigail was a source of gossip: "I think Madame Helvetius must be very melancholy now Franklin as she used to call him is gone." (Franklin had been a frequenter of the somewhat tawdry salon of Madame Helvetius, and he had asked her to marry him. She refused.) Abigail also provided political news: "Mr. Osgood, Mr. Walter Livingston and Mr. Arthur Lee are the commissioners of the Treasury . . . it is said the commissioners will have a difficult task to bring order out of the confusion in which the financier left the office." For Abigail, Jefferson was a sympathetic ear. In response to the attacks against John Adams in the British press, Jefferson wrote, "Indeed the man must be of rock who can stand all this; to Mr. Adams it will be but one victory the more." They also shopped for each other, sending goods back and forth across the Channel.

As the representative of a former enemy, Adams wasn't having an easy time of it in England, though he had been respectfully received by the king, and Abigail and Nabby were introduced at a royal reception. (The two women spent a good deal of time and energy figuring out what to wear. Abigail ended up feeling fairly ridiculous in her enormous hoop skirt and with feathers in her hair that brushed against the carriage roof.) The newspapers made fun of the American ambassador for his frugality and wondered when he would host the expected dinner for the diplomatic corps. (Not knowing how she'd pay for the feast, Abigail postponed it until an American ship arrived serendipitously carrying an enormous turtle that could make a meal.) And the British government was giving Adams a hard time in commercial negotiations. Abigail told Jefferson, "In this country there is a great want of many French commodities: good sense, good nature, political wisdom and benevolence." Jefferson had reason to agree with her when he went to London early in 1786. As ambassador to France, Jefferson was presented at court by Adams. King George saw the author of the Declaration of Independence and turned his back on the two Americans, infuriating Jefferson, who wrote that the British "require to be kicked into common good manners."

As far as Abigail was concerned, neither France nor England could measure up to her own country. "I am really surfeited with Europe, and most heartily long for the rural cottage, the purer and honester manners of my native land, where domestic happiness reigns unrivalled, and virtue and honor go hand in hand." Abigail especially missed her sisters, though they wrote often and she would send them special treats from England. One piece of silk for Betsey came with a note: "I was deliberating some time whether it should be virgin white or sky blue." Abigail explained: "Upon the whole, I concluded you had more pretensions to the sky than to the appellation annexed to the white." Fairly frisky stuff for a Puritan woman. Despite her sisters' loving care, Abigail worried about her sons at home. John Quincy, after years traveling the world, was having a hard time adjusting to Harvard, where he somewhat haughtily let it be known he considered his teachers unprepared for their jobs. Abigail remonstrated, "Your whole time has been spent in the company of men of literature and science. How unpardonable would it have been in you, to have been a blockhead."

For her part, Nabby was enjoying "domestic happiness" in London. Her fiancé in America had not responded to her letters, so Nabby eventually officially broke off the engagement. But John Adams's aide, Colonel William Smith, had fallen in love with the boss's daughter. In June 1786 they were married. Though the couple saw John and Abigail daily, Abigail missed having her daughter in the house. She wrote to Jefferson, trying to persuade him to send Patsy for a visit, but Jefferson replied, "I cannot part with my daughter." During her London sojourn, Abigail was able to fulfill one of her longest-held desires—she met Catharine Macaulay, the English heroine of the American cause. Showing her true rebel nature, Macaulay had married a man half her age, causing quite a

scandal. (During the war an Englishman had face-
tiously proposed another marriage for the contro-
versial historian. When American general Charles
Lee had been captured by the British, one of the
captor's fellow countrymen suggested that Lee either be hanged or marry Catharine Macaulay. Not a
pretty choice in the English wag's estimation.)
Macaulay and her young husband had toured
America in 1785, but Abigail was already in Europe at the time. Mercy Otis Warren had written
John Adams about her erstwhile mentor that
Macaulay's "independency of spirit led her to suppose she might associate for the remainder of life,
with an inoffensive, obliging youth, with the same
impunity a gentleman of three score and ten might
marry a damsel of fifteen." Talk about a double
standard. Though she was somewhat shocked at
the unorthodox marriage, Abigail was excited to
entertain the former Mrs. Macaulay and her
"obliging youth." In fact, Abigail took to hosting a
good many people at Grosvenor Square. The captain of every U.S. ship that came into port received
an invitation to dine at the ambassador's residence.
Abigail was so desperate for news from home that
she was scouring the highways and byways for
Americans.

The news from Massachusetts alarmed Abigail.
Economic conditions were so bad that farmers in
the western part of the state were losing their
property. To stop the foreclosure process, bands of
hundreds of armed men, led by Daniel Shays, were
closing down the courts by force. When Shays's

men threatened to raid the federal arsenal in Springfield, Massachusetts, Henry Knox, as secretary of war, was authorized by Congress to raise an army to quell the insurrection. In the end the Massachusetts uprising failed, but only in the face of overwhelming force. Abigail sent Jefferson newspaper accounts about what came to be called Shays' Rebellion, with her commentary, "Ignorant, wrestless desperadoes, without conscience or principals, have led a deluded multitude to follow their standard. . . . Instead of the laudable spirit which you approve, which makes a people watchful over their liberties . . . these mobish insurgents are for sapping the foundation and destroying the whole fabric at once." Jefferson's famous reply, "I like a little rebellion now and then," foreshadowed what would become a deep political rift between the dear friends. But at that time the families were about to grow closer, not further apart.

Jefferson had arranged for his daughter Polly to join him in Paris. Her ship would land in England, and he had asked Abigail Adams to take care of the little girl until he could collect her. Jefferson greatly enjoyed the companionship of his older daughter Patsy, who sent him newsy notes when he was gone from Paris. One told the story of a gentleman "that killed himself because he thought his wife did not love him. . . . I believe that if every husband in Paris was to do as much there would be nothing but widows left" (Jefferson at the time was seeing a great deal of a married woman, Maria Cosway, whose official unavailability must have been quite convenient, since Jefferson family lore has it that on her deathbed his wife asked him never to marry again.)

For two years little Polly had steadfastly refused to leave her aunt and uncle and cousins in Virginia. But Jefferson didn't want his child to grow up as a stranger to him, so Polly was tricked into traveling. Her cousins went aboard ship with her, and then, when she fell asleep, they went ashore and the ship set sail. When she woke up, the nine-year-old found herself at sea, with only Sally Hemings, a fourteen-year-old slave, as a companion. After what must have been quite a shock, the girls had a good time on their crossing—so much so that Polly had to be tricked again to get off the ship. It was a teary little girl that Abigail Adams greeted in June 1787. "At present everything is strange to her," Abigail wrote to Polly's father. "She was so much attached to the Captain and he to her that it was with no small regret that I separated her from him. . . . I show her your picture. She says she does not know it, how should she when she should not know you." That was precisely why Jefferson had summoned his daughter to Paris. Abigail urged Jefferson to bring Patsy with him when he came to get Polly, thinking her sister would cheer the little girl up. Instead, Jefferson sent a French aide to London, knowing that another wrenching moment was in store for Polly. "By this time she will have learned again to love the hand that feeds and comforts her, and have formed an attachment to you. She will think I am made only to tear her from all her affections." Abigail was clearly appalled that Jefferson had not come himself, quoting Polly to her father: "She told me this morning, that as she had left all her friends in Virginia to come over the ocean to see you, she did think you would have taken the pains to have come here for her, and not have sent a man whom she cannot understand." The poor child had "been so often deceived that she will not quit me a moment least she should be carried away." Not only was Abigail cross with Jefferson, but she was enchanted by Polly and didn't want to lose her so soon. The idea that the child should go to a French convent seemed cruel to Abigail, but she didn't think Jefferson had a choice: "The girl she has with her wants more care than the child, and is wholly incapable of looking properly after her." Sally Hemings, Abigail thought, should return to Virginia. With great reluctance, when it became clear that Jefferson would stick to his plan to have his aide bring his daughter to Paris, Abigail sent Polly to her father.

Even without Polly Jefferson in the house, there was plenty to occupy Abigail's attention. Nabby had produced a baby boy that spring, and word had come from America that a convention had been called to rewrite the Articles of Confederation. The United States needed a new form of government. When John Adams heard about the convention, he quickly wrote the "Defense of the Constitutions of Government of the United States of America." Abigail helped him with the work, but warned him that it would be unpopular, that his call for a strong central government under a single executive would earn him the epithet of "monarchist." As usual, her political instincts were better than his. But John pressed ahead with his treatise, knowing that the changes afoot in America would finally call him home.

CHAPTER SIX

1787–1789: Constitution and the First Election

MARY WHITE MORRIS

Assembling in Philadelphia

Shays' Rebellion served as a wake-up call to many of the Founders—a demonstration of just how inadequately the new government under the Articles of Confederation was functioning. For all intents and purposes, thirteen separate state legislatures ran the country—printing their own money, assessing their own taxes, establishing tariffs among the states, failing to provide for the common defense or pay down the public debt. Nine states maintained their own navies. When a

courier triumphantly brought the news of Cornwallis's surrender to Congress, members had to
reach into their own pockets to pay the messenger;
there was nothing but worthless paper money in
the treasury. Without the rallying cry of independence and the common enemy of England, the
states found no thread to pull them together into a
nation. Civil unrest in Philadelphia, led by unpaid,
unhappy Revolutionary War veterans, had caused
the Congress to flee, just as it had from the British,
moving first to Princeton, New Jersey, then to Annapolis, Maryland, then to Trenton, New Jersey,
then (after the British evacuated) to New York
City.

Fortunately for the members, the Congress was
welcome in those towns. When it moved to Princeton in 1783, Annis Boudinot Stockton, by then a
widow, had moved back into her house, Morven,
which had been wrecked by the enemy, after she
restored it to its former graciousness. She offered it
as lodging for members of Congress, making available "the whole house in which she lives, stables."
(Trentonians were a little more wary of the lawmakers. A Trenton advertisement offering congressional housing asked "to be excused from providing
dinners, as Congress do not dine at common family
hours." No kidding. Even then, they couldn't be
counted on to stop talking in proper time for a
meal.) Annis's brother, Elias Boudinot, was president of the Congress at the time. So Annis hosted
most of the important politicians of the day, including George and Martha Washington, at Mor-

ven, where she continued to write her poetry. (Morven served for many years as the New Jersey governor's mansion and still stands in Princeton as a historic site.) In one poem sent to Washington after the provisional peace treaty with Britain was ratified by Congress, Annis prays for the General's "return to Vernon's soft retreat":

And oh! If haply in your native shade,
One thought of Jersey enters in your mind,
Forget not her on Morven's humble glade,
Who feels for you a friendship most refin'd.

There wasn't much by way of "soft retreat" when George Washington finally returned to Mount Vernon. The property was a mess, and, having refused to take any money but expenses for himself and Martha—which were considerable—for his almost nine years in the army, his finances were in shambles. And the house was overrun by family and guests. Martha's two little grandchildren, Eleanor, called Nelly, and George Washington Parke Custis, lived with them, plus her niece, Fanny Bassett, who soon married George's nephew. One of Washington's nieces, the somewhat obstreperous Harriot, also moved in. And there was a constant parade of visitors, so much so that Mount Vernon was essentially run as an inn— 423 people visited in one year, according to Washington's records. George had "so much business of his own and the publics," Martha wrote her sister-in-law, "that I fear he will never find leisure to go see his friends." When Lafayette came to pay his respects, he sent as a "house present" a pack of French hounds. Martha hated them. She also seemed less than thrilled to entertain Catharine Macaulay Graham and her young husband. Macaulay was making her grand tour of America and had visited her longtime correspondent, Mercy Otis Warren, who sent her with a letter of introduction to Mount Vernon. Martha thanked Mercy "for introducing a lady so well known in the literary world" and added, "she now returns to make happy those whom she left." That was probably a relief.

The general did take a stand against one relative moving in—his mother. Old and not very well off, Mary Washington was living alone in Fredericksburg, Virginia, when the family decided it would be best for her to go live with her son John. Then John died, and George was terrified that his mother might come to Mount Vernon. The letter he wrote to keep her away would have discouraged any potential visitor: "My house is at your service, and [I] would press you most sincerely and most devoutly to accept it, but I am sure, and candor requires me to say, it will never answer your purposes . . . for in truth it may be compared to a well resorted tavern, as scarcely any stranger who are going from north to south, or from south to north, do not spend a day or two at it." He then went on to explain that Mary would have three choices: first, to be always dressed for "people of distinction," second, to appear in "dishabille," or third, to be "a prisoner in your own chamber." He concluded that she wouldn't like the first choice, he wouldn't like the second, and neither one of them would like the third. Even though George had graciously invited Martha's mother to live with them, an invitation she declined, for whatever unspoken reason he clearly didn't want his own mother around. And his rather stark assessment of what her life would be like at Mount Vernon seems to have done the trick—Mary Washington stayed put. (She died of breast cancer while her son was president. George declared a period of "republican mourning.") But poor Martha—there she was feeding all those people going from north to south and south to north, and never able to hang around in "dishabille" in her own house. (One visitor described what she did wear: "She was dressed in a plain black satin gown, with long sleeves, figured lawn apron and handkerchief, gauze French night cap with black bows—all very neat, but not gaudy.")

While running his "well resorted tavern," Washington kept a close eye on politics—and he didn't like what he saw. "The disinclination of the individual states to yield competent powers to Congress for the federal government," he worried in 1784, "will, if there be not a change in the system, be our downfall as a nation. . . . I think we have opposed Great Britain, and have arrived at the present state of peace and independency to very little purpose." To try to bring states together George and Martha Washington hosted an important event that started the country on the road toward a Constitutional Convention. In March 1785 commissioners from Maryland and Virginia met at Mount Vernon to hammer out the regulation of commerce on the Potomac River and Chesapeake Bay. They later invited Pennsylvania to join in the agreement they forged. It was a sign that the states could cooperate when they recognized a self-interest.

But it would still be a couple of years before the weakness of the government under the Articles of Confederation met a crisis big enough to spur change. Along the way some states urged action—the Massachusetts legislature called for a convention to reform the confederation as early as July 1785, and in January 1786 Virginia invited the other states to a commercial conference. Later that year a series of steps aimed at strengthening the union was proposed in Congress, but members, fearful the proposals would be defeated, never submitted them to the states. Then the enlarged commission on interstate commerce formed at Mount Vernon met in Annapolis in September 1786 and recommended a meeting in Philadelphia the next May to "take into consideration the trade and commerce of the United States." Meanwhile the postwar economy was in the dumps, and some of the Founders were beginning to worry that their enemies might have been right—America was ungovernable. In 1786 John Jay wrote: "Our affairs seem to lead to some crisis, some revolution, something I cannot foresee or conjecture. I am uneasy and apprehensive, **more so than during the war.**"

Then came Shays' Rebellion in the fall of 1786. By the time it was quashed the states knew they could no longer tolerate the current situation, and in February 1787 Congress endorsed the resolution passed in Annapolis the preceding September—a Convention would meet in Philadelphia on May 14.

The Convention was called for the purpose of revising the Articles of Confederation, since anything more dramatic would have scared off many of the old rebels against England who looked with gimlet eyes on a powerful central government. But a massive restructuring of the system was what some of the men meeting in Philadelphia had in mind. Prime among them was Alexander Hamilton, the former aide to George Washington who had become a leader in the New York legislature and ardent advocate of centralization. Hamilton had been militating for a Constitutional Convention for at least seven years, since he was a young man in the army and had written a seventeen-page letter to a friend outlining his ideas. Over the years, as he rose in prominence, Hamilton refined his theories of government and wrote them up for the newspapers, over the signature "The Continentalist." It's remarkable that this young man, who was foreign-born and well known to be illegitimate, could become so influential in the new America, and it could be seen as something of a symbol of meritocracy, of throwing off European class distinctions. In truth, Hamilton was accepted as readily as he was because he had married well.

Elizabeth Schuyler was the product of two old

Dutch Hudson Valley families. Her mother was Catherine Van Rensselaer Schuyler, whom we last met rushing against refugee traffic to her home in Saratoga to burn the wheat fields before the British could harvest them. Betsey's father, Philip, was for a period of time head of the Northern Command. Though friendly with the royal governor of New York, Philip Schuyler became a Revolutionary leader early on, serving in the Continental Congress. When George Washington left Philadelphia to take command of the army in 1775, he was accompanied by Major General Philip Schuyler. At that point Schuyler's daughter Betsey was eighteen years old, the second daughter in the family, the plain and quiet one stuck between two vivacious beauties. Still, Betsey had her charms. An aide to Washington described her as "a brunette with the most good natured dark lovely eyes that I ever saw, which threw a beam of good temper and benevolence over her entire countenance." Though they lived in a mansion in Albany, with a country estate in Saratoga, the Schuylers dealt with the rigors of the frontier and fostered friendship with the Indian nations. The Schuyler girls were no hothouse flowers; Betsey seems to have been a bit of a tomboy, and all of the distinguished visitors to the Schuyler homes commented on the "lively behavior" of the general's daughters.

As the Battle of Saratoga drew near in the autumn of 1777, and the British moved into the territory, the notorious story of the murder of a local woman, Jane McCrea, terrified the Americans.

Jane was engaged to a Tory who had joined the British army, and hoping to meet up with him, refused to flee as the redcoats approached. She ended up murdered and scalped by Indians working with the British, and her death became a rallying cry for patriots. Not long after the murder, Catherine Schuyler defied danger and made her heroic ride to Saratoga to collect some valuables and burn the fields, insisting that "a General's wife should know no fear." The British finished the job of destroying the Schuyler's Saratoga property. During the Battle of Saratoga, Burgoyne and his boys set fire to the Schuyler house, even though Philip was no longer in command of the American army in the North, having been removed ignominiously in a political move. After Burgoyne's defeat, when he was taken prisoner, the British general and many of his aides were brought, at Philip's instruction, to the Schuyler household in Albany, where they were received as honored guests by Catherine and her daughters. Imagine! The Schuyler women were entertaining the enemy who had just burned down their country house, but Philip thought a fellow general, even from the other side, deserved his hospitality and courtesy. Burgoyne later wrote of his first encounter with Schuyler after the battle: "I expressed my regret at the event which had happened, and the reasons which had occasioned it. He desired me to think no more about it; said the occasion justified it, according to the rules and principles of war and he should have done the same." Easy for him to say, but Catherine must have had some slightly less "gentlemanly" thoughts as she was called on to play hostess. The American military aide who accompanied the Brits to Albany observed that the generals and their retinues "give Mrs. Schuyler no small trouble." It was up to the little Schuyler boys to exact a tiny measure of revenge, recounted later by the French traveler and writer the Marquis de Chastellux. The second son, a seven-year-old, "a spoiled little child, as are all American children—very willful, mischievous, and likeable . . . opened the door of the room, burst out laughing on seeing these Englishmen collected there; and, shutting the door behind him, said to them, 'You are all my prisoners.' This innocent remark was cruel to them and rendered them more melancholy than they had been the evening before." Poor dears.

Soon after the Battle of Saratoga, General Washington dispatched his young aide-de-camp, Alexander Hamilton, to Albany to wrest some brigades from the victorious General Horatio Gates, who had taken over command from Schuyler in time to claim triumph for the battle. While Hamilton was fencing with Gates, who wanted to keep all his battalions in Albany with grandiose plans to launch an attack on British-held Canada, he visited the Schuyler mansion. Years later Betsey's youngest sister, who wasn't born at the time of the 1777 visit, composed this portrait of the dashing military man: "His features gave evidence of thought, intellectual strength and a determined mind. [His] high expansive forehead, a nose of the Grecian mold, a dark bright eye and lines of a mouth expressing decision and courage completed the contour of a face never to be forgotten."

Whether Betsey had forgotten Hamilton or not we don't know, but a couple of years later she found herself constantly in his company. Her older sister Angelica was already married (the first of four Schuyler girls to jump out the window and elope), and Betsey was eager to escape Albany. In February 1780 the twenty-three-year-old went to visit her aunt in Morristown, New Jersey, where Washington's army was camped. This was the winter of the famous three-hour dance of George Washington and Kitty Greene, and unmarried women were husband hunting among the young officers. Betsey's dear friend Kitty Livingston was there as well. Despite his reputation as a ladies' man (remember, Martha Washington named her tomcat in Morristown "Hamilton"), Alexander was in the market for a wife as well, having asked his friend John Laurens to find him a South Carolina bride: "She must be young, handsome (I lay most stress upon a good shape), sensible (a little learning will do), well-bred . . . chaste and tender. . . . As to fortune, the larger the stock of that the better."

Soon after Betsey arrived in camp, Hamilton gave a clear-eyed assessment of her to John Laurens: "She has good nature, affability and vivacity unembellished with that charming frivolousness which is justly deemed one of the principal accomplish-

ments of a **belle.** In short, she is so strange a creature that she possesses all the beauties, virtues and
graces of her sex without any of those amiable defects." Not exactly a swoon, but clearly smitten. In
fact he claimed to be "the veriest **inamorato** you
perhaps ever saw." Philip Schuyler, who was serving in Congress in Philadelphia, came to Morristown as well, as an adviser to Washington, and he
took kindly toward Hamilton, despite the young
man's lack of illustrious family background. By
April, Alexander had asked for Betsey's hand.
Schuyler's response? You have to ask her mother,
the formidable Catherine Schuyler. Bravely, Hamilton approached his future mother-in-law: "I leave
it to my conduct rather than expressions to testify
the sincerity of my affection for her, the respect I
have for her parents, the desire I shall always feel to
justify their confidence and merit their friendship."

The friendship of the rich and powerful
Schuyler–Van Rensselaer tribe gave Hamilton the
backing he needed in all his future endeavors. But
it was not just a marriage of convenience for the
young man. His roving eye notwithstanding, he
told his friend John Laurens, "believe me, I am a
lover in earnest." With her mother's approval Betsey went home to Albany to prepare for her wedding, and Hamilton sent one love letter after
another ("I love you more and more every hour";
"You engross my thoughts too entirely to allow me
to think of anything else"). It was in one of those
letters that he wrote her of the encounter with
Peggy Arnold the day her husband escaped, and

Hamilton's firm belief that the hysterical wife of the traitor was indeed innocent. Betsey must have found the intrigue distressing from several angles—not only had America been betrayed by a general they all knew, but the man in custody and later hanged was a special friend of hers. Once when he was under house arrest as a prisoner of war, Major Andre had lived with the Schuyler family and enchanted the then-teenage Betsey.

Hamilton was able to maneuver a leave in December 1780 and the couple was married at the Schuyler family home in Albany, with the groom's friends John Laurens and the Marquis de Lafayette in attendance. It was an excellent match for Hamilton. It was not just that he married into wealth and power; Betsey's devotion and good sense supported him for years. In writing a biography of Hamilton, one of his grandsons, Allan McLane Hamilton, concluded: "The surroundings and circumstances of Elizabeth Schuyler's life had all tended to prepare her for her future as Hamilton's wife. Had she been any other than what she was, despite all his genius and force of character, Hamilton could never have attained the place he did."

The young couple joined the army camp at New Windsor, where Betsey participated in Martha Washington's sewing circle. But Hamilton was growing restive as an aide-de-camp—he desperately wanted a command of his own—and he used a curt remark by Washington as an excuse to quit. (The general had said he wanted to speak to Hamilton, who finished some business before responding. "In a very angry tone," Alexander explained to his father-in-law, Washington barked, " 'Colonel Hamilton,' said he, 'you have kept me waiting at the head of the stairs these ten minutes. I must tell you, sir, you treat me with disrespect.' ") The bruised young man went back to the Schuyler home and engaged himself in writing a lengthy treatise on government and money, which was published in the **New York Packet.** He also whiled away some hours with the three-months pregnant Betsey's older sister, the beguiling Angelica Church. But eventually Hamilton returned to camp and was able to prevail upon Washington to entrust him with a command. In August 1781 off he went to Yorktown, without saying good-bye to Betsey who was with her parents in Albany. "I am wretched at the idea of flying so far from you without a single hour's interview, to tell you all my pains and all my love. . . . I must go without seeing you—I must go without embracing you;—alas! I must go." In truth, seemingly heartsick Hamilton was desperate to see action, to confront the enemy. Betsey certainly had no such desire, but the same month Alexander wrote that letter, his pregnant wife and her family unwillingly saw some action themselves. Philip Schuyler was always in danger of being kidnapped by the British or their loyalist and Indian sympathizers, so he kept armed guards at the house in Albany. But that August when Angelica was visiting with her little boy, she hid the guards' guns to keep them away from her child. When the enemy raided the house and the guards were defenseless, the family rushed upstairs to hide. Catherine Schuyler then realized that in her hurry she'd left her new baby downstairs in the cradle. Daughter Peggy ran down to rescue her baby sister and dashed back up the stairs. As family stories tell it, when one of the Indian marauders saw her, he hurled his tomahawk and cut a gash in the stair banister, and a gash is still visible at the Schuyler Mansion in Albany today. Philip Schuyler called out the window for help and was saved by townsfolk, though the kidnappers did make off with one of his men and a plate.

In September 1781 Hamilton reached Maryland, where he wrote Betsey that he was leaving for Yorktown the next day but was sure he would see her by November. Itching for battle, he added: "every day confirms me in the intention of renouncing public life, and devoting myself wholly to you. Let others waste their time and their tranquility in a vain pursuit of power and glory; be it my object to be happy in a quiet retreat with my better angel." Right. Hamilton's wish for glory on the field of action was granted. He performed heroic acts of derring-do at Yorktown and won much praise for his bravery, though, he assured Betsey, "There will be, certainly, nothing more of this kind." And for him and many in the army after Yorktown there was not. His active duty ended with Cornwallis's surrender in October 1781. But Hamilton's dear friend John Laurens was killed in South Carolina the next year, in the last land war of the Revolution. It was John's death that had caused his sister Martha Laurens to abandon her plans to marry her Frenchman, Caladon deVerne, and join her father, Henry, who was negotiating peace in Paris.

After the war Betsey and her husband and their new baby, Philip, lived with her parents in Albany while Hamilton studied for the bar. It was a happy time for them, as Alexander wrote to a friend: "You cannot imagine how domestic I am becoming. I sigh for nothing but the company of my wife and baby." Sharing the Schuyler library with Hamilton was another young man cramming for entrance to the bar—Aaron Burr, who had arrived with a letter of introduction to Schuyler. The men had known each other when Burr briefly served on Washington's staff. Now they were battling over books; soon they would be contesting cases in New York courtrooms—much less lethal fights than what was to come. When the war was finally over, Hamilton joined his old chief George Washington on the march into New York on November 25, 1783, long thereafter celebrated as Evacuation Day—the day the British departed from the city.

The Hamiltons set up housekeeping on Wall Street where a little girl, Angelica, and another boy, Alexander, soon joined their brother Philip. Betsey, on learning that the artist Ralph Earl was in debtors' prison, took pity on him and went to the jail to pose for a portrait. She convinced so many other "society ladies" to do the same that Earl earned enough to gain his release. Alexander stayed active in public affairs, holding various offices and working regularly with Robert Morris, who had been the financier of the Revolution, and with his father-in-law, who held political offices as well. Hamilton kept arguing for more power for Congress, for a central bank, for the payment of the debt. When the conference on commerce met in Annapolis, Hamilton was there, pushing for a full-blown Constitutional Convention. In May 1787 when the conclave in Philadelphia finally convened, Hamilton wasn't interested in half measures. But it would take all summer for the majority of men meeting in the Pennsylvania State House to agree with him.

One of the first delegates to arrive was thirty-two-year-old Rufus King of Massachusetts. The year before he had married Mary Alsop, the daughter of a wealthy New Yorker whose house King lived in while serving in Congress. A nineteenth-century chronicler of the **Republican Court,** Rufus Griswold, described her as "remarkable for her personal beauty; her face was oval, with finely formed nose, mouth, and chin, blue eyes, a clear brunette complexion, black hair and fine teeth." King's courtship of Mary Alsop had been the talk of the town—John Jay wrote to his sister-in-law Kitty Livingston in early 1786 that he was sure the sixteen-year-old would soon marry. And so she did. One of the bridesmaids reported on the nuptials to a relative of the groom: "The wedding was very splendid . . . and at the supper was produced for the first time wine which had been purchased and put aside at the birth of the bride, for this very occasion. The pipe containing it had been bricked up in one of the arches of the house . . . and had escaped the scrutiny of the British officers who had made their headquarters there. The rest of Mr. Alsop's wine was not so fortunate." John Adams, writing from England to Rufus King, had a more sober assessment of that union plus a few other recent interstate romances: "It will be unnatural if federal purposes are not answered by all these intermarriages." Seeking a stronger federal union, Adams saw some hope in the "intermarriage" of a New Yorker with a man from Massachusetts.

Sharing the commitment to federalism was Charles Cotesworth Pinckney, who sailed to Philadelphia with his new bride, Mary Stead Pinckney. Charles's first wife, Sarah Middleton Pinckney, who had suffered through the Revolution with his mother, Eliza, had died in 1784, leaving him with three small daughters. While he and his brother Thomas were busy trying to patch war-ravaged South Carolina back together, Charles sent his children to live at Hampton, his sister Harriott Pinckney Horry's plantation. Eliza Pinckney was living there as well since her house in Charleston had been hit by a cannonball and Belmont plantation had been completely destroyed. Eliza wrote to Harriott's son, who was studying in England, that she had neither "in country or town a place to lay my head . . . nor was I able to hire a lodging." But, she added, she was ready to forgive and forget in the hope that the postwar scarcity would be met with "equal the fortitude with which the greatest number even of our sex sustained the great reverse of fortune they experienced." Fortitude on Eliza's part would be required after Charles turned over the rearing of his children to his mother. In 1786 the forty-year-old widower married the highly intelligent, politically sophisticated, and still single thirty-four-year-old Mary Stead, who brought a tidy inheritance into the marriage. The children came to live with them in Charleston for a while, but then the Constitutional Convention beckoned and the couple left for Philadelphia and the children returned to their grandmother.

William Livingston, still governor of New Jersey as he had been since 1776, lent some heft to the gathering, at the age of almost sixty-four. Livingston's bevy of daughters continued to take an active part in the political and social life of the nation. The political part was fine with their father, the social part was cause for comment: "My principal secretary of state, who is one of my daughters," Livingston complained in early 1787, "is gone to New York to shake her heels at the balls and assemblies of a metropolis which might as well be—more studious of paying its taxes than of instituting expensive diversions." The governor's real gripe wasn't with his daughter but with New York, which had imposed a tariff on boats coming from New Jersey carrying fuel for the city's fires. New York had also been particularly obstinate about paying taxes to the Continental Congress, but New Jersey wasn't much better.

Of course the man contributing the most gravitas

to the Convention was George Washington. The general had started working for reform of the Articles of Confederation from his post as commander in chief when he experienced firsthand the inadequacies of a system that kept his soldiers begging for food and clothes. The fifty-five-year-old Washington's comrade in arms from the predominantly Anti-Federalist state of Virginia was thirty-six-year-old James Madison, who had been preparing studiously for the meeting by reading hundreds of books on philosophy and government sent to him from Paris by his friend Thomas Jefferson, plus the newly published **Defense of the Constitutions of Government of the United States of America,** written by John Adams. A bachelor, Madison showed up eleven days early for the session, so he was already in Philadelphia when bells rang out in greeting of the hero of the Revolutionary War. This time Martha decided to stay home at Mount Vernon. "Mrs. Washington has become too domestic and too attentive to two little grandchildren to leave home," Washington wrote to the man who would be his host in Philadelphia, Robert Morris, the moneyman during the Revolution and a delegate to the Convention. (Ironically the Morris house where Washington stayed was the one that General Howe had used as headquarters when his army occupied Philadelphia. After the British left, the house had been commandeered by Benedict Arnold.) Upon his arrival in the city, Washington's first courtesy call was to Philadelphia's own great statesman, and the oldest delegate, eighty-one-year-old Benjamin Franklin.

Welcoming the Visitors

When Benjamin Franklin arrived back in Philadelphia from his long sojourn in Europe in September 1785, he recorded in his journal that he was greeted by "a crowd of people with huzzas, and accompanied with acclamation quite to my door. Found my family well." That was all he had to say about seeing his daughter, Sally, for the first time in almost nine years and meeting most of his grandchildren. A few days later he wrote hurriedly to his sister Jane Mecom in Boston, announcing his safe arrival and apologizing for his brief note: "I am continually surrounded by congratulating Friends, which prevents my adding more." Franklin was the toast of the town, feted by all. Before he was there a week he had been recruited to run for the Supreme Executive Council of Pennsylvania. By the time he had been home a month, he had been elected president (governor) of Pennsylvania. Jane now realized that she would not be spending her old age with her brother: "I was in hopes you would have resolutely resisted all solicitations to burden yourself any more with the concerns of the public, and flattered myself if I were with you I should enjoy a little familiar domestic chit chat like common folks, but now I imagine all such attempts would be an intrusion, and I may as well content myself at this distance with the hopes of receiving once in while a kind letter from you." As annoyingly whining as that letter is, Jane was right. She and her brother did not see each other ever again, even though Ben had returned to America. They did keep up their correspondence—much of it about the infinitely fascinating crown soap, which Ben thought Jane could manufacture to supplement her small income from the rental of her house. (Franklin would also ask his sister about various relatives, since all kinds of people claiming to be kin were looking for favors. She sent him a list, then amended it to tell him that one man who had written to Ben was, in fact, related but was a "good for nothing impudent lazy fellow, just like his father.")

Sally Bache, on the other hand, was at the center of the swirl. All of the people visiting her celebrated father had to be attended to, made comfortable, and fed, even though she had a houseful of little children. By the time he had been home a year, Franklin was building new houses and adding on to the one they were living in, "it being too small for our growing family," as he told Jane. The burden on Sally must have grown much greater once the Convention met in Philadelphia and the affable old man invited his fellow delegates to dinner (he bragged to Jane that his new dining room could "dine a company of 24 persons"), along with the constant stream of callers from out of town. One visitor to the house wrote an account of his meeting Franklin, the former darling of the French court, sitting under the mulberry tree in his yard, surrounded by people including three of his grandchildren—"they seemed to be excessively fond of their grandpapa." Sally served tea. Franklin started to tell an anecdote about what had happened at the Convention that day and had to be reminded of the pledge of secrecy the delegates had sworn to. Apparently, a self-appointed censor regularly attended Ben's dinners, ready to change the subject when the doctor launched into some story about the secret deliberations. If Sally thought the extra load occasioned by her father's fame would be somewhat offset by an opportunity to finally bask in his affection, she soon learned she would have to share that as well. Ben brought his surrogate daughter in England, Polly Stevenson Hewson, and her family to live in a house in Philadelphia so he could spoil her children along with his daughter's.

Maintaining the secrecy of the Convention must have been pretty difficult given the socializing that went on in Philadelphia among politically sophisticated men and women. Apologizing to Annis Stockton for not answering a letter sooner, Washington described the swirl: "What with my attendance in Convention, morning business, receiving and returning visits, and dining late with the numberless [personages] etc, which are not to be avoided in so large a city as Philadelphia, I have scarcely a moment." It seems likely that George Washington and his host, Robert Morris, went over the day's events in the evening, when it would have been perfectly natural for Mary, called Molly, Morris to join in. Mary White had been nineteen years old and a Philadelphia belle when she married the prospering thirty-five-year-old merchant Robert Morris in 1769. Seeing young Molly White at a Philadelphia society event, one of the stalwarts of the community penned an impromptu poem:

In lovely White's most pleasing form,
What various graces meet!
How blest with every striking charm!
How languishingly sweet!

So Molly was a catch, but so was Morris, who had emigrated from England as a boy and formed a partnership with a member of one of Philadelphia's most prominent families, Thomas Willing. The firm of Willing and Morris, eventually the largest importers in America, owned its own fleet of ships. In that partnership and others, Morris accumulated so much wealth that by the time of the Constitutional Convention he was recognized as the richest man in America. He was also one of the most politically active, entering early into the Revolutionary struggle, serving in the Continental Congress and signing the Declaration of Independence. Molly's letters to him and to her mother show a young woman keeping up with politics while producing babies every two years and occasionally fleeing from the British. "Mr. Hancock intends resigning his seat in Congress, and going home," she confided to her mother in April 1777. "They meant to have complimented Mr. Morris with the Presidentship, but he told the gentleman who informed him of it he could not serve, as it would interfere entirely with his private business." The Washingtons stayed with the Morrises when they were in Philadelphia during the war, and Sarah Jay's sister, Kitty Livingston, lived with them while the Jays were in Europe and the British were rampaging through New Jersey. Molly Morris and Sally Jay sent letters back and forth, mainly about people and fashion, but also about politics. After penniless refugees from Charleston arrived in Philadelphia in 1781, Molly wrote that she hoped the country would "cheerfully execute the plan of Congress for a loan to relieve their necessities as the most delicate way of doing it, and the one they prefer." Congressional loans were something Molly Morris knew a good deal about, since her husband was busy financing them.

Robert Morris was made "superintendent of finance" for the Confederation of American States in 1781 when its credit had collapsed and its paper currency was worthless. No one would do business with America—it was broke. Morris knew drastic steps were necessary. He was the one who established the Bank of North America that George Washington tried to convince Esther Reed to invest in. A central bank proved to be the first step toward genuine federal government. Private credit was the only kind anyone trusted, and Morris staked his own on the country. He issued his own currency, what came to be called "Morris's Notes," which were accepted as money more readily than the paper printed by the government. He also managed to buy supplies for the hard-pressed army and provided the ships to carry soldiers to Yorktown, leading one foreign commentator to judge that "the Americans certainly owed, and still owe, as much acknowledgment to the financial operations of Robert Morris, as to the negotiations of Benjamin Franklin, or even to the arms of Washington." The next year Morris proposed a comprehensive plan for dealing with public debt, through tax collection by a central government.

As the moneyman, the so-called financier of the Revolution, Morris was sought after by all distinguished visitors to Philadelphia. He and Molly were considered the host and hostess of the country. Samuel Breck, author of an essay about the era, **Recollections,** described entertainment at the Morris home: "No badly cooked or cold dinners at their tables; no pinched fires upon their hearths; no paucity of waiters; no awkward loons [louts] in their drawing rooms. We have no such establishments now. God in his mercy gives us plenty of provisions, but it would seem as if the devil possessed the cooks." One visitor from Paris, the Prince de Broglie, told of being taken to the Morris house for tea by the French ambassador: "I partook of most excellent tea, and I should be even now drinking it, I believe, if the Ambassador had not charitably notified me at the twelfth cup that I must put my spoon across it when I wished to finish with this sort of warm water." It must have gotten pretty tiresome, but impressing foreign dignitaries was useful for the struggling young republic, which needed European goodwill as well as foreign capital and credit.

When the Constitutional Convention assembled, it was Robert Morris who proposed George Washington for president (Franklin was supposed to make the motion but he was out sick), and the election was unanimous. The general sat in his chair on the raised dais, never uttering a word during the four months the Convention met, until the last day. Washington's conversation at the time came after hours, with the men and women of Philadelphia. His diaries seldom mention the work he was there to do, but they do record his comings and goings: "dined with Mr. and Mrs. Morris," "drank tea at Doctor Shippin's with Mrs. Livingston's party," "accompanied Mrs. Morris to Doctor Redman's, three miles in the country where we drank tea and returned," "drank tea at Mr. Bingham's & went to the play" (John Dryden's version of **The Tempest**), "in company with Mr. Robert Morris and his Lady and Mr. Gouverneur Morris I went up to Trenton on another Fishing party," "drank tea with Mrs. Bache," "drank tea at Mr. Powel's." Finally, on the last day of the Convention, Washington wrote: "Met in Convention when the Constitution received the Unanimous assent of 11 states and Col. Hamilton's from New York . . . did some business with, and received the papers from the secretary of the Convention, and retired to meditate on the momentous work."

As temporary home to the men accomplishing the "momentous work," Philadelphia had a lot to offer. The nation's biggest city, with a population of close to forty thousand, boasted theaters, bookstores, a library, taverns, a circus, plus "Mr. Peale's Museum" where the artist displayed his own work and biological specimens. And, as Washington's diaries indicate, the city "possessed a very gay and fashionable circle, despite the large Quaker element in its population, and . . . was distinguished for its hospitality and generous living," in the assessment of a nineteenth-century social historian. Leading the circle, along with Molly and Robert Morris, was his partner's family—the Willings. Thomas Willing's mother was a member of the prominent Shippen family, his sister Eliza was married to the "Mr. Powel" mentioned by Washington, and Willing's daughter Anne was the wife of "Mr. Bingham." William Bingham had made a large fortune in the West Indies, partly by acting as an agent for Willing and Morris, and then taken his wife for a protracted stay in Paris, where she struck up a friendship with Thomas Jefferson, and London, where Abigail Adams was quite taken with her, often writing home about her. Once, after dinner with Lafayette, Abigail described what Anne was wearing: "her dress was of black velvet, with pink satin sleeves and stomacher, a pink satin petticoat, and over it a shirt of white crape, spotted all over with gray fur." Quite an outfit. Judging Mrs. Bingham "the finest woman I ever saw," Abigail had her reservations about the beauty: "one has only to lament too much dissipation of frivolity of amusement, which have weaned her from her native country, and given her a passion and thirst after all the luxuries of Europe." Anne Bingham brought that passion back home to the enormous mansion the couple built in Philadelphia where she held a European-style salon, entertaining all important visitors with conversation about politics and fashion, and was considered as "unquestionably the head of American society."

In her continuing correspondence with Thomas Jefferson, Anne challenged his statement that American women should stay out of politics except "to soothe and calm the minds of their husbands returning ruffled from political debate." To the contrary, the combative young woman argued, the women of France meddled in politics and found it improved their lot: "they have obtained that rank of consideration in society, which the sex are entitled to, and which they in vain contend for in other countries." The lovely Mrs. Bingham was used to having her way. When a new theater was opened in Philadelphia, she proposed to buy a private box "at any cost to be fixed by the manager," decorate it, lock it, and keep the key, so that only she and her friends could use it. The theater's owner, thinking such a privilege would fly in the face of republican principles, refused the request "and thus forfeited the patronage of the most influential woman in

Philadelphia." Miffed at the rebuff, Anne boycotted the theater from then on.

Eliza Powel, Anne Bingham's aunt, appears a far
more sober-minded matron. She was a great friend
of both George and Martha Washington and, later,
Abigail Adams, who considered "Mrs. Powel of all
the ladies she has met the best informed." The
Marquis de Chastellux, who seems to have spent
some time with just about every family in America
during his travels, wrote that Eliza was "well read
and intelligent; but what distinguished her most is
her taste for conversation," and he viewed her and
Samuel Powel as equals, "unusually well matched
in understanding, taste and knowledge." (In the
first published edition of his work, the Frenchman
had this to say about Eliza: "Contrary to American
custom, she plays the leading role in the family . . .
she has wit and a good memory, speaks well and
talks a great deal; she honored me with her friendship and found me very meritorious because I mer-
itoriously listened to her." Chastellux later said he
was sorry for his "innocent" little joke because he
had "since conceived great esteem and friendship
for her.") George Washington kept up a correspondence with Eliza, whose judgment he trusted,
something that would become highly significant
once he was president.

Also in Philadelphia at the time of the Constitutional Convention was a young woman who would
turn out to be more influential politically than any
of the reigning Philadelphia doyennes. Nineteen-
year-old Dolley Payne had moved to the city four

years earlier with her parents and seven brothers and sisters. A Quaker family, the Paynes had been slaveholders in Virginia but, due to religious scruples about the institution of slavery, Dolley's father, John Payne, had freed his slaves and moved to Philadelphia where he became a laundry starch merchant. The family was struggling in Philadelphia, and certainly not part of the dazzling society of the Willings and Morrises. It was only when Philadelphia took its brief turn as the nation's capital that Dolley would meet and marry the young man who was making such a splash at the Convention, James Madison.

Madison and his colleagues spent the long summer wondering whether the Convention would ever bear fruit. There were so many divisions—big states versus small states chief among them. And there were so many arguments—over direct election of representatives, over whether there should be a chief executive, over whether men who served in government should be paid or should be subject to a religious test, over slavery, over admission of new states, over the definition of treason, over ratification, and, most important, over the basic issue of whether a national government should exist at all. And the debates all were waged in the stifling hot room of the State House because the pledge of secrecy prevented the delegates from taking their passionate views outside the hall. The secrecy rule caused controversy both inside and outside the sessions, but even some newspapers agreed that opening the debates to the press would result in an aborted Convention. (It's something of an object lesson to those of us who've covered Congress to know if ancestors of our ilk had reported on the ancestors of the lawmakers, we probably wouldn't be governed by this remarkable charter.) At one particularly contentious point in the proceedings Benjamin Franklin suggested that a chaplain come daily to pray over the assemblage. The unceremonious response: there's no money to pay a chaplain. (The delegates themselves were not being paid. There might have also been some hesitation about bringing in someone from the outside, since the chaplain of the Continental Congress during the Revolution, Jacob Duche, turned out to be an enemy agent who tried to convince Washington to abandon his cause and side with the British.)

Most of the framers accepted the fact that they were moving well beyond what they had been called together to do—amend the Articles of Confederation—and they knew if they succeeded they would create a whole new form of government, never seen before. "A very large field presents to our view without a single straight or eligible road that has been trodden by the feet of nations," the North Carolina delegates reported to their governor in late June, "several members of the Convention have their wives here and other gentlemen have sent for theirs. This seems to promise a summer's campaign. Such of us as can remain here from the inevitable avocation of private business, are resolved to continue, whilst there is any prospect of being able to serve the state and union." One member who did find it necessary to return home to attend to business was Alexander Hamilton. On July 10 Washington wrote to his former aide telling him that he wished Hamilton were there, adding in anguish, "I almost **despair** of seeing a favorable issue to the proceedings of the Convention." Partly because of Washington's stature with the delegates, the Convention muddled on through, producing a "favorable issue" by eventually accepting the compromises that made possible a Constitution bringing together so many disparate interests. The delegates hoped General Washington's clout would work with the country as well. Charles Cotesworth Pinckney wrote to his sister Harriet Horry: "I have no doubt that his reputation and that of many respectable characters I see in the Convention will dispose our fellow citizens to judge favourably of such issues as we shall adopt." Facing a deadline because the Pennsylvania Assembly needed the meeting hall, a Committee on Style and Arrangement was appointed to write the final document. But in much the same manner that Thomas Jefferson wrote the Declaration of Independence, though a committee was assigned to draft it, one man chose the words that are the Constitution: Gouverneur Morris.

Writing It Down

In some ways the man from Philadelphia, a young business associate of Robert Morris, was the obvious choice for the author of the Constitution. Gouverneur Morris, who wasn't related to Robert, but who had worked as his deputy in the Finance Office and was an ardent supporter of a national government, had spoken more than any single member of the Convention, despite his spending the month of June away from Philadelphia tending to personal business. But in other ways, Morris was an unlikely pick. A well-known ladies' man and wealthy sophisticate, the thirty-five-year-old Morris was not the sort of upright stolid fellow many of the Founders were. "The Tall Boy," as Morris was called, had lost a leg in a carriage accident and his wooden leg somehow added to his devil-may-care air. (One story had it that Morris lost the leg diving out of a married woman's window. His friend John Jay wrote from Spain that it would have been better if Morris "had lost **something** else.") To men of the Puritan tradition like John Adams, Morris seemed far too dedicated to the pursuit of pleasure, and not dedicated enough to republican principles. But George Washington liked him, and everyone knew Morris could write. Taking the cumbersome twenty-three articles approved by the Convention and shaping them into six succinct sections, plus a ratification instrument, Morris crafted the document in four days. He is the man responsible for the words of the Preamble: "We the people of the United States in order to form a more perfect union, establish justice, insure domestic tranquility, provide for the common defense, promote the general welfare, and secure the blessings of liberty to ourselves and our posterity, do ordain and establish this Constitution for the United States of America." They give you goose bumps. But the stirring sentiments were not just felicitous phrases, they were a political statement. Originally a roll call of states introduced the document: "We the undersigned delegates of the states of New Hampshire, Massachusetts-Bay. . . ." Not only was that beginning boring, it was dangerous to purposes of national government. The states were recognized as the source of legitimacy. With "We the people of the United States," Morris essentially went over the heads of the states to the people. He also finessed the questions of what to do about Rhode Island, which didn't send any delegates to Philadelphia, and how to handle states that might not ratify.

Gouverneur Morris was single at the time of the Constitutional Convention. He had been one of a long line of men, including Alexander Hamilton, who set their sights on Kitty Livingston. And he was one of a long line rejected by the New Jersey governor's daughter. Over the years his name had been linked with those of various married women, but when he hit his fifties without ever bringing home a bride, he seemed a confirmed bachelor for life. Then, just a month shy of his fifty-eighth birthday, Morris surprised his friends and family, especially the relatives who expected to enjoy an inheritance, by deciding to tie the knot. It was not just **that** Morris married, it was **whom** he married that shocked his social set. Anne Cary Randolph, a cousin of Jefferson and a sister-in-law of Jefferson's daughter Martha, had been cast as the villain in what might have been the greatest scandal of eighteenth-century America.

Anne, called Nancy, was a member of the distinguished and large Randolph family of Virginia. Her father had entertained George Washington and Lafayette, and Thomas Jefferson spent a considerable part of his boyhood on the Randolph plantation. Gouverneur Morris had come around as well, when Nancy was a girl of thirteen and he was doing business in Virginia. Nancy Randolph's privileged girl life came to an end in 1790 when her father remarried a little more than a year after his first wife died. The new bride, not much older than her sixteen-year-old stepdaughter, made it clear she wanted no teenage girl around, so Nancy moved in with her sister and brother-in-law on their plantation called, of all things, "Bizarre." Nancy's sister, Judith, had married their cousin Richard Randolph the year before, and Richard's brother Theodorick was wooing Nancy, so he decided to take up residence at Bizarre as well. Complicating this already complicated situation was the fact that another Randolph brother, John, was also interested in Nancy and was far from pleased when he learned that she planned to marry Theodorick. Much more dangerous for Nancy, Judith's husband, Richard, had also fallen in love with her. Then, in early 1792, Theodorick died of tuberculosis. Soon relatives, including Patsy Jefferson who had married Nancy and Judith's brother Thomas Randolph, were worried about Nancy's health—her spirits were low, she seemed to be gaining weight, she wasn't her old self. But she went with Judith and Richard, and Richard's brother John, to a house party at a cousin's plantation. During the night Nancy's screams wakened the household. When the hostess went to see what was wrong, Richard blocked the door. A couple of days later the Randolphs returned to Bizarre.

The rumor mill started churning. Slaves at the plantation spread the story that they had found a dead white baby on the woodpile. The word all over Virginia was that Nancy had borne Richard's child and he had murdered it. Nancy stayed stubbornly silent about the gossip swirling around her. "Amidst the distress of her family she alone is tranquil," her sister-in-law Patsy Jefferson Randolph told her father, "I am one of the few who have always **doubted** the truth of the report." Thomas Jefferson had urged his daughter to support "your poor afflicted friend." Richard decided he had to do something to answer the whispered accusations, and what he chose to do was truly stupid. He placed a notice in the **Virginia Gazette** declaring that he would "refute the calumnies which have been circulated" by appearing in Cumberland Court and "render myself a prisoner before the **court,** or any magistrate of the county there **pres-**

ent, to answer in the due course of law, **any charge of crime which any person or persons whatsoever shall then and there think proper to allege against me.**" Apparently Richard Randolph was surprised when he showed up at Cumberland Court and the sheriff was there waiting for him. Charged with "feloniously murdering a child said to be borne of Nancy Randolph," he was thrown in jail. A week later at a sensational trial where Richard was represented by Patrick Henry and John Marshall, the dream team of the era, a stream of Randolph cousins testified that they thought Richard and Nancy seemed imprudently fond of each other, and that they suspected Nancy was pregnant, but that Nancy and her sister Judith had a warm and loving relationship. Judith swore that the pair was innocent; so did John. The slaves were not allowed under Virginia law to testify against white men. With no real evidence against Richard, and two superb lawyers supporting him, that "trial of the century" ended in acquittal. Judith, Richard, and Nancy all went home to Bizarre.

Three years later, at the age of twenty-six, Richard Randolph suddenly died. All Nancy and Judith could report to his brother John was that Richard suffered a high fever, followed by a severe stomach pain. John took over the operation of Bizarre and made it so prosperous that he attracted the attention of prominent men in the area who asked him to run for Congress. At the age of twenty-six John Randolph was elected and became one of the most brilliant and erratic members. His speeches were laced with clever venom, making him eminently quotable, if not likable. The relationship between the sisters grew increasingly strained, as Judith brooded about how much of the infamous story alleged in the trial was true. Each sister sent letters to relatives describing the tension in the household. John Randolph, having been rejected as a lover by Nancy, took Judith's part and finally, in 1805, unceremoniously threw his cousin out. Writing to Randolph about it years later, Nancy gave her version of his harsh actions: "You came into my room one evening, after you had been a long time in your chamber with my sister, and said . . . 'Nancy, when do you leave this house? The sooner the better, for you take as many liberties as if you were in a tavern.' On this occasion, as on others, my course was silent submission. I was poor, I was dependent . . . I replied with the humility suitable to my forlorn condition, 'I will go as soon as I can.' You stalked haughtily about the room, and poor, unprotected Nancy retired to seek the relief of tears."

She had nowhere to go. Think of it, a twenty-nine-year-old well-bred woman on her own with no resources. It wasn't as if she could go out and find a job. There weren't any jobs for someone like her. She was hardly suitable as a governess or tutor; she was suspected of incestuous adultery and murder. First, she went home to her now dead father's plantation and found it stripped of furniture and abandoned. Then she drifted on to Richmond where she used what little money she had to rent a room from a respectable family. When she sent John a letter complaining that her nephew at school in Richmond was not allowed to see her, John came to call. Nancy later reminded John of the scene: "You sat on my bedstead, I cannot say my bed, for I had none, I was too poor. When weary, my limbs rested on a blanket spread over the sacking." After seeing her, John dispatched the nephew to offer Nancy one hundred dollars but she refused it, "my feelings were too indignant to receive a boon at the hands of those by whom I had been so grievously wounded." She was destitute but proud. She moved away from Virginia, landing in Newport, Rhode Island, where her poverty overcame her pride—she asked for a loan of fifty dollars but never heard a word from her family. "I was then so far off, my groans could not be heard in Virginia. You no longer apprehended the reproaches which prompted your ostentatious offer at Richmond. Yes, sir, you were silent." But John Randolph had not been silent back in Virginia. Fearing "reproaches" for turning a woman, a relative, out of house and home, the congressman had spread vicious lies about his cousin. Nancy had murdered Richard, he told anyone who would listen, and there was more—she had taken up with a slave at Bizarre as his mistress; she had lived in a house of ill repute in Richmond.

The stories traveled on the congressional grapevine and followed Nancy wherever she went. Hoping to escape them, she looked for someone traveling to Europe who wanted a female companion but found no takers. Her brother sent her a little money now and then, and, eventually, she met a friendly woman who ran a boardinghouse in New York. When she moved to a room in the boarding-house, Nancy wrote to the one person she thought might be helpful—Gouverneur Morris, the man she had met back home on the plantation when she was thirteen years old. He traveled from his estate, Morrisania, in what's now the Bronx, into the city to meet the now thirty-four-year-old Miss Randolph. He needed a housekeeper to keep his rowdy servants in check and thought a "reduced gentle-woman" could do the trick. But he wanted to meet that gentlewoman first, to see how he liked her. After he came to call, in the fall of 1808, Morris corresponded with Nancy, trying to convince her to take the position. "Pride may exclaim 'Miss Randolph cannot descend to the rank of a servant under whatever name, or however elevated and distinguished.'" He knew about the scandal attached to her but brushed it off: "I once heard but have no distinct recollection of events which brought distress into your family. Do not dwell on them now. If ever we happen to be alone you shall tell your tale of sorrow when the tear from your cheek may fall in my bosom." He even wrote her a poem about her troubles, reminding her that the world was capricious:

And feeble insults of a day
May pine beneath the world's disdain,
But when that world has passed away
The soul immortal shall remain.

What was Nancy to make of it? After all, Morris was a notorious rake; what was he really proposing for her? He answered by admitting some interest: "Time in taking away the ardor has not wholly quelled the rashness of youth"; but then promised her, "I can only answer that I will love you as little as I can." And he assured her, he had never acted with impropriety toward any of his housekeepers, even though one had been "a well made, good looking woman." So in April 1809 Nancy Randolph moved to Morrisania. On Christmas Day she and Gouverneur Morris were married. Years later Nancy remembered, "I glory in stating that I was married in a gown patched at the elbows, being one of the only two I had in the world."

The determined bachelor didn't take the dramatic step of marrying a scandalous woman almost half his age without consulting anyone. He wrote to Richard Randolph's surviving former defense lawyer, John Marshall, now chief justice of the United States Supreme Court, asking the truth about Miss Randolph. Marshall replied that Nancy had been a victim of "rumor with her usual industry," which had spread stories that "were probably invented by the malignant." The chief justice declared Virginia opinion divided on Nancy's guilt or innocence but pointed out that she had lived with her sister, who would have been the most injured party if the story were true, for many years after the trial. That seems to have been enough for Morris. But not for his putative heirs. A niece wrote to express her dismay with his choice, wondering why he hadn't consulted her. Morris shot back, "if the world were to live with my wife, I should certainly have consulted its tastes; but as that happens not to be the case, I thought I might, without offending others, endeavor to suit myself, and look rather into the head and heart than into the pocketbook." The relatives became even more alarmed when Nancy produced Gouverneur Morris II in February 1813. Morris was ecstatic, sending love poems to his wife and son when he traveled, but Nancy was such an easy target for rumormongers. One of Morris's nephews, David Ogden, put it out that the baby wasn't really his uncle's at all but the child of a servant at Morrisania. And he claimed that Nancy was trying to murder Morris's kin. The man Ogden chose to tell his lies to was none other than John Randolph.

After their baby was born, Nancy and her husband, who lived in luxury and were entertaining many of the Founders, had reached out to her Randolph family, despite their treatment of her. The Randolphs had had a tough time—Judith's house, Bizarre, had burned down; one of her sons who was both deaf and mute had become mentally ill, the other showed signs of tuberculosis; John Randolph had been defeated for Congress. Judith's son Tudor, who was at Harvard, went to visit Morrisania at his aunt's invitation. When the Morrises saw how sick he was, they asked Judith and John to come join him. Judith and Tudor stayed on at the estate for a few months, while John went in to New York to a boardinghouse. It was while Randolph was at the boardinghouse that David Ogden and another Morris nephew visited him. When they added their poisonous prevarications to Randolph's own list of lies, something must have snapped in the once-rejected lover. All of the pent-up vitriol Randolph could no longer spew at members of Congress came flowing out at Nancy.

He tried to ruin her. He sent Nancy a letter, care of Gouverneur, accusing her of every imaginable crime, starting with bearing an illegitimate baby and forcing his brother Richard to deal with it: "His hands received the burden, bloody from the womb, and already lifeless. Who stifled its cries, God only knows and you. His hands consigned it to an uncoffined grave." He charged her with murdering Richard, and he claimed Judith believed that as well. He slammed one accusation on top of another about how horrible she had been at Bizarre, forcing them to evict her, "your intimacy with one of the slaves, your '**dear** Billy Ellis,' thus you commenced your epistles to this Othello! attracted notice." He pronounced her a prostitute, "a vampire that, after sucking the best blood of my race, has flitted off to the North, and struck her harpy fangs into an infirm old man. To what condition of being have you reduced him? Have you made him a prisoner in his own house that there he may be witness of your lewd amours, or have you driven away his friends and old domestics that there may be no witness of his death? . . . If he be not both blind and deaf, he must sooner or later unmask you unless **he too die of cramps** in his **stomach.**"

Morris seemed utterly unperturbed by the hateful missive; he wrote a friend that his wife had told him she had borne a stillborn baby, the child, she said, of her fiancé Theodorick. And Morris suspected John hated Nancy "because she's happy." But Nancy was at first devastated, then furious. She wrote to Morris's nephews warning them to back off; then she composed a forty-page response to John Randolph. She sent copies of it and John's letter to his political opponents in Virginia, where more copies quickly circulated. Like her serpent-tongued cousin, Nancy minced no words: "It was your troublesome attention which induced Richard to inform you of my engagement [to Theodorick]. . . . I was left at Bizarre, a girl, not seventeen, with the man she loved. I was betrothed to him and considered him as my husband in the presence of that God whose name you presume to invoke on occasions the most trivial and for purposes most malevolent. We should have been married if death had not snatched him away a few days after the scene which began the history of my sorrows." She said Richard knew everything and that "Neither your brother or myself had done anything to excite enmity yet we were subjected to an unpitying persecution. The severest scrutiny took place. You know it. He was acquitted to the joy of numerous spectators, expressed in shouts of exultation. This, sir, passed in a remote county of Virginia more than twenty years ago. You have revived the slanderous tale in the most populous city in the United States."

She went on to knock down his accusations one by one, concluding, "I observe, sir, in the course of your letter allusion to one of Shakespeare's best tragedies . . . for a full and proper description of what you have written and spoken on this occasion, I refer you to the same admirable author. He will tell you it is a tale told by an idiot, full of sound and fury, signifying nothing." Good for Nancy. In sending along a copy of the letter to Senator William B. Giles, Nancy sought further sympathy: "Mr. Randolph's unprovoked attack on me commenced when I was borne down with the fatigue of nursing his nephew who was continually relapsing." Nancy clearly won in this battle of the Randolphs. Almost half a century later, social historian Rufus Griswold wrote that anyone who read the much-passed-around correspondence "will not easily forget the clever and dramatic management of Mrs. Morris, by which Randolph was exposed and outwitted."

The next year Gouverneur Morris died, having cut his evil nephews out of his will. But David Ogden still managed to have a hold on Nancy because her husband had cosigned a mortgage with the ne'er-do-well. Her estate was so reduced paying off the loan that she was afraid she'd be carted off to debtors' prison. But she once again scrimped and saved, forgoing the annuity Morris had provided for her, collected even the smallest of debts due her husband, and eventually, by planting corn, raising cattle, sheep, and hogs, and renting out pastures, she made the fields around Morrisania income producing. When her son came of age she was able to turn over his father's estate free and clear. She might have been helped by her husband, according to a ghost story of Nancy's. A couple of men knocked on her door one night looking for something valuable Morris had absconded with in his time in France. The shade of Gouverneur Morris stepped out of his portrait, goes the tale, scared off the harassers, and showed his wife where to find the treasure.

The young delegate to the Constitutional Convention had no way of knowing how interesting his love life would turn out to be back in 1787. What he was worrying about then was getting the words down on paper in time for the delegates to sign the document and disband, which they did on September 17, 1787. It was Eliza Powel's question to Benjamin Franklin about what kind of government the Convention had produced that sparked his famous answer, "a republic, Madam, if you can keep it." Three days later Franklin provided a somewhat longer assessment of the four-month-long session for his sister Jane: "You will see the Constitution we have proposed in the papers. The forming of it so as to accommodate all the different interests and views was a difficult task; and perhaps after all it may not be received with the same unanimity in the different states [as in] the Convention. . . . We have however done our best, and it must take its chance." The framers knew the Constitution would not be received with anything like unanimity; the ratification battle was on.

Ratification

Each signer of the new charter headed for his own state to fight for its endorsement. In an attempt to influence the whole nation, Alexander Hamilton, John Jay, and James Madison took up their pens and published what have come down in history as **The Federalist Papers**. (Betsey Hamilton often recopied her husband's drafts to make them more legible.) But much of the strategizing took place in private, at Mount Vernon. Charles Cotesworth Pinckney and his wife, Mary, stopped off on the way back to South Carolina from Philadelphia, among other supporters of the Constitution who came to call constantly. "We have not a single article of news but politics which I do not concern myself about," Martha Washington complained to her niece during the ratification battle. "I wish you could see the papers that come here every week as you are fond of reading them." Martha and George Washington had no illusions about what the outcome of the debate would mean for their personal future. If nine states ratified the Constitution, George Washington would be elected as the first president. A guest at Mount Vernon in October 1787 wrote to Thomas Jefferson in Paris that Washington "appears to be greatly against going into public life again," but, the letter continued, "I am fully of the opinion he may be induced to appear once more on the public stage of life. I form my opinion from what passed between us in a very long and serious conversation as well as from what I could gather from Mrs. Washington on the same subject."

Pennsylvania called its ratification convention for November, and friends from Philadelphia gathered at Mount Vernon. After her visit Eliza Powel mused to Martha: "I am clearly of the sentiment that our sex were never intended for the great affairs of life. They have happy talents for suggesting and can see the ends of the chain, but it requires masculine powers to discern the intermediate links and connect them with propriety." Eliza would use her talent "for suggesting" with her friend George Washington when it was needed. Robert and Gouverneur Morris combined a trip to Mount Vernon with business in Virginia and so were out of the state when Pennsylvania rowdily ratified the Constitution, the debate punctuated by rioting in the streets. On December 12 Molly Morris wrote to her husband: "As you know . . . I am something of a politician and could not forbear informing you that the federal government is agreed to by our convention. They finished last evening. Great demonstrations of joy were expressed by the populace. They did not forget YOU. We had three cheers." Delaware had been the first state to approve the Constitution, but Pennsylvania was the first big state, and its ratification was significant, but the voices of the Anti-Federalists, as they styled themselves, were growing louder; and the very question of union was up for grabs. Massachusetts would be the scene of the next major convention contest. In Europe, where the diplomats were keeping as close an eye on the proceedings as possible, Abigail Adams wrote to Thomas Jefferson: "By letters this day received from Boston it appears that a convention was agreed to by both houses, and that it is to meet the second Wednesday in January." When the convention in Massachusetts did meet, the opponents of the Constitution had the support of an articulate ally—Mercy Otis Warren.

The Warrens had been going through some hard years. Their oldest son, James, suffered a mental breakdown even as his parents were celebrating independence; then he recovered enough to go to war, be hit by a cannonball, and have part of his leg amputated. Their other sons also faced disease and difficulty—one was taken prisoner by the British, one contracted tuberculosis, one had trouble finding work. When in 1781 the Warrens bought their old nemesis Thomas Hutchinson's house in Milton Hill, it at first seemed a stroke of happy irony, but purchase of the estate brought on such large debts that the couple sold it and moved back to Plymouth seven years later. And James Warren was viewed by his colleagues in the Revolutionary cause as something of a quitter for his refusal to serve in public office, though he did run for Massachusetts governor in 1785 and was defeated.

But Mercy had stayed busy, working on her history of the Revolution and writing plays. First, in 1784, came **The Ladies of Castile,** featuring a heroine engaged in political struggles. The next year she published **The Sack of Rome;** again a woman played a pivotal part. Unlike Mercy's earlier plays, which were meant to be read, not performed, she was interested in seeing **The Sack of Rome** on the stage. She appealed to her old friend John Adams, asking if he could find a producer in London; he replied that "nothing American sells here." Then Shays' Rebellion, followed by the Constitutional Convention, brought Mercy publicly back into politics. Henry Warren, her son, and her nephew, Harrison Otis, both served in the militia that quelled the uprising, but the Warrens were nonetheless seen by some of their friends as supporters of Shays. When James Warren returned to the state legislature in 1787 and was elected Speaker of the House, he showed some sympathy for the western Massachusetts farmers and voiced criticism for the way they were handled. As Warren was defending the civil liberties of the rioters, the Constitutional Convention was gathering in Philadelphia.

Mercy Warren had been unhappy for some time with post-Revolutionary America. "We have weathered the shocks of war—we have hazarded all, and waded through rivers of blood to establish the independence of America and maintained the freedom of the human mind. But alas! If we have any national character, what a heterogeneous mixture," she exclaimed to Elbridge Gerry as early as

1783, "where are the virtues that will make a balance sufficient to support a commonwealth." Despite her concerns about the current government, Mercy was wary of the Convention from the beginning, as she made clear in letters to Catharine Macaulay. The secrecy of the proceedings bothered the defender of rights; Mercy questioned what the delegates were up to "when they ordered their doors to be locked, their members inhibited from all communications abroad, and when proposals were made that their journals should be burnt, lest their consultations and debates be viewed by the scrutinizing eye of a free people."

When she actually saw the proposed new form of government the "Old Republican," as some of the Anti-Federalists were called, she found little she liked. The idea of a central government over such a large country seemed absurd to her, the Senate too oligarchical, the terms of office too long; and where, she demanded, was a bill of rights? Jane Mecom wrote to her brother from Boston: "You perceive we have some quarrelsome spirits against the Constitution, but it does not appear to be those of superior judgment." Mercy Warren tried to convince the country that those with "superior judgment" opposed ratification. Over the pseudonym "A Columbian Patriot," she published **Observations on the New Constitution, and on the Federal and State Conventions.** By the time the pamphlet hit the streets in February 1788, some swift political deal making by proponents of the Constitution in Massachusetts, plus suggestions for amendments, had given them the edge in the ratification fight there. Mercy had her eye on the seven states that had not yet ratified. The pamphlet was printed in New York newspapers and reprinted in other states. It lashed out at the very idea of representative government, saying of the legislators, "the people have an undoubted right to reject their decisions, to call for a revision of their conduct, to depute others in their room." The Old Patriot echoed the words of the Declaration of Independence in her assertion of "unalienable rights" and insisted that "the origin of all power is in the people, and that they have an incontestable right to check the creatures of their own creation," meaning the elected officials. Mercy would approve of recalls.

Sentiments like those expressed by Mercy Warren and other Anti-Federalists made George Washington wonder whether there would ever be a new Constitution. Throughout the spring of 1788 he continued to receive his allies at Mount Vernon, for reasons of both politics and pleasure. Molly and Robert Morris's boys had returned from school in Europe, after five years away, but their father wasn't in Philadelphia to greet them. He had been in Virginia tending to his tobacco business for close to six months and Molly was getting increasingly irritated at his long stay away from home: "It is indeed too long now that you have been absent from us. I find my patience indeed, my dear Mr. Morris, most exhausted." She wanted to know "whether I and the boys are to meet you at Mount Vernon or whether your return home will be so soon as to make it unnecessary." George Washington's diary gives us the answer. His entry for Saturday, May 17: "Mrs. Morris, Miss Morris and her two sons (lately arrived from Europe) came here about eleven o'clock."

On May 23 South Carolina became the eighth state out of the nine needed to ratify the Constitution, with Governor Thomas Pinckney leading the fight for the charter, and Henry Laurens, Jr. and Martha's husband, David Ramsay, supporting him. In June battles royal were under way in New York and Virginia. The Jays and Hamiltons threw dinner parties to lobby Convention delegates. "We are entertaining many important people," Betsey told her folks, "the talk at the dinner table is all of the Constitution." Madison was making the case in his home state of Virginia, but he was up against such powerful men as Patrick Henry, George Mason, Richard Henry Lee, and young James Monroe. John Marshall sided with Madison, and everyone knew where George Washington stood. Still, from his command post at Mount Vernon, the general sent letters to the Convention, and received reports from it, keeping the express riders on the move. Then Virginia's governor, Edmund Randolph, one of the few delegates to the Constitutional Convention who had refused to sign the final document, changed his position. He could endorse the charter with the understanding that amendments, a bill of rights, would be added. Randolph took a lot of heat for the switch, but it was effective.

When the New York Convention met in Poughkeepsie, John Jay kept his wife apprised of the proceedings, and Sally, who was at Liberty Hall with
her parents and children, sent him news of what
was happening elsewhere. First she let him know
that his propaganda in favor of the Constitution
was getting good play: "The pamphlet entitled an
address to the inhabitants of New York, etc. has
been received in this state with great approbation,
nor has the tribute of applause been with-held
from the author that usually accompanies his writings." She knew he needed bucking up because he
was in an uphill battle. "The opposition to the proposed Constitution appears formidable, the more
so from numbers than other considerations," Jay
somewhat churlishly reported. "I do not despair on
the one hand, although I see much room for apprehension on the other." Then, on June 21, 1788,
New Hampshire, with Josiah Bartlett leading the
supporters, became the ninth state to ratify. The
Constitution was officially the law of the land. Sally
was excited to hear the news, which she included in
a postscript to a newsy family letter: "I have just
heard that New Hampshire has adopted the proposed Constitution, and congratulate you upon it. I
wish it may prove a stimulus to your convention
and should rejoice still more were they to anticipate
Virginia." Virginia and New York remained crucial—such large states needed to be brought into
the fold.

On June 25, by a vote of 89 to 79, Virginia accepted the Constitution, with a list of suggested

amendments that became the basis for the Bill of Rights. On the twenty-eighth George Washington recorded in his diary: "The inhabitants of Alexandria having received the news of the ratification of the proposed Constitution by this state, and that of New Hampshire . . . determined on public rejoicings, part of which to be in a dinner, to which this family was invited." Alexander Hamilton had managed to postpone a vote in the New York Convention until word came from Virginia and New Hampshire, hoping that ratification by Virginia would force New York's hand. Sally Jay was eager to know if it had: "every one is anxious to hear the effect which the accession of Virginia has had upon your convention, and the expectation of having my own curiosity gratified on that subject, as well as my solicitude about your health increases my impatience to hear from you." The effect of Virginia's vote was what Hamilton and Jay had counted on. Still it was close, 30 to 27, when New York cast its lot with the other states on July 26.

As the states ratified, celebrations—some carefully planned, some impromptu—broke out around the country. In August the men of Waterford, New York, processed in honor of the Constitution. The next day the women of Waterford followed suit. Newspapers around the country picked up the story of women marching for a political purpose. Even Mercy Warren fell in line behind the Constitution once it officially became law. Still, to Catharine Macaulay, she worried whether it would ever work: "We are too poor for

monarchy—too wise for despotism, and too dissipated, selfish, and extravagant for republicanism."
It took some diehards against the Constitution
years to accept it. North Carolina only signed on
after the Congress had approved a Bill of Rights, in
November 1789. Rhode Island didn't ratify until
May 1790, and then only under economic pressure
from the other New England states. Whatever the
concerns, the new government would soon be in
place. In November the Congress created by the
Articles of Confederation, having named New
York City as the temporary nation's capital, adjourned for the last time. Elections would be called
under the Constitution. There was no question as
to who would win for president, but there was
some politicking around the second spot.

Abigail and John Adams had left London in May,
eager to return home, but unclear about John's future. Thomas Jefferson was sad to see them go: "I
have considered you while in London as my neighbor, and look forward to the moment of your departure from thence as to an epoch of much regret
and concern for me . . . the days will seem
long . . . before I too am to rejoin my native country," he wrote to Abigail. "It will lighten them to
me if you will continue to honor me with your correspondence." Abigail replied, thanking Jefferson
for his kindness and friendship, adding, "retiring to
my own little farm feeding my poultry and improving my garden has more charms for my fancy than
residing at the Court of St. James where I seldom
meet with characters so inoffensive as my hens and

chickens, or minds so well improved as my garden." In fact, Abigail had no intention of returning to her "little farm." "You never can live in that house when you return," her sister Mary had flatly told her a year earlier. "Mr. Adams will be employed in the public business . . . that house will not be large enough for you." So Abigail was primed when her cousin Cotton Tufts sent word that a large house in their hometown of Braintree, Massachusetts, was for sale. She told him to buy it and sent instructions for painting and papering, then packed up her furniture and headed for home. (Nabby and her husband and child sailed for New York.)

When Abigail and John Adams arrived in Boston, they were amazed at their reception. Crowds of citizens gathered to greet them; Governor Hancock, who had never been a friend, treated them like royalty. They finally managed to get home to Braintree where the house was nowhere near ready for them, and when the furniture finally arrived, it was damaged. (Sounds like the typical move today.) Compared with the grand houses they had lived in abroad, the new house seemed awfully small. Abigail warned her daughter to "be sure you wear no feathers" if she came for a visit—they would hit the ceiling. By fall the couple had more or less settled in, and Abigail traveled to New York where Nabby had just delivered a second baby. While there, the grandmother tacked on some political reporting to her domestic duties. About politics, she pledged to John: "I design to be vastly prudent

I assure you, hear all and say little." Not very likely.
John Jay called on her at Nabby's in-laws, she visited with Sally Jay and Lucy Knox, and Abigail
heard encouraging news about her husband's vice
presidential prospects from Alexander Hamilton.

On January 7, 1789, George Washington recorded in his diary: "Went up to the election of an
Elector of President and Vice-President." He
knew his time as a private citizen wouldn't last
much longer. The newly created House of Representatives and Senate met on March 4, but, as
Pennsylvania senator Robert Morris wrote to his
wife, "There were only eight Senators and thirteen
assembly men, and before we can proceed to business there must be twelve Senators and thirty
members of the assembly." Finally, on April 6, the
two houses of Congress met to count the ballots of
the Electoral College. The results: George Washington, 69; John Adams, 34. Washington still holds
the title of the only president to receive the unanimous vote of the electors. Messengers went out to
inform officially the first president and vice president of the United States of their assignments.
John Adams was formally notified on April 12,
George Washington on April 14. That night the
general went to see his mother in Fredericksburg
for the last time. Then, on April 16, the old war-
horse left for one more battle. "About ten o'clock I
bade adieu to Mount Vernon, to private life, and to
domestic felicity; and with a mind oppressed with
more anxious and painful sensations than I have
words to express, set out for New York," he sighed

in his diary, "with the best dispositions to render service to my country in obedience to its call, but with less hope of answering its expectations." Martha Washington was even less happy. "I am truly sorry to tell that the General is gone to New York," she wrote to a nephew on April 20, "when or whether he will ever come home again, God only knows. I think it was much too late for him to go into public life again, but it was not to be avoided. Our family will be deranged as I must soon follow him." And so she soon did, in a triumphal procession to New York, where Martha Washington took on the undefined and difficult role of the first First Lady.

CHAPTER SEVEN

After 1789:
Raising a Nation

MARTHA WASHINGTON

Assembling in New York

People turned out in droves to get a glimpse of President-elect George Washington as his carriage traveled triumphantly from Mount Vernon to New York. All along the route the general was greeted by the ringing of church bells, the roaring of cannons, the ritual of ceremony. When he crossed the Delaware River, as he had done in the dead of night so many years before to surprise the British at Trenton, Washington passed under a soaring, evergreen-swathed arch erected on the bridge. The women of the city had collected the money for the huge structure and directed its construction, which featured a banner proclaiming "THE DEFENDER OF THE MOTHERS WILL BE THE PROTECTOR OF THE DAUGHTERS." The women and girls of Trenton, all dressed in white, strew petals as they serenaded the first president:

> Virgins fair and matrons grave,
> Those thy conquering arm did save,
> Build for thee triumphal bowers;
> Strew, ye fair, his way with flowers!
> Strew your hero's way with flowers.

Washington expressed "his acknowledgements to the matrons and young ladies who received him in so novel and grateful a manner at the Triumphal Arch" and, writing of himself in the third person, promised the women of Trenton, "the innocent appearance of the white-robed choir who met him with the gratulatory song, have made such an impression on his remembrance as, he assures them, will never be effaced." I bet not. A gleaming barge, piloted by thirteen men also garbed in white, carried him across the Hudson from New Jersey to New York in a parade where "boat after boat and sloop after sloop, gaily dressed in all their naval ornaments, added to our train, and made a most splendid appearance," a member of the greeting committee wrote to his wife. "As we approached the harbor our train increased, and the huzzahing and shouts of joy seemed to add life to this brilliant scene. At this moment a number of porpoises came playing amongst us, as if they had risen up to know what was the cause of all this happiness. We now discovered the shores to be crowded with thousands of people—men, women, and children—nay, I may venture to say, tens of thousands . . . heads standing as thick as ears of corn before the harvest." Washington then walked the half-mile to the house Congress had arranged for him: "The houses were filled with gentlemen and ladies the whole distance . . . and the windows, to the highest stories, were illuminated by the sparkling eyes of innumerable companies of ladies, who seemed to vie with each other in showing their joy on this great occasion."

It was an auspicious, if over the top, beginning. But on Inauguration Day, April 30, the president put the pageantry aside and appeared in a plain American-made brown suit to take his simple oath. Every act was symbolic, and this one signaled that the pomp of European courts would not be practiced in the new republic. There was, however, a resplendent inaugural ball. Many years later, Betsey Hamilton still remembered it in glowing detail: "I was at the inauguration ball . . . which was given early in May at the Assembly Rooms on Broadway, above Wall Street. It was attended by the President and Vice-President, the Cabinet officers, a majority of the members of Congress, the French and Spanish Ministers, and military and civil officers, with their wives and daughters. Mrs. Washington had not yet arrived in New York from Mount Vernon, and did not until three weeks later. On that occasion every woman who attended the ball was presented with a fan, prepared in Paris, with ivory frame and when open displayed a likeness of Washington in profile." Doesn't sound all **that** down-home.

A good deal of hand-wringing was going on about just what rules of protocol. Washington's advisers discussed exactly how he and his wife should entertain, whether they should accept private invitations or gifts, and how they should be addressed. The Senate debate over titles revealed a division in the just-formed government between those who were ready to pattern the system after a monarchy and thought a grand title like "His Serene Highness" was appropriate and those who insisted on fidelity to "republican principles" in favor of the simpler "President of the United States," which was what the much more democratic House of Representatives had opted for. One Senate committee actually proposed "His Highness the President of the United States of America, and Protector of their Liberties," and John Adams argued so strenuously for an elaborate presidential title that the politicians took to calling the vice president "His Rotundity." Benjamin Franklin had another suggestion for the vice president: "His Superfluous Excellency." Many a vice president over the centuries has agreed with that assessment. Washington had been thinking about the issues of etiquette and dress for some time. He had written on the subject to New Jersey poet Annis Stockton the previous summer when she sent a message of congratulations on the ratification of the Constitution. In reply, he congratulated the men and women who had made the new nation possible, then posed a question: "And now that I am speaking of your sex, I will ask whether they are not capable of doing something towards introducing federal fashions and national manners?" To make this new system work, Washington knew he would have to depend on the ladies, and one lady in particular. His wife would be required to set a tone both dignified and democratic. And in May, after she had organized everything at Mount Vernon and put her niece Fanny in charge, Martha Washington left home, as she had so many times before, to join her husband.

With her ten-year-old granddaughter and eight-year-old grandson in tow, and George's nephew Robert Lewis escorting her, Martha embarked on what turned out to be another grand procession to New York. In Baltimore the fact that she was feted with fireworks and serenaded by musicians was considered big news by several journals. In Pennsylvania "we were met by the President of the state with the city troop of horse and conducted safe to Grays Ferry, where a number of ladies and gentlemen came to meet me," Martha wrote to Fanny. The entourage proceeded to Philadelphia, where church bells rang, cannons fired, and citizens cheered. In response, First Lady Martha Washington delivered her maiden speech: "Standing in the carriage [she] thanked the troops who had escorted her, and the citizens also." The traveling party stayed with Molly Morris, who along with her two daughters accompanied Martha to New York, with newspaper reporters trailing the carriage. After stopping on the way for a visit with the Livingstons at Liberty Hall, the women were met by their husbands on the New Jersey side of the Hudson River. George Washington and Robert Morris escorted their wives to New York on "the fine barge you have seen so much said of in the papers with the same oars men that carried the P. to New York," Martha wrote home. Her grandson seemed dazed by "the great parade that was made for us all the way we came. The governor of the state met me as soon as we landed, and led me up to the house, the paper will tell you how I was complimented on my landing." She was "complimented" by a huge crowd chanting, "God Bless Lady Washington." If Martha Washington hadn't realized that she would be playing a very public role before that enthusiastic greeting, she certainly knew it after. But she didn't need lessons in political savvy—the wealthy Mrs. Washington arrived wearing a homespun gown, a forerunner of Pat Nixon's good Republican cloth coat.

The very next day, official visitors arrived to be "received" by Lady Washington. Soon a schedule was set up for receptions at the Cherry Street house. Tuesday would be the day for the president to greet gentlemen guests; on Fridays Mrs. Washington would entertain anyone who wanted to come, providing they were properly dressed. One visitor reported that the receptions "were numerously attended by all that was fashionable, elegant, and refined in society; but there were no places for the intrusion of the rabble in crowds, or for the mere coarse and boisterous partisan—the vulgar electioneerer—or the impudent place hunter." Only two days after she arrived in New York, Martha hosted the first official reception of the republic, part of a schedule so busy that she complained to Fanny, "I have not had one half hour to myself since the day of my arrival. My first care was to get the children to a good school which they are both very much pleased at." Think of it: she had young children to worry about while trying to figure out her new job. And they weren't particularly easy children. Later that summer Martha described Nelly Custis as "a little wild creature." And then, as now, the president's wife had to worry about her appearance: "My hair is set and dressed every day," she told her niece, and while she was first lady she ordered "a set of teeth . . . make them something bigger and thicker in front and a small matter longer."

The Congress had provided a house for the chief executive, but not so for the vice president. (An official vice-presidential residence was not established until 1974.) And John Adams was puzzled about where to live, since his salary had not yet been decided. He stayed at the home of Sally and John Jay, who would be the first chief justice of the Supreme Court, while he waited to learn what his circumstances would be. Jauntily, he assured Abigail, back home in Braintree, that "we can conform to our circumstances. And if they determine that we must live on little, we will not spend much." Easy for him to say. She was busy trying to sell off property so she could move: "I have been trying to dispose of the stock on hand, but no purchaser appears." But Abigail was more interested in what was happening in New York than what her own trials and tribulations might be at home: "When I read the debates of the House, I could not but be surprised at their permitting them to be open, and thought it would have been a happy circumstance if they could have found a Dr. Johnson for the Editor of them." She clearly wasn't impressed by the rhetoric of the new representatives. John wanted that wit by his side. He sent ever more urgent letters insisting that she come to New York as soon as possible.

With the help of his son-in-law, William Smith, John had found a house about a mile outside of town, in what now would be Greenwich Village. It had no furniture, so Abigail would have to ship theirs from home, and he wanted her to get right on it. Forget dealing with the property, he pleaded, just come: "As to money to bear your expenses you must if you can borrow of some friend enough to bring you here. If you cannot borrow enough, you must sell horses, oxen, sheep, cows, anything at any rate rather than not come on. If no one will take the place leave it to the birds of the air and beasts of the field." She somewhat impatiently explained that packing up their furniture and leaving was not that easy. Still, Abigail was keeping a close eye on the players in New York, and she didn't like what she was reading about Congressman James Madison: "I do not like his politics," she pronounced. Madison was beginning to break away from Washington and Hamilton, his allies at the Constitutional Convention, to champion individual and states' rights. Congress was only a couple of months old, and nascent partisanship was already brewing. John sweetened the pot for his wife's move to New York: he invited their daughter, son-in-law, and grandchildren to live with them. Having finally found someone to occupy their house in Braintree, and with her son Charles and niece Louisa Smith as company, Abigail moved to New York in June and immediately went to call on Martha Washington.

Somewhat rapturously, Abigail wrote to her sister Mary about the visit: "She received me with great ease and politeness. She is plain in her dress, but that plainness is the best of every article. . . . Her hair is white, her teeth beautiful, her person rather short than otherways, hardly so large as my ladyship, and if I was to speak sincerely, I think she is a much better figure. Her manners are modest and unassuming, dignified and feminine, not the tincture of hauteur about her." Abigail and Martha would spend a good deal of time together in the coming years, on both official and unofficial occasions.

The official entertaining was onerous, to say the least. Protocol demanded that the women pay calls on each other and receive calls from visitors. They also dutifully held regular receptions, called levees, stuffy and tedious affairs. Here is Abigail's description of Martha Washington's Friday-night entertainment: "The form of the reception is this, the servants announce and [an aide to the president] receives every lady at the door and hands her up to Mrs. Washington, to whom she makes a most respectful curtsey and then is seated without noticing any of the rest of the company. The President then comes up and speaks to the Lady, which he does with a grace, dignity and ease that leaves Royal George far behind him. The company are entertained with ice creams and lemonade and retire at their pleasure performing the same ceremony when they quit the room." Women used the occasion of the receptions to get the attention of the president, according to his grandson: "There were some well remembered belles of that day who imagined themselves to be favorites with him." One particularly memorable evening was recounted by Betsey Hamilton: "Ostrich plumes, waving high overhead, formed a part of the evening head-dress of a fashionable belle at that time. Miss McEvers . . . had plumes unusually high. The ceiling of the drawing room of the president's house near Franklin Square was rather low, and Miss McEvers' plumes were ignited by the flames of the chandelier. Major Jackson, Washington's aide-de-camp, sprang to the rescue of the young lady and extinguished the fire by smothering it with his hand."

As Abigail became a regular attendee at Martha's "public day," she assumed her own place: "My station is always at the right hand of Mrs. W. . . . I find it sometimes occupied, but on such an occasion the President never fails of seeing that it is relinquished for me, and having removed ladies several times, they have now learnt to rise and give it me, but this is between ourselves, as **all distinction** you know is unpopular." Abigail instituted her own Monday-night receptions, plus Wednesday-night dinners; other women held weekly gatherings as well. Lucy Knox, whose husband became secretary of war, chose Wednesday. (Lucy had grown so fat that Nabby Adams Smith had written to her mother the year before: "Her size is enormous, I am frightened when I look at her; I verily believe her waist is as large as three of yours, at least.") Sally Jay, the wife of the first chief justice, entertained on Thursday. (Nabby was kinder to Sally: "Mrs. Jay dresses gaily and showily, but is very pleasing upon a slight acquaintance.") Tuesday it was the turn of the wife of the British consul-general. Though much of it sounds silly, these weekly events served a purpose. Their formality seemed appropriate to diplomats and dignitaries accustomed to royal courts abroad. But they were open to all well-dressed comers, lending a democratic air to what came to be called the republican court.

In addition to George and Martha's receptions, there were formal dinners as well. And what dinners they were. One guest described a dinner at the president's house: "There was an elegant variety of roast beef, veal, turkey, ducks, fowls, hams, etc.;

puddings, jellies, oranges, apples, nuts, almonds, figs, raisins, and a variety of wines and punch." Putting all that together required quite a staff. For a while Washington was able to prevail on Samuel Fraunces, the owner of the tavern where the general had said good-bye to his officers, to serve as his majordomo, but then Fraunces left and the first couple was reduced to advertising in the newspapers:

A Cook

Is wanted for the family of the President of the United States. No one need apply who is not perfect in the business, and can bring indubitable testimonials of sobriety, honesty and attention to the duties of the station.

The cook didn't have to worry about recipes— Martha had plenty of those, including the ones collected in a cookbook owned by her first mother-in-law and passed along to her. It must have been compiled in the seventeenth century, but there's much in it that's recognizable.

Congress had determined that the first family should accept no private invitations, in order to avoid the appearance of favoritism, and Martha was finding her confinement fairly miserable. "I live a very dull life here and know nothing that passes in the town," she told Fanny in October 1789. "Indeed I think I am more like a state prisoner than anything else. There are certain bounds set for me which I must not depart from, and as I can not do as I like, I am obstinate and stay at home a great deal." Betsey Hamilton remembered hearing something similar from the president's wife: " 'They call me First Lady in the land and think I must be extremely happy,' she would say almost bitterly at times and add, 'They might more properly call me the Chief State Prisoner.' " How many first ladies since then have felt the same way?

The social life of the administration predictably came under attack from the Anti-Federalist press, but the receptions and dinners provided places for politicians to come together outside the halls of Congress, where there was a huge amount of work to be done. The executive departments had to be established, plus the federal judiciary, and members had promised a bill of rights. As Congress established departments, the president officially named Cabinet members. Henry Knox was confirmed as secretary of war and Alexander Hamilton as the first secretary of the treasury in September. While he was waiting for Congress to establish the office, the thirty-two-year-old Hamilton had spent the summer working on a plan for the national debt. He also seems to have spent some time wooing his wife's sister, Angelica Church, who was visiting in New York from her home in England without her husband and children.

If Hamilton and Angelica were having an affair, it seems unlikely that Betsey, who by now had four children, knew anything about it. She wrote her sister an anguished letter when Angelica sailed for London, begging her "to make your absence short." Betsey said Angelica should tell her husband, John Church, "of the happiness he will give me in bringing you to me, not to me alone but to fond parents, sisters, friends, and to my Hamilton who has for you all the affection of a fond own brother." Or perhaps as something else. Despite his declarations of undying love for Betsey, later events made clear that naming a tomcat after him would still be an apt joke on Alexander Hamilton.

It took until early the next year for Thomas Jefferson to assume the job of secretary of state. Jefferson had stayed in Paris through the opening shots of the French Revolution, delighting in the storming of the Bastille and leaving with some reluctance. He and his daughters had arrived back at Monticello in December 1789, after a leisurely trip through Virginia from the port city of Norfolk. Along the way, while visiting friends and relatives, Patsy took up with her cousin Thomas Randolph, and since Jefferson needed to be in New York to take on his new assignment, the couple arranged a hasty wedding. Thomas Randolph, like his sister Nancy, had found himself an outcast from home after his father married a young bride. So the couple stayed at Monticello.

Soon after Washington named his cabinet, he consulted with some members—Hamilton, Knox, and Jay, who was acting as secretary of state until Jefferson arrived—about the advisability of a tour through the Northeast during the coming congressional recess to learn "the temper and disposition of the inhabitants towards the new government."

The president's advisers all thought it was a good idea, and after a pleasant family outing with the Adams household, Washington set off on October 15 for a trip that sounds very much like one a politician would make today. He was led on tours of farms, fisheries, and "manufactories," wined and dined by local politicians, and visited by veterans. Also included in the president's diary are careful notations on all the "ladies" he met. In Cambridge, Massachusetts, arches over the street proclaimed "To the Man who unites all hearts" and "To Columbia's favorite Son." Another arch "was handsomely ornamented and over the Center of it a canopy was erected twenty feet high with the American Eagle perched on top." The women wore sashes with the American eagle at one end, the French fleur-de-lis at the other, and the initials "G. W." in gold in the middle. Modern presidential advance staff have nothing on the first president.

In New Hampshire, Washington preserved for posterity that he attended an "assembly where there were about 75 well dressed, and many of them very handsome ladies—among whom (as was also the case at the Salem and Boston Assemblies) were a greater proportion with much blacker hair than are usually seen in the Southern States." Aside from the ladies, Washington saw much to give him encouragement on his tour, as he wrote to Catharine Macaulay: "I have lately made a tour through the Eastern States. I found the country, in a great degree, recovered from the ravages of war, the towns flourishing, and the people delighted with a government instituted by themselves and for their own good. . . . By what I have just observed, I think you will be persuaded that the ill-boding politicians who prognosticated that America would never enjoy any fruits from her independence, and that she would be obliged to have recourse to a foreign power for protection, have at least been mistaken." It gives you a sense of how precarious the idea of nationhood still was.

The president returned to New York on November 13, "where I found Mrs. Washington and the rest of the family all well. And it being Mrs. Washington's Night to receive visits, a pretty large company of ladies and gentlemen were present." No wonder Martha felt like a prisoner. Her husband comes home from a long trip, and she has to entertain the city. But Martha was putting the best face on her situation. Having received a letter from Mercy Otis Warren praising her as the person "who by general consent would be more likely to obtain the suffrages of the sex," Martha replied that though she would have preferred to be at Mount Vernon, where she had hoped "we should have been left to grow old in solitude and tranquility together," she and George had accepted their new life. "In his late tour through the eastern states, by every public and by every private information which has come to him, I am persuaded that he has experienced nothing to make him repent his having acted from what he conceived to be alone a sense of indispensable duty." She was determined to be happy, Martha insisted, and convinced "that the greater part of our happiness or misery depends upon our dispositions, and not upon our circumstances." It was a philosophy that had served the now fifty-eight-year-old matron well all of her life.

On April 17, 1790, a year after George Washington left Mount Vernon, Benjamin Franklin died. Thomas Jefferson, on his way from Monticello to New York in March, had stopped off in Philadelphia to see his old friend and mentor and found him "on the bed of sickness from which he never rose." At age eighty-four, Franklin knew the end had come, and when his daughter, Sally, offered encouraging words about him living many years longer, he replied, "I hope not."

Jane Mecom received the news of her brother's death from Sally's husband, Richard Bache, who informed her of the "event which I know will be a sore affliction to your affectionate breast. . . . Madam, I do most sincerely condole with you on the loss of so excellent a friend and brother. . . . We had been in daily expectation of his getting better, but nature was at last worn out." Twenty thousand mourners, the largest gathering in the history of the continent, showed up at the old statesman's funeral on April 21. Then there was the will: "My fine crab-tree walking-stick, with a gold head curiously wrought in the form of the cap of liberty, I give to my friend, and the friend of mankind, General Washington. If it were a scepter, he has merited it and would become it." To his sister Jane Mecom, Franklin left the house she lived in in Boston plus a healthy annuity. To his grandson Benjamin Franklin Bache, the old publisher left his typesetting and printing materials. To his daughter, Sally Bache, and her husband, Richard, he left his Philadelphia real estate and household goods. Franklin also willed to Sally a gift to him from the French government—a miniature of Louis XVI surrounded by 408 diamonds with the proviso "that she would not form any of those diamonds into ornaments either for herself or daughters, and thereby introduce or countenance the expensive, vain, and useless fashion of wearing jewels in this country." He never let up, even in death. But Sally had the last word. She didn't make the diamonds into jewelry—she sold them, and just about everything else her father left her, including the house Deborah had so nervously decorated. Sally took the money and ran—she and Richard went on an extended trip to England, the country for which her father had abandoned his family for so many years.

Not long after Franklin's death, George Washington appeared to be dying as well. In May 1790 he developed pneumonia, and the doctors called to attend to him didn't think the president would make it. It was a terrifying development for the country, as Abigail Adams told her sister after Washington pulled through: "At this early day when neither our finances are arranged nor our government sufficiently cemented to promise duration, his death would I fear have had most disastrous consequences." It seems unfathomable now, but then the death of the president could have caused the dissolution of the nation. In a letter to Mercy Otis Warren, Martha Washington said the only person who wasn't worried was her husband: "He seemed less concerned himself as to the event, than perhaps almost any other person in the United States."

Abigail was right to worry about the finances not being arranged. The issue of the national debt was causing rifts in Congress that would soon develop into the formation of distinct political parties. Alexander Hamilton's three-part plan to deal with the millions of dollars borrowed during the Revolution was the hottest topic of the day. Hamilton heard from his sister-in-law Angelica Church in London: "I am impatient to hear in what manner your budget has been received, and extremely anxious for your success." Abigail Adams was equally anxious: "I hope to see an adoption of all the state debts, and ways and means devised to pay them," she wrote to her uncle Cotton Tufts. She saw that decision as "one of the main pillars upon which the duration of the government rests." Abigail joined Sally Jay for her first trip to hear a congressional debate on the treasury secretary's financial propositions. Women were so regularly attending sessions of Congress that a "Ladies' Gallery" had been set aside for them. (A section of seats in the balconies above the House and Senate still bear the name "Ladies' Gallery," but anyone can now sit in them.)

Hamilton's plan to reimburse other countries what was owed them, plus pay the domestic debt

352 / Cokie Roberts

incurred by the Continental Congress, was fairly well accepted. But his proposal that the federal government assume state debts, estimated at $25 million, met with fierce resistance. Having already begun paying off what they had borrowed, the southern states had no desire to be taxed in order to bail out their northern compatriots. In the Senate, Hamilton had the support of his father-in-law, Philip Schuyler, and the other senator from New York, Rufus King, who had moved from Massachusetts to take up residence in his wife's state. But in the House, Hamilton faced a formidable opponent—his old collaborator, James Madison, who had the votes to defeat the treasury secretary. Ironically, it was Madison's mentor, Jefferson, who brokered the deal that saved the day. Jefferson hosted a dinner party where representatives of the southern states agreed to go along with the debt assumption if members from the northern states agreed to a permanent national capital on the Potomac River, bordering Virginia and Maryland. Congress voted for the compromise and decided to move to Philadelphia until the new federal city was ready for occupancy.

New Yorkers, who were going to lose the substantial economic benefits derived from hosting the government, were livid. They suspected that Robert Morris, with all of his financial interests in Philadelphia, was responsible for the relocation of the capital, and newspaper cartoons cruelly caricatured the senator from Pennsylvania. As mastermind behind the move, Morris had some help from his wife, Molly. One night at dinner at the president's house, a trifle was served for dessert that had been made with spoiled cream. Molly Morris tasted it and announced that the capital had to move to Philadelphia because you couldn't get any decent cream in New York.

Molly Morris might have been happy with the decision, but Abigail Adams was distressed. First of all, Philadelphia—the nation's biggest city—was an expensive place to live, and the family was hurting for money. Abigail blamed John for their financial troubles: "If Doctor Tufts and my ladyship had been left to the sole management of our affairs, they would have been upon a more profitable footing," she bragged to her sister. But Abigail's real complaint wasn't financial—it was emotional. She loved her house and gardens in New York and didn't want to leave them: "I feel low spirited and heartless," she complained to Mary. "I am going amongst another new set of company, to form new acquaintances, to make and receive a hundred ceremonious visits, not one of ten from which I shall derive any pleasure or satisfaction." And her daughter and grandchildren would be staying in New York. Alexander and Betsey Hamilton would be leaving family behind as well. Betsey's father, Philip Schuyler, would have no reason to relocate to Philadelphia after his Senate defeat by Aaron Burr. Martha Washington, who had already moved once during the year to a bigger house in New York, accepted the decision with equanimity: "I have been so long accustomed to conform to events which are governed by the public voice," she wrote to a friend, "I hardly dare indulge any personal wishes which cannot yield to that." It was the story of her life.

Philadelphia and South

Martha Washington had no reason to dread moving to Philadelphia the way Abigail Adams did. During the war the general's wife had spent many a pleasant stay there and made many friends. The first family rented from Robert and Molly Morris the house Washington had stayed in during the Constitutional Convention. It needed a good deal of work to accommodate all of the family and staff, and while Martha and George paid a visit to Mount Vernon, the president instructed his secretary on what was needed: "Mrs. Morris, who is a notable lady in family arrangements, can give you much information in all the conveniencies about the house and buildings; and I dare say would rather consider it as a compliment to be consulted in these matters (as she is so near) than a trouble to give her opinion of them." Even with Molly Morris on the case, the house wasn't ready when the Washingtons moved in. Abigail Adams, who also arrived to find work in progress, wrote Nabby that she had heard "I am much better off than Mrs. Washington will be when she arrives, for that house is not likely to be completed this year." Adams had taken a house outside of town because it was cheaper than the ones in the city. Unoccupied for four years, it was cold and everyone in the family was sick, but Abigail exclaimed to Mary, "In the midst of all this, the gentlemen and ladies solicitous to manifest their respect were visiting us every day from 12 to 3 o'clock in the midst of rooms heaped with boxes, trunks, cases, etc." The calling had already begun, and the weekly receptions resumed immediately, with Nelly Custis now old enough now to help her grandmother by passing the sugar and cream. (Nelly still seemed somewhat untamed. Eliza Powel once told her, "You look as if your clothes were thrown on with a pitchfork!")

The official dinners were a little grander than the ones in New York; after all, there was Philadelphia society to compete with. And there were Philadelphia prices to cope with. Lucy Knox had ordered furniture to be made in New York and shipped. "We have had two severe storms," Abigail Adams told her daughter. "Poor Mrs. Knox is in great tribulation about her furniture. The vessel sailed the day before the first storm." (The furniture must have made it—a mahogany wardrobe Lucy bought that spring is on display at Montpelier, the General Henry Knox Museum in Maine.) The $3,000 a year paid to Cabinet members presented a challenge to the families that weren't personally wealthy. Seeing Betsey Hamilton gamely trying to manage the family finances, one of Alexander's friends teased him: "I have learned from a friend of yours that she has as much merit as your treasurer as you have as treasurer of the wealth of the United States." Despite the inconveniences, the families of the administration soon settled in, and by March, after legislation establishing a national bank had been approved and Vermont had entered the union as the fourteenth state, Abigail seemed downright excited: "Our public affairs never looked more prosperous. The people feel the beneficial effects of the new government by an increasing credit both at home and abroad and a confidence in their rulers." She told her sister about dinner at the Washingtons' the night before: "The President sets off this week on a tour to those parts of his dominions which he has not yet visited, Georgia and North Carolina." Washington was embarking on another grand tour—this time of the South.

On March 21, 1791, soon after Congress recessed, President Washington was off on a four-month journey to determine whether reports of southern dissatisfaction with his presidency were true. If they were, Washington had threatened to resign. As with his northern trip, the president would stay only at public inns rather than accept offers of hospitality from individuals who might seem to be currying favor. (That's the reason for all those "GEORGE WASHINGTON SLEPT HERE" signs up and down the East Coast.) In the South, where such hospitality was expected and happily extended, most travelers stayed in private homes, and inns were few and far between. They also weren't very good—in his diary, Washington refers repeatedly to his lodgings as "indifferent." (There was one notable exception along the way, in North Carolina: "Went to a Colonel Allan's supposing it to be a public house; where we were very kindly and well entertained without knowing it was at his expense, until it was too late to rectify the mistake." The entourage had unwittingly dropped in on a private home!) As with his northern tour, Washington was seeing the sights, including a new canal connecting the cities of Richmond and Westham, Virginia, and taking the political pulse of the region. "In the course of my inquiries," he wrote on April 12, "I cannot discover that any discontents prevail among the people at large, at the proceedings of Congress." And as with the other tour, the president was greeted with great ceremony and entertained at endless balls all over the South. This time too, wherever he went, he commented on the ladies. But there were a couple of ladies in particular to whom Washington wanted to pay his respects.

After the general's caravan made its way into South Carolina on April 27, 1791, Thomas Pinckney, who was then a member of Congress, was alerted by a friend that Washington "will go tomorrow to Georgetown and intends dining at Mrs. Horry's on Sunday." The president stopped in the port town of Georgetown, South Carolina, which he judged to have not more than five or six hundred people, and was "introduced to upwards of fifty ladies who had assembled on the occasion." On May 1 his entourage "left Georgetown about six o'clock, and crossing the Santee Creek at the town and the Santee River twelve miles from it," he recorded in his diary, "we breakfasted and dined at Mrs. Horry's."

When the president arrived at Harriott Pinckney Horry's plantation, Hampton, he was greeted by the lady of the house and her mother, Eliza Pinckney. The women and the girls of the family sported sashes and headbands with Washington's picture and words of welcome. The portico of the plantation house had recently been enlarged, reflecting the profits that Harriott, who had been managing the property for years with the help of her mother, was extracting from her rice plantings. Though indigo remained a cash crop, the loss of the British price supports made it less valuable. Still, Washington was so interested in the blue dye that the next month he sent the women a plow to improve the planting of indigo seeds. (Since his diary tells us that he stayed at Hampton for two meals, the president must have liked the food. Harriott Horry was a famous cook, and her recipe book survives. It includes instructions on how to "Dress a Calves Head.") As he prepared to leave Hampton, the president commented on a young oak near the house. Harriott explained that it interfered with the view, and she planned to cut it down. Commenting that man could not make an oak, Washington entreated her to keep it, and so she did. The Washington Oak still stands at the Hampton Plantation Historic Site. If only it could talk!

The presidential party then moved on to Charleston. Washington was escorted into the city by Charles Cotesworth Pinckney "in a twelve oared barge, rowed by twelve American captains of ships, most elegantly dressed." The next day the president "was visited about two o'clock by a great number of the most respectable ladies of Charleston—the first honor of the kind I had ever experienced and it was as flattering as it was singular." It's quite a mental image, the proper general surrounded by Charleston belles. The first federal census, completed several months earlier, had revealed that Charleston was the fourth-largest city in America at the time with a population of 16,000, following Philadelphia with 42,000 people, New York with 33,000, and Boston with 18,000. And the ladies of the city turned out in force to provide a royal reception for the president. On May 4, 1791, Washington "in the evening went to a very elegant dancing assembly at the Exchange—at which were 256 elegantly dressed & handsome ladies." The next day he "went to a concert at the Exchange at which there were at least 400 ladies—the number and appearances of which exceeded anything of the kind I had ever seen." Harriott Horry had dashed into the city to partake in the festivities.

Then it was on to Georgia for a reunion with a lady of long acquaintance. On May 12, on his way to Savannah, the general "called upon Mrs. Greene, the widow of the deceased General Greene (at a place called Mulberry Grove) and asked how she did." Life had been challenging, to put it mildly, for Kitty Greene since the end of the war. Nathanael had returned to Rhode Island a hero, but a poverty-stricken hero. Along with friends and relatives, he had made investments that had all gone bad, and he was deeply indebted to the merchants of Charleston for the uniforms he had purchased on his personal credit for the soldiers in his command. In gratitude for his service, the southern states provided Greene with large land grants, but those properties were heavily mortgaged to pay off his debts. Still, it was a happy time—the first time Nathanael had ever seen all four of his children, and he was a loving and playful father. A passerby reported seeing the war hero, his (of course) pregnant wife, and their children all in the yard playing "Puss in the Corner." Eventually, however, it became clear that the family would have to move to one of the southern properties in an attempt to make it profitable. In 1785, with Kitty pregnant yet again, Greene traveled to Georgia to scout out the situation and wrote home woefully of "the enormous sums I owe and the great difficulty of obtaining money. I seem to be doomed to a life of slavery and anxiety; but if I can render you happy it will console me." When Nathanael went back to Newport, the Greenes' sixth child, Catharine, was born, and then died of whooping cough some weeks later. Kitty was deeply depressed when the family set sail for Savannah with a tutor for the children accompanying them, a young Yale graduate named Phineas Miller.

The Mulberry Grove plantation, fifteen miles up the Savannah River from the city, had been confiscated during the war from the royal governor of Georgia and had stood abandoned since. So it took some doing to recultivate fields that had lain fallow for ten years and make the house habitable. It was such hard work, Nathanael wrote to Henry Knox, that Kitty had switched "from the gay lady to the sober housewife." Soon, though, the rice plantation was up and running, and Kitty was merrily receiving the constant stream of visitors a southern family entertained. One, a Georgia politician named Isaac Briggs, was bowled over by his hostess. He had heard in New England that Mrs. Greene "had no more gravity than an air balloon in her acting and thinking," Briggs wrote to a friend, "that she cared for nothing but flirting, rattling and riding about." He had concluded, to the contrary, that she was an "object of envy . . . she is honest and unaffected enough to confess that she is a woman, and it seems to me the world dislikes her for nothing else." By the spring of 1786, even though Kitty had lost another baby late in pregnancy, it looked like the family fortunes might be turning. The plantation was in full bloom in June when the Greenes went to a friend's in Savannah for dinner. On the way home Nathanael complained of a bad headache. A week later, at the age of forty-four, he was dead.

There she was, a debt-ridden thirty-two-year-old widow with five children in a strange state with no family anywhere nearby. Kitty toyed with the idea of moving back to Rhode Island, but she had no way to support herself there. Over the next

couple of years she traveled back and forth between Mulberry Grove and Newport, trying to settle her husband's estate. George Washington
offered to take over the education of her oldest
child, George Washington Greene, as did Lafayette. After Henry Knox urged her to accept Lafayette's offer, she sent her twelve-year-old son off
to France. She then enrolled the two oldest girls in
boarding school in Bethlehem, Pennsylvania, and
left her youngest boy, Nat, who had been born at
Morristown, in Rhode Island with the executor of
the estate, Jeremiah Wadsworth. After a visit to
Mount Vernon, the widow Greene returned to Mulberry Grove with the baby, Louisa, and Phineas
Miller. The gossips had a grand time linking her
name with those of several men, and this time the
gossips were at least partly right. Kitty's correspondence with the married congressman Wadsworth
makes clear that she had a romantic relationship
with the man she was dependent on as the estate's
chief creditor as well as its executor. She also was
counting on him to introduce in Congress her petition for repayment of General Greene's war expenses.

To promote her petition, Kitty traveled to New
York, where she stayed with her old friends Henry
and Lucy Knox, as she had so many years before at
the beginning of the war. George Washington's diaries include many an entry with Kitty Greene's
name as a guest for dinner or a member of the
president's party at the theater. George and Martha
Washington both enjoyed Kitty's company, but

they warned her that her romantic life was likely to cause her problems with the politicians who were considering her case. She had started living intimately and traveling openly with the children's old tutor, and now her business manager, Phineas Miller. But the young widow didn't want to get married. She needed the title of "Lady Greene" to prosecute her cause, and if she won, the settlement would be hers. If she married, it would be her husband's.

When Washington pulled up at Mulberry Grove on an elaborately decked-out barge, rowed by ship captains wearing hats with "LONG LIVE THE PRESIDENT" emblazoned on the bands, Kitty's petition before the Congress was still pending. Alexander Hamilton, who was giving her advice, warned of a problem—Greene hadn't asked permission from Congress before he signed the notes for his soldiers' uniforms. "I love you too well not to be candid with you," the secretary of the treasury told her. Washington's supporters in Congress must have known where he stood on the matter, and the president and the petitioner certainly had some time to talk about it during the visit. Three days later, on May 15, 1791, after a wildly enthusiastic reception by the citizens of Savannah, including "about 100 well dressed and handsome ladies," Washington returned to dine at "Mulberry Grove—the seat of Mrs. Greene." That December, Kitty took her case personally to Philadelphia. She presented documents and prepared debate, and she watched members of Congress fight over her fate, with their own political scores to settle of more concern to them than her plight. Finally, in March, the House of Representatives approved the bill indemnifying Nathanael Greene's estate by a vote of 33 to 24. The Senate soon followed suit, and President Washington readily signed it. A message from the president was read into the proceedings of the House on April 27, 1792, announcing that the bill was now law. Kitty Greene was in the gallery. She wrote to her lawyer in Georgia that she felt "as saucy as you please—not only because I am independent, but because I have gained a complete triumph over some of my friends who did not wish me success—and others who doubted my judgment managing the business—and constantly tormented me to death to give up my **obstinacy** as it was called—they are now as mute as mice. . . . O how sweet is revenge!"

Later that year, on a visit to New York, Kitty asked Ezra Stiles, the president of Yale University, to recommend a tutor for some friends in Georgia. It was Stiles who had sent Phineas Miller to the Greene family. This time the man Stiles chose was Eli Whitney. Whitney and three of the Greene children traveled back to Georgia with Kitty and Phineas Miller. (Fourteen-year-old Cornelia Greene accepted the invitation of George and Martha Washington to spend the year with them in Philadelphia.) Before moving in with the family whose children he had been hired to tutor, Whitney stopped at Mulberry Grove for a visit. He liked it so much, and Kitty Greene and Phineas Miller were so taken with his genius, that Whitney abandoned the tutoring job altogether and stayed on at the plantation as a toolmaker. When visiting Georgia planters fretted about the difficulty of removing seeds from cotton, Whitney went to work. He built a laboratory in the house that only he, Miller, and Kitty could enter and set about inventing a machine to remove the cottonseeds. One night he brought down a small prototype to the dinner table for a demonstration. It removed the seeds, but the cotton stuck to the works of the machine. In what was a "Eureka!" moment for Whitney, Kitty grabbed a hearth brush to sweep off the fiber as the gin separated out the seeds. It was a suggestion that completed the concept. (The Massachusetts Institute of Technology School of Engineering's "Inventor of the Week" program goes further: "Experts on invention agree that Eli Whitney could not have developed the cotton gin—the quintessential American invention—without Greene's advice. In fact, some believe that Whitney stole the credit for what was essentially Greene's invention.") One thing is certain: Whitney couldn't have done anything without Kitty's cash. After she staked him and Phineas to the capital to form the firm of Miller and Whitney, Eli went off to Philadelphia to obtain a patent and then on to New Haven to start manufacturing the cotton gins.

That same year, 1793, George Washington Greene came home from revolution-wracked France for the first time in five years. His boarding school had closed; his patrons, the Marquis and

Marchioness de Lafayette, were locked up in separate prisons. Kitty, thrilled to have him home, was utterly devastated a short while later when he drowned in the Savannah River. What followed was a trying time when the firm of Miller and Whitney was plagued by disasters. In an attempt to raise capital, Kitty invested in a fraudulent land company and once again found herself broke. While her finances were unraveling, Kitty and Phineas traveled in 1796 to Philadelphia, where she finally took the advice of her old friends the Washingtons: with George and Martha as witnesses, she and Phineas were married. After selling everything she could sell, Kitty lost Mulberry Grove and moved with Miller and her children to Nathanael Greene's other southern property, Cumberland Island, off the coast of Georgia. By selling timber, Kitty was able to establish her family on the island, but she struggled to make it while saddled with old debt. Then, in 1803, Phineas Miller died. But that same year the South Carolina legislature bought the patent for the cotton gin from the firm of Miller and Whitney for $50,000. Once again, Kitty Greene was sitting pretty.

Kitty's tumultuous tale was just beginning when George Washington visited her on those fine May days in 1791. After he left Mulberry Grove, he headed home, stopping at Revolutionary War battlefields along the way. Summing up what he had learned on his travels, the president was satisfied: "The manners of the people," he wrote on June 4, "were orderly and civil. And they appeared to be happy, contented and satisfied with the general government under which they were placed." Washington would find less contented souls when he returned to Philadelphia. Not only was the political situation growing tense, the city also suffered that summer through its first major yellow fever epidemic.

While George Washington toured the South, his fellow Virginians, Thomas Jefferson and James Madison, took a trip of their own—through New York and New England. The secretary of state and his acolyte, the congressman from Virginia, were doing some political organizing, drumming up opposition to administration policies, particularly Alexander Hamilton's financial proposals. Jefferson had lured a young Princeton classmate of Madison's, Philip Freneau, to Philadelphia and given him a minor position at the State Department. But Freneau's real job was to start a newspaper to combat the staunchly Federalist **Gazette of the United States**. The **National Gazette,** like Jefferson, railed against a strong central government, in favor of states' rights, and it boisterously supported the revolutionaries in France. In Congress, Madison, under Jefferson's guidance, led what was forming into a political party against Hamilton's forces, who were branded as monarchists. The party was variously called Anti-Federalist, Democratic, or Republican at first, until Republican was finally settled on, in contrast to Hamilton's Federalists. Washington was of course distressed by the dissension in his Cabinet. Also distressing was news from the West that an expedition under General Arthur St. Clair had been defeated by Indians and that farmers, up in arms over the Whiskey Act, a Hamilton-inspired law taxing liquor and stills, had attacked tax collectors in western Pennsylvania. Another, much more decorous revolt was going on as well—among the women.

Ladies of Letters

After all those years of Abigail Adams demanding a better education for women, it was finally happening. The Revolution had served to convince the country that women would be called on to take on unexpected roles that they might better fulfill if they were more formally educated. And the new republic, if it were to function as the Founders envisaged, would require the participation of its citizens. But someone would have to train those citizens. That someone was a mother. John Adams's advice to Nabby when she was a young woman, that "it is by the female world that the greatest and best characters among men are formed," was becoming accepted wisdom. To better form their sons' characters, women would have to be educated. Dr. Benjamin Rush, signer of the Declaration of Independence, battlefield physician during the war, and son-in-law of Annis Stockton, made that argument in an address, "Thoughts upon Education," to the Young Ladies' Academy of Philadelphia in 1787. He had helped establish the school, which, like the one Kitty Greene's girls attended in Bethlehem, Pennsylvania, was one of a growing number of "female academies" in America at the end of the eighteenth century. It was a time when women, as a result of their revolutionary experiences, began to advocate publicly for equal education.

Our old friend Catharine Macaulay published her **Letters on Education** in 1790 detailing an exhaustive educational curriculum for every age: "At age fourteen: Rollin's **Ancient History** in French, English history, Livey's history in Latin. . . . At age eighteen: Plato (**Dialogues,** only) . . . in Greek; Caesar's **Commentaries** . . . in Latin: Harria and Monboddo on Language. . . ." Boys and girls, men and women, were to study the same subjects and participate in the same sports in Macaulay's ideal world. That same year in this country, **Massachusetts Magazine** printed Judith Sargent Murray's poem and essay "On Equality of the Sexes." It was one of several periodicals that treated themes of women's education and accomplishments. **American Museum,** for example, printed an article about Deborah Sampson, the woman who disguised herself as a man during the Revolution. George Washington's account ledger records a subscription to that magazine. Judith Murray, who later became famous for articles she wrote "narrated" by **The Gleaner,** claimed that the Revolution had caused her to think about women's roles in America. ("The law acknowledges no **separate** act of a **married** woman," she complained to her brother.) She actually wrote her essay on equality in 1779, though it wasn't published for more than a decade.

Raised in Gloucester, Massachusetts, Judith Sargent was widowed when she married John Murray, the head of the Universalist Church in America, in 1788. And she had been writing for magazines for years (favorable reviews of Mercy Otis Warren's plays were among her articles) when her call for equality appeared in the March and April 1790 issues of **Massachusetts Magazine.** If women were in any way inferior to men, she argued, it was because they weren't afforded the same opportunities: "Will it be said that the judgment of a male of two years old, is more sage than that of a female's of the same age? I believe the reverse is generally observed to be true. But from that period what partiality! . . . As their years increase the sister must be wholly domesticated, while the brother is led by the hand through all the flowery paths of science." Those views would have been considered wildly radical before the Revolution, when Abigail Adams chided John about the ridicule surrounding the idea of women's education. But by the time they were published in 1790, the first lady of the land had enrolled her ten-year-old granddaughter in a New York school where she was taught arithmetic, geography, French, and English along with the "womanly arts" of embroidery, dancing, and drawing. Martha Washington wrote to Mercy Otis Warren that though she would rather be at Mount Vernon, in New York "my grandchildren have . . . good opportunities for acquiring a useful and accomplished education." Not only was Judith Murray a guest at a reception in the president's home, but Martha Washington paid a surprise call on the feminist a few days later, so they could talk some more. (On the same visit to the capital, Judith, like many women, went to watch debates in the House of Representatives and clucked over members "walking to and fro . . . reading the newspapers— lolling upon their writing stand, picking their nails . . . ogling the gallery." Listen to tourists emerging from the House galleries today and you'll hear similar comments.)

The September 1790 issue of **Massachusetts Magazine** featured a positive review of a new book—by Mercy Otis Warren. As an indication of how times had changed, Mercy for the first time published under her own name. She dedicated her **Poems, Dramatic and Miscellaneous** to George Washington, who accepted the request for the implied endorsement, "duly sensible of the merits of the respectable and amiable writer." When the book was published, Mercy shot off copies to her friends in high places. Though he hadn't had time to read it all, the president told her, "from the parts I have read, and a general idea of the pieces, I am persuaded of its gracious and distinguished reception by the friends of virtue and science." The secretary of state had also been busy but had read enough "to foresee that it will soothe some of my moments of rest from drudgery. I will add another illustrious name to the roll of female worthies made for the ornament as well as vindication of their sex." The secretary of the treasury chimed in: "In the career of dramatic composition at least, female genius in the United States has outstripped the male." The vice president too congratulated his old friend Mercy.

The Adams and Warren families had gone their separate ways when James and Mercy opposed the Constitution and the men who supported it. Abigail, never one to forgive and forget, was appalled when Mercy asked John to find a job for one of her sons. "A certain Lady," Abigail indignantly wrote to her sister, "wrote him that he now had it in his power to . . . successfully help his friends and that she is sure of his patronage. . . . You cannot mistake who the Lady was. I know no other equally ambitious." With John Adams's letter in praise of her book, the icy relations between the Warrens and Adamses thawed. In 1796 Abigail dropped in on the Warrens for the first time in almost twelve years, surprising her old friend and mentor. "Whither friendly, political or accidental I know not," Mercy snipped, "but she appeared very **clever**." But Mercy's assessment of the Adams presidency in her massive **History of the American Revolution,** published in 1805, created another period of hostility between the old allies.

With women's education becoming more widespread, women like Judith Sargent Murray writing regularly about the status of her sex, and Mercy Otis Warren promoting her book, educated American women were ready targets when Mary Wollstonecraft's **Vindication of the Rights of Women** torpedoed in from England in 1792. Though the call for women's political and civil rights stirred up a torrent of controversy, it was Wollstonecraft's personal life that attracted the most vituperative attacks, since she was known to have had one illegitimate child and to have conceived a second child before she married the baby's father. (That child, Mary Wollstonecraft Shelley, grew up to write **Frankenstein** and marry Percy Bysshe Shelley.)

Despite one politician's dismissal of her as "a vulgar, impudent hussy," everybody read Mary Wollstonecraft. Aaron Burr told his wife (he had married his friend Mrs. Prevost, the widow of an English soldier) that "I made haste to procure it, and spent the last night, almost the whole of it, in reading it." Eliza Powel's diary records a purchase of the **Vindication.** Making a crack to Abigail about their son Thomas seeing too much of the ladies, John Adams interjected: "Pardon me! Disciple of Wollstonecraft." David Ramsay piously proclaimed that his wife, Martha Laurens Ramsay, "**read** Wollstonecraft's **Rights of Women** but **studied** the Bible." Annis Stockton told her daughter Julia Rush that she had had a hard time finding a copy of the work in Princeton: "I suppose it is an old thing with you—I wonder you never sent me your critique. . . . I am sure that no one can read it but they may find something or other that will correct their conduct and enlarge their ideas." Stockton, whose poems were widely published in newspapers like the **New York Mercury** and the **Pennsylvania Chronicle** and periodicals like the **New American Magazine, Columbian Magazine,** and **American Museum,** had long been an advocate for women's education and ran something of an intellectual and political salon for men and women at Morven.

Though political and civil rights would be a long time coming for American women, Mary Wollstonecraft clearly had an impact. So did the improvement in women's education, which was already, at the end of the eighteenth century, giving women "ideas." One young woman, Priscilla Mason, in what must have been a startling "Salutatory Oration," addressed her fellow graduates and guests at the Young Ladies' Academy of Philadelphia the year after **Vindication** was published. (Conjure up the mental image—girls, probably all in white, proud parents and teachers, local dignitaries, maybe including Benjamin Rush . . . the girls stand and thank their teachers and families . . . then it's Priscilla's turn.) "Our high and mighty lords (thanks to their arbitrary constitutions) have denied us the means of knowledge, and then reproached us for the want of it." And though she conceded that women's education was improving, Priscilla asked where a female orator, as she clearly considered herself, could use her talents: "The Church, the Bar, the Senate are shut against us. Who shut them? **Man;** despotic man, first made us incapable of duty, and then forbid us the exercise. Let us by suitable education, qualify ourselves for these high departments. They will open before us." It would have been wonderful to see the faces of the all-male teachers.

Though the church, the bar, and the Senate remained closed for a long time to come, women could actually vote in one state at the end of the eighteenth century—New Jersey. The state constitution adopted in 1776 did not explicitly include women in its suffrage section, but it didn't exclude them either. Then in 1790 a state election law inserted the words "he or she" when referring to voters: "No person shall be entitled to vote in any other township or precinct, than that in which he or she doth actually reside." In their post-Revolutionary raised political consciousness, women property holders (which meant single or widowed women, since married women could not own property) started showing up at the polls, and no one seemed to think anything of it. In 1800 an attempt to codify the right in congressional as well as state and local elections was deemed redundant. But this was New Jersey, and as partisanship grew increasingly bitter, elections got dirtier. Finally, many more women than were eligible to vote cast ballots in one blatantly rigged Essex County election, and in 1807 legislators used the excuse of fraud to limit the franchise to "free, white, male citizens of this state, of the age of twenty-one years," thus guaranteeing "the safety, quiet, good order and dignity of the state." Something New Jersey elections have not exactly been known for in the centuries since. The partisanship that led to voter fraud in New Jersey had been percolating throughout George Washington's first term. But by the time the second presidential election year of 1792 began, members of Congress and the cabinet were engaged in full-blown party warfare.

Election Year

The year began auspiciously enough with the appointment of the first ambassadors under the new government. For the Court of St. James's, the president chose Thomas Pinckney, who had studied in England as a boy. Gouverneur Morris, who was already in Paris on private business, was named as envoy to France. Thomas Jefferson's ally William Short was dispatched to the Netherlands. Though Pinckney was pleased with the appointment, his wife, Betsey, was horrified at the idea. Not only would she be leaving her South Carolina friends and family, she would be living in England—the country that had laid waste to her state and occupied her mother's home. One friend wrote that the once brave Betsey could not stop crying. But she had no choice. The twenty-nine-year-old Mrs. Pinckney packed up her children and moved across the ocean with her husband, who, as the representative of America, had his work cut out for him. Europe was roiling with the French Revolution, and the United States was assumed to be aiding the rebels. The old rabble-rouser Thomas Paine had published his **Rights of Man** attacking monarchy with an endorsement by none other than the secretary of state. Jefferson insisted that his letter approving of Paine's pamphlet had been printed without his permission, but his glowing praise for the incendiary tract certainly made the already suspect upstart republic even more suspect in the courts of Europe. Jefferson's praise for Paine also caused a rift with his old colleague John Adams. Bored as vice president, Adams, fearful of mob rule, had written a series of wildly unpopular articles published in the Federalist **Gazette of the United States,** which sneered at democratic majorities and scoffed at the cry for equality in France. In Jefferson's accolade for **The Rights of Man,** he rejoiced that it would answer "the political heresies which have sprung up among us." An exchange of letters between Jefferson and Adams papered over their personal differences for the time being, but their political differences were real.

But it wasn't Adams whom Jefferson and Madison aimed their political arrows at—it was Hamilton. In March 1792, Madison moved in Congress to remove Hamilton from his position at Treasury. When that effort failed, the secretary of state went to the president urging him to fire Hamilton, who, Jefferson said, was dividing the country between "Republican federalists" and "Monarchical federalists." Washington, shocked at the suggestion, was probably alerted by Jefferson's visit to the fact that the secretary of state was the source of the diatribes against Hamilton in the Republican press. On several occasions the president tried to no avail

to convince his cabinet officers to stop their bicker-
ing. Rather than cooperating with a man he
adamantly disagreed with, Jefferson toyed with retirement. He wrote to his daughter Patsy, who was
now the mother of a little girl, that he might soon
be returning to Monticello, "where I may once
more be happy with you, with Mr. Randolph, and
dear little Anne, with whom even Socrates might
ride on a stick without being ridiculous."

But Jefferson stayed on in the ever more rancorous
administration, privately guiding his allies in the
ever more raucous Congress. "As to politics, they
begin to grow pretty warm," Abigail Adams wrote
to her sister in March 1792, blaming southerners for
"all the attacks upon the Secretary of the Treasury
and upon the Government." But Abigail was relieved that her husband wasn't in the opposition's
sights: "The Vice President, they have permitted to
sleep in peace this winter, whilst the minister at
War, and the Secretary of the Treasury have been
their game." (Henry Knox sided with Alexander
Hamilton in the cabinet; Attorney General and fellow Virginian Edmund Randolph was on Jefferson's
team.) Most of all, Abigail observed, "the members
are . . . weary and long for a recess."

Finally, the Congress did recess, and Abigail
Adams, along with her husband, went home to
Braintree, now renamed Quincy, for the first time
in almost three years. Martha Washington also
went with George to Mount Vernon that summer,
writing ahead to her niece Fanny, "I have not a
doubt but we shall have company all the time we

are at home. I wish you to have all the china looked over, the closet cleaned and the glasses all washed." (Even when the Washingtons weren't home, strangers dropped by all the time. At one point, Martha chided Fanny, "the President seemed a good deal surprised at the quantity of wine that you have given out, as it never was his intention to give wine or go to any expense to entertain people that came to Mount Vernon out of curiosity.") Betsey Hamilton, pregnant with her fifth child, headed to the Schuyler family home in Albany, leaving her husband behind in Philadelphia. While sending Betsey declarations of devotion ("Think of me— dream of me—and love me, my Betsey, as I do you"), Hamilton was seeing another woman.

Maria Reynolds had first come into his life the summer before when he was busy writing his "Report on Manufactures." He later said that she claimed to be vaguely related to the Livingston family and asked for his help, telling him her husband had left her for another woman and she was destitute. He told her he would bring her money at her boardinghouse that night. When he did, she invited him in. So started one of the most notorious affairs in American history. After a few months Maria's husband, James Reynolds, showed up and started blackmailing the treasury secretary. Whether it was a setup all along is not certain, but Hamilton kept seeing Maria while paying off her husband. He didn't end the affair until August 1792, soon after Betsey delivered the baby.

A few months later James Reynolds, after being

charged with perpetrating a fraud, appealed to Hamilton to intercede with the law. When Hamilton refused, the scam artist's partner in the fraud told the Speaker of the House that Reynolds had the goods on Hamilton—accusing him of speculating with federal funds. The Speaker consulted a couple of trusted allies in Congress, including James Monroe, a good friend of Madison's and Jefferson's. This rump congressional committee called on Maria Reynolds, who gave them some letters she said were from Hamilton. When he saw Senator Aaron Burr in his office, Hamilton must have known that the delegation of lawmakers who had come to confront him wasn't a friendly one. Burr said he was acting as the lawyer for James Reynolds. When shown Maria's "evidence," Hamilton asked them to come to his house that evening. There he produced his letters from Maria, which made clear the nature of the relationship. He had cheated on his wife, not his country. The embarrassed congressmen agreed to drop the whole matter. But James Monroe took the letters with him and passed them along to Thomas Jefferson. Monroe kept the letters as a stockpiled weapon, waiting for the right chance to fire them.

While members of Congress were back in their districts campaigning for reelection during the summer of 1792, an election for governor of New York was underway. The incumbent, George Clinton, had been a leader of the Anti-Federalist forces during the battle over ratification of the Constitution, writing articles combating the **Federalist Papers**. At the ratification convention Clinton almost prevailed against the forces of Alexander Hamilton, Philip Schuyler, and John Jay. Though Clinton, now allied with the Republicans, had been governor since 1777 (and is now called the Father of New York), Federalist John Jay decided to challenge him. Jay waged his campaign even as he served as chief justice of the Supreme Court. In those days justices had to "ride the circuit," presiding over courtrooms around the country. While Jay was on the circuit, his wife, Sally, provided news of the election.

In May she reported, "It is said by both parties that if the votes are not lost in the country in which Judge Cooper resides, Mr. Clinton will lose the election, but it seems some mistake or other renders that questionable." The Clinton forces were playing dirty, rigging the returns. A commission was appointed to review the vote. At first, Sally thought it was going in John's favor: "This evening I obtain an account of the examination of the votes this day. Judge Hobart is so sanguine, that he is sure of a majority for you, even though the Otsego votes should be lost. You will doubtless be pleased at having a majority in the City of New York, and County of West Chester, as being the places in which you are most known." But then, eight days later, she was less sure: "If the suffrages of the people are admitted, they give you a majority of 400 votes, but if the County of Otsego are to lose theirs, Clinton will have the majority of a small number." Vote-counter Sally was mortified because some of her relatives were working against her husband, including her brother Brockholst who as Jay's young secretary had been such a thorn in their sides back in Spain: "Oh how is the name of Livingston to be disgraced! . . . Those shameless men, blinded by malice, ambition and interest have conducted themselves with such indecency during the election and daily since the canvassing of the votes." The eleven commissioners included only three "in favor of you," she explained, but concluded, "whether you are, or are not Governor, it appears that you are the choice of the people." By the next night Sally disgustedly reported: "When Governor Clinton was 108 votes ahead, it was thought dangerous to examine the votes of Tioga County, it being reduced to a certainty that that county alone would give you a majority independent of the votes of Otsego, another quibble was therefore invented, and they were likewise set aside." Sounds like some elections I've covered. The bitterness caused by charges that Clinton stole the New York election only added to the partisanship when Congress reconvened back in Philadelphia.

The social life in Philadelphia had never slowed down. Abigail Adams complained that she would "spend a very dissipated winter if I were to accept one half the invitations I receive." But now all those parties served a civilizing purpose. The homes of Anne Bingham, Molly Morris, and Eliza Powel were places where members of both parties came together and, out of courtesy if nothing else, were forced to treat their opponents with respect.

Though the three families were all Federalists (Morris and Bingham were in the Senate, and Powel was mayor of Philadelphia), their entertainments were bipartisan. Remember, Anne Bingham had kept up a correspondence with Thomas Jefferson after she left France. (And he sent her French face cream.) It's not that the parties were devoid of politics—all three women were more than willing to engage in political arguments themselves. John Adams told Abigail of a political conversation he had engaged in with Anne Bingham and the information from France she was able to transmit. And Eliza Powel "eagerly and passionately" took on the president on many occasions. But arguing politics at a party is very different from the same debate in the halls of Congress or on the campaign trail. Getting together over drinks and a good dinner at the end of the day tends to tame animosities.

Washington particularly liked the evenings with his old Philadelphia friends. And finding something Washington liked about being president was the foremost concern of politicians of both parties. The president was ready to hang it up and go home. Early in 1792 he had asked Madison to prepare a farewell address for him, but then he put it aside. The one thing Jefferson and Hamilton could agree on was that the country needed Washington, that without him the Union might disintegrate. (Of course, they were doing their best to stir up the dissension that could lead to disintegration.) They each pleaded with the president to run for reelection. But perhaps more persuasive than the politicians in convincing Washington to make the run for a second term was a woman whose judgment he trusted—Eliza Powel.

As late as November 1792, when he was still telling her that he was determined to retire, Eliza composed a letter detailing the "consequence of the sentiments that you had confided to me." First she threatened him, telling him that "the well earned popularity that you are now in possession of will be torn from you by the envious and malignant should you follow the bent of your inclinations." People would say that he cared only about himself, that the job could do nothing to add to his fame. "The Anti-Federalist would use it as an argument for dissolving the Union, and would urge that you, from experience, had found the present system a bad one, and had, artfully, withdrawn from it that you might not be crushed under its ruins." Then she appealed to his patriotism: "Will you withdraw your aid from a structure that certainly wants your assistance to support it? Can you, with fortitude, see it crumble to decay?" Then she played on his pride: "At this time, you are the only man in America that dares to do right on all public occasions . . . your very figure is calculated to inspire respect and confidence in the people." And then she raised doubts about his judgment: "Have you not, on some occasions, found the consummation of your wishes the source of the keenest of your sufferings?" This outpouring from a friend carried no self-interested politics with it. Washington would run for a second term.

There was no question about his reelection, but what about the not very popular vice president, John Adams? The Republicans fielded Governor George Clinton, fresh from his spurious victory in New York, in the hopes of ousting the heir apparent. Jefferson stayed on the sidelines; Hamilton vigorously supported Adams. On December 5, 1792, electors from fifteen states (Kentucky had joined the Union in June) met in Philadelphia to count the ballots. The results: Washington 132, Adams 77, Clinton 50. Abigail had been right to worry about the southern states. That was where 80 percent of Clinton's vote came from. From back home in Massachusetts, she wrote to John in Philadelphia: "After what took place in New York with respect to the election of Mr. Jay, I had no expectation but that the same party would oppose your election to the vice presidency. But I did not think that they would have led Virginia by the nose so completely. . . . I own I cannot feel that cordiality towards those states which I do for those who have been unanimous towards you." Abigail, as always, understood the politics better than her husband did.

A Second Washington Term

Washington might have received the unanimous vote of the electors, but the newspapers were another matter altogether—as were the so-called Democratic Societies springing up around the country in support of the French Revolution. Congress, bolstered by the election of more devotees of Jefferson, called for an official investigation of activities at the Treasury Department, beginning the itch to investigate that has ever since been the hallmark of the out-of-office party. Abigail Adams, who did not return to Philadelphia with John after their summer vacation in Quincy, told her husband how Boston newspapers were playing the story: "I was told in Boston that there was a Club, who were in constant correspondence with the Secretary of State. Those papers are leveled at the Government and particularly against Hamilton, who will however I hope stand his ground."

There was foreign news to report as well. Nabby had moved to England, where her ne'er-do-well husband was trying to collect debts owed his family. Abigail passed on with commentary her daughter's rendition of what was happening in Europe: "Mrs. Pinckney complains of the impudence of trades people in the country . . . perhaps these people [the Pinckneys] have been accustomed to slaves, and expect the same servility. Mr. Morris renders himself very obnoxious in France by an active and officious zeal in favor of the aristocracy. . . . [Nabby] had visited Mrs. Bache who was well and vastly pleased with England." Abigail had decided against moving back to Philadelphia for the second term. Her health was bad, and their finances were shot. Renting houses and entertaining had placed the family $2,000 in debt. With Abigail home in Massachusetts, minding the property, the

Adamses were able to save some money. But as always when they were separated, Abigail missed her husband. In the cold weather she teased him that she had "the advantage of you, I have Louisa for a bedfellow but she is cold comfort for the one I have lost." And there's some wistfulness in her request to her John to "present me affectionately to all my friends, particularly to Mrs. Washington whom I both love and respect."

Mrs. Washington had recently learned that her niece Fanny's husband, who was George's nephew, had died of tuberculosis. Instead of being able to rush to the grieving widow, left alone with three small children, as she would have liked, Martha felt duty-bound to stay by her husband's side in Philadelphia. As someone who had been widowed young herself, Martha tried to console her niece from afar: "You have, my dear Fanny, received a very heavy affliction; but while it pleases God to spare the President he will be a friend to you and to the children." The family in Philadelphia was in mourning, declining invitations to friends' events.

But there was one group of people Martha continued to see—Revolutionary War veterans. In his account of the presidential years, George Washington Parke Custis recalled that veterans stopped by the house almost every day. His grandmother would greet the old soldiers, give them some food and maybe some money, and reminisce with them about old times. And on holidays, veterans "were cordially welcomed as old friends" by Lady Washington. Many of the men were angry about the

Congress's refusal to give them back pay, and Martha, as she did all through the war, smothered their resentment with her kindness. The veterans weren't the only group that called on the first lady for help. She received letters from artists, sculptors, tradespeople, cranks, and, of course, relatives, soliciting her help. The editors of **Ladies' Magazine** sent her their first volume with the request that she would be "an encourager and patron of the work."

For President Washington's second inaugural on March 4, 1793, Martha and all of her grandchildren were on hand. Not long after, word arrived from Europe that King Louis XVI had been beheaded in January and England had declared war on France. Despite the reports of blood in the streets of Paris, American public opinion was firmly on the side of France—the "republic" versus the monarchy, the ally versus the enemy. In April the new French government's envoy, Citizen Edmond-Charles-Édouard Genet, arrived in Charleston to much fanfare and then proceeded up the coast to Philadelphia, stirring up pro-French sentiments as he traveled. People in Philadelphia, aping everything French, started calling themselves "Citizen" and "Citess." It was a dicey situation for the government. The Franco-American alliance forged during the Revolution had pledged U.S. support for France in case of war with Britain. But war was the last thing the struggling new country needed, and trade with Britain was essential. Washington declared neutrality, with the assent of

Hamilton, who supported Britain, and Jefferson, who backed France.

At just about the same time Citizen Genet set out from Charleston for Philadelphia, a group of Pinckney women were making the same trip. But for a much sadder reason. Eliza Pinckney was suffering from breast cancer and needed to see the best doctors the country had to offer. Her daughter Harriott Horry and three granddaughters (two named Harriott) all accompanied the intrepid Eliza, who was now probably seventy years old. (The date of her birth is uncertain.) After ten days at sea, the entourage arrived in Philadelphia on April 20, 1793, where they took rooms in a house "opposite Mr. Bingham's garden." In addition to the doctors, all of Philadelphia came to call. Betsey Hamilton, Anne Bingham, Eliza Powel, Lucy Knox, and, at different times, their husbands paid homage to the remarkable old lady. So, despite the urgent issues he was dealing with, did the president. "General Washington was extremely kind," Harriott Horry wrote in her journal, "and said as Mrs. Washington was sick, he offered in her name as well as his own everything in their power to serve us and begged we would use no ceremony."

Harriott returned the calls and visited Mrs. Washington on May 9, when she also accepted the doctor's invitation to "walk with him to see some of his cancerous patients who were cured, and some who were then under cure that I might ask them what questions I chose of the pains etc. which they suffered." Seeing the other breast cancer patients encouraged Harriott about her mother's prospects. The next day, when Eliza was "very sick indeed and extremely weak. Doctor Tate perceived that his medicine began to operate upon the cancer." A couple of weeks later Eliza Pinckney died. From Harriott's journal, it would appear that the end came as a blessing: "Dear mother continued to suffer extremely with the sick stomach and vomiting, and for several hours was in great agony when it pleased Almighty God to take her to himself." She was buried in St. Peter's graveyard on May 27, 1793, far from the Low Country she had cultivated and cherished. George Washington, at his request, was a pallbearer. Eliza Pinckney's great-great-granddaughter, Harriott Horry Ravenal, concluded after writing the account of her ancestor's life: "The women of all the colonies had committed to them a great though an unsuspected charge: to fit themselves and their sons to meet the coming change (self-government) in law and soberness; not in riot and anarchy as did the unhappy women of the French Revolution."

At the time of Eliza Pinckney's death the French Revolution was tearing American politics apart. Washington was coming under constant attack in Jefferson's paper, and the secretary of state told the president in July that he would be leaving the administration at the end of the year. Citizen Genet, who was enjoying public adulation, thumbed his nose at America's neutrality by hiring sailors and purchasing equipment for privateers—ships that would attack British commercial vessels. And he was launching the ships from U.S. waters. When Washington tried to stop the "incorrigible" thirty-year-old envoy, as even Jefferson called Genet, he threatened to go over the heads of the government directly to the public. More and more pro-French (and anti-Hamilton) Democratic Societies were springing up around the country. The cabinet demanded that France recall the young "diplomat." (His replacement, representing the next wave of French radicals, arrived with orders to arrest Genet. The Frenchman asked for asylum, stayed in America, and married Governor Clinton's daughter.)

Adding to the political turmoil in Philadelphia, a virulent yellow fever epidemic hit the city that summer. The young wife of the president's secretary, who lived with the first family and was a great favorite of Martha Washington's, died from the disease. Alexander and Betsey Hamilton, who sent the children to Albany that summer but stayed in Philadelphia with her husband, contracted it but survived. (Martha sent over three bottles of old wine as a restorative, with a note to Betsey: "We have a plenty to supply you as often as you please to send for it.") As summer wore on, the death toll rose to upward of fifty people a day. Anyone who could leave the city did, including Secretary Jefferson, Secretary Knox, and Attorney General Randolph.

George Washington thought it would set a bad example if he fled but tried to convince Martha and the children to repair to Mount Vernon. She refused to go without him, forcing the president to relent, and in September the family left for Virginia, urging their friend Eliza Powel to come with them. Eliza consulted her husband, who said he was not "impressed with the degree of apprehension" their friends felt about yellow fever, and he saw no point in leaving the only place where there were doctors who knew anything about the disease. (They didn't—they treated victims with bleeding and purging, which just made them weaker.) As for Eliza: "The conflict between duty and inclination is a severe trial of my feelings; but as I believe it is always best to adhere to the line of duty, I beg to decline the pleasure . . . in accompanying you to Virginia." Duty, always duty, ever present. Eliza worried that her husband might become ill while she was away and she would never forgive herself if she weren't there to care for him. It was a legitimate fear—Samuel Powel died of yellow fever at the end of September. In all, about five thousand people lost their lives in Philadelphia in the summer of 1793, and when Martha Washington returned to the city in the fall, she told her niece that the people were still in shock: "They have suffered so much that it can not be got over soon by those that were in the city—almost every family has lost some of their friends—and black seems to be the general dress of the city."

While the Washington family was home in Virginia, the president took a short trip into the future capital city, the District of Columbia, which was under construction. He laid the cornerstone for the building that would become for generations the symbol of American democracy—the United States Capitol. (Nobody knows where the cornerstone is—it's been lost somewhere under the Capitol.) The plan to move out of Philadelphia must have looked prescient at that point. But it wouldn't happen in Washington's presidency; he would have to return to Philadelphia and the partisan battles raging there. Pro-French sentiment continued strong, but fortunately for the administration, it was all talk and no action. As John Adams reported to Abigail: "We are afraid to go to war, though our inclinations and dispositions are strong enough to join the French Republicans. It is happy that our fears are a check to our resentments; and our understandings are better than our hearts." In March 1794 Martha wrote home to Fanny: "There is a new French minister arrived about ten days ago—he seems to be a plain grave and good looking man—but can't speak a word of English." That was probably a relief after the gregarious Genet. But Britain kept provoking the former colonies, seizing U.S. ships in order to shut down trade with the West Indies. The Federalists leaned on Washington to name a special envoy to Britain to try to hammer out a commercial treaty. The president chose Chief Justice John Jay.

Once again Sally Jay learned of her husband's position from the newspapers, and once again she was furious: "The utmost exertion I can make is to be silent; excuse me if I have not philosophy or patriotism to do more. I heard of the nomination yesterday; so did the children." But this time with a houseful of children and the hopes that it would be a short assignment, Sally wouldn't go along. Instead, she begged him to take their son Peter, who had stayed in America when his parents went to Spain and France: "I cannot say I perceive your objections to taking with you our son," she pushed. Peter Augustus Jay, newly graduated from college, did make the trip with his father. In an attempt to diffuse war talk, the Washington administration made other diplomatic appointments as well. John Quincy Adams was picked for the Netherlands, where he had spent so much time with his father as a boy. (His mother, Abigail, wrote to Martha Washington: "At a very early period in his life I devoted him to the public.") James Monroe would go to France to replace Gouverneur Morris, who was seen as too pro-royal. Monroe brought his wife, the former Elizabeth Kortright, with him. The Virginia congressman had married the New York beauty in 1786, and the couple had expected to settle in Virginia until politics changed their course. Elizabeth, like Sally Jay before her, was hailed in Paris as **la belle Américaine.** One friend of America must have considered Elizabeth Monroe very **belle** indeed—the Marquis de Lafayette. Lafayette was in exile, and his wife was in jail. Her mother and grandmother had both been beheaded when Elizabeth Monroe intervened on behalf of the Marchioness, who could expect a trip to the guillotine as well. James Monroe, as a diplomat, knew he couldn't interfere in French domestic affairs, but his wife could. Elizabeth Monroe, in the official American carriage, went to the prison where Adrienne Lafayette was held and asked to speak to her. That show of interest resulted in the Marchioness's release. She joined her husband in exile. Their oldest son, George Washington Lafayette, escaped the vicissitudes of the revolution in America, living first with Alexander and Betsey Hamilton and then with George and Martha Washington.

Even though he was leading the opposition to administration policies in Congress, James Madison had reason to spend some time at the Washington home after the summer of 1794. That's when he met the young widow Dolley Payne Todd. Dolley's Quaker family had fallen on hard times, causing her mother to open a boardinghouse to support herself and her children. At her father's instruction, Dolley had married a man who could provide for her, and she had two children by John Todd. Then he and their infant son died in the yellow fever epidemic of 1793, leaving her with a little boy and a brother-in-law who was trying to steal her inheritance. One of her mother's former boarders, lawyer and senator Aaron Burr, came to her rescue. He told her that James Madison, called Jemmy, had asked to meet the beautiful widow Todd. Dolley and Jemmy met and were married in September 1794.

Dolley Madison must have been well known to the Washingtons, because a couple of years earlier her sister had married George's nephew, who had come to Philadelphia to serve on the president's staff. There's even a story, which came down in Dolley's family, that Martha Washington encouraged her to marry Madison, even though he was seventeen years her senior. The two women did become friends, exchanging gifts and recipes, and Dolley was soon at the center of Philadelphia political life. She used her dinners as opportunities to glean information for, and soothe opposition to, her husband. She used her smarts and social graces for many years on the American political scene, serving as Thomas Jefferson's hostess when he became president and then as first lady herself through Madison's two terms. Living well into the nineteenth century, Dolley Madison served as an American icon for decades.

While romance was blossoming in Philadelphia, rebellion was brewing in western Pennsylvania. Farmers furious at the tax on liquor and stills took after the "revenuers," tarring and feathering tax collectors or burning their homes. Pennsylvania officials thought they could handle the matter themselves, but at Hamilton's recommendation, Washington ordered a militia of some thirteen thousand troops to quash the "Whiskey Rebellion." George Washington and Alexander Hamilton went back into battle mode to lead the troops. Martha didn't seem too concerned in a letter to Fanny: "The insurgents in the back country have carried matters so high that the President has been obliged to send a large body of men to settle the matter— and is to go himself tomorrow to Carlyle to meet the troops." The main purpose of the letter was to answer Fanny's request for advice about marrying Washington's secretary, Tobias Lear, whose wife had died in the yellow fever epidemic. Martha was hesitant to weigh in, even though she liked Lear, and she knew her husband wouldn't want to give advice either: "He never has, nor never will, as you have often heard him say, inter meddle in matrimonial concerns." Just in rebellions.

The insurgents in western Pennsylvania dispersed in the face of the army. (And Fanny Washington did marry Tobias Lear.) Two hundred rebels were arrested, twenty-five charged with treason, and two convicted; one a madman and one an incompetent, both were pardoned by Washington. But the Republicans in Congress were not ready to pardon General Washington when he returned and blamed the Democratic Societies for the uprising. The Republicans fumed but took no action, and as the year ended, John Adams told Abigail: "This session of Congress is the most innocent I ever knew. We have done no harm." There was no news: "I know not what to write to you, unless I tell you that I love you, and long to see you." Think how she would have killed to read those words back when he was abroad and she was so miserable managing everything on her own in Massachusetts.

Thomas Jefferson had left the cabinet at the end of 1793 and retreated to Monticello. Henry Knox retired to private life at the end of 1794. Lucy's loyalist family had owned a large tract of land in Maine, where she and Henry moved and constructed a mansion. It's hard to imagine what the folks in the country thought of the redoubtable Mrs. Knox, with "her hair in front . . . craped up at least a foot high, much in the form of a churn, bottom upward, and topped off with a wire skeleton in the same form, covered with black gauze, which hangs in streamers down her back." That hairdo must have been hard enough to pull off in Philadelphia. But a visitor to Montpelier, the Knox estate in Maine, wrote that the better you knew Lucy, the better you liked her: "Seeing her in Philadelphia you think of her only as a fortunate player at whist; at her house in the country you discover that she possesses sprightliness, knowledge, a good heart and excellent understanding." Lucy Knox had thirteen children, only three of whom survived to adulthood.

Next to depart from the cabinet, in January 1795, was Alexander Hamilton. Angelica Church had the nerve to take her sister Betsey Hamilton to task for the resignation: "I am inclined to believe that it is your influence that induces him to withdraw from public life. That so good a wife, so tender a mother, should be so bad a patriot is wonderful!" In fact, it was Hamilton himself who wanted to return to New York to make some money. The cabinet salary of $3,000 a year didn't support a family with five children in Philadelphia. Once Hamilton made it clear that the choice was his, Angelica had the grace to admit to Betsey her real reason for being sorry to see him resign: "I was very proud to have the American Ministers entreating me for information from America. I did boast of very long letters and give myself some airs of importance." There was talk in Federalist circles of promoting Hamilton for high office, maybe sidestepping John Adams and fielding Hamilton for president. But a reporter at the pro-Republican Philadelphia newspaper the **Aurora** (published by Benjamin Franklin Bache on the printing press willed to him by his grandfather) let Hamilton know that he had seen the letters in the Reynolds affair that James Monroe had kept. The threat had its desired effect: Hamilton discouraged any discussion about him running for anything, instead devoting his time and talents to working for ratification of the Jay Treaty.

John Jay had reached an accommodation with Britain that infuriated the Republicans when they learned the details in March 1795. Even though it guaranteed British withdrawal from forts they were still occupying in the Northwest Territory and provided for substantially improved trade arrangements, the treaty was silent on the question of the British hijacking sailors from American ships. By signing it, America made clear that there would be no war with Britain. The French Revolution would have to fend for itself. The Republican press, particularly the **Aurora,** denounced the treaty, John Jay, and George Washington. But the Senate ratified on a straight party-line vote. The opponents then took their case to the House in an effort to block the appropriations to implement the measure. The counterattack, orchestrated by Hamilton, was led by Federalist Theodore Sedgewick (yes, the same man who argued the slave Mumbet's case for freedom), but what turned the tide for the treaty was a dramatic speech by Massachusetts Federalist Fisher Ames. At the end of it, John Adams told Abigail, "not a dry eye, I believe, in the House except some of the jackasses who had occasioned the necessity of the oratory. . . . The situation of the man excited compassion, and interested all hearts in his favor. The ladies wished his soul had a better body." The treaty appropriation won by a single vote, dealing the Republicans a devastating defeat. And John Jay was elected governor of New York.

Another treaty that year was met with considerably more enthusiasm. Thomas Pinckney had been sent to Spain, where he was able to extract an agreement on the southern and western boundaries of the United States, secure free navigation of the Mississippi River, and obtain cargo deposit rights at the New Orleans port. But Pinckney's success was marred for him by the death the year before of his thirty-two-year-old wife, Betsy. She had not wanted to go to England, and she turned out to be right. Left with five young children to care for, Thomas married Betsy's younger sister, who was widowed as well, a few years later, in 1797. But first, another presidential election year was dawning, when Pinckney would play a significant role.

As 1796 began, the question again was, What would Washington do? Would he run for reelection? John Adams thought not. "In perfect secrecy between you and me, I must tell you that I now believe the President will retire," he confided to Abigail in January. "The consequence to me is very serious and I am not able as yet to see what my duty will demand of me. . . . My country has claims—my children have claims and my own character has claims upon me." As speculation grew about Washington's plans, Adams was wooed by the other politicians. "I am Heir Apparent you know and a succession is soon to take place." He warned Abigail that this news was still secret and then raised doubts about what he would do: "I have no very ardent desire to be the butt of party malevolence. Having tasted of that cup I found it bitter, nauseous and unwholesome." The prospect of Washington leaving office no longer carried the risk of causing disunion. Even with the partisanship and division, Adams was quite sanguine about the future of the country: "If Jay or even Jefferson . . . should be the man, the Government will go on as well as ever." It was quite a change from four years earlier and reflected a certain stability that the nation had achieved, even as the possibility loomed of war with France as a result of the Jay Treaty.

It didn't take long, however, for Adams to start fretting. "Electioneering begins to open her campaign," he wrote home in February. "If Washington continues I suppose Jefferson and Jay may both be set up for Vice President. If he renounces, they will set up for President and Vice President both, and let the lot come out as it will." Of course, he didn't mean it. Adams was dying to be president. And Abigail was eager for him to get the job, but she wasn't so sure about being first lady. She was worried that she wouldn't be able to keep her mouth shut: "I have been so used to a freedom of sentiment that I know not how to . . . look at every word before I utter it, and to impose a silence upon myself, when I long to talk." His reply: "I have no concern your account but for your health. A woman **can** be silent when she will." Still, Abigail encouraged John, telling him that "the President's birthday was celebrated with more than usual festivity in Boston, and many other places. In the toasts drank, they have for once done justice to the V.P. It is a toast that looks . . . to a future contemplated event." She was eager for him to be president, but not to take the number two spot again. "Who in their senses could suppose that you would continue to serve in your present station with any other than Washington." Briefly, the idea of further public service made Abigail feel sorry for herself; she complained that this country had "obliged me to more sacrifices than any other woman in the country, and this I will maintain against anyone who will venture to come forward and dispute it with me." But outrage at the political opposition caused her quickly to change her tune: "Whilst I see the desire of equity, order and good government, rising up to oppose war, anarchy and confusion, I feel ready to make every personal sacrifice in aid of the cause."

George Washington had had enough of "war, anarchy and confusion," particularly from the newspapers. Benjamin Franklin Bache's (his enemies called him "Lightning Rod Junior") **Aurora** stuck as a permanent thorn in the president's side, and he complained that the newspapers were hounding him out of office: "I am attacked for persevering steadily in measures which to me appear necessary to preserve us, during the conflicts of belligerent powers, in a state of tranquility." Every president since has had the same complaint about the press.

The first lady, like all first ladies since, came in for her share of criticism as well. Her receptions, which had been so carefully calibrated by the president's advisers when he first took office, now were attacked as "monarchical." Talk about a no-win situation. First Martha was required to host these levees, then she was attacked for doing it. (As Nelly Custis grew up, her grandmother enlisted her more and more to help with the entertainment—including playing the harpsichord at dinner. Nelly griped to a friend, "We have a large company of the **Honorable Congress** to dine with us, & I must not be so remiss as to go out in the evening as they like to hear music although they do not know one note from another.") Martha's grandson remembered his grandmother growing ever more irritated with the political opposition. In his **Memoirs and Recollections of Washington,** George Washington Parke Custis told a story of Martha checking to see who had been visiting Nelly. "Her attention was arrested by a blemish on the wall, which had been newly painted a delicate cream color. 'Ah! it was no federalist,' she exclaimed, looking at the spot just above the settee; 'none but a filthy democrat would mark a place with his good for nothing head in that manner!'" The next year, when Adams was president, a diplomat's wife described the new first lady: "She has spirit enough to laugh at Bache's abuse of her husband, which poor Mrs. Washington could not." Sounds like the prickly Abigail was putting on a good show.

Martha Washington also had personal reasons for wanting to retire from the job of first lady. Her niece Fanny, whom she truly loved, died in March 1796, and Martha was mourning her loss. So she was greatly relieved when, in September, George Washington made his resignation official by sending his Farewell Address to the Philadelphia newspaper **Daily American Advertiser,** with the explanation: "While choice and prudence invite me to quit the political scene, patriotism does not forbid it." The president never actually delivered the famous speech, which has come down in history as a collection of cautionary instructions about the divisiveness of political parties and the dangers of foreign entanglements, but its publication signaled the start of the first real campaign for president. The Republicans, under the guidance of Madison, put forward the name of Thomas Jefferson, who stayed home at Monticello and let the politicking take place at a distance. Aaron Burr was their choice for vice president; the Federalists went with John Adams and Thomas Pinckney.

But the way elections worked at that time, the man with the highest number of votes won the presidency, and the one with the second highest number became vice president. It was not only possible but likely that one party would hold the highest office, while the other party took the second spot. Alexander Hamilton could not tolerate the prospect of his old nemesis Jefferson reaching the highest post in the land. He surreptitiously started organizing northern Federalists to vote for Thomas Pinckney instead of Adams, on the assumption that the South Carolinian would get southern votes from both parties. John Adams never believed the stories of Hamilton's perfidy, but Abigail did, and she eventually received proof of Hamilton's actions in a letter from a friend. She chided her husband, "You may recollect, that I have often said to you, H. is a man ambitious as Julius Caesar. A subtle intriguer, his abilities would make him dangerous if he was to espouse a wrong side. His thirst for fame is insatiable. I have ever kept my eye upon him."

It must have given Abigail some satisfaction when the next year Hamilton was thoroughly humiliated. The Republican press publicly accused him of paying off James Reynolds to keep secret his illegal securities activities. Hamilton was forced to issue a statement: "The charge against me is a connection with one James Reynolds for purposes of speculation. My real crime is an amourous connection with his wife. This confession is not made without a blush." Hamilton's political career was saved only because Betsey publicly stood by her man. She did, however, try to remove all traces of the scandal by buying up copies of her husband's published confession so she could destroy them. Apparently there was a brisk business in printing the pamphlets for the sole purpose of selling them to Betsey. Alexander Hamilton's life ended in 1804 when he was killed in a duel with Aaron Burr. But Betsey lived until the middle of the nineteenth century, working all the while to burnish Hamilton's name. She never forgave James Monroe, the man who had held on to Maria Reynolds's letters and given them to the newspapers. When Betsey Hamilton was an old woman, former president Monroe dropped by her house one day hoping to put the past behind them. "No lapse of time," she told him, "no nearness to the grave makes any difference."

When the electors met on December 7, 1796—this time with the new state of Tennessee added to the nation—no one had any idea who would win. As the day dawned, Abigail prayed: "On the decisions of this day, hangs perhaps the destiny of America, and may those into whose hands the sacred deposit is committed be guided and directed by that wisdom which is from above." The votes would not be officially counted until February, but the results leaked out throughout December. By the twentieth, Adams was fairly sure that he would be president: "It is supposed to be certain that Mr. Jefferson cannot be P[resident,] and a narrow squeak it is as the boys say, whether he or P[inckney] shall be Daddy Vice." Now that it seemed real, Abigail had genuine qualms; she was beginning to think that retirement would be better "than to be fastened up hand and foot and tongue to be shot at as our Quincy lads do at the poor geese and turkeys." By December 27 John was able to report that he would win with seventy-one votes and that "Jefferson will be Daddy Vice." Abigail was delighted with those results despite her differences with Jefferson: "Though wrong in politics, though formerly an advocate for Tom Paine's **Rights of Man** and though frequently mistaken in men and measures, I do not think him an insincere or a corruptible man. My friendship for him has ever been unshaken." On February 9, 1797, the electoral tally was announced, and it was a "narrow squeak," but for president, not vice president: Adams 71, Jefferson 68, Pinckney 59, Burr 30. That day the new president-elect wrote his wife: "The die is cast and you must prepare yourself for honorable trials." Among her trials—trying to keep her mouth shut. Of course, Abigail Adams would be unsuccessful in that effort.

On March 4, 1797, George Washington accompanied John Adams and Thomas Jefferson to their inauguration. It was a resounding reminder that this was no monarchy. No king was dead—these were new leaders by choice. Crowds jammed into the chamber of the House of Representatives to witness the voluntary and peaceful transfer of power: "The Sight of the Sun setting full orbit and another rising no less splendid, was a novelty," John exulted to Abigail. The only dry eye in the House was Washington's: "Methought I heard him think Ay! I am fairly out and you fairly in! See which of us will be happiest."

George Washington had reason to be happy. Not only were he and Martha going home to rest at Mount Vernon, but the great experiment they had helped create was now working. A new nation had been fought for, on the field of battle and in the forum of free debate, and it would survive. And its success was in no small part due to the efforts of the women. George Washington himself recognized the contributions of women when he wrote to Annis Stockton, celebrating the men we now call the Founding Fathers, "Nor would I rob the fairer sex of their share in the glory of a revolution so honorable to human nature, for indeed, I think you ladies are in the number of the best patriots America can boast." A salute from the Father of the Country to its Founding Mothers.

Cast of Characters

As this book is about the women who influenced the Founding Fathers, almost all of them are recognizable only because of the men in their lives. These are the mothers, wives, sisters, daughters, and friends of the men who signed the Declaration of Independence, fought in the Revolutionary War, attended the Constitutional Convention, and served in the new government. With the exception of the few women of the period who published their work, especially the highly influential Mercy Otis Warren, we wouldn't know about most of the major players in this story were it not for the men they corresponded with. Here, then, as sorry as I am to define these wonderful women by their male attachments, is the Who's Who among Founding Mothers.

SIGNERS OF THE DECLARATION OF INDEPENDENCE

JOHN ADAMS—husband of Abigail Smith Adams

JOSIAH BARTLETT—husband of Mary Bartlett

BENJAMIN FRANKLIN—husband of Deborah Read Franklin, brother of Jane Franklin Mecom, friend of Catharine Ray Greene, father of Sarah Franklin Bache

BUTTON GWINNETT—husband of Anne Gwinnett

THOMAS JEFFERSON—husband of Martha Wayles Jefferson; father of Martha Jefferson Randolph and Maria Jefferson Eppes; cousin of Anne Randolph Morris

FRANCIS LEWIS—husband of Elizabeth Annesley Lewis

ARTHUR MIDDLETON—brother of Sarah Middleton Pinckney

ROBERT MORRIS—husband of Mary White Morris

GEORGE ROSS—uncle-in-law of Betsy Ross

BENJAMIN RUSH—husband of Julia Stockton Rush, son-in-law of Annis Boudinot Stockton

RICHARD STOCKTON—husband of Annis Boudinot Stockton, father of Julia Stockton Rush

SOLDIERS AND STATESMEN IN THE REVOLUTIONARY PERIOD

BENEDICT ARNOLD—husband of Margaret Shippen Arnold

NATHANAEL GREENE—husband of Catharine Littlefield Greene

JOHN JAY—husband of Sarah Livingston Jay, son-in-law of Susannah French Livingston, brother-in-law of Susan Livingston Symmes and Catharine Livingston Ridley

HENRY KNOX—husband of Lucy Flucker Knox

HENRY LAURENS—father of Martha Laurens Ramsay

MORGAN LEWIS—son of Elizabeth Annesley Lewis, son-in-law of Margaret Beekman Livingston

CHARLES COTESWORTH PINCKNEY—son of Eliza Lucas Pinckney, brother of Harriott Pinckney Horry, husband of Sarah Middleton Pinckney and then Mary Stead Pinckney

THOMAS PINCKNEY—son of Eliza Lucas Pinckney, brother of Harriott Pinckney Horry, husband of Elizabeth Motte Pinckney, Frances Motte Pinckney, son-in-law of Rebecca Brewton Motte

JOSEPH REED—husband of Esther deBerdt Reed

PHILIP SCHUYLER—husband of Catharine Van Rensselaer Schuyler; father of Elizabeth Schuyler Hamilton and Angelica Schuyler Church

GEORGE WASHINGTON—husband of Martha Dandridge Custis Washington

SIGNERS OF THE CONSTITUTION

ALEXANDER HAMILTON—husband of Elizabeth Schuyler Hamilton, son-in-law of Catharine Van Rensselaer Schuyler, brother-in-law of Angelica Schuyler Church

RUFUS KING—husband of Mary Alsop King

WILLIAM LIVINGSTON—husband of Susannah French Livingston; father of Susan Livingston Symmes, Sarah Livingston Jay, and Catharine Livingston Ridley

JAMES MADISON—husband of Dolley Payne Todd Madison

GOUVERNEUR MORRIS—husband of Anne Randolph Morris

PLAYERS IN THE NEW GOVERNMENT

AARON BURR—son of Esther Edwards Burr

WILLIAM BINGHAM—husband of Anne Willing Bingham

SAMUEL POWEL—husband of Elizabeth Willing Powel

JOHN RANDOLPH—cousin of Anne Randolph Morris and Martha Jefferson Randolph

THOMAS RANDOLPH—husband (and cousin) of Martha Jefferson Randolph, brother of Anne Randolph Morris

WOMEN WRITERS

CATHARINE MACAULAY

JUDITH SERGENT MURRAY

ANNIS BOUDINOT STOCKTON

MARY KATHERINE STODDARD

MERCY OTIS WARREN

PHILLIS WHEATLEY

OTHER WOMEN OF COURAGE

DEBORAH CHAMPION

MARGARET CORBIN

LYDIA DARRAGH
ELIZABETH FREEMAN (MUMBET)
EMILY GEIGER
NANCY HART
MARY HAYS (MOLLY PITCHER)
DICEY LANGSTON
SYBIL LUDDINGTON
BEHETHLAND MOORE
DEBORAH SAMPSON
PRUDENCE WRIGHT

Recipes

The Recipe for the Franklin Family Crown Soap

The Letters of Benjamin Franklin and Jane Mecom, edited and with an introduction by Carl Van Doren (Princeton, N.J.: Princeton University Press, 1950), pp. 251-52.

it must be taken of yr mould which [**word torn off**] is to be Redy Repared with some small [?] tises in the sides clos to the botom [?] to Let of any Ley first you cant avoid putting in with the curd there is also to be taked in a cours Lining [?] Smooth [?] which when the sides of the mould are taken off will Peal off with out any wast of wax the time for cooling will be acording to the Quantity, it ought to be cut as soon as throw cool Least it grow two hard, & not before because it will then twist & be more apt to crack, the Gages for cutting up must be in size I think about Six Inches Long & three Broad & in thikness about three quarters of an Insh I have not the Gage by me therefore cannot be Positive but when they are first cut up the wey about half a Pound they are Stampd Emediatly Every slab of it is cut or the surfice will Dry & not take the Impreshon so well, I think you must Remember

the Large Slabs are cut with a strong Brass wier (for Iron is Equally Prenicous to this as to the Dye) and the small cakes [with?] strong thrid or silk & as it is all most Imposable to cut them Perfictly of a size we have a small Gage Just fitt for won cake that we Pare any that needs it

N B the stamp as also the wier is touchd with a Litle Sweet oyl now & then as it needs it, the wax must not have been coulered before hand with any thing to make it Green: if the Plank the moulds are made with are not very thick they will soon warp & be unfitt for use, no other wood is suitable as Pine

Martha Washington's Recipes

From Poppy Cannon and Patricia Brooks, **The Presidents' Cookbook: Practical Recipes from George Washington to the Present** (New York: Funk & Wagnalls, 1968).

Martha Washington's Crab Soup

Certain favorite dishes of one Presidential family have come down through the years and have, through continued use, become favorites of many Presidential families. This is such a dish. Martha Washington served it to her seafood-loving husband. Later it became a favorite soup of Franklin

Roosevelt. And a White House chef served it to President and Mrs. Dwight Eisenhower, who also admired it.

Fresh crabs	Salt and pepper
Butter	Milk
Flour	Cream
Hard-boiled eggs	Sherry
Lemon rind, grated	Worcestershire sauce

Boil enough crabs in salted water to make ½ pound (or use 1 cup canned or frozen) crabmeat. Combine 1 tablespoon butter, 1½ tablespoons flour, 3 hard-boiled eggs that have been mashed, rind of one lemon grated, and salt and pepper to taste. Bring 4 cups milk to boil in a saucepan. Then pour it slowly into the egg mixture. Add the crabmeat to the milk–egg mixture and cook gently five minutes. Add ½ cup heavy cream; remove from the heat before it reaches a full boil. Add ½ cup sherry and a dash of Worcestershire sauce. Serve piping hot. **Six servings.**

Chicken Sauce

We would call this an Oyster Sauce for Chicken.

Oysters	Salt and pepper
Burgundy wine	Lemon juice
Mace	Butter
Onion	Slice of bread

Drain 2 dozen oysters (1 pint) well. Cook the oyster liquor, ½ cup Burgundy, ⅛ teaspoon mace, and 1 small shredded onion together until the onion is tender. Add salt and pepper to taste, the juice of ½ lemon, 2 tablespoons butter, 1 slice grated bread, and the oysters. Cook until the oysters are plump and crinkled, but do not boil. Pour over individual servings of roast or broiled chicken.

Hearty Choak Pie

Translation: Artichoke pie. This old English recipe comes from an old recipe book in Martha Washington's family. The coffin used, lest you become alarmed, was a pastry-lined dish or pan shaped like a (you guessed it!) coffin. The **verges** mentioned is verjuice or green juice—any sour juice of a green fruit used in place of vinegar. Grape juice was commonly used this way.

Artichokes	Sugar
Pastry	Verges (green juice)
Butter	Cinnamon
Marrow bones	Ginger

Take 12 harty choak [artichoke] bottoms, good and large and boil them. Discard the leaves and core, and place the bottoms on a coffin of pastry, with 1 pound butter and the marrow of 2 bones in big pieces, then close up the coffin, and bake it in the oven. Meanwhile, boil together ½ pound sugar, ½ pint verges, and a touch of cinnamon and ginger. When the pie is half-baked, put the liquor into it, replace it in the oven until it is fully baked.

Recipes from Eliza Pinckney and Harriott Pinckney Horry

From **A Colonial Plantation Cookbook: The Receipt Book of Harriott Pinckney Horry,** 1770, edited with an introduction by Richard J. Hooker (Columbia, S.C.: University of South Carolina Press, 1984), p. 46.

To Dress a Calves Head

Boil the head till the Tongue will Peal, then cut half the Head into small pieces, about the size of an oyster, then stew it in Strong Gravy, with a large Ladle full of Claret, and a handfull of sweet herbs, a little lemon peal, a pieces of Onion and Nutmeg. Let all These stew till they are tender: Take the other half of the head and boil it, scratch it across, strew over it grated Bread and sweet herbs with a little lemon Peal: Lard it with Bacon, and wash it over with the Yolks of Eggs, and strew over it a little grated Bread and Place it in the middle of your dish. Then put a pint a pint [**sic**] of strong Gravy into your stew pan with three Anchovies, a few

Capers a good many Mushrooms a good quantity of sweet Butter, and a quart of large Oysters; stew the Oysters in their own liquor with a Blade of Mace and a little white wine, keep the largest to fry, and shred a few of the smallest; then Beat the Yolks of Eggs [2] and Flour, dip them in and fry them in Hogs Lard, make little Cakes of the Brains and dip them in and fry them, then pour the stew'd meat in the dish with the other half of the head, and lay the fried Oysters, Brains and Tongue, with little bits of crispt bacon, and force meat Balls, on the Top and all about the meat garnish with horseradish and Barberries and serve it hott.

Brown Frigasee

Take Rabbits or Chickens, season them with salt, Pepper, and a little Mace, then put half a pound of Butter in your pan, Brown it, and dredge it with flower; cut up your Chickens put them in and fry them Brown and have ready a quart of good strong gravy, Oysters, Mushrooms, three Anchovies a chalot or two, a bunch of sweet herbs, and a glass of Claret. Season it high, and when they are boil'd enough take out the herbs, Chalots and Anchovies Bones, shred a lemon small and put in, and when your Chickens are almost brown enough, put them in and let them stew altogether keeping them shaking all the time its on the fire, and when it is as thick as cream, take it up and have ready to lay over it some Bitts of crispt Bacon, Fry Oysters in Hogs lard to make them look Brown, dip them in the Yolks of Eggs and Flour, and a little grated Nutmeg; and Forcemeat Balls: Garnish with Lemon and flowers and serve it

Notes

INTRODUCTION

The comprehensive books on colonial women used throughout this work are: **No Small Courage: A History of Women in the United States**, edited by Nancy F. Cott (New York: Oxford University Press, 2000); Elizabeth F. Ellet, **The Women of the American Revolution** (New York: Baker & Scribner, 1849); and **Noble Deeds of American Women; with Biographical Sketches of Some of the More Prominent**, edited by J. Clement, with an introduction by Mrs. L. H. Sigourney (Buffalo, N.Y.: Jewett, Thomas and Co., 1851); Mary Beth Norton, **Liberty's Daughters: The Revolutionary Experience of American Women, 1750–1800** (Ithaca, N.Y.: Cornell University Press, 1980); Linda K. Kerber, **Women of the Republic: Intellect and Ideology in Revolutionary America** (Chapel Hill: University of North Carolina Press, 1980); and Carol Berkin, **First Generation Women in Colonial America** (New York: Hill and Wang, 1996).

xvii "fly to the woods with our children": **The Book of Abigail and John**, edited by and with an introduction by L. H. Butterfield, Marc Friedlaender, and Mary-Jo Kline (Cambridge, Mass.: Harvard University Press, 1975), p. 83.

xviii Peru or Mexico to Spain: Frances Leigh Williams, **A Founding Family: The Pinckneys of South Carolina** (New York: Harcourt Brace Jovanovich, 1978), p. 12.

xviii "my affairs died": **Benjamin Franklin and Women: A Series of Essays**, edited by Larry Tise (University Park: Pennsylvania State University Press, 1998), p. 35.

xix Nathanael Greene: John F. Stegeman and Janet A. Stegeman, **Caty: A Biography of Catharine Littlefield Greene**, foreword by Harvey H. Jackson (Athens: University of Georgia Press, 1977) p. 69.

xix "Awake, awake, Sir Billy": Sally Smith Booth, **The Women of '76** (New York: Hastings House, 1973), p. 104.

xix "In bed with Mrs. L——g": Linda Grant De-Pauw, **Founding Mothers: Women of America in the Revolutionary Era** (Boston: Houghton Mifflin, 1975), p. 187.

xx independence and then government: Jeffrey Richards, **Mercy Otis Warren** (New York: Twayne, 1995) p. 15.

xxi "America can boast": George Washington to Annis Boudinot Stockton, August 31, 1788, available at University of Virginia, The Papers of George Washington, gwpapers.virginia.edu/constitution/1788/stock.html.

xxi "defeat the women": Dorothy Denneen Volo and James M. Volo, **Daily Life During the American Revolution** (Westport, Conn.: Greenwood Press, 1947), p. 229.

xxii because men wanted them to: DePauw, **Founding Mothers**, p. 219.

CHAPTER ONE
STIRRINGS OF DISCONTENT

Sources for biographical information are: Harriott Horry Ravenal, **Women of Colonial and Revolutionary Times: Eliza Pinckney** (New York: Charles Scribner's Sons, 1896); Frances Leigh Williams, **Plantation Patriot: A Biography of Eliza Lucas Pinckney** (New York: Harcourt, Brace & World, 1967); and Frances Leigh Williams, **A Founding Family** (New York: Harcourt Brace Jovanovich, 1978).

3 "much business": Eliza Lucas to Mrs. Boddicott May 2, 1740, **The Letterbook of Eliza Lucas Pinckney 1739–1762**, edited and with a new introduction by Elise Pinckney, with the editorial assistance of Marvin R. Zahniser (Columbia: University of South Carolina Press, 1997), p. 7.

3 "I always shall": Eliza Lucas to Mary Bartlett, June 1742, ibid., p. 41.

4 "but eighteen": Eliza Lucas to Col. George Lucas, 1740, ibid., p. 6.

4 "and export them": Eliza Lucas to Mary Bartlett, 1742, ibid., p. 35.

5 "suit Carolina": Ibid.

5 "to build fleets": Eliza Lucas to Mary Bartlett, 1972, ibid., p. 38.

5 "one may hit": Ibid.

6 "the fire the other day": Eliza Lucas to Mary Bartlett, March–April 1742, ibid., p. 33.

7 "more peaceably inclined": Ravenal, **Eliza Pinckney**, p. 11.

8 "applied to in earnest": Ibid., p. 105.

8 "breach of prudence": Ibid., p. 100.

9 "do more for her country": Ibid., p. 107.

10 "lover of all mankind": Ibid., pp. 116–18.

11 played cards much too much: Eliza Pinckney to Mrs. Gabriel Manigault, December 1753–January 1754, **Letterbook**, p. 80.

11 "to an American": Ravenal, **Eliza Pinckney**, p. 149.

12 "on some accounts more valuable": Eliza Pinckney to Lady Carew, February 7, 1757, Pinckney, **Letterbook**, p. 88.

13 "existed between mortals": Eliza Pinckney to Dr. Kirk Patrick, February 1760, ibid., p. 132.

13 "weak to complain": Eliza Pinckney to Mrs. Kina, May 1759, ibid., p. 119.

13 "lost only one": Eliza Pinckney to Mrs. Evance, June 19, 1760, ibid., p. 153.

14 "to do you good": Eliza Pinckney to P. Harles and Thomas Pinckey, August 1758, ibid., p. 95.

14 "of his age capable": Eliza Pinckney to Mr. Gerrard, February 1760, ibid., p. 136.

14 "our impatience is here": Eliza Pinckney to Mrs. Kina, February 27, 1762, ibid., p. 175.

14 "and his consort": Ibid.

15 "the Little Rebel": Ravenal, **Eliza Pinckney,**
p. 247.

15 "and the attachment strong": Ibid., p. 249.

EVERYDAY LIFE FOR COLONIAL WOMEN
Major source books for this chapter are: Mary Beth
Norton, **Liberty's Daughters: The Revolutionary**
Experience of American Women, 1750–1800
(Ithaca, N.Y.: Cornell University Press, 1980);
Linda K. Kerber, **Women of the Republic: Intel-**
lect and Ideology in Revolutionary America
(Chapel Hill: University of North Carolina Press,
1980); and Harry Clinton Green and Mercy Wolcott
Green, **The Pioneer Mothers of America: A**
Record of the More Notable Women of the Early
Days of the Country and Particularly of the
Colonial and Revolutionary Periods (New York:
Putnam's Sons, 1912).

17 economy entirely run by women: Laurel
Thatcher Ulrich, **A Midwife's Tale: The Life of**
Martha Bullard 1785–1812 (New York: Vintage
Press, 1990), p. 84.

17 "exceedingly brilliant": John Adams to Abigail
Adams, April 25, 1778, **The Adams Papers:**
Adams Family Correspondence, vol. 3, edited by
L. H. Butterfield (Cambridge, Mass.: Belknap
Press of Harvard University Press, 1973), p. 17.

18 "to ridicule female learning": Abigail Adams to John Adams, June 30, 1778, ibid., p. 52.

18 control her property: John F. Stegeman and Janet A. Stegeman, **Caty: A Biography of Catharine Littlefield Greene**, foreword by Harvey H. Jackson (Athens: University of Georgia Press, 1977), p. 160.

21 **She Stoops to Conquer:** Evarts Boutell Greene, **Revolutionary Generation 1763–1790** (New York: Macmillan, 1943), p. 153.

21 New York Hospital in 1773: Ibid., p. 152.

A SOLID CITIZEN

Biographical material and quotations from letters in this chapter are taken from **The Journal of Esther Edwards Burr 1754–1757**, edited and with an introduction by Carol F. Karlsen and Laurie Crumpacker (New Haven, Conn.: Yale University Press, 1984); and Sharon M. Harris editor, **American Women Writers to 1800** (New York: Oxford University Press, 1996).

23 "this nine years past": Jonathan Edwards, "On the Great Awakening," December 12, 1743, available at National Humanities Institute, "Who We Are: The Story of America's Constitution," www.nhinet.org/ccs/docs/awaken.htm.

25 **Pamela** was a favorite: March 11, 1755, **Journal of Esther Edwards Burr**, p. 98; Pinckney, **Letterbook**, p. 47.

25 "a woman than of a man": April 1, 1755, **Journal of Esther Edwards Burr**, p. 105.

25 "that is certain": April 30, 1755, ibid., p. 114.

26 "making a disturbance": October 2, 1754, ibid., p. 46.

26 "really hurried": October 5, 1754, ibid., p. 50.

26 "the sisterhood": January 22, 1756, ibid., p. 184.

26 "a few days past": February 21, 1755, ibid., p. 93.

26 "very low spirited": July 17, 1755, ibid., p. 134.

26 "Too gloomy to write": August 9, 1755, ibid., p. 142.

26 "some weeks past": December 12, 1755, ibid., p. 176.

26 "I felt so dull": October 17, 1754, ibid., p. 55.

26 **"old, dead horse"**: October 2, 1755, ibid., p. 156.

27 "worldly minded and devilish": June 22, 1755, ibid., p. 12.

27 "but in deeds and practice!": January 19, 1755, ibid., p. 82.

27 "the house of God": November 10, 1754, ibid., p. 61.

27 "not on God": December 1, 1754, ibid., p. 68.

27 "being very bad": December 4, 5, 6, 1754, ibid., p. 70.

27 "filled again": December 10, 1754, ibid., p. 71.

27 "very near to me": April 19, 1755, ibid., p. 111.

28 "to go out": April 13, 1756, ibid., p. 192.

28 student in housewifery: November 25, 1755, ibid., p. 170.

28 "TO MARRY THAN TO": January 6, 1755, ibid., p. 79.

28 "'the Jesuit!'": June 13, 1755, ibid., p. 123n.

29 "his afflicted family!": November 1754, ibid., p. 60.

29 "to turn Papist": August 8–9, 1755, ibid., p. 142.

30 "hear the like!": January 29, 1755, ibid., p. 86.

30 "brought forth a mouse": March 3, 1755, ibid., p. 96.

30 "against their governors": November 29, 1755, ibid., p. 171.

30 "in this country": Ibid.

31 "to make me easy": December 20, 1755, ibid., p. 178.

31 "the **barbarous** retches": July 17, 1755, ibid., p. 135.

31 "in fear every minute": September 2–3, 1756, ibid., p. 220.

31 "gloom to everything": September 7, 1756, ibid., p. 221.

32 "I can't devise": April 13, 1756, ibid., p. 192.

32 "ten months old": February 28, 1755, ibid., p. 95.

33 for hire in Newark: July 29, 1756, ibid., p. 214.

33 "An Army to breakfast": May 16, 17, 18, 19, 1757, ibid., p. 260.

33 "would be my joys": April 11, 1757, ibid., p. 256.

34 "talked him quite silent": April 12, 1757, ibid., p. 257.

35 "bring him to terms": September 2, 1757, ibid., p. 274.

PHILADELPHIA BUSINESS WOMAN

Information on Deborah Franklin is taken from Carl Van Doren, **Benjamin Franklin** (New York: Viking Press, 1938); Walter Isaacson, **Benjamin Franklin: An American Life** (New York: Simon & Schuster, 2003); **Benjamin Franklin and Women**, edited by Larry Tise (University Park: Pennsylvania State University Press, 1998); and H. W. Brands, **The First American** (New York: Doubleday, 2000). Quotations from the correspondence of Jane Mecom are taken from Carl Van Doren, **The Letters of Benjamin Franklin and Jane Mecom** (Princeton, N.J.: Princeton University Press/ American Philosophical Society, 1950).

37 "took to wife": P. M. Zall, **Founding Mothers: Profiles of Ten Wives of America's Founding Fathers** (Washington, D.C.: Heritage Books, 1991), p. 2.

38 "this was precisely what she had grasped": Cabanis, **American National Biography** (New York: Oxford University Press/American Council of Learned Societies, 2003).

38 The recipe survives: **Letters of Benjamin Franklin and Jane Mecom,** Van Doren, p. 130.

38 "fortune to me": Isaacson, **Benjamin Franklin,** p. 78.

39 buckwheat cakes: Sheila Skemp, "Family Partnerships: The Working Wife, Honoring Deborah Franklin" in **Benjamin Franklin and Women,** p. 27.

40 "upon you greater honors": Abiah Franklin and Jane Mecom to Benjamin Franklin, October 14, 1751, in Van Doren, **Letters of Benjamin Franklin and Jane Mecom,** p. 46.

40 "a spinning wheel": Benjamin Franklin to Jane Mecom, January 6, 1726, ibid. p. 35.

41 "baronet's ladies": Jane Mecom to Deborah Franklin, January 29, 1758, ibid. p. 65.

42 "regularly discharged from New York": Deborah Franklin to the commander of the British forces, January 9, 1758, in Zall, **Founding Mothers,** p. 8.

42 "look after your interest": Isaacson, **Benjamin Franklin**, p. 179.

43 "long and bitter dissensions": Benjamin Franklin to Deborah Franklin, January 10, 1758, quoted in Skemp, "Family Partnerships," p. 30.

43 "Mrs. F. to accompany me": Isaacson, **Benjamin Franklin**, p. 202.

44 "that I don't perceive them": William Greene Roelker, **Benjamin Franklin and Catharine Ray Greene: Their Correspondence 1755–1790** (Philadelphia: American Philosophical Society Independence Square, 1949), p. 14.

45 **"When younger arms invite him"**: Isaacson, **Benjamin Franklin**, p. 216.

45 "circumspect in all your behavior": Ibid., p. 218.

45 "a letter from you": Deborah Franklin to Benjamin Franklin, February 1765, in Zall, **Founding Mothers**, p. 9.

46 "everything is with you": Deborah Franklin to Benjamin Franklin, April 1765, ibid., p. 10.

46 "something to say": Ellet, **Women of the American Revolution**, p. 1:334.

47 "show a proper resentment": Zall, **Founding Mothers**, p. 5.

47 "courage you showed": Isaacson, **Benjamin Franklin**, p. 225.

47 "exceeded your fear": Jane Mecom to Deborah Franklin, June 25, 1767, in Van Doren, **Letters of Benjamin Franklin and Jane Mecom**, p. 89.

47 "heads and bosoms": Jane Mecom to Benjamin Franklin, November 8, 1766, ibid., p. 94.

48 "our top ladies": Jane Mecom to Margaret Stevenson, May 9, 1967, ibid., p. 97.

48 "a **husband's love letter**": Deborah Franklin to Benjamin Franklin, October 8, 1765, in Zall, **Founding Mothers,** p. 10.

48 "if you had been at home yourself": Deborah Franklin to Benjamin Franklin, January 12, 1766, ibid., p. 11.

48 "children seem distracted": Ellet, **Women of the American Revolution**, p. 1:335.

49 "a considerable time": Ibid.

49 "Oh, that you were at home!": Deborah Franklin to Benjamin Franklin, May 16, 1767, in Zall, **Founding Mothers**, p. 11.

49 "my best judgment": **The Papers of Benjamin Franklin**, vol. 14, **January 1 Through December 31, 1767**, edited by Leonard W. Labaree (New Haven, Conn.: Yale University Press, 1970), p. 136.

50 "a proper one": Benjamin Franklin to Deborah Franklin, May 23, 1967, ibid., p. 167.

50 "brushed over again with the same color": Benjamin Franklin to Deborah Franklin, June 22, 1767, ibid., pp. 193–95.

51 "for a living as we have done": Benjamin Franklin to Richard Bache, August 5, 1767, ibid., p. 221.

51 "on this happy occasion": Isaacson, **Benjamin Franklin**, p. 238.

51 "that can make her happy": Jane Mecom to Benjamin Franklin, December 1, 1767, in Van Doren, **Letters of Benjamin Franklin and Jane Mecom**, p. 99.

51 "to be maintained": Benjamin Franklin to Jane Mecom, January 21, 1768, ibid., p. 103.

51 "to a parson": Deborah Franklin to Benjamin Franklin, January 13, 1767, in Zall, **Founding Mothers**, p. 11.

51 "sixty years old": Deborah Franklin to Benjamin Franklin, January 21, 22, 1768, ibid., p. 12.

52 "one moment's trouble": Deborah Franklin to Benjamin Franklin, August 16, 1770, ibid., p. 12.

52 "longer than this fall": Deborah Franklin to Benjamin Franklin, October 14, 1770, ibid., p. 13.

52 "affectionate wife D Franklin": Deborah Franklin to Benjamin Franklin, October 14, 1770, ibid., p. 13.

52 "is stuffed into them": Jane Mecom to Benjamin Franklin, November 7, 1768, ibid., p. 107.

53 "ministerial displeasure": Benjamin Franklin to Jane Mecom, September 26, 1774, Van Doren, **Letters,** p. 147.

53 "cannot now be repaired": Zall, **Founding Mothers,** p. 7.

53 "Be content with that": Ibid.

CHAPTER TWO
REBELLIOUS WOMEN

The source book for the history of the Revolutionary War is Howard H. Peckham, **The War for Independence: A Military History** (1958; reprint, Chicago: University of Chicago Press, 1979).

55 "ladies in this town": Alfred M. Young, "The Women of Boston," in **Women in Politics in the Age of the Democratic Revolution,** edited by Har-

riet B. Applewhite and Darline G. Levy (Ann Arbor: University of Michigan Press, 1993), p. 196.

56 "your traffic be dull": Hannah Griffits, "The Female Patriots," reprinted in **Milcah Martha Moore's Book**, edited by Catherine La Courreye Blecki and Karin A. Wulf (University Park: Pennsylvania State University Press, 1997), pp. 172–73, available at "Women and Social Movements in the United States, 1775–2000," womhist.binghamton.edu/amrev/doc1.htm.

56 "refuse to buy from William Jackson": Young, "Women of Boston," p. 195.

57 "salvation of a whole continent": Mary Beth Norton, **Liberty's Daughters: The Revolutionary Experience of American Women 1750–1800** (Boston: Little, Brown, 1980), p. 166.

57 six o'clock in the evening: **Essex Gazette**, May 23, 1769, available at "Women and Social Movements in the United States, 1775–2000," womhist.binghamton.edu/amrev/doc3.htm.

57 "of your own make and spinning": Young, "Women of Boston," p. 197.

57 fancy ball in Williamsburg, Virginia: Helen Bryan, **First Lady of Liberty: Martha Washington** (New York: John Wiley & Sons, 2002), p. 160.

58 "our country requires it": "Boston Ladies' Boycott Agreement," in **Boston Evening Post**, February 12, 1770, available at "Women and Social Movements in the United States, 1775–2000," womenhist.binghamton.edu/amrev/doc2.htm.

58 "entertaining them later at her home": Linda Kerber, "History Can Do It No Justice," in **Women in the Age of the American Revolution**, edited by Ronald Hoffman and Peter J. Albert (Charlottesville: University Press of Virginia/U.S. Capital Historical Society, 1989), p. 23.

60 signed by Carolinians abroad: Harriott Horry Ravenal, **Women of Colonial and Revolutionary Times: Eliza Pinckney** (New York: Charles Scribner's Sons, 1896), p. 252.

60 "all adult persons of both sexes": Young, "Women of Boston," p. 204.

60 "clap their hands": Norton, **Liberty's Daughters**, p. 159.

60 **"Then farewell Liberty most dear"**: Young, "Women of Boston," pp. 203–4.

61 "A Lady's Adieu to Her Tea Table": Linda Grant DePauw and Conover Hunt, with the assistance of Miriam Schneir, **Remember the Ladies: Women in America 1715–1850** (New York: Viking Press, 1976), p. 83.

61 "for the public good": Edenton Ladies' Agreement, October 27, 1774, **Morning Chronicle and London Advertiser**, January 16, 1776, available at "Women and Social Movements in the United States, 1775–2000," womenhist.binghamton.edu/ amrev/doc4.htm.

61 a well-publicized cartoon of the time is to be believed: Cartoon from the Library of Congress Prints Division.

61 "fatal consequence is to be dreaded": Arthur Iredell to James Iredell, January 31, 1775, Charles E. Johnson Collection, Division of Archives and History, Raleigh, N.C.; reprinted in **The Papers of James Iredell**, vol. 1, **1776–1777**, edited by Don Higginbotham (Raleigh: North Carolina Division of Archives and History, 1976), pp. 282–84.

62 "that inspired it": Ravenal, **Eliza Pinckney**, p. 256.

62 "and the sooner, the better": John Adams to Abigail Adams, July 6, 1774, **The Adams Papers: Adams Family Correspondence**, vol. 1, **December 1761–May 1776**, edited by L. H. Butterfield; Marjorie E. Sprague, assistant editor (Cambridge, Mass.: Harvard University Press, 1963), pp. 129–30.

63 "the house of Colonel Pond": Ellet, **Women of the American Revolution**, p. 2:117.

64 "transformation into balls": Ibid., pp. 2:116–17.

65 dangerous cause of the new nation: DePauw, **Remember the Ladies,** p. 87.

PROPAGANDIST FOR THE REVOLUTION

Basic biographical information in this section is taken from Ellet, **Women of the American Revolution**, vol. 1; Rosemarie Zagarri, **A Women's Dilemma: Mercy Otis Warren and the American Revolution** (Wheeling, Ill: Harlan Davidson, 1995); Jeffrey Richards, **Mercy Otis Warren** (New York: Wayne Publishers, 1995); **American Women Writers to 1800,** edited by Sharon M. Harris (New York: Oxford University Press, 1996); and Lester M. Cohen, "Mercy Otis Warren: The Politics of Language and the Aesthetics of Self," **American Quarterly** (Johns Hopkins University Press) 35, no. 5 (winter 1983): 481–98. Biographical information on Catharine Macaulay is taken from **The Blackwell Encyclopedia of the American Revolution**, edited by Jack P. Greene and J. R. Pole (Cambridge, Mass.: Basil Blackwell Inc., 1991).

68 according to an eighteenth-century historian: William Gordon, **The History of the Rise, Progress, and Establishment of the Independence of the United States of America** (London, 1788); see Richards, **Mercy Otis Warren**, p. 10.

68 "with infamy": Zagarri, **Women's Dilemma,** p. 43.

69 **"make them slaves":** Young, "Women of Boston," p. 212.

71 **"sexes sage advice":** Mercy Warren to Abigail Adams, February 1774, in Butterfield, **Adams Papers,** p. 1:99.

71 One of her needlework accomplishments: Pilgrim Hall Museum, Plymouth, Mass.

72 "all slaves by nature?": Zagarri, **Women's Dilemma,** p. 16.

72 life-sized statue of her in his church: Sally Smith Booth, **The Women of '76** (New York: Hastings House, 1973), pp. 14–15.

73 "their female efforts": Ishbel Ross, **Sons of Adam, Daughters of Eve: The Role of Women in American History** (New York: Harper & Row, 1969), p. 115.

74 "happy institution": Ellet, **Women of the American Revolution,** p. 1:77.

74 "manes of liberty": Mercy Warren to Abigail Adams, August 9, 1774, in Butterfield, **Adams Papers,** p. 1:138.

75 "bolden language of the other sex": Richards, **Mercy Otis Warren,** p. 43.

75 "of your foggy islands": Henry Steele Commager and Richard B. Moss, **The Spirit of '76: The Story of the American Revolution as Told by Participants** (Cambridge, Mass.: Da Capo Press, 1968), p. 250.

76 "victory over tyranny": Mercy Warren to Abigail Adams, January 28, 1775, in Butterfield, **Adams Papers**, p. 1:181.

76 "to successful tyranny,": Ibid. p. 181.

76 "first of British slaves": Abigail Adams to Mercy Warren, February 3, 1775, ibid., p. 1:183.

76 "morality have failed": Abigail Adams to Mercy Warren, February 3, 1775, ibid., p. 1:185.

76 "female character suffer?": Richards, **Mercy Otis Warren**, pp. 95–96.

77 "virtue and patriotism": James Warren to Mercy Warren, April 7, 1775, ibid., p. 5.

77 **"bless each hero's name"**: Harris, **American Women Writers to 1800**, p. 383.

77 "citizens be poured out": Richards, **Mercy Otis Warren**, p. 38.

78 "with mangled bodies": Ellet, **Women of the American Revolution**, pp. 1:94–95.

79 "blood of thy children": Abigail Adams to Mercy Warren, May 2, 1775, in Butterfield, **Adams Papers**, p. 1:190.

79 "so noble a part": Mercy Warren to Abigail Adams, May 25, 1775, ibid., p. 1:198.

80 "fill the streets": James Warren to Mercy Otis Warren, June 18, 1775, "The Decisive Day Is Come," Massachusetts Historical Society www.masshist.org/bh/warrenpltext.html.

80 "merciless foe": Ellet, **Women of the American Revolution**, p. 1:96.

81 "bosom of their brethren": Mercy Otis Warren to Catharine Macaulay, August 24, 1775, available at Gilder Lehrman Online Exhibits, www.digital-history.uh.edu/exhibits/ dearmadam.

81 "resolution of yours": Ellet, **Women of the American Revolution**, p. 1:80.

81 "done to America": Ibid., p. 1:81.

82 "unfeeling heart": Abigail Adams to Mercy Warren, July 24, 1775, in Butterfield, **Adams Papers**, p. 1:254.

83 "easy deportment": Ellet, **Women of the American Revolution**, p. 1:82.

83 "particular transactions": Mercy Otis Warren to Abigail Adams, December 11, 1775, in Butterfield, **Adams Papers,** p. 1:339.

83 Pennsylvania and Virginia: Melissa Lukeman Bohrer, **Glory, Passion, and Principle: The Story of Eight Remarkable Women at the Core of the American Revolution** (New York: Atria Books, 2003), p. 46.

83 **"With gold unfading, WASHINGTON! be thine":** Available at James Madison Center, www.jmu.edu/Madison/Wheatley.htm.

83 Latin and ancient history: www.womenshistory.about.com/bio/biblio_phillis_wheatley. html.

84 **"in my parents' breast!":** Quoted in **American Women Writers to 1800,** Harris, (New York: Oxford University Press, 1996), p. 332.

85 "favoured by the Muses": Available at James Madison Center, www.jmu.edu/Madison/Wheatley.Washingtonreply.htm.

85 "Commonwealth of America": Ellet, **Women of the American Revolution,** p. 1:83.

85 "in every production": Mercy Warren to Abigail Adams, February 7, 1776, in Butterfield, **Adams Papers,** p. 1:343.

86 "glad of your opinion": Abigail Adams to Mercy Warren, April 13, 1776, ibid., pp. 1:377–78.

87 "of that unhappy town": Mercy Warren to Abigail Adams, April 17, 1776, ibid., p. 1:385.

87 "very disagreeable disorder": Abigail Adams to John Adams, April 21, 1776, ibid., p. 1:391.

88 "before he is aware": Ellet, **Women of the American Revolution**, p. 1:100.

88 "I need say no more": Abigail Adams to John Adams, June 17, 1776, in Butterfield, **Adams Papers**, p. 2:16.

88 his wife's disapproval: Richards, **Mercy Otis Warren**, p. 15.

POLITICAL PHILOSOPHER

General biographical information is taken from Sally Smith Booth, **The Women of '76** (New York: Hastings House, 1973); Lynne Withey, **Dearest Friend: A Life of Abigail Adams** (New York: Touchstone, 2001); Edith B. Gelles, **Portia: The World of Abigail Adams** (Bloomington: Indiana University Press, 1992); Natalie S. Bober, **Abigail Adams: Witness to a Revolution** (New York: Simon & Schuster, 1995); and P. M. Zall, **Founding Mothers: Profiles of Ten Wives of America's Founding Fathers** (Washington, D.C.: Heritage

Books, 1991). Quotations from letters between Abigail and John Adams and by Abigail Adams are all taken from **The Adams Papers**: Adams Family Correspondence, vols. 1 and 2, edited by L. H. Butterfield (Cambridge, Mass.: Harvard University Press, 1963). For more information on the Adams family, see Paul C. Nagel, **The Adams Women: Abigail and Louisa Adams, Their Sisters and Daughters** (Cambridge, Mass.: Harvard University Press, 1987).

89 "give you up our names": Abigail Adams to John Adams, Butterfield, **Adams Papers**, p. 1:263.

89 "I cannot but laugh": John Adams to Abigail Adams, April 14, 1776, ibid., p. 1:382.

89 "the laws of England": Abigail Adams to Mercy Warren, April 27, 1776, ibid., p. 1:397.

90 "I never could have talked": Abigail Adams to John Adams, October 22, 1775, ibid., p. 1:310.

91 "I have observed in you": John Adams to Abigail Adams, April 17, 1764, ibid., p. 1:35.

91 "like a lack of breeding": Abigail Adams to John Adams, April 30, 1764, ibid., p. 1:42.

91 "whatever you please to call them": John Adams to Abigail Adams, May 7, 1764, ibid., p. 1:44.

91 "legs of a lady": Abigail Adams to John Adams, May 9, 1764, ibid., p. 1:47.

92 burst into tears: Withey, **Dearest Friend**, p. 38.

92 cousin in London: Abigail Adams to Isaac Smith Jr., in Butterfield, **Adams Papers**, p. 1:67.

93 "one of her own sex and country": Abigail Adams to Isaac Smith Jr., January 4, 1770, ibid., pp. 1:76–77.

94 "landing of it": Abigail Adams to Mercy Warren, December 5, 1773, ibid., p. 1:88.

94 "such is the spirit that prevails": Ibid.

94 "respecting the tea": Abigail Adams to John Adams, December 30, 1773, ibid., p. 1:90.

94 celebrate it with a poem: Abigail Adams to Mercy Warren, February 27, 1774, ibid., p. 1:99.

94 "a shilling a week": John Adams to Abigail Adams, May 12, 1774, ibid., p. 1:107.

94 outside of Boston: John Adams to Abigail Adams, June 2, 1774, ibid., p. 1:109.

95 "friends of liberty": John Adams to Abigail Adams, July 1, 1774, ibid., p. 1:118.

95 "in the struggle": Ibid., p. 1:119.

95 "without horror": Abigail Adams to John Adams, August 19, 1774, ibid., p. 1:142.

95 "innocent creatures": Mary Cranch to Abigail Adams, August 20, 1774, ibid., p. 1:142.

96 compatriots in Massachusetts: John Adams to Abigail Adams, September 8, 1774, ibid., p. 1:150.

96 "breastworks, etc. etc.": Abigail Adams to John Adams, September 14, 1779, ibid., p. 1:151.

96 "is prepared for us": John Adams to Abigail Adams, September 20, 1774, ibid., p. 1:161.

97 "upon this subject": Abigail Adams to John Adams, September 1774, ibid., p. 1:162.

97 "liberty or death": Abigail Adams to Catharine Macaulay, 1774, ibid., p. 1:177.

97 "upon the sea coast": Abigail Adams to Mercy Warren, May 2, 1775, ibid., p. 1:190.

97 "idle reports and frivolous alarms": John Adams to Abigail Adams, April 30, 1775, ibid., p. 1:189.

97 "love to them, and to all": John Adams to Abigail Adams, May 1, 1775, ibid., p. 1:192.

98 "imagine how we live": Abigail Adams to John Adams, May 24, 1775, ibid., p. 1:205.

98 "Continental expense": John Adams to Abigail Adams, June 10, 1775, ibid., p. 1:214.

98 "before Boston": John Adams to Abigail Adams, June 17, 1775, ibid., p. 1:215.

99 "sufficient supply": Abigail Adams to John Adams, June 16, 1775, ibid., p. 1:217.

99 "battle must ensue": Abigail Adams to John Adams, June 18, 1775, ibid., p. 1:222.

99 "Battle of Bunker's Hill": John Quincy Adams to Joseph Sturuf, March 1846, ibid., p. 1:223n.

99 "drop in the bucket": Abigail Adams to John Adams, June 20, 1775, ibid., p. 1:223.

99 "Can they realize what we suffer?": Abigail Adams to John Adams, June 22, 1775, ibid., p. 1:225.

100 "bled with them and for them": Abigail Adams to John Adams, July 5, 1775, ibid., p. 1:239.

100 "you are an heroine": John Adams to Abigail Adams, July 7, 1775, ibid., p. 1:242.

101 "the great public": Abigail Adams to John Adams, July 16, 1775, ibid., pp. 1:246–47.

101 British newspapers: Ibid., p. 1:256n.

101 "to negotiate with": John Adams to Abigail Adams, July 24, 1777, ibid., p. 1:255.

102 "we could maintain it": John Adams to Abigail Adams, July 23, 1775, ibid., p. 1:253.

102 "wickedness of the man": Abigail Adams to John Adams, July 25, 1775, ibid., pp. 1:261–62.

102 "deemed the Lukewarms": Ibid., p. 1:263.

103 "small sacrifice to the public": Abigail Adams to Mercy Warren, August 27, 1775, ibid., p. 1:275.

103 "support me": John Adams to Abigail Adams, October 1, 1775, ibid., p. 1:290.

103 "their grandmother": John Adams to Abigail Adams, October 13, 1775, ibid., p. 1:300.

103 "make out so well": Abigail Adams to Mercy Warren, October 19, 1775, ibid., p. 1:302.

103 "more than six": Abigail Adams to John Adams, October 21, 1775, ibid., p. 1:308.

103 "not washed away": Abigail Adams to John Adams, October 25, 1775, ibid., p. 1:313.

104 "I won't say": John Adams to Abigail Adams, November 14, 1775, ibid., p. 1:320.

104 "to all their devices": Abigail Adams to John Adams, November 12, 1775, ibid., p. 1:324.

105 "as well as other things": Abigail Adams to John Adams, November 27, 1775, ibid., p. 1:330.

105 separation from Britain: Abigail Adams to John Adams, December 10, 1775, ibid., p. 1:336.

105 "if he quit": Abigail Adams to Mercy Warren, January 1776, ibid., p. 1:423.

105 "in a separation": Abigail Adams to John Adams, March 16, 1776, ibid., p. 1:357.

106 "with impunity": Abigail Adams to John Adams, March 31, 1776, ibid., pp. 1:369–70.

107 "heroes would fight": John Adams to Abigail Adams, April 14, 1776, ibid., p. 1:382.

108 "liberal principles": Abigail Adams to Mercy Warren, April 12, 1776, ibid., p. 1:397.

108 "to be broken": Abigail Adams to John Adams, May 7, 1776, ibid., p. 1:402.

108 "Latin and Greek": John Adams to Abigail Adams 2nd, April 18, 1776, ibid., p. 1:388.

108 "else you undertake": John Adams to Abigail Adams, April 28, 1776, ibid., p. 1:398.

108 "very apropos": John Adams to Abigail Adams, May 27, 1776, ibid., pp. 1:419–20.

109 "gentlemen to fortify": John Adams to Abigail Adams, May 12, 1776, ibid., p. 1:406.

109 "of her husband": John Adams to Abigail Adams, May 22, 1776, ibid., p. 1:412.

109 serve the country: Abigail Adams to John Adams, June 3, 1776, ibid., p. 2:4.

110 "'free and independent states'": John Adams to Abigail Adams, July 3, 1776, ibid., p. 2:28.

110 "of our country": Abigail Adams to John Adams, July 14, 1776, ibid., p. 2:46.

110 "children a father?": John Adams to Abigail Adams, July 20, 1776, ibid., p. 2:54.

111 "face appeared joyful": Abigail Adams to John Adams, July 21, 1776, ibid., p. 2:56.

111 "throw it to you": John Adams to Abigail Adams, July 29, 1776, ibid., p. 2:68.

112 "learned women": Abigail Adams to John Adams, August 14, 1776, ibid., p. 2:94.

112 "shape or other": John Adams to Abigail Adams, August 25, 1776, ibid., p. 2:110.

113 "Amazons in America": Abigail Adams to John Adams, September 20, 1776, ibid., p. 2:129.

CHAPTER THREE
AT THE FRONT

115 eyewitness account: Ray Raphael, **A People's History of the American Revolution: How Common People Shaped the Fight for Independence** (New York: New Press, 2001), p. 124.

115 "in the Revolutionary War": Linda Grant De-Pauw, **Remember the Ladies: Women in America 1750–1815** (New York: Viking Press, 1976), p. 90.

116 rum or whiskey: **Notable American Women, 1607–1950: A Biographical Dictionary**, edited by Edward T. James; Janet Wilson, associate editor (Cambridge, Mass.: Belknap Press of Harvard University Press, 1971), p. 385.

116 receive that honor: DePauw, **Remember the Ladies**, p. 90.

116 men received, of course: Ibid., p. 89.

117 baggage wagons: George Washington Papers, Library of Congress, www.memory.loc.gov.

117 "frequent marches": Ibid.

117 "soldiers to desert": Ibid.

117 local mortician: Sally Smith Booth, **The Women of '76** (New York: Hastings House, 1973), p. 153.

117 Washington's army: Melissa Lukeman Bohrer, **Glory, Passion, and Principle: The Story of Eight Remarkable Women at the Core of the American Revolution** (New York: Atria Books, 2003), p. 134.

118 to thwart disaster: Phebe A. Hanaford, **Daughters of America; or, Women of the Century** (Augusta, Me.: True and Co., 1883), p. 56.

118 "the American army": Henry Steele Commager and Richard B. Moss, **The Spirit of '76: The Story of the American Revolution as Told by Participants** (Cambridge, Mass.: Da Capo Press, 1968), p. 464.

119 information verbally: Hanaford, **Daughters of America**, p. 61.

119 troops in South Carolina: DePauw, **Remember the Ladies**, p. 90.

119 information to George Washington: Raphael, **People's History of the American Revolution**, p. 124.

119 enemy troop movements: Linda Kerber, "History Can Do It No Justice," in **Women in the Age of the American Revolution**, edited by Ronald Hoffman and Peter J. Albert (Charlottesville: University Press of Virginia/U.S. Capital Historical Society, 1989), p. 5.

119 intelligence to the Americans: Sue Heinemann, **Timeline of American Women's History** (New York: Berkeley Group, 1996), p. 256.

120 "to a female bosom": Elizabeth Ellet, **The Women of the American Revolution** (New York: Baker & Scribner, 1849), p. 2:126.

120 "find a home": Ibid., p. 2:134.

120 her military service: Ibid.

121 "do not hesitate to grant relief": Booth, **Women of '76**, pp. 269–70.

121 "devil of a wife": Ellet, **Women of the American Revolution**, p. 2:233.

122 "are all true": Kerber, "History Can Do It No Justice," p. 79 and 79n.

122 civilian panic: Carol Berkin, **First Generations: Women in Colonial America** (New York: Hill & Wang, 1996), p. 183.

122 "what her country called for": Kerber, "History Can Do It No Justice," p. 25.

122 not harvest them: Heinemann, **Timeline of American Women's History**, p. 256.

123 "his cheeks as he passed along": Linda Kerber and Jane Sherron de Hart, **Women's America: Refocusing the Past**, 5th ed. (New York: Oxford University Press, 2000), pp. 109–10.

123 military campaign of the Revolution: Helen Bryan, **First Lady of Liberty: Martha Washington** (New York: John Wiley & Sons, 2002).

AT CAMP WITH THE GENERALS' WIVES
One useful source in this section is Harry Clinton Green and Mercy Wolcott Green, **The Pioneer Mothers of America: A Record of the More Notable Women of the Early Days of the Country and Particularly of the Colonial and Revolutionary Periods**, 3 vols. (New York: G. P. Putnam's Sons, 1997). Biographical information on Martha Washington comes from Helen Bryan, **First Lady of Liberty: Martha Washington** (New York: John Wiley & Sons, 2002). Quotations from her letters are taken from **Worthy Partner: The Papers of Martha Washington**, compiled by Joseph E. Fields (Westport, Conn.: Greenwood Press, 1994).

124 "George Washington": George Washington to Martha Washington, June 18, 1775, Fields, **Worthy Partner**, p. 159.

125 was now in charge: Martha Custis to Robert Cary and Company, August 20, 1757, ibid., p. 5.

125 "no ordinary mortal": Margaret C. Conkling, **Mary and Martha Washington: Memoirs of the Mother and Wife of Washington** (Auburn, Me.: Derby, Miller & Co., 1850), pp. 77–78.

125 "amid a wide and bustling world": Bryan, **First Lady of Liberty**, p. 128.

126 "I know George will": Mary V. Thompson, "Martha Washington in the American Revolution: Becoming the New Nation's First Lady (As if I Had Been a Very Great Somebody)," Mount Vernon Ladies' Association, February 6, 2002 (slightly revised March 7, 2002), p. 4.

126 "in my power to avoid it": George Washington to Martha Washington, June 18, 1775, Fields, **Worthy Partner**, p. 159.

126 a form of lobbying: Bryan, **First Lady of Liberty**, pp. 185–86.

126 returning to Mount Vernon: Ibid., p. 187.

126 "way of revenge on me": Thompson, "Martha Washington in the American Revolution," p. 8.

127 "city of New York": Alice Curtis Desmond, **Martha Washington: Our First Lady** (New York: Dodd, Meade, 1943), p. 142.

127 in the dead of winter: Bryan, **First Lady of Liberty**, p. 191.

127 "a very great somebody": Martha Washington to Elizabeth Ramsay, December 30, 1775, Fields, **Worthy Partner**, p. 164.

127 "sound of a gun": Ibid.

Much of the biographical information on Catharine Littlefield Greene is from John F. Stegeman and Janet A. Stegeman, **Caty: A Biography of Catharine Littlefield Greene**, foreword by Harvey H. Jackson (Athens: Brown Thrasher Books, University of Georgia Press, 1977). Some of the biographical material on Lucy Knox comes from Diana Forbes-Robertson, **Lady** (Washington, D.C.: American Heritage, 1966).

129 British-occupied Boston: Carl Van Doren, **The Letters of Benjamin Franklin and Jane Mecom** (Princeton, N.J.: Princeton University Press American Philosophical Society, 1950), p. 164.

130 "taking their vessels": Martha Washington to Anna Maria Bassett, January 31, 1776, Fields, **Worthy Partner**, p. 167.

130 time out for entertainment: Martha Washington to Mercy Otis Warren, April 2, 1776, ibid., p. 168.

130 despite the disease: Bryan, **First Lady of Liberty**, p. 205.

131 "chosen to make the flag": See "The Betsy Ross Homepage," Independence Hall Association, www.ushistory.org.

131 was secure: Ibid.

131 fight under a single standard: Linda Grant De-Pauw, **Founding Mothers: Women of America in the Revolutionary Era** (Boston: Houghton Mifflin, 1975), p. 162.

131 **Harper's Monthly** in 1873: See "About Women's History: Comprehensive Research Guide," www.womenshistory.about.com.

131 "This fact is officially recorded": Green and Green, **Pioneer Mothers of America**, p. 96.

132 statue of George III: Stegeman and Stegeman, **Caty**, p. 34.

132 "so contemptible": Mary Beth Norton, **Liberty's Daughters: The Revolutionary Experience of American Women 1750–1800** (Boston: Little, Brown, 1980), p. 223.

133 gallons of it, missing: Booth, **Women of '76**, p. 161.

133 "still going there": Martha Washington to Anna Maria Bussett, August 28, 1776, Fields, **Worthy Partner**, p. 172.

133 "share of happiness": Stegeman and Stegeman, **Caty**, p. 38.

133 nowhere to hide: Ibid., p. 39.

134 in her homespun: Bryan, **First Lady of Liberty**, p. 212.

134 "happy in each other": Thompson, "Martha Washington in the American Revolution," p. 35.

135 flirt with his friends: Stegeman and Stegeman, **Caty**, p. 44.

135 "comforts have been derived": Bryan, **First Lady of Liberty**, p. 215.

135 "to my heart": Stegeman and Stegeman, **Caty**, p. 45.

136 "quite a woman of business": Norton, **Liberty's Daughters**, p. 223.

137 "equal command": Document 2437, Gilder Lehrman Institute of American History, www.gilderlehrman.org/teachers/modules1.html.

137 "does I must go": Martha Washington to Burwell Bassett, December 22, 1777, in Fields, **Worthy Partner**, p. 175.

137 human condition was not much better: Thompson, "Martha Washington in the American Revolution," p. 43.

137 "No bread, no soldier": Ibid., p. 42.

137 arrived on the scene: Bryan, **First Lady of Liberty**, p. 225.

138 "comforts to them in her power": Ibid., p. 227.

138 "they were at first": Martha Washington to Mercy Otis Warren, March 7, 1778, Fields, **Worthy Partner**, p. 178.

138 "would be complete": Ibid., p. 177.

138 wiped out: Bryan, **First Lady of Liberty**, p. 228.

139 keep up morale: Thompson, "Martha Washington in the American Revolution," p. 46.

139 pledging assistance: Bryan, **First Lady of Liberty**, p. 231.

139 "celebrating the important Event": George Washington General Orders, May 5, 1778, www.memory.loc.gov.

139 gill of rum for each soldier: Thompson, "Martha Washington in the American Revolution," p. 49.

ON THE HOME FRONT

Quotations from Mary Bartlett's letters are taken from **The Papers of Josiah Bartlett**, edited by Frank C. Mevers (Hanover, N.H.: University Press of New England, published for the New Hampshire Historical Society, 1979).

140 "business with Congress": Josiah Bartlett to Mary Bartlett, June 21, 1778, Mevers, **Papers of Josiah Bartlett**, p. 189.

140 "suffered to accomplish": Mary to Josiah, May 17, 1776, ibid., p. 59.

140 headed for Canada: Josiah to Mary, May 18, 1776, ibid., p. 60.

141 she told her husband: Mary to Josiah, June 30, 1776, ibid., p. 80.

141 "fate of America": Mary to Josiah, July 16, 1776, ibid., p. 92.

141 "defending America": Mary to Josiah, July 20, 1776, ibid., p. 97.

141 "if I'm alive": Mary to Josiah, September 9, 1776, ibid., p. 117.

142 "it must be at such a time": Abigail Adams to Mercy Warren, January 1, 1777, **The Adams Papers: Adams Family Correspondence**, vol. 2, **June 1776–March 1778**, edited by L. H. Butterfield (Cambridge, Mass.: Harvard University Press, 1965), in p. 150.

142 "all this melancholy": John Adams to Abigail Adams, February 3, 1777, ibid., p. 2:153.

142 "join the army": Abigail Adams to John Adams, February 8, 1777, ibid., p. 2:157.

142 "being full": Abigail Adams to John Adams, February 12, 1777, ibid., p. 2:160.

142 "part of the world": John Adams to Abigail Adams, February 18, 1777, ibid., p. 2:164.

142 "industry and economy": Mercy Warren to Abigail Adams, March 1, 1777, ibid., p. 2:167.

142 "sufferings of their ancestors": Abigail Adams to John Adams, March 8, 1777, ibid., p. 2:172.

143 "beyond all bounds": John Adams to Abigail Adams, May 14, 1777, ibid., p. 2:238.

143 "felt than expressed": Abigail Adams to John Adams, March 9, 1777, ibid., p. 2:173.

143 "past my comprehension": John Adams to Abigail Adams, March 14, 1777, ibid., p. 2:175.

144 "gust for them": John Adams to Abigail Adams, April 2, 1777, ibid., p. 2:195.

144 "similar circumstances": Abigail Adams to John Adams, April 17, 1777, ibid., p. 2:212.

144 "with horror": Abigail Adams to John Adams, May 18, 1777, ibid., p. 2:241.

145 "my circumstances": Abigail Adams to John Adams, June 15, 1777, ibid., p. 2:266.

145 "in my absence": John Adams to Abigail Adams, June 16, 1777, ibid., p. 2:267.

145 "dread its arrival": Abigail Adams to John Adams, June 23, 1777, ibid., p. 2:270.

145 "young patriot": Mercy Warren to Abigail Adams, July 7, 1777, ibid., p. 2:276.

145 "Heaven only knows": Abigail Adams to John Adams, July 9, 1777, ibid., p. 2:277.

145 "mind and heart": John Adams to Abigail Adams, July 10, 1777, ibid., p. 2:278.

146 "with its ancestors": Abigail Adams to John Adams, July 16, 1777, ibid., p. 2:282.

146 "female beauty": John Adams to Abigail Adams, July 20, 1777, ibid., p. 2:285.

146 "in the grave": Abigail Adams to John Adams, July 23, 1777, ibid., p. 2:287.

146 "affected me": John Adams to Abigail Adams, July 28, 1777, ibid., p. 2:292.

147 "spectators of the whole transaction": Abigail Adams to John Adams, July 31, 1777, ibid., p. 2:295.

147 drive up the price: Raphael, **People's History of the American Revolution**, p. 118.

147 "our own country": John Adams to Abigail Adams, August 11, 1777, in Butterfield, **Adams Papers**, p. 2:305.

148 "Philadelphia a long time ago": John Adams to Abigail Adams, August 11, 1777, ibid., p. 2:306.

148 just bad news about war: Abigail Adams to John Adams, September 17, 1777, ibid., p. 2:343.

148 took over the city: John Adams to Abigail Adams, September 30, 1777, ibid., p. 2:349.

149 offering to her country: Abigail Adams to John Adams, October 25, 1777, ibid., p. 2:358.

149 "my own personal happiness": Abigail Adams to Isaac Smith Jr., October 30, 1777, ibid., p. 2:364.

149 "with the demand of my country?": Abigail Adams to James Lovell, December 15, 1777, ibid., p. 2:371.

150 "prevented my taking her": Ibid., p. 2:376n.

150 "weakness of the advisor": Mercy Warren to Abigail Adams, January 29, 1778, ibid., p. 2:376.

150 "already consented": Mercy Warren to Abigail Adams, January 8, 1778, ibid., p. 2:379.

151 "that yours has": Hannah Storer to Abigail Adams, February 24, 1778, ibid., p. 2:395.

151 "of your tickets": Mevers, **Papers of Josiah Bartlett**, Josiah to Mary Bartlett, May 21, 1778, p. 178.

151 "this way from Philadelphia": Mary Bartlett to Josiah Bartlett, June 4, 1778, ibid., p. 183.

152 "is chiefly over": Josiah Bartlett to Mary Bartlett, June 7, 1778, ibid., p. 184.

152 "and etc. etc.": Josiah Bartlett to Mary Bartlett, ibid., p. 190.

152 "anxious to hear the event": Josiah Bartlett to Mary Bartlett, August 18, 1778, ibid., p. 207.

152 "by seeing you at home": Mary Bartlett to Josiah Bartlett, August 21, 1778, ibid., p. 212.

153 "dressed that way": Josiah Bartlett to Mary Bartlett, August 24, 1778, ibid., p. 214.

153 "middling well": Mary Bartlett to Josiah Bartlett, August 28, 1778, ibid., p. 216.

153 huge rise in prices: Mary Bartlett to Josiah Bartlett, September 26, 1778, ibid., p. 227.

154 "prepare for the winter": Josiah Bartlett to Mary Bartlett, October 10, 1778, ibid., p. 229.

155 "fortified themselves strongly": Jane Mecom to Benjamin Franklin, August 15, 1778, Carl Van Doren, **The Letters of Benjamin Franklin and Jane Mecom** (Princeton, N.J.: Princeton University Press/American Philosophical Society, 1950), in p. 183.

155 "before your abode is mine": Sarah Livingston Jay to John Jay, September 3, 1777, Richard Morris, **John Jay: The Making of a Revolutionary: John Jay Unpublished Papers 1745–1780**, vol. 1 (New York: Harper & Row, 1975), in p. 442.

156 sensitive documents unmolested: Elizabeth F. Ellet, **The Women of the American Revolution** (New York: Baker & Scribner, 1849), p. 2:115; see also Margaret Truman, **Women of Courage** (New York: William Morrow, 1976), p. 38.

156 wanted to punish patriots: Green and Green, **Pioneer Mothers**, p. 133.

158 "had she been slain in battle": Julia Delafield, **Biographies of Francis Lewis and Morgan Lewis** (New York: Anson P. F. Randolph & Co., 1877), p. 50.

CHAPTER FOUR
ON THE HOME FRONT

160 determined to succeed: R. L. Barbour, **South Carolina's Revolutionary War Battlefields: A Tour Guide** (Gretna, La.: Pelican Publishing, 2002), p. 26.

160 "virtuous liberty": Harriott Horry Ravenal, **Eliza Pinckney** (New York: Charles Scribner's Sons, 1896), p. 270.

160 north from Florida: Elise Pinckney, ed., "Letters of Eliza Lucas Pinckney, 1768–1782," **South Carolina Historical Society** 76 (July 1975): 153n.

160 "here entirely alone": Ravenal, **Eliza Pinckney,** p. 273.

161 "a severe blow!": Eliza Pinckney to Thomas Pinckney, May 17, 1779, in Pinckney, "Letters of Eliza Lucas Pinckney," p. 157.

161 grant it to the slaves: Howard H. Peckham, **The War for Independence: A Military History** (1958; reprint, Chicago: University of Chicago Press, 1979), p. 105.

161 "a little will make us that": Pinckney, **Letters,** p. 157.

161 Georgia and South Carolina: Barbour, **South Carolina's Revolutionary War Battlefields,** p. 55.

162 "felons of the town": Ravenal, **Eliza Pinckney,** p. 282.

162 "'British officers'": Ibid., p. 283.

162 "men in camp": Ibid., p. 284.

163 "crimson and gold": Ibid., p. 285.

163 "by the enemy": Ibid., p. 287.

163 "your husband's fortitude": Ibid., p. 288.

164 "safe with Gen. Washington": Ibid., p. 290.

164 "save your limb": Eliza Pinckney to Thomas Pickney, August 1780, Pinckney, "Letters of Eliza Lucas Pinckney," p. 159.

164 "I was near you": Ibid.

164 "hearty and well": Eliza Pinckney to Thomas Pinckney, September 17, 1780, ibid., p. 162.

164 "comfort than we have lately known!": Eliza Pinckney to Elizabeth Motte Pinckney, ibid., p. 163.

164 "I feel much for her": Eliza Pinckney to Thomas Pinckney, October 4, 1780, ibid., p. 165.

165 wounded husband: Ravenal, **Eliza Pinckney**, p. 295.

165 rest of the war: Ibid., p. 298.

166 "good of her country": Lee Memoirs quoted in **Spirit of '76: The Story of the American Revolution as Told by Participants**, edited by Henry Steele Commager and Richard B. Morris, (New York: DaCapo Press, 1995), p. 1181.

166 their target: Ravenal, **Eliza Pinckney**, p. 299.

166 "injury she had received": Sally Smith Booth, **The Women of '76** (New York: Hastings House, 1973), p. 257.

166 knitting needles: Ravenal, **Eliza Pinckney**, p. 300.

167 "my singular case": Eliza Pinckney to Dr. Garden, May 14, 1782, Pinckney, "Letters of Eliza Lucas Pinckney," p. 169.

167 "not got a penny": Ibid., p. 170.

AT CAMP

167 "trip northward": Martha Washington to Bartholomew Dandridge, November 2, 1778, **Worthy Partner: The Papers of Martha Washington**, compiled by Joseph E. Fields (Westport, Conn.: Greenwood Press, 1994), p. 180.

167 four years: Mary V. Thompson, "Martha Washington in the American Revolution: Becoming the New Nation's First Lady (As if I Had Been a Very Great Somebody)," Mount Vernon Ladies' Association, February 6, 2002 (slightly revised March 7, 2002), p. 53.

168 anniversary in January: Ibid., p. 54.

168 "speaks of you highly": Ibid., p. 55.

168 "to have you with me": John F. Stegeman and Janet A. Stegeman, **Caty: A Biography of Catharine Littlefield Greene**, foreword by Harvey H. Jackson (Athens: University of Georgia Press, 1977), p. 68.

169 "without sitting down": Ibid., p. 69.

169 "Mrs. Knox is fatter than ever": Helen Bryan, **First Lady of Liberty: Martha Washington** (New York: John Wiley & Sons, 2002), p. 234.

169 too fond of wine: Stegeman and Stegeman, **Caty**, p. 70.

169 trimmed in blue: Bryan, **First Lady of Liberty**, p. 336.

169 "in those quarters": Martha Washington to John Parke and Eleanor Custis, March 19, 1779, in Fields, **Worthy Partner**, p. 181.

169 once again was pregnant: Stegeman and Stegeman, **Caty**, p. 71.

169 reaching twelve feet: Thompson, "Martha Washington in the American Revolution," p. 62.

170 "but hay": Bryan, **First Lady of Liberty**, p. 239.

170 Nathanael Ray Greene: Stegeman and Stegeman, **Caty**, p. 75.

170 "are still just a man!": Ibid., p. 76.

171 eye for the ladies: Thompson, "Martha Washington in the American Revolution," p. 65.

171 "will be acceptable to her": Martha Washington to Elizabeth Schuyler, (no month) 1780, in Fields, **Worthy Partner**, p. 182.

171 with guns at the ready: Bryan, **First Lady of Liberty**, p. 240.

171 "in six months": Thompson, "Martha Washington in the American Revolution," p. 66.

171 "distressed me exceedingly": Martha Washington to Burwell Bassett, July 18, 1780, in Fields, **Worthy Partner**, p. 183.

POLITICAL ACTIVISM

Esther Reed's letters were collected by her grandson, who compiled them with biographical information in William Reed, **The Life of Esther DeBerdt, Afterwards Esther Reed of Pennsylvania** (Philadelphia: C. Sherman, Printer, privately printed, 1853).

172 "The Sentiments of an American Woman": "The Sentiments of an American Woman," 1780, available at "Women and Social Movements in the United States, 1775–2000," womhist.binghamton.edu/amrev/doc6.htm.

172 "By an American Woman": Sharon M. Harris, **American Women Writers to 1800** (New York: Oxford University Press, 1996), p. 258.

172 Delaware and Massachusetts: Reed, **Life of Esther DeBerdt Reed**, p. 41.

173 "to relieve you": Esther DeBerdt to Joseph Reed, August 10, 1765, ibid., p. 59.

173 "for a long time": Esther DeBerdt to Joseph Reed, November 9, 1765, ibid., p. 67.

174 "taxing yourselves": Esther DeBerdt to Joseph Reed, February 7, 1766, ibid., p. 74.

174 "fiercely on the side of America": Esther DeBerdt to Joseph Reed, December 12, 1766, ibid., p. 107.

174 "without me": Esther DeBerdt to Joseph Reed, February 19, 1767, ibid., p. 110.

174 "counsels of politicians": Joseph Reed to Esther DeBerdt, April 5, 1767, ibid., p. 113.

174 "impossible to say": Esther DeBerdt to Joseph Reed, August 1768, ibid., p. 129.

175 "emigrant to Oregon": Ibid., p. 152.

175 "our heavy one": Esther Reed to Dennis DeBerdt, April 1772, ibid., p. 172.

175 "indifferent here": Esther Reed to Dennis DeBerdt, June 15, 1771, ibid., p. 168.

176 "don't expect that": Esther Reed to Dennis DeBerdt, October 20, 1772, ibid., p. 181.

176 "for the public": Esther Reed to Dennis De-Berdt, May 14, 1774, ibid., p. 193.

176 "of civil war": Esther Reed to Dennis De-Berdt, November 2, 1774, ibid., p. 203.

176 "and who against": Esther Reed to Dennis DeBerdt, February 13, 1775, ibid., p. 207.

177 "family concerns": Esther Reed to Dennis DeBerdt, March 14, 1775, ibid., p. 209.

177 "will terminate": Ibid., p. 210.

177 his law practice: Elizabeth F. Ellet, **The Women of the American Revolution** (New York: Baker & Scribner, 1849), p. 1:42.

177 "to die or be free": Esther Reed to Dennis DeBerdt, June 24, 1775, **Life of Esther DeBerdt Reed**, p. 216.

178 "to be victorious": Esther Reed to Dennis De-Berdt, July 22, 1775, ibid., p. 219.

178 "without a murmur": Esther Reed to Dennis DeBerdt, September 8, 1775, ibid., p. 228.

178 "though true in general": Ibid., p. 229.

178 "English nation?": Dennis DeBerdt to Jos. Reed, October 4, 1775, ibid., p. 228.

179 "circles of acquaintance": Esther Reed to Dennis DeBerdt, October 28, 1778, ibid., p. 240.

179 "utmost to defend ourselves": Ibid., p. 234.

180 "commanded by noblemen": Ellet, **Women of the American Revolution,** p. 1:44.

180 "to our retreat": Esther Reed to Dennis De-Berdt, March 1777, in Reed, **Life of Esther DeBerdt Reed,** p. 258.

180 "shot under him": Ibid., p. 260.

181 "the day before": Jos. Reed to Dennis De-Berdt, May 24, 1778, ibid., p. 286.

181 "**all** things well": Esther Reed to Mrs. Cox, June 16, 1778, ibid., p. 291.

181 "entwined in politics": Esther Reed to Dennis DeBerdt, September 16, 1779, ibid., p. 298.

181 troop morale: Thompson, "Martha Washington in the American Revolution," p. 67.

181 how to proceed: Mary Beth Norton, **Liberty's Daughters: The Revolutionary Experience of**

American Women, 1750–1800 (Ithaca, N.Y.: Cornell University Press, 1980), p. 179.

182 "Soldier more pleasant": Harris, **American Women Writers to 1800,** p. 259.

182 fund drive proceeded: Ellet, **Women of the American Revolution**, p. 152.

183 "strength and courage": "A Letter from a Lady in Philadelphia to Her Friend in This Place," June 20, 1780, in **Maryland Gazette**, July 21, 1780, available at "Women and Social Movements in the United States, 1775–2000," womhist.binghamton.edu/amrev/doc12.htm.

183 "side of the water": Sarah Franklin Bache to Mrs. Gray, July 1, 1780, Kane Family Letters, Historical Society of Pennsylvania, available at "Women and Social Movements in the United States, 1775–2000," womhist.binghamton.edu/amrev/doc16.htm.

184 "call for them": Phebe A. Hanaford, **Daughters of America; or, Women of the Century** (Augusta, Me.: True and Co., 1883), p. 54.

184 "to get rid of them": Norton, **Liberty's Daughters**, p. 180.

184 "accept her offering": Reed, **Life of Esther DeBerdt**, p. 320.

184 "Continental Army": "The Ladies of Trenton Assemble, 1780," in **Documents Relating to the Revolutionary History of the State of New Jersey**, edited by William Nelson, vol. 4 (Trenton, N.J.: State Gazette Publishing Co., 1914), available courtesy of the New Jersey Historical Society at www.scc.rutgers.edu/njwomenshistory/Period_2/Trenton.htm.

185 "with lukewarmness": Booth, **Women of '76**, p. 266.

185 "at present engaged in": Ronald Hoffman, in collaboration with Sally D. Mason, **Princes of Ireland, Planters of Maryland: A Carroll Sage, 1500–1782** (Chapel Hill: University of North Carolina Press, 2000), p. 379.

185 women of Philadelphia: Ibid.

186 "mark of respect": Norton, **Liberty's Daughters**, p. 182.

186 "of those virtuous feelings": Thompson, "Martha Washington in the American Revolution," p. 70. A copy of the letter in Martha Jefferson's handwriting is on the website of the University of North Carolina.

186 Martha Jefferson's that survives: Norton, **Liberty's Daughters**, p. 184.

187 "to anything else": Thompson, "Martha Washington in the American Revolution," p. 68.

187 "wishes on the subject": Esther Reed to George Washington, July 4, 1780, in Reed, **Life of Esther DeBerdt Reed**, p. 319.

187 "made into shirts": George Washington Papers, Library of Congress, www.memory.loc.gov.

188 "union with the gentlemen": Ibid.

188 "his own disposal": Esther Reed to George Washington, July 31, 1780, in Reed, **Life of Esther DeBerdt Reed**, p. 323.

188 "their pay": George Washington Papers, Library of Congress, www.memory/loc.gov.

188 "to give them": Esther Reed to Jos. Reed, August 22, 1780, in Reed, **Life of Esther DeBerdt Reed**, p. 311.

189 "should it be otherwise": Jos. Reed to Esther Reed, August 26, 1780, ibid., p. 313.

189 "of citizens followed": Ibid., p. 331.

189 "I lost her forever": Jos. Reed to Dennis DeBerdt, 1781, ibid., p. 332.

190 "lady who made it": Marquis de Chastellux, **Travels in North America in the Years 1780, 1781, 1782**, translated by Howard C. Rice Jr., vol. 1 (Chapel Hill: University of North Carolina Press, 1963), p. 135.

190 "as they are amiable": George Washington Papers, Library of Congress, www.memory. loc.gov.

190 "warmest inclinations": Norton, **Liberty's Daughters**, p. 184.

ENEMY AGENT

191 pretty daughters: Carl Van Doren, **Secret History of the American Revolution** (Garden City, N.Y.: Garden City Publishing Co., 1941), p. 186.

191 family was driven out: James Parton, **Noted Women of Europe and America: Authors, Artists, Reformers, and Heroines, Queens, Princesses, and Women of Society, Women Eccentric and Peculiar, from the Most Recent and Authentic Sources** (Hartford, Conn.: Phoenix Publishing Co., 1883), p. 197.

191 Shippen household: Ibid., p. 198.

192 "Turkish" costumes: Van Doren, **Secret History of the American Revolution**, p. 184.

192 only changing the names: Ibid., p. 186.

192 "lays close siege to Peggy": Ellet, **Women of the American Revolution**, p. 2:214.

193 "how to kiss": Van Doren, **Secret History of the American Revolution**, p. 187.

194 "Revolutionary patriot": Ellet, **Women of the American Revolution**, p. 2:216.

194 "former government": Van Doren, **Secret History of the American Revolution**, p. 196.

194 "and other nonsense": Ibid., p. 440.

194 would be protected: Ibid., p. 203.

195 "particular compliments": Ibid., p. 442.

195 "to be further employed": Ibid., p. 454.

195 "impaired by time or accident": Ibid.

195 French fleet on its way: Ibid., p. 262.

195 over three years' time: Parton, **Noted Women of Europe and America**, p. 203.

196 "Sir Henry Clinton from Rhode Island": Ibid., p. 467.

196 "with New England": Ibid., p. 468.

196 along to the enemy: Ibid., p. 280.

196 arrival at West Point: Ibid., p. 287.

196 rest of the party had rarely seen: Ibid., p. 303.

197 "not to wait for me": Ibid., p. 204.

197 men around her: Van Doren, **Secret History of the American Revolution**, pp. 347–48.

198 "unacquainted with the plan": Ibid., p. 349.

198 "that he is now safe": Parton, **Noted Women of Europe and America,** p. 206.

198 Peggy Arnold's guilt continued: Ibid., p. 207; Van Doren, **Secret History of the American Revolution,** p. 350.

199 "present war": Van Doren, **Secret History of the American Revolution,** p. 383.

199 "genteel life": Ibid., p. 384.

199 "which were very meritorious": Ibid., p. 386.

WAITING FOR PEACE

200 "How unhappy is war to domestic happiness": Stegeman and Stegeman, **Caty,** p. 81.

200 and say good-bye: Ibid., p. 82.

201 were also in need of her: Bryan, **First Lady of Liberty,** p. 249.

201 struck again in April: Fawn M. Brodie, **Thomas Jefferson: An Intimate History** (New York: W. W. Norton & Co., 1974), pp. 142–43.

201 having the house razed: Bryan, **First Lady of Liberty,** p. 249.

202 a few weeks before—and flee: Brodie, **Thomas Jefferson,** p. 146.

202 control the water: Howard H. Peckham, **The War for Independence: A Military History** (1958, reprint, Chicago: University of Chicago Press, 1979), pp. 160–66.

202 "fine Hyson tea": Thompson, "Martha Washington in the American Revolution," pp. 81–82.

203 to wait the British out: Peckham, **War for Independence,** pp. 169–74.

204 live at Mount Vernon: Bryan, **First Lady of Liberty,** p. 256.

204 "not to be surmounted": Thompson, "Martha Washington in the American Revolution," p. 89.

205 "five miles from headquarters": Stegeman and Stegeman, **Caty,** p. 92.

205 all along the way: Ibid., pp. 93–94.

205 almost two years: Ibid., p. 94.

206 "even with the ladies": Ibid., p. 95.

206 turncoats in his camp: Ibid., pp. 96–97.

207 "yellow buttons and gold facings": Ibid., p. 99.

207 "had all crept into one bed together": Ibid., p. 101.

208 sail back to Philadelphia: Ibid., p. 105.

208 honored with gold medals: Bryan, **First Lady of Liberty,** p. 260.

208 "upon the road": Thompson, "Martha Washington in the American Revolution," p. 96.

208 attempt to placate the troops: Bryan, **First Lady of Liberty,** p. 261.

209 "but for want of tape": Martha Washington to Major General Henry Knox, March 6, 1783, in Fields, **Worthy Partner,** p. 189.

CHAPTER FIVE
WIDOWS AND ORPHANS TO DIPLOMACY

211 "rendering themselves agreeable": William Greene Roelker, **Benjamin Franklin and Cath-**

arine Ray Greene: Their Correspondence, 1755–1790 (Philadelphia: American Philosophical Society, 1949), p. 103.

211 "were advancing towards us": Carl Van Doren, **The Letters of Benjamin Franklin and Jane Mecom** (Princeton, N.J.: Princeton University Press, 1950), p. 169.

212 more accurate news: Elizabeth F. Ellet, **The Women of the American Revolution** (New York: Baker & Scribner, 1849), p. 1:338.

212 "with fine walks in it": Benjamin Franklin to Jane Mecom, October 5, 1777, in Van Doren, **Letters of Benjamin Franklin and Jane Mecom**, p. 171.

212 "home and for repose": Benjamin Franklin to Catharine (Ray) Greene, February 28, 1778, in Roelker, **Benjamin Franklin and Catharine Ray Greene**, p. 87.

213 "as that of the moon": Benjamin Franklin to Jane Mecom, October 25, 1779, ibid., p. 103.

213 "every cock's tail": Sally Smith Booth, **The Women of '76** (New York: Hastings House, 1973), p. 266.

213 "amazing lately": Ellet, **Women of the American Revolution**, p. 1:342.

214 "the schools in France": Benjamin Franklin to Jane Mecom, April 22, 1779, in Van Doren, **Letters of Benjamin Franklin and Jane Mecom,** p. 191.

214 "future kind letters": Jane Mecom to Benjamin Franklin, July 27, 1779, ibid., p. 195.

214 "favor of the ladies": Jane Mecom to Benjamin Franklin, June 23, 1779, ibid., p. 192.

214 "very long time": Roelker, **Benjamin Franklin and Catharine Ray Greene,** p. 96n.

214 "peace is established": Jane Mecom to Benjamin Franklin, September 12, 1779, in Van Doren, **Letters of Benjamin Franklin and Jane Mecom,** p. 197.

214 "much alarmed": Benjamin Franklin to Jane Mecom, October 25, 1779, ibid., p. 199.

215 "caused in America": Ibid.

216 "in their fortune": Jane Mecom to Sarah Bache, October 1780, ibid., p. 202.

217 "of our new allies": Catharine Ray Greene to Benjamin Franklin, January 1, 1781, in Roelker, **Benjamin Franklin and Catharine Ray Greene,** p. 107.

217 "has ravaged Richmond": Catharine Ray Greene to Benjamin Franklin, January 31, 1781, ibid., p. 109.

217 "to be very powerful": Jane Mecom to Benjamin Franklin, June 17, 1782, in Van Doren, **Letters of Benjamin Franklin and Jane Mecom**, p. 213.

217 "from our land": William and Catharine Greene to Benjamin Franklin, June 25, 1782, in Roelker, **Benjamin Franklin and Catharine Ray Greene**, p. 117.

218 "upon him to consent": Abigail Adams to John Thaxter, February 15, 1778, in **The Adams Papers: Adams Family Correspondence**, vol. 2, **June 1776–March 1778**, edited by L. H. Butterfield (Cambridge, Mass.: Harvard University Press, 1965), p. 390.

218 "between the male and female sex": Abigail Adams to John Thaxter, February 15, 1778, ibid., p. 391.

218 "communicated to a **woman**": Ibid., p. 392.

218 "too often the case": John Thaxter to Abigail Adams, March 6, 1778, ibid., p. 401.

218 "I admire the ladies here": John Adams to Abigail Adams, April 25, 1778, in **The Adams Papers: Adams Family Correspondence**, vol. 3, edited by L. H. Butterfield (Cambridge, Mass.: Belknap Press of Harvard University Press, 1973), p. 17.

219 "of my own country": Abigail Adams to John Adams, June 30, 1778, ibid., p. 52.

219 "would have failed me": Abigail Adams to John Adams, September 29, 1778, ibid., p. 95.

219 "drop of your blood": Abigail Adams to John Adams, October 25, 1778, ibid., p. 111.

220 "of your absence": Abigail Adams to John Adams, November 11–23, 1778, ibid., p. 119.

220 "really makes me unhappy": John Adams to Abigail Adams, December 18, 1778, ibid., p. 138.

220 "more of my love letters there": John Adams to Abigail Adams, January 18, 1779, ibid., p. 149.

221 "patience and submission": Abigail Adams to James Lovell, January 4, 1779, ibid., p. 147.

221 "convey them to me": Abigail Adams to James Lovell, January 4, 1779, ibid., p. 148.

222 "with a secret": John Adams to Abigail Adams, February 13, 1779, ibid., p. 170.

222 "and malicious politicians": John Adams to Abigail Adams, February 20, 1779, ibid., p. 174.

222 "of either sex": John Adams to Abigail Adams, February 1779, ibid., p. 183.

222 "continuance in Europe": Mercy Otis Warren to Abigail Adams, July 6, 1779, ibid., p. 209.

223 "commission was vacated?": Abigail Adams to James Lovell, July 15, 1779, ibid., p. 210.

223 "very, very affectionately": James Lovell to Abigail Adams, July 16, 1779, ibid., p. 212.

224 "and four pence": Howard W. Felton, **Mumbet** (New York: Dodd, Mead & Co., 1970), p. 8.

225 "Good mother, farewell": Information on Elizabeth Freeman available at "Africans in America," www.pbs.org/wgbh/aia/part2/2p39.html.

225 Irish linen sold better than Dutch: Abigail Adams to John Adams, July 5, 1780, Butterfield, **Adams Papers,** p. 372.

225 charging too much for some handkerchiefs: Mercy Otis Warren to Abigail Adams, December 21, 1780, in **The Adams Papers: Adams Family Correspondence,** vol. 4, edited by L. H. Butterfield (Cambridge, Mass.: Belknap Press of Harvard University, 1973), p. 42.

226 "a writer of votes": Abigail Adams to John Adams, July 5, 1780, in Butterfield, **Adams Papers,** vol. 3, p. 372.

226 "from state to state": Abigail Adams to John Thaxter, July 21, 1780, ibid., p. 378.

226 "stabs of calumny": Abigail Adams to Mercy Otis Warren, February 28, 1780, ibid., p. 288.

227 "minister to join him": Alice Lee Snippen to Elizabeth Welles Adams, June 17, 1781, in Butterfield, **Adams Papers,** vol. 4, p. 154.

228 "wounded I bleed": Abigail Adams to James Lovell, June 30, 1781, ibid., p. 166.

228 "country and your friend": Abigail Adams to Elbridge Gerry, July 20, 1781, ibid., p. 183.

228 "chagrin must arise": James Lovell to Abigail Adams, August 10, 1781, ibid., p. 194.

228 "Lovell and Gerry": Abigail Adams to John Adams, August 1, 1781, ibid., p. 191.

229 "Tutor and Companion": Joanna Bowen Gillespie, **The Life and Times of Martha Ramsay 1759–1811** (Columbia: University of South Carolina Press, 2001), p. 46.

230 "womanish fears": Gregory D. Massey, **John Laurens and the American Revolution** (Columbia: University of South Carolina Press, 2000), p. 53.

230 "domestic duties": Ibid.

230 "incessantly for peace": Gillespie, **Life and Times of Martha Ramsay,** p. 81.

231 "concerning these matters": Ibid., p. 80.

231 "Britain and her colonies": Ibid., p. 75.

232 "and respectable father": Massey, **John Laurens and the American Revolution**, p. 189.

232 "end in their favor": Gillespie, **Life and Times of Martha Ramsay**, p. 89.

232 "wished to relieve you": Ibid., p. 93.

232 "'in servitude'": In a letter from Henry Laurens to Henry Laurens Jr., August 20, 1782, ibid., p. 95.

232 "reputation at home": Henry Laurens to Henry Laurens Jr., August 22, 1782, ibid., p. 97.

233 "death of another child": Henry Laurens to James Laurens, November 17, 1782, ibid., p. 101.

233 "American woman": Henry Laurens to William Drayton, February 13, 1783, ibid., p. 103.

WIVES AND DAUGHTERS TO DIPLOMACY
234 "has no objections": Gouverneur Morris to Catharine Wilhelmina Livingston, January 11, 1773, in Richard B. Morris, **John Jay: The Making of a Revolutionary, Unpublished Papers 1745–1780** (New York: Harper & Row, 1980), p. 1:123.

235 "sustained by the appointment": John Jay to Sarah Livingston Jay, December 23, 1775, ibid., p. 1:212.

235 "hope the best": Sally Jay to John Jay, March 23–24, 1777, ibid., p. 1:380.

236 "an elegant amusement": Sarah Livingston Jay to John Jay, June 17, 1777, ibid., p. 1:413.

236 before she was married: P. M. Zall, **Founding Mothers: Profiles of Ten Wives of America's Founding Fathers** (Washington, D.C.: Heritage Books, 1991), p. 89.

236 "controlled by his minions": Sarah Livingston Jay to Henry Brockholst Livingston, August 18, 1777, in Morris, **John Jay**, p. 1:438.

236 "being a husband": Sarah Livingston Jay to Susannah Livingston, March 16, 1778, ibid., p. 1:467.

237 "to the public": Sarah Livingston Jay to John Jay, December 28–30, 1778, ibid., p. 1:517.

237 "obscurity and dullness": Sarah L. Jay to John Jay, February 12, 1779, ibid., p. 1:555.

237 "from the mantelpiece": Sarah L. Jay to John Jay, March 5, 1779, ibid., p. 1:572.

238 Gibraltar was in Spanish hands: Susan Mary Alsop, **Yankees at the Court: The First Americans in Paris** (New York: Doubleday & Co., 1982), p. 204.

238 "with equal force": William Livingston Jr. to Sarah Livingston Jay, October 16, 1779, in Morris, **John Jay**, p. 1:677.

238 "about to walk in": George Washington to Sarah Livingston Jay, October 7, 1779, ibid., p. 1:656.

239 "complete them": Sarah Livingston Jay to Susannah French Livingston, December 12–26, 1779, ibid., p. 1:681.

239 "crabs, fresh fish and oysters": Ibid.

240 "of the inhabitants": Sarah L. Jay to Peter Jay, January 9, 1780, ibid., p. 1:687.

240 other vermin: Alsop, **Yankees at the Court**, p. 203.

240 "to my assistance!": Sarah L. Jay to Catharine W. and Susannah Livingston, March 4, 1780, in Morris, **John Jay**, p. 1:692.

241 John Jay would not be officially received: Alsop, **Yankees at the Court**, p. 205.

241 "with the tinkling": Sarah L. Jay to Susannah Livingston, August 28, 1780, in Morris, **John Jay**, p. 1:706.

241 "found murdered there": Sarah L. Jay to Susannah Livingston, August 28, 1780, ibid., p. 1:708.

242 "that her opinion prevails": Booth, **Women of '76**, p. 213.

242 "of distinguished beauty": Anne Hollingsworth Wharton, **Salons Colonial and Republican** (Philadelphia: J. B. Lippincott, 1900), p. 63.

242 "splendid court of Madrid": Ellet, **Women of the American Revolution**, p. 1:103.

243 "so nobly struggled": Sarah Livingston Jay to Susannah French Livingston, May 13, 1780, in Morris, **John Jay**, p. 1:695.

243 "Is he healthy?": Ibid.

243 "similar occasions": Sarah Livingston Jay to Susannah French Livingston, August 28, 1780, ibid., p. 1:710.

243 "without friends": Ibid., p. 1:709.

244 "became a mother": Ibid., p. 1:711.

244 "charming countrywomen": Mary Beth Norton, **Liberty's Daughters: The Revolutionary Experience of American Women, 1750–1800** (Ithaca, N.Y.: Cornell University Press, 1980), p. 187.

245 "visit this summer": Susannah Livingston to Sarah Livingston Jay, May 27, 1781, in Morris, **John Jay**, p. 2:186.

245 "in the family": Ibid., p. 2:187.

245 "books from Philadelphia": Peter Augustus Jay to Sarah Livingston Jay, July 18, 1781, ibid., p. 2:194.

246 than any monarchy: Sarah Livingston Jay to William Livingston, June 24, 1781, ibid., p. 2:190.

247 "him that trouble": William Livingston to Sarah Livingston Jay, August 21, 1781, ibid., p. 2:200.

247 "delighted with the water": Ibid.

248 terms of peace: Alsop, **Yankees at the Court**, p. 235.

249 "to send for him": Sarah Livingston Jay to Susannah French Livingston, August 28, 1782, in Morris, **John Jay**, p. 2:465.

249 "I was too timid": Ibid., p. 2:466.

249 "to be a queen": Sarah Livingston Jay to Mary White Morris, November 14, 1782, ibid., p. 2:476.

249 opera with Benjamin Franklin: Alsop, **Yankees at the Court**, p. 196.

250 "some delightful scenes": Sarah Livingston Jay to Catharine W. Livingston, December 14, 1782, in Morris, **John Jay**, p. 2:590.

250 "its great advantages": Mary Morris to Sarah Livingston Jay, June 1, 1783, quoted in Zall, **Founding Mothers**, pp. 75–76.

250 American Indian Messenger: Alsop, **Yankees at the Court**, p. 267.

250 "guest next month": John Jay to Catharine W. Livingston, July 1, 1783, in Morris, **John Jay**, p. 2:607.

251 "Happiness to all Mankind": Alsop, **Yankees at the Court**, p. 272.

252 "glorious and honorable": Howard H. Peckham, **The War for Independence: A Military History** (1958; reprint, Chicago: University of Chicago Press, 1979), p. 194.

252 "employments of public life": Ibid., p. 196.

253 "two years in Europe": **The Book of Abigail and John**, edited and with an introduction by L. H. Butterfield, Marc Friedlaender, and Mary-Jo Kline (Cambridge, Mass.: Harvard University Press, 1975), p. 377.

253 "inhabitant of this state": Abigail Adams to John Adams, April 10, 1782, in Butterfield, **Adams Papers**, vol. 4, p. 306.

254 "heroic of yours": Abigail Adams to John Adams, June 17, 1782, ibid., p. 328.

254 "than any others": John Adams to Abigail Adams, August 14, 1783, in **Book of Abigail and John**, p. 360.

255 "intentions of Philadelphia": John Adams to Abigail Adams, September 7, 1783, ibid., p. 363.

255 "her head turned by it": John Adams to Abigail Adams, July 17, 1783, ibid., p. 357.

255 "disgrace to you": Abigail Adams to John Adams, December 15–17, 1783, ibid., p. 372.

255 "who was his mother?": John Adams to his daughter Abigail Adams, August 13, 1783, ibid., p. 360.

256 "including teaching": Edith B. Gelles, **Portia: The World of Abigail Adams** (Bloomington: Indiana University Press, 1992), p. 118.

257 "loss of our cow": Abigail Adams to Elizabeth Smith Shaw, July 10[?], 1784, in **Book of Abigail and John**, p. 383.

257 "I was yesterday": John Adams to Abigail Adams, July 26, 1784, ibid., p. 391.

257 "upon the other": Abigail Adams to Mary Smith Cranch, July 30, 1784, ibid., p. 395.

257 "has in store for me": Abigail Adams to John Adams, July 30, 1784, ibid., p. 396.

258 "pencil of the other": Abigail Adams to Mary Cranch, [c. January 7, 1784, exact date not known], ibid., p. 397.

258 turn of the nineteenth century: Norton, **Liberty's Daughters**, pp. 232–34.

259 "I have promised": Fawn M. Brodie, **Thomas Jefferson: An Intimate History** (New York: W. W. Norton, 1974), p. 126.

259 "unpardonable rage for retirement": Quoted ibid., p. 163.

260 **"shortly to make":** Elizabeth Langhorne,

Monticello: A Family Story (Chapel Hill, N.C.: Algonquin Books, 1989), p. 22.

260 "violent burst of grief": Quoted in **Wives of the Signers** (excerpted from **Pioneer Mothers**) (Aledo, Tex.: WallBuilder Press, 1997), pp. 246–47.

261 "fourteen to one": Langhorne, **Monticello**, p. 27.

262 "worthy of my love": Ibid., p. 28.

262 "discover a pin amiss": Brodie, **Thomas Jefferson**, p. 176.

262 "enter on all fours": Zall, **Founding Mothers**, p. 122.

262 her father visited her every day: Brodie, **Thomas Jefferson**, p. 187.

263 "dancing here and there like a Merry Andrew": Natalie S. Bober, **Abigail Adams: Witness to a Revolution** (New York: Aladdin Paperbacks, 1995), p. 130.

263 "made up in two days": Brodie, **Thomas Jefferson**, p. 188.

264 "him and his daughter": Ibid., p. 190.

264 "Uncle Eppes house": Ibid., p. 191.

264 "love you so much": Ibid.

264 "in the dumps": Ibid., p. 192.

264 "ones of the earth": Bober, **Abigail Adams,** p. 134.

265 "what may be necessary and right": Lester J. Cappon, Thomas Jefferson to Abigail Adams, June 21, 1785, **The Adams-Jefferson Letters** (Chapel Hill: University of North Carolina Press, 1959), p. 35.

265 "as she used to call him is gone": Abigail Adams to Thomas Jefferson, August 21, 1785, ibid., p. 56.

265 "financier left the office": Abigail Adams to Thomas Jefferson, September 6, 1785, ibid., p. 62.

265 "one victory the more": Thomas Jefferson to Abigail Adams, September 25, 1785, ibid., p. 70.

266 against the carriage roof: Lynne Withey, **Dearest Friend: A Life of Abigail Adams** (New York: Touchstone, 2001), p. 177.

266 "wisdom and benevolence": Abigail Adams to Thomas Jefferson, November 24, 1785, in Cappon, **Adams -Jefferson Letters,** p. 100.

266 "common good manners": Brodie, **Thomas Jefferson**, p. 195.

266 "go hand in hand": Ibid., p. 119.

267 "annexed to the white": Bober, **Abigail Adams**, p. 146.

267 "been a blockhead": Ibid., p. 145.

267 "part with my daughter": Thomas Jefferson to Abigail Adams, August 9, 1786, in Cappon, **Adams–Jefferson Letters,** p. 149.

268 wag's estimation: Booth, **Women of '76,** p. 109.

268 "damsel of fifteen": Ibid., p. 288.

269 "fabric at once": Abigail Adams to Thomas Jefferson, January 29, 1787, in Cappon, **Adams–Jefferson Letters,** p. 168.

269 "little rebellion now and then": Thomas Jefferson to Abigail Adams, February 22, 1787, ibid., p. 173.

269 "but widows left": Brodie, **Thomas Jefferson,** p. 237.

270 never to marry again: Zall, **Founding Mothers,** p. 121.

270 as a companion: Brodie, **Thomas Jefferson**, p. 217.

270 "not know you": Abigail Adams to Thomas Jefferson, June 16, 1787, in Cappon, **Adams-Jefferson Letters**, p. 178.

270 "all her affections": Thomas Jefferson to Abigail Adams, July 1, 1787, ibid., p. 179.

271 "should be carried away": Abigail Adams to Thomas Jefferson, July 6, 1787, ibid., p. 183.

271 "properly after her": Ibid.

CHAPTER SIX
ASSEMBLING IN PHILADELPHIA

274 money in the treasury: Catharine Drinker Bowen, **Miracle at Philadelphia** (Boston: Little, Brown, 1966), p. 5.

274 "the whole house in which she lives, stables": Linda K. Kerber, **Women of the Republic: Intellect and Ideology in Revolutionary America** (Chapel Hill, N.C.: University of North Carolina Press, 1980), p. 62.

274 "at common family hours": Ibid.

275 **"feels for your friendship most refin'd":** Women's Project of New Jersey, Inc., 2002,

www.scc.rutgers.edu/njwomenshistory/Period_2/s
tocktonpoem_gw.htm.

275 423 people visited in one year: David L. Ribblett, **Nelly Custis, Child of Mount Vernon**
(Mount Vernon, Va.: Mount Vernon Ladies' Association, 1993), p. 9.

275 "to go see his friends": Martha Washington to
Hannah Bushrod Washington, June 22, 1784,
**Worthy Partner: The Papers of Martha Wash-
ington,** compiled by Joseph E. Fields, (Westport,
Conn.: Greenwood Press, 1994), p. 194.276

276 French hounds: Helen Bryan, **Martha Washington, First Lady of Liberty** (New York: John
Wiley & Sons, 2002), p. 276.

276 "those whom she left": Martha Washington to
Mercy Otis Warren, June 9, 1785, in Fields, **Worthy Partner,** p. 196.

276 "a day or two at it": George Washington to
Mary Ball Washington, February 15, 1787, in
Bryan, **Martha Washington,** p. 280.

276 "a prisoner in your own chamber": Ibid.

277 "but not gaudy": Onley Winsor to Mrs. Olney
Winsor, March 31, 1788, in John P. Kaminisky and
Gaspare J. Saladino, eds., **The Documentary His-**

tory of the Ratification of the Constitution, vol. 8 (Madison: State Historical Society of Wisconsin, 1988), p. 523; part of an unpublished compilation of testimonials about and descriptions of Martha Washington, by Mary V. Thompson (Mount Vernon, Va.: Mount Vernon Ladies' Association), p. 9.

277 "to very little purpose": Rufus Wilmot Griswold, **The Republican Court** (New York: D. Appleton & Company, 1854), pp. 42–43.

278 "commerce of the United States": Bowen, **Miracle at Philadelphia,** p. 9.

278 **"more so than during the war":** Griswold, **The Republican Court,** p. 43.

279 outlining his ideas: Bowen, **Miracle at Philadelphia,** p. 8.

280 "her entire countenance": J. Munsell, **Memoirs of Lt. Col. Tench Tilghman** (Albany, N.Y.: 1876), p. 89, quoted in Allan McLane Hamilton, **Life of Alexander Hamilton** (New York: Charles Scribner's Sons, 1910), p. 95.

280 "lively behavior": Mary Gay Humphries, **Catharine Schuyler** (New York: Charles Scribner's Sons, 1897), p. 149.

281 "know no fear": Ibid., p. 154.

281 "done the same": Ibid., p. 160.

282 "no small trouble": Ibid.

282 "evening before": François Jean de Beauvoir, Marquis de Chastellux, **Travels in North America in the Years 1780, 1781, 1782,** translated by Howard C. Rice Jr. (Chapel Hill: University of North Carolina Press, 1963), pp. 1:220–21.

283 "never to be forgotten": Willard Sterne Randall, **Alexander Hamilton** (New York: Harper-Collins, 2003), p. 143.

283 "the larger stock of that the better": Alice Curtis Desmond, **Alexander Hamilton's Wife** (New York: Dodd, Mead & Co., 1952), pp. 91–92.

284 "**inamorato** you perhaps ever saw": Randall, **Alexander Hamilton,** p. 189.

284 "merit their friendship": Hamilton, **Life of Alexander Hamilton,** p. 126.

284 "lover in earnest": Randall, **Alexander Hamilton,** p. 194.

284 "every hour": Hamilton, **Life of Alexander Hamilton,** p. 127.

284 "of anything else": Ibid., p. 133.

285 "the place he did": Ibid., p. 103.

286 "you treat me with disrespect": Alexander Hamilton to Philip Schuyler, February 18, 1781, in Randall, **Alexander Hamilton,** p. 223.

286 "I must go": Hamilton, **Life of Alexander Hamilton,** p. 142.

287 "better angel": Ibid., p. 143.

287 "more of this kind": Randall, **Alexander Hamilton,** p. 244.

288 "my wife and baby": Humphries, **Catherine Schuyler,** p. 199.

288 gain his release: Desmond, **Alexander Hamilton's Wife,** p. 138.

289 "and fine teeth": Griswold, **The Republican Court,** p. 100.

289 would soon marry: John Jay to Catharine Livingston Ridley, March 20, 1786, in Robert Ernst, **Rufus King American Federalist** (Chapel Hill: University of North Carolina Press, 1968), p. 66.

290 "not so fortunate": Ibid., pp. 66–67.

290 "these intermarriages": John Adams to Rufus King, June 14, 1786, ibid., p. 68.

291 "fortune they experienced": Harriott Horry Ravenal, **Eliza Pinckney** (New York: Charles Scribner's Sons, 1896), pp. 309–10.

291 "expensive diversions": Griswold, **The Republican Court,** pp. 83–84.

291 for the city's fires: Randall, **Alexander Hamilton,** pp. 311–12.

291 wasn't much better: Bowen, **Miracle at Philadelphia,** p. 5.

292 "to leave home": George Washington to Robert Morris, May 5, 1787, in Ribblett, **Nelly Custis,** p. 13.

WELCOMING THE VISITORS

293 "my family well": Carl Van Doren, **Benjamin Franklin** (New York: Viking Press, 1938), p. 728.

293 "my adding more": Benjamin Franklin to Jane Mecom, September 19, 1785, in **The Letters of Benjamin Franklin and Jane Mecom,** edited and with an introduction by Carl Van Doren (Princeton, N.J.: Princeton University Press, 1950), p. 237.

294 "letter from you": Jane Mecom to Benjamin Franklin, October 1, 1785, ibid., p. 240.

294 "just like his father": Jane Mecom to Benjamin Franklin, March 9, 1787, ibid., p. 292.

294 "our growing family": Benjamin Franklin to Jane Mecom, September 21, 1786, ibid., p. 282.

294 "of 24 persons": Benjamin Franklin to Jane Mecom, May 30, 1787, ibid., p. 295.

295 "fond of their grandpapa": Van Doren, **Benjamin Franklin,** p. 750.

295 secret deliberations: Bowen, **Miracle at Philadelphia,** p. 22.

295 "I have scarcely a moment": George Washington to Annis Boudinot Stockton, June 30, 1787, in John C. Fitzpatrick, ed., **The Writings of George Washington from the Original Manuscript Sources, 1745–1799,** available at www.memory.loc.gov.

296 "How languishingly sweet!": Charles Henry Hart, **Mary White–Mrs. Robert Morris,** in **Pennslyvania Magazine of History and Biography** 2, 1878, p. 157.

297 "his private business": Ibid., pp. 160–61.

297 "one they prefer": Molly Morris to Sarah Jay, 1781, in P. M. Zall, **Founding Mothers**: (Washington, D.C.: Profiles of **Ten Wives of America's Founding Fathers** Heritage Books, 1991), p. 75.

298 "arms of Washington": Griswold, **The Republican Court,** p. 37. Biographical information on

Robert Morris is from Eleanor Young, **Forgotten Patriot, Robert Morris** (New York: The Macmillan Company, 1950).

298 "possessed the cooks": Anne Hollingsworth Wharton, **Salons Colonial and Republican** (Philadelphia: J.B. Lippincott, 1900), p. 131.

299 "of warm water": Hart, **Mary White—Mrs. Robert Morris,** p. 166.

300 "momentous work": Donald Jackson and Dorothy Twohig, eds., **The Diaries of George Washington,** vol. 5, **July 1786–December 1789** (Charlottesville: University Press of Virginia, 1979): June 10, p. 168; June 16, p. 169; July 9 and 10, p. 175; August 3, p. 180; August 13 and 17, p. 181; September 17, p. 185.

300 "generous living": Wharton, **Salons Colonial and Republican,** p. 81.

301 "gray fur": Griswold, **The Republican Court,** p. 295.

301 "luxuries of Europe": Wharton, **Salons Colonial and Republican,** p. 142.

301 "the head of American society": Elizabeth Ellet, **Queens of American Society** (Philadelphia: Porter & Coates, 1867), p. 142.

301 "in other countries": Mary Beth Norton, **Liberty's Daughters** (Ithaca, N.Y.: Cornell University Press, 1980), pp. 190–91.

301 "woman in Philadelphia": Wharton, **Salons Colonial and Republican,** pp. 151–52.

302 "the best informed": Anne Hollingsworth Wharton, **Through Colonial Doorways** (Philadelphia: J. B. Lippincott, 1893), p. 225.

302 "taste and knowledge": Chastellux, **Travels in North America,** p. 1:136.

302 "friendship for her": Ibid., pp. 136n, 302n.

304 Jacob Duche: Reverend Jacob Duche to George Washington, October 8, 1777, www.candst. tripod.com/duche.htm.

305 "the state and union": Bowen, **Miracle at Philadelphia,** p. 103.

305 "of the Convention": Ibid., p. 140.

305 "as we shall adopt": Charles Cotesworth Pinckney to Harriott Pinckney Horry, May 30, 1787, in Frances Leigh Williams, **A Founding Family** (New York: Harcourt Brace Jovanovich, 1978), p. 225.

WRITING IT DOWN

Biographical information in this section is from Bowen, **Miracle at Philadelphia,** and Richard Brookhiser, **Gentleman Revolutionary: Gouverneur Morris—The Rake Who Wrote the Constitution** (New York: Free Press, 2003); and Alan Pell Crawford, **Unwise Passions** (New York: Simon & Schuster, 2000).

306 "had lost **something** else": Brookhiser, **Gentleman Revolutionary,** p. 61.

307 "Massachusetts-Bay": Bowen, **Miracle at Philadelphia,** p. 240.

309 "the truth of the report": Martha Jefferson Randolph to Thomas Jefferson, May 16, 1793, quoted in Fawn Brodie, **Thomas Jefferson, An Intimate History** (New York: W. W. Norton & Company, 1974), p. 256.

309 "poor afflicted friend": Thomas Jefferson to Martha Jefferson Randolph, April 28, 1793, ibid.

310 **"allege against me":** Crawford, **Unwise Passions,** pp. 77–78.

310 "of Nancy Randolph": Ibid., p. 82.

311 "the relief of tears": Anne Randolph Morris to John Randolph, January 16, 1815, in Zall, **Founding Mothers,** pp. 113–14.

312 "over the sacking": Ibid., p. 115.

312 "you were silent": Ibid.

313 "reduced gentlewoman": Anne Randolph Morris to Joseph C. Cabell, May 30, 1828, in Zall, **Founding Mothers,** p. 117.

313 "and distinguished": Gouverneur Morris to Anne Cary Randolph, March 1809, in Brookhiser, **Gentleman Revolutionary,** p. 183.

313 "fall in my bosom": Gouverneur Morris to Anne Cary Randolph, March 3, 1809, ibid., p. 184.

313 **"The soul immortal shall remain":** Gouverneur Morris to Anne Cary Randolph, March 3, 1809, in Crawford, **Unwise Passions,** p. 193.

314 "as little as I can": Gouverneur Morris to Anne Cary Randolph, March 9, 1809, in Brookhiser, **Gentleman Revolutionary,** p. 184.

314 "good looking woman": Gouverneur Morris to Anne Cary Randolph, March 3, 1809, in Crawford, **Unwise Passions,** p. 194.

314 "in the world": Anne Randolph Morris to Joseph C. Cabell, May 30, 1828, in Zall, **Founding Mothers,** p. 117.

314 "by the malignant": John Marshall to Gou-

verneur Morris, December 12, 1809, in Crawford, **Unwise Passions,** p. 197.

315 "into the pocketbook": Gouverneur Morris to Gertrude Meredith, January 10, 1810, ibid., p. 201.

316 "uncoffined grave": John Randolph to Anne Randolph Morris, October 31, 1814, ibid., p. 236.

317 "in his **stomach**": Ibid., pp. 239–40.

317 "because she's happy": Gouverneur Morris to Randolph Harrison, May 25, 1815, ibid., p. 242.

317 "of my sorrows": Anne Randolph Morris to John Randolph, January 16, 1815, in Zall, **Founding Mothers,** p. 112.

318 "in the United States": Ibid., p. 113.

318 "signifying nothing": Ibid., p. 116.

318 "was continually relapsing": Ibid.

318 "exposed and outwitted": Griswold, **The Republican Court,** p. 207n.

319 Morrisania income producing: Crawford, **Unwise Passions,** p. 265.

319 find the treasure: Ibid., p. 218.

319 "if you can keep it": Brookhiser, **Founding Father,** p. 122.

319 "take its chance": Benjamin Franklin to Jane Mecom, September 20, 1787, in Van Doren, **Letters of Benjamin Franklin and Jane Mecom,** p. 298.

RATIFICATION
320 make them more legible: Desmond, **Alexander Hamilton's Wife,** p. 145.

320 "fond of reading them": Martha Washington to Fanny Bassett Washington, February 25, 1788, in Fields, **Worthy Partner,** p. 205.

321 "on the same subject": Dorothy Twohig, **George Washington's Diaries: An Abridgement** (Charlottesville: University Press of Virginia, 1999), p. 326.

321 "them with propriety": Eliza Powel to Martha Washington, November 31, 1787, in Fields, **Worthy Partner,** p. 198.

321 "had three cheers": Molly Morris to Robert Morris, December 12, 1787, in Zall, **Founding Mothers,** p. 77.

322 "Wednesday in January": Abigail Adams to Thomas Jefferson, December 5, 1787, in Lester J. Cappon, ed., **The Adams-Jefferson Letters** (Chapel

Hill: University of North Carolina Press, 1959), p. 213.

323 "nothing American sells here": Rosemarie Zagarri, **A Woman's Dilemma: Mercy Otis Warren and the American Revolution** (Wheeling, Ill.: Harlan Davidson, 1995), p. 138.

324 "support a commonwealth": Mercy Otis Warren to Elbridge Gerry, June 6, 1783, in C. Harvey Gardiner, ed., **A Study in Dissent: The Warren-Gerry Correspondence, 1776–1792** (Carbondale: Southern Illinois University Press, 1968), pp. 162–63.

324 "of a free people": Zagarri, **A Woman's Dilemma**, p. 118.

324 "of superior judgment": Jane Mecom to Benjamin Franklin, November 9, 1787, in Van Doren, **Letters of Benjamin Franklin and Jane Mecom,** p. 301.

325 "others in their room": Jeffrey H. Richards, **Mercy Otis Warren** (New York: Twayne, 1995), p. 122.

325 "of their own creation": Ibid.

326 "make it unnecessary": Molly Morris to Robert Morris, May 4, 1788, in Zall, **Founding Mothers,** p. 80.

326 "about eleven o'clock": Twohig, **George Washington's Diaries,** p. 329.

326 "of the Constitution": Desmond, **Alexander Hamilton's Wife,** p. 143.

326 riders on the move: Bowen, **Miracle at Philadelphia,** p. 295.

327 "usually accompanies his writings": Sally Livingston Jay to John Jay, June 19, 1788, John Jay Collection, Rare Book and Manuscript Library, Columbia University Library, provided by Mary-Jo Kline, Columbia University.

327 "for apprehension on the other": John Jay to Sally Livingston Jay, June 21, 1788, John Jay Collection.

327 "they to anticipate Virginia": Sally Livingston Jay to John Jay, June 25, 1788, John Jay Collection.

328 "family was invited": Twohig, **George Washington's Diaries,** p. 330.

328 "hear from you": Sally Livingston Jay to John Jay, July 7, 1788, John Jay Collection.

328 Waterford followed suit: Susan Branson, **These Fiery Frenchified Dames** (Philadelphia: University of Pennsylvania Press, 2001), pp. 19–20.

329 "extravagant for republicanism": Zagarri, **A Woman's Dilemma,** p. 123.

329 other New England states: Arthur M. Schlesinger Jr., **The Almanac of American History** (Greenwich, Conn.: Brompton Books Corporation, 1993), p. 157.

329 "with your correspondence": Thomas Jefferson to Abigail Adams, February 2, 1788, in Cappon, **The Adams-Jefferson Letters,** p. 222.

330 "as my garden": Abigail Adams to Thomas Jefferson, February 26, 1788, ibid., p. 228.

330 "enough for you": Mary Cranch to Abigail Adams, June 13, 1787, in Edith B. Gelles, **Portia: The World of Abigail Adams** (Bloomington: Indiana University Press, 1992), p. 122.

330 "wear no feathers": Natalie S. Bober, **Abigail Adams: Witness to a Revolution** (New York: Aladdin Paperbacks, 1995), p. 155.

331 "hear all and say little": Ibid., p. 206.

331 "Elector of President and Vice-President": Twohig, **George Washington's Diaries,** p. 336.

331 "of the assembly": Hart, **Mary White–Mrs. Robert Morris,** pp. 171–72.

331 of their assignments: Schlesinger, **The Almanac of American History,** p. 153.

331 for the last time: Bryan, **Martha Washington,** p. 287.

332 "answering its expectations": Twohig, **George Washington's Diaries,** p. 338.

332 "soon follow him": Martha Washington to John Dandridge, April 20, 1788, in Fields, **Worthy Partner,** p. 213.

CHAPTER SEVEN

ASSEMBLING IN NEW YORK

334 **"Strew your hero's way with flowers":** Rufus Wilmot Griswold, **The Republican Court** (New York: D. Appleton & Co., 1854), p. 17.

334 "will never be effaced": Ibid., p. 130.

335 "on this great occasion": Ibid., pp. 131–33.

336 "likeness of Washington in profile": Interview by historian Benson J. Lossing for "The Last Surviving Belle of the Revolution," in **Hours with the Living Men and Women of the Revolution** (New York, 1889), pp. 150–56, quoted in P. M. Zall, **Founding Mothers: Profiles of Ten Wives of America's Founding Fathers** (Washington, D.C.: Heritage Books; 1991), p. 168.

336 "Protector of their Liberties": Griswold, **Republican Court**, p. 152.

336 "His Rotundity": Lynne Withey, **Dearest Friend: A Life of Abigail Adams** (New York: Simon & Schuster, 2001), p. 212.

336 "His Superfluous Excellency": Natalie S. Bober, **Abigail Adams: Witness to a Revolution** (New York: Simon & Schuster, 1995), p. 160.

337 "federal fashions and national manners?": George Washington to Annis Boudinot Stockton, August 31, 1788, available at University of Virginia, "The Papers of George Washington," gwpapers.virginia.edu/constitution/1788/stock. html.

337 news by several journals: Carl Sferrazzo Anthony, **First Ladies: The Saga of the Presidents' Wives and Their Power, 1789–1961** (New York: William Morrow,1990), p. 37.

337 "gentlemen came to meet me": Martha Washington to Fanny Bassett Washington, June 8, 1789, in **Worthy Partner: The Papers of Martha Washington**, compiled by Joseph E. Fields (Westport, Conn.: Greenwood Press, 1994), p. 215.

337 "and the citizens also": Anthony, **First Ladies**, p. 38.

338 "complimented on my landing": Martha Washington to Fanny Bassett Washington, June 8, 1789, in Fields, **Worthy Partner**, p. 215.

338 "God Bless Lady Washington": David L. Ribblett, **Nelly Custis: Child of Mount Vernon** (Mount Vernon, Va.: Mount Vernon Ladies' Association, 1993), p. 15.

339 "impudent place hunter": Griswold, **Republican Court**, p. 165n.

339 first official reception of the republic: Helen Bryan, **First Lady of Liberty: Martha Washington** (New York: John Wiley & Sons, 2002), p. 292.

339 "very much pleased at": Martha Washington to Fanny Bassett Washington, June 8, 1789, in Fields, **Worthy Partner**, p. 215.

339 "a little wild creature": Martha Washington to Fanny Bassett Washington, summer 1789, ibid., p. 217.

339 "My hair is set and dressed every day": Martha Washington to Fanny Bassett Washington, June 8, 1789, ibid., p. 215.

339 "small matter longer": Martha Washington to Mr. Whitelock, April 14, 1774, ibid., p. 265.

340 "we will not spend much": John Adams to Abigail Adams, April 22, 1789, **Adams Family Papers: An Electronic Archive** (Boston: Massachusetts Historical Society, 2002), available at http://www.masshist.org/digitaladams.

340 "for the Editor of them": Abigail Adams to John Adams, May 1, 1789, ibid.

340 "beasts of the field": John Adams to Abigail Adams, May 14, 1789, ibid.

341 "I do not like his politics": Abigail Adams to John Adams, May 26, 1789, ibid.

341 "of hauteur about her": Abigail Adams to Mary Cranch, May 28, 1789, in **New Letters of Abigail Adams, 1788–1801**, edited and with an introduction by Stewart Mitchell (Boston: Houghton Mifflin, 1947), p. 13.

342 "they quit the room": Abigail Adams to Mary Cranch, August 9, 1789, ibid. p. 19.

342 "be favorites with him": Mary V. Thompson, "Martha Washington as First Lady" (Mount Vernon, Va.: Mount Vernon Ladies' Association, 2002), p. 3.

342 "smothering it with his hand": Elizabeth Hamilton to B. J. Lossing, in Zall, **Founding Mothers**, p. 172.

343 "you know is unpopular": Abigail Adams to Mary Cranch, January 5, 1790, in Mitchell, **New Letters**, p. 35.

343 "three of yours, at least": Griswold, **Republican Court**, p. 95.

343 "upon a slight acquaintance": Ibid., p. 92.

344 "variety of wines and punch": Poppy Cannon and Patricia Brooks, **The Presidents' Cookbook: Practical Recipes from George Washington to the Present** (New York: Funk & Wagnalls, 1968), p. 2.

344 **"duties of the station"**: Ibid., p. 4.

345 "stay at home a great deal": Martha Washington to Fanny Bassett Washington, October 23, 1789, in Fields, **Worthy Partner**, p. 220.

345 "the Chief State Prisoner": Elizabeth Hamilton to B. J. Lossing, quoted in Zall, **Founding Mothers**, p. 171.

346 "a fond own brother": Elizabeth Hamilton to Angelica Schuyler Church, November 8, 1789, in **Papers of Alexander Hamilton**, edited by H. C. Syrett (New York, 1961–87), pp. 20:502, 166.

346 "towards the new government": **George Washington's Diaries: An Abridgement**, edited

by Dorothy Twohig (Charlottesville: University Press of Virginia, 1999), p. 341.

347 "American Eagle perched on top": Ibid., p. 350.

347 "G.W." in gold in the middle: Griswold, **Republican Court**, p. 192.

347 "seen in the Southern States": Twohig, **George Washington's Diaries**, p. 356.

348 "at least been mistaken": George Washington to Catharine Macaulay Graham, January 9, 1790, available at TeachingAmericanHistory.org, http://teachingamericanhistory.org/library/index.asp?document=353.

348 "gentlemen were present": Twohig, **George Washington's Diaries**, p. 358.

348 "suffrages of the sex": Rosemary Zagarri, **A Woman's Dilemma: Mercy Otis Warren and the American Revolution** (Wheeling, Ill.: Harlan Davidson, 1995), p. 93.

349 "upon our circumstances": Martha Washington to Mercy Otis Warren, December 26, 1789, in Fields, **Worthy Partner**, pp. 223–24.

349 "which he never rose": Carl Van Doren, **Benjamin Franklin** (New York: Viking Press, 1938), p. 778.

349 "I hope not": Ibid., p. 779.

349 "at last worn out": Richard Bache to Jane Mecom, April 19, 1790, in **The Letters of Benjamin Franklin and Jane Mecom**, edited by Carl Van Doren (Princeton, N.J.: Princeton University Press, 1950), p. 341.

349 funeral on April 21: Arthur M. Schlesinger Jr., **The Almanac of American History** (Greenwich, Conn.: Brompton Books Corp., 1993), p. 157.

349 "would become it": Van Doren, **Benjamin Franklin**, p. 762.

350 "jewels in this country": Ibid., p. 761.

350 abandoned his family for so many years: Larry E. Tise, "Liberty and the Rights of Women: Sarah Franklin's Declaration of Independence," in **Benjamin Franklin and Women: A Series of Essays**, edited by Larry Tise (University Park: Pennsylvania State University Press, 1998), pp. 38–40.

350 "disastrous consequences": Abigail Adams to Mary Cranch, May 30, 1790, in Mitchell, **New Letters**, p. 49.

351 "person in the United States": Martha Washington to Mercy Otis Warren, June 12, 1790, in Fields, **Worthy Partner**, p. 226.

351 "anxious for your success": Alice Curtis Desmond, **Alexander Hamilton's Wife** (New York: Dodd, Mead & Co., 1952), p. 160.

351 "government rests": Abigail Adams to Cotton Tufts, January 18, 1790, in Phyllis Lee Levin, **Abigail Adams: A Biography** (New York: Thomas Dunne Books, 2001), p. 262.

353 couldn't get any decent cream in New York: Mary Gay Humphries, **Catherine Schuyler** (New York: Charles Scribner's Sons, 1897), pp. 217–18.

353 "a more profitable footing": Abigail Adams to Mary Cranch, October 10, 1790, in Mitchell, **New Letters**, p. 61.

353 "pleasure or satisfaction": Abigail Adams to Mary Cranch, October 3, 1790, ibid., p. 59.

354 "cannot yield to that": Martha Washington to Janet Montgomery, January 29, 1791, in Fields, **Worthy Partner**, p. 230.

PHILADELPHIA AND SOUTH
354 "her opinion of them": Steven Decatur Jr., **Private Affairs of George Washington** (Cambridge, Mass.: Riverside Press, 1933), p. 162.

354 "completed this year": Griswold, **Republican Court**, p. 251.

355 "with boxes, trunks, cases, etc.": Abigail Adams to Mary Cranch, December 12, 1790, in Mitchell, **New Letters**, p. 66.

355 "on with a pitchfork!": Ribblett, **Nelly Custis**, p. 20.

355 "before the first storm": Griswold, **Republican Court**, p. 251.

356 "wealth of the United States": Desmond, **Hamilton's Wife**, p. 162.

356 "Georgia and North Carolina": Abigail Adams to Mary Cranch, March 12, 1791, in Mitchell, **New Letters**, p. 71.

356 Washington had threatened to resign: Decatur, **Private Affairs**, p. 212.

356 his lodgings as "indifferent": Twohig, **George Washington's Diaries**, pp. 384, 388, 391.

357 "to rectify the mistake": Ibid., p. 383.

357 "at the proceedings of Congress": Ibid.

357 "Mrs. Horry's on Sunday": John Rutledge Jr. to Thomas Pinckney, April 28, 1791, in Frances Leigh Williams, **A Founding Family** (New York: Harcourt Brace Jovanovich, 1978), p. 292.

357 "assembled on the occasion": Twohig, **George Washington's Diaries**, p. 384n.

358 "dined at Mrs. Horry's": Ibid., p. 385.

358 planting of indigo seeds: Williams, **Founding Family**, p. 293.

358 "Dress a Calves Head": **A Colonial Plantation Cookbook: The Receipt Book of Harriott Pinckney Horry,** 1770, edited and with an introduction by Richard J. Hooker (Columbia: University of South Carolina Press, 1984), p. 46.

358 entreated her to keep it, and so she did: Harriott Horry Ravenal, **Eliza Pinckney** (New York: Charles Scribner's Sons, 1896), p. 312.

359 "it was singular": Twohig, **George Washington's Diaries**, p. 385.

359 Boston with 18,000: Schlesinger, **Almanac of American History**, p. 156.

359 "I had ever seen": Twohig, **George Washington's Diaries**, pp. 385–86.

359 "asked how she did": Ibid., p. 386.

360 "Puss in the Corner": Elizabeth F. Ellet, **The Women of the American Revolution** (New York: Baker & Scribner, 1849), p. 1:71.

360 "it will console me": Nathanael Greene to Catharine Littlefield Greene, April 14, 1785, in John F. Stegeman and Janet A. Stegeman, **Caty: A Biography of Catharine Littlefield Greene** (Athens: University of Georgia Press, 1977), p. 115.

361 "sober housewife": Sally Smith Booth, **Women of '76** (New York: Hastings House, 1973), p. 295.

361 "her for nothing else": Isaac Briggs to Joseph Thomas, November 23, 1785, in Stegeman and Stegeman, **Caty**, p. 121.

363 "be candid with you": Alexander Hamilton to Catharine Littlefield Greene, March 8, 1791, ibid., p. 149.

363 "and handsome ladies": Twohig, **George Washington's Diaries**, p. 386.

363 "Grove—the seat of Mrs. Greene": Ibid., p. 387.

364 "O how sweet is revenge!": Catharine Littlefield Greene to Nathaniel Pendleton Jr., May 25, 1792, in Stegeman and Stegeman, **Caty**, p. 155.

365 "Greene's invention": See Lemelson-MIT Program, www.web.mit.edu/invent.

367 "they were placed": Twohig, **George Washington's Diaries**, p. 391.

LADIES OF LETTERS

368 "characters among men are formed": John Adams to his daughter, Abigail Adams, August 13, 1783, in **The Book of Abigail and John**, edited and with an introduction by L. H. Butterfield, Marc Friedlaender, and Mary-Jo Kline (Cambridge, Mass.: Harvard University Press, 1975), p. 360.

368 "Thoughts upon Education": Mary Beth Norton, **Liberty's Daughters** (Ithaca, N.Y.: Cornell University Press, 1980), pp. 267–68.

369 "Harria and Monboddo on Language": Catharine Macaulay, **Letters on Education**, Letters 14 and 15, available at "Sunshine for Women,"www.pinn.net/~sunshine/march99/macaly2.html.

369 during the Revolution: Norton, **Liberty's Daughters**, p. 247.

369 a subscription to that magazine: Decatur, **Private Affairs**, p. 197.

369 "act of a **married** woman": Judith Sargent Murray to Winthrop Sargent, November 23, 1791, in Susan Branson, **These Fiery Frenchified Dames**

(Philadelphia: University of Pennsylvania Press, 2001), p. 33.

370 "flowery paths of science": Sharon M. Harris, ed., **American Women Writers to 1800** (New York: Oxford University Press, 1996), p. 151.

370 embroidery, dancing, and drawing: Ribblett, **Nelly Custis**, pp. 16–17.

370 "and accomplished education": Martha Washington to Mercy Otis Warren, June 12, 1790, in Fields, **Worthy Partner**, p. 226.

371 could talk some more: Judith Sargent Murray to her parents, August 1, 1790, in **From Gloucester to Philadelphia in 1790: Observations, Anecdotes, and Thoughts from the Eighteenth-Century Letters of Judith Sargent Murray**, edited by Bonnie Hurd Smith (Cambridge, Mass.: Judith Sargent Murray Society, 1998), pp. 245–60, quoted in Mary V. Thompson, "Testimonials About Martha Washington" (Mount Vernon, Va.: Mount Vernon Ladies' Association), p. 11.

371 "ogling the gallery": Branson, **Frenchified Dames**, p. 132.

371 "and amiable writer": George Washington to Mercy Otis Warren, June 4, 1790, available at Library of Congress, "American Memory: Historical

Collections for the National Digital Library," www.memory.loc.gov.

371 "of virtue and science": George Washington to Mercy Otis Warren, November 4, 1790, available ibid.

371 "vindication of their sex": Thomas Jefferson to Mercy Otis Warren, November 15, 1790, available ibid.

372 "outstripped the male": Zagarri, **Woman's Dilemma**, p. 138.

372 "equally ambitious": Abigail Adams to Mary Cranch, July 12, 1789, in Mitchell, **New Letters**, pp. 15–16.

372 "but she appeared very **clever**": Zagarri, **Woman's Dilemma**, p. 149.

373 "a vulgar, impudent hussy": Norton, **Liberty's Daughters**, p. 251.

373 "in reading it": Aaron Burr to Theodosia Prevost Burr, February 16, 1793, in Linda K. Kerber, **Women of the Republic** (Chapel Hill: University of North Carolina Press, 1980), p. 224.

373 purchase of the **Vindication**: Norton, **Liberty's Daughters**, p. 251n.

373 "Pardon me! Disciple of Wollstonecraft": John Adams to Abigail Adams, January 22, 1794, in **Adams Family Papers** (electronic).

373 "but **studied** the Bible": Joanna Bowen Gillespie, **The Life and Times of Martha Laurens Ramsay, 1759–1811** (Columbia: University of South Carolina Press, 2001), p. 114.

373 "and enlarge their ideas": Annis Stockton to Julia Rush, March 22 (no year), in Branson, **Frenchified Dames**, pp. 44–45.

374 and **American Museum**: **American National Biography**, published by Oxford University, www.libarts.ucok.edu/history.

374 "They will open before us": "Oration," May 15, 1793, **The Rise and Progress of the Young-Ladies' Academy of Philadelphia,** in quoted in Harris, **American Women Writers to 1800**, pp. 71–72.

375 "she doth actually reside": 1790 Election Law, available at "New Jersey Women's History," www.scc.rutgers.edu/womenshistory.

375 was deemed redundant: Norton, **Liberty's Daughters**, p. 191.

375 "age of twenty-one years": "Who Shall Not Vote," available at "New Jersey Women's History," www.scc.rutgers.edu/womenshistory.

375 "good order and dignity of the state": Norton, **Liberty's Daughters**, p. 193.

ELECTION YEAR

376 Betsey could not stop crying: Frances Leigh Williams, **A Founding Family** (New York: Harcourt Brace Jovanovich, 1978), p. 297.

377 "sprung up among us": Fawn M. Brodie, **Thomas Jefferson: An Intimate History** (New York: W. W. Norton & Co., 1974), p. 261.

377 "Monarchical federalists": John Ferling, **A Leap in the Dark: The Struggle to Create the American Republic** (New York: Oxford University Press, 2003), p. 345.

378 "without being ridiculous": Thomas Jefferson to Martha Jefferson Randolph, January 15, 1792, in Brodie, **Thomas Jefferson**, p. 263.

378 "upon the Government": Abigail Adams to Mary Cranch, March 29, 1792, in Mitchell, **New Letters**, pp. 80–81.

378 "long for a recess": Abigail Adams to Mary Cranch, April 20, 1792, ibid., p. 83.

379 "the glasses all washed": Martha Washington to Fanny Bassett Washington, July 1, 1792, in Fields, **Worthy Partner**, p. 238.

379 "out of curiosity": Martha Washington to Fanny Bassett Washington, November 30, 1794, ibid., p. 281.

379 "my Betsey, as I do you": Desmond, **Hamilton's Wife**, p. 169.

381 "renders that questionable": Sarah Livingston Jay to John Jay, May 17, 1792, John Jay Collection, Rare Book and Manuscript Library, Columbia University Library, provided by Mary-Jo Kline.

381 "you are most known": Sarah Livingston Jay to John Jay, June 2, 1792, John Jay Collection.

382 "likewise set aside": Sarah Livingston Jay to John Jay, June 10–12, 1792, John Jay Collection, provided by Allan Weinreb, John Jay Homestead State Historic Site.

382 "invitations I receive": Griswold, **Republican Court**, p. 327.

383 she was able to transmit: John Adams to Abigail Adams, December 2, 1796, in **Adams Family Papers** (electronic).

383 the president on many occasions: Branson, **Frenchified Dames**, p. 135.

383 old Philadelphia friends: Decatur, **Private Affairs,** p. 290.

383 but then he put it aside: Ferling, **Leap in the Dark,** p. 351.

384 judgment he trusted—Eliza Powel: Richard Brookhiser, **Founding Father: Rediscovering George Washington** (New York: Free Press, 1996), p. 84; Helen Bryan, **First Lady of Liberty: Martha Washington** (New York: John Wiley & Sons, 2002), p. 322.

384 "keenest of your sufferings?": Elizabeth Willing Powel to George Washington, November 17, 1792, in **The Papers of George Washington, Presidential Series,** vol. 11, **August 1792–January 1793,** edited by Christine Sternberg Patrick (Charlottesville: University of Virginia Press, 2002), p. 395.

385 "unanimous towards you": Abigail Adams to John Adams, December 29, 1792, **Adams Family Papers** (electronic).

A SECOND WASHINGTON TERM
386 "pleased with England": Abigail Adams to John Adams, February 9, 1793, in **Adams Family Papers** (electronic).

386 $2,000 in debt: Withey, **Dearest Friend,** p. 224.

387 "one I have lost": Abigail Adams to John Adams, December 29, 1792, in **Adams Family Papers** (electronic).

387 "love and respect": Abigail Adams to John Adams, February 22, 1793, ibid.

387 "you and to the children": Martha Washington to Fanny Bassett Washington, February 18, 1793, in Fields, **Worthy Partner**, p. 244.

387 reminisce with them about old times: Thompson, "Martha Washington as First Lady," p. 6.

387 "welcomed as old friends": Anthony, **First Ladies**, p. 54.

388 "patron of the work": Editors of **Ladies' Magazine** to Martha Washington, May 18, 1793, in Fields, **Worthy Partner**, p. 249.

389 "opposite Mr. Bingham's garden": Unpublished diary of Mrs. (Harriott) Daniel Horry, April 20, 1793; typescript provided by the South Carolina Historical Society.

389 "would use no ceremony": Ibid., May 7, 1793.

389 "which they suffered": Ibid., May 9, 1793.

390 "operate upon the cancer": Ibid., May 10, 1793.

390 "her to himself": Ibid., June 10, 1793.

390 was a pallbearer: Frances Leigh Williams, **A Founding Family** (New York: Harcourt Brace Jovanovich, 1978), p. 332.

390 "of the French Revolution": Harriott Horry Ravenal, **Eliza Pinckney** (New York: Charles Scribner's Sons, 1896), p. 322.

391 "incorrigible": Ferling, **Leap in the Dark**, p. 361.

391 "please to send for it": Martha Washington to Elizabeth Schuyler Hamilton, September 1793, in Fields, **Worthy Partner**, p. 53.

392 "you to Virginia": Elizabeth Willing Powel to Martha Washington, August 9, 1793, ibid., p. 251.

392 yellow fever at the end of September: Ibid., p. 252n.

392 "general dress of the city": Martha Washington to Fanny Bassett Washington, January 14, 1794, ibid., p. 254.

393 "better than our hearts": John Adams to Abigail Adams, January 22, 1794, in **Adams Family Papers** (electronic).

393 "a word of English": Martha Washington to Fanny Bassett Washington, March 2, 1794, in Fields, **Worthy Partner**, p. 260.

394 "did the children": Sally Livingston Jay to John Jay, April 18, 1794, John Jay Collection, Rare Book and Manuscript Library, Columbia University, provided by Mary-Jo Kline.

394 "taking with you our son": Sally Livingston Jay to John Jay, April 22, 1794, ibid.

394 "devoted him to the public": Withey, **Dearest Friend**, p. 230.

395 joined her husband in exile: Edith P. Mayo, general editor, **The Smithsonian Book of the First Ladies** (New York: Henry Holt & Co., 1996).

396 exchanging gifts and recipes: Anthony, **First Ladies**, p. 56.

396 American icon for decades: Ibid.; Paul M. Zall, **Dolley Madison: A Volume in the Presidential Wives Series** (New York: Nova History Publications, 2001).

396 "to meet the troops": Martha Washington to Fanny Bassett Washington, September 29, 1794, in Fields, **Worthy Partner**, p. 277.

397 "in matrimonial concerns": Ibid., p. 276.

397 both were pardoned by Washington: Ferling, **Leap in the Dark**, p. 373.

397 "and long to see you": John Adams to Abigail Adams, December 5, 1794, in **Adams Family Papers** (electronic).

398 "down her back": Booth, **Women of '76**, pp. 294–95.

398 "and excellent understanding": Griswold, **Republican Court**, p. 50.

398 "a patriot is wonderful!": Desmond, **Hamilton's Wife**, p. 181.

399 "some airs of importance": Ibid., p. 182.

400 "soul had a better body": John Adams to Abigail Adams, April 30, 1796, in **Adams Family Papers** (electronic).

401 "claims upon me": John Adams to Abigail Adams, January 7, 1796, ibid.

401 "bitter, nauseous and unwholesome": John Adams to Abigail Adams, January 20, 1796, ibid.

401 "go on as well as ever": John Adams to Abigail Adams, February 15, 1796, ibid.

401 "lot come out as it will": John Adams to Abigail Adams, February 20, 1796, ibid.

402 "when I long to talk": Abigail Adams to John Adams, February 20, 1796, ibid.

402 "A woman **can** be silent when she will": John Adams to Abigail Adams, March 1, 1796, ibid.

402 "station with any other than Washington": Abigail Adams to John Adams, February 28, 1796, ibid.

402 "dispute it with me": Abigail Adams to John Adams, March 2, 1796, ibid.

402 "in aid of the cause": Abigail Adams to John Adams, April 28, 1796, ibid.

403 "Lightning Rod Junior": Ferling, **Leap in the Dark**, p. 394.

403 "in a state of tranquility": Griswold, **Republican Court**, p. 413.

403 "note from another": Ribblett, **Nelly Custis**, p. 28.

404 "head in that manner!": Bryan, **First Lady of Liberty**, p. 333.

404 "Mrs. Washington could not": Mrs. Henrietta Liston to her uncles, July 12, 1797, in "A Diplomat's Wife in Philadelphia: Letters of Henrietta Liston, 1796–1800," edited by Bradford Perkins, **William and Mary Quarterly** (October 1954): 592–632, 613, in Thompson, "Testimonials About Martha Washington," p. 15.

404 "patriotism does not forbid it": See EarlyAmerica.com, http.//earlyamerica.com/mile stones/farewell.

405 "my eye upon him": Abigail Adams to John Adams, December 31, 1796, in **Adams Family Papers** (electronic).

405 "without a blush": Desmond, **Hamilton's Wife**, p. 191.

406 selling them to Betsey: Zall, p. 161.

406 "makes any difference": Ibid., p. 163.

406 "which is from above": Abigail Adams to John Adams, December 7, 1796, in **Adams Family Papers** (electronic).

406 "shall be Daddy Vice": John Adams to Abigail Adams, December 20, 1796, ibid.

407 "poor geese and turkeys": Abigail Adams to John Adams, December 23, 1796, ibid.

407 "Jefferson will be Daddy Vice": John Adams to Abigail Adams, December 27, 1796, ibid.

407 "has ever been unshaken": Abigail Adams to John Adams, January 15, 1797, ibid.

407 "yourself for honorable trials": John Adams to Abigail Adams, February 9, 1797, ibid.

408 "will be happiest": John Adams to Abigail Adams, March 5, 1797, ibid.

408 "America can boast": George Washington to Annis Boudinot Stockton, August 31, 1788, available at University of Virginia, "The Papers of George Washington," gwpapers.virginia.edu/ constitution/1788/stock.html.

Photograph Credits

CHAPTER ONE

DEBORAH READ FRANKLIN
Portrait by Benjamin Wilson ca. 1758–1759
Permission to reprint from The American
Philosophical Society Library

CHAPTER TWO

MERCY OTIS WARREN
about 1763; John Singleton Copley American,
1738–1815;
oil on canvas; 126.05 x 100.33cm (49 $\frac{5}{8}$ x 39 $\frac{1}{2}$ in.);
Permission to reprint from the Museum of Fine
Arts, Boston
Bequest of Winslow Warren; 31.212.
Photograph © 2004 Museum of Fine Arts Boston.

CHAPTER THREE

ABIGAIL SMITH ADAMS
Permission to reprint from The Granger
Collection, New York

CHAPTER FOUR

SARAH FRANKLIN BACHE
Permission to reprint from The American
Philosophical Society

CHAPTER FIVE

SARAH LIVINGSTON JAY
Courtesy of John Jay Historic Site, New York State
Office of Parks, Recreation and Historic
Preservation

CHAPTER SIX

MARY WHITE MORRIS
Permission to reprint from The Library Company
of Philadelphia

CHAPTER SEVEN

MARTHA WASHINGTON
© Bettmann/CORBIS

Index